Identity Flexibility During Adulthood

Jan D. Sinnott
Editor

Identity Flexibility During Adulthood

Perspectives in Adult Development

Springer

Editor
Jan D. Sinnott
Towson University
Baltimore, MD, USA

ISBN 978-3-319-55656-7 ISBN 978-3-319-55658-1 (eBook)
DOI 10.1007/978-3-319-55658-1

Library of Congress Control Number: 2017950293

Printed on acid-free paper

This Springer imprint is published by Springer Nature
The registered company is Springer International Publishing AG
The registered company address is: Gewerbestrasse 11, 6330 Cham, Switzerland

Preface

After changes, after changes, we are more or less the same….

~Simon & Garfunkel, "The Boxer" ("missing verse")

Be like water
run deep run clear
fill any space to its own dimensions
respond to the moon, to gravity…
take the coast by storm…
go underground…
eat boulders quietly…. ~Kendra Ford

We humans, especially we modern Western humans, struggle with the idea of identity. As children, we are asked what we will be when we get older, and we name something concrete and then wait to miraculously become it for the rest of our lives. As adolescents and young, emerging adults, we struggle to "find ourselves" and to "create ourselves" before too much more of life passes.

During adulthood as "stuff happens," our identities are more or less challenged. This is frightening, because we thought we *knew* who we were, because we dislike change, and because we don't want to contemplate losing parts of the self. The creation of identity turns out to be an ill-structured logical problem without clear boundaries or solutions. When we finally become accustomed to the ill-structured nature of identity, the realization that life is finite puts an even larger existential identity challenge in our paths.

With every lesson about who we are comes the feeling of dread: What if I am not the person I thought I was before? To survive adulthood as a "self," we need to keep that self somewhat flexible without losing it entirely. This does not feel easy and may sometimes feel impossible. How can we understand cognitively this thing called an identity when it both is and is not at the same time?

In this book, I have tried to gather the wisdom of many writers who all accepted the challenge of talking about creating a flexible adult self and identity during adulthood. These authors come at this challenging question from many different perspectives using different tools. Some survey existing literature and theory and then summarize prior work in a meaningful way. Some discuss their own research; some reflect on personal experiences that have demanded a flexible identity. As I spoke with potential authors, I was surprised by the great variety of their approaches to the problem of maintaining/transforming an identity in the face of ongoing challenges to that identity during adult life. I continue to be impressed with the real wisdom shown in addressing these challenges and demands by individuals who each try to create a flexible but ongoing adult identity and "eat boulders quietly."

How This Book Is Organized

The First Two Chapters

The first two chapters in this volume offer a structure we can use to think about identity flexibility during adulthood. This book begins with a summary of theory about the nature of identity in which we can ground our explorations. Evangeline Wheeler starts us off with her chapter "On the Stability of Identity Interacting with the Impermanence of Time." She addresses the making of identity, external identity (the identity of ourselves with others), internal identity (the identity of aspects of ourselves within ourselves), and identity as memory over time. In each of these "identity spaces," we see ideas and uncertainty with more research needed. The challenge of social intersection with individual development over time makes the formation and nature of identity especially challenging.

The second chapter addresses a particular interest of mine, namely, "The Cognitive Underpinnings of Identity Flexibility in Adulthood." As I developed the adult cognitive-developmental theory of postformal logical thought and noticed the many potential applications of this theory, I gradually realized that postformal logic is involved in knowing the evolving self. To make matters even more interesting, here is a place where cognition, emotion, social/interpersonal factors, and individual's beliefs about something greater than that mortal individual self all intersect, transform, and are known. Constructing this *concept* of the transforming self is one of the intriguing processes explored in this chapter.

Remaining Chapters

The remaining chapters in this book cover such a wide variety of issues and themes, all centered on the flexibility of adult identity, that they are arranged in alphabetical order on the basis of the first author's last name. See the table of contents and the information about each author, as well as the keywords for each chapter. Here, I'll give a brief description of each chapter to stimulate your appetite for these many ideas.

Sherry Beaumont writes about "Identity Flexibility and Wisdom in Adulthood: The Roles of a Growth-Oriented Identity Style and Contemplative Processes." Contemplative processes are ways of understanding and accepting the nature of one's inner and outer reality through direct experience in the given moment. This style of identity processing is oriented toward the development of personal growth and ultimately brings about compassion and wisdom.

Emerging adulthood is becoming an important focus of psychologists. In his chapter, Luke Boardman makes "An Experiential Exploration of Identity During Emerging Adulthood" with the subtitle "The Impact of Growth Experiences on Emerging Adult Characteristics." Gathering exploratory data led him to the conclusion that emerging adulthood emphasizes identity flexibility and is a stage of testing oneself in reference to the world, ending, hopefully, in the state of being a responsible adult. Growth experiences may have a significant role to play in this process.

A subcategory of identity theories that has become a rich source of ideas in adult identity development and flexibility involves Black identity, especially Black immigrant identity. "Bridging the Gap: Black Immigrant Identities and Dreams of Home" is the title of the chapter contributed by Leonie J. Brooks. This chapter highlights the multidimensional experience of Black immigrants in the United States as it relates to the complex process of establishing and maintaining evolving national, racial, and ethnic identity in a predominantly white context. Brooks uses her own experience as well as quotes and experience from interviewees to illustrate the complexity of this identity creation.

Cameron Camp writes about "Flexibility in Persons with Dementia." The focus of this chapter is on the capacity of persons diagnosed with dementia to exhibit flexibility in their actions, thinking, attitudes, and creative capacities, including the capacity to shape and reshape identity. In contrast to the way many patients are seen as "those who are demented," Camp offers a series of examples from his work where dementia sufferers think of themselves, for example, as beer brewers in a beer-making club, as activity planners, and as dog trainers. International explorations have demonstrated that individuals with dementia don't limit themselves to identifying with their diagnoses but also see themselves as learners when they are asked *what they want to learn* and offered a chance to learn that. Being a resident leader for activities expands identity beyond "patient" to "leader."

In later adulthood, if not before, we confront life's existential questions, issues surrounding spirituality, and our relations with the transcendent in terms of our own definitions. From this challenge, we see the inherent contradictions in the self when relating to the transcendent. The false self (a reference point focused on personal achievement grounded in the ego) cannot grasp this series of contradictions, but the true self (a reference point that is utterly within you and utterly beyond you at the same time) can resolve the contradictions and paradoxes. These are just some of the ideas presented by John Cavanaugh in his chapter entitled "Spirituality as a Framework for Confronting Life's Existential Questions in Later Life."

While there has been scholarly interest in social identity, most studies focus on Western countries and dominant ethnic groups in non-Western countries. Gareth Davey offers a qualitative analysis of identity among the Badaga people of South India, a non-dominant disadvantaged group. Limited research has been conducted on the identity of groups such as this who may construct identity in different ways grounded in different cultural and historical practices. His chapter is entitled "Rural-Urban Migration, Quality of Life, and Identity."

Many of us find a real challenge to our ongoing identities when we become parents. Maria Fracasso writes about this important area of growth in her chapter entitled "The Concurrent Paths of Parental Identity and Child Development". She discusses the experience so widely shared of being forever changed upon becoming a parent, and remaining a parent is various ways for life!

Gender is one of the first identities we learn, and it is usually binary (e.g., man/woman). In their research, Paz Galupo, Lexi Pulice-Farrow, and Johanna L. Ramirez examine gender identity flexibility among 197 transgender individuals by exploring the gender identity labels they choose and the descriptions they provide for their gender identity and experience. This chapter is entitled "Like a Constantly Flowing River: Gender Identity Flexibility Among Non-binary Transgender Individuals." Galupo et al. suggest that the way gender-nonconforming individuals describe their gender identity may contribute to the way we conceptualize identity flexibility overall.

An examination of "Identity Stories to Jettison" is contributed by Louis Green. As she says, what we believe is true can shape, delineate, and limit consciousness. Using examples from personal stories, the ideas of the Zanders published by the Harvard Business School, and poetry, she suggests we consider dropping three assumptions: that I am alone, that my identity is fixed, and that there will never be enough. Without these, we can thrive. Rather than writing in a scholarly style, Green offers the gift of personal experiences using an everyday language and tone. This variety in tone is one of the positive features of this volume and the variety of authors who contributed to it.

Carol Hoare contributed the chapter entitled "Work and Identity Flexibility." This chapter considers the turbulence of today's work environment and how its uncertainty requires flexibility in employees' identities. Three ways workers can reshape their work-based identities are examined, including those of *knowledge upgrading*, *adapting to changing role functions*, and *transitioning to positions that better express their identity needs*. Identity flexibility becomes a survival mechanism.

The changes in identity experienced when one moves from student to professional are explored by Shaina Kumar in her chapter entitled "Moving from Student to Professional: Thoughts on Roadblocks and Keys to Success." Shaina uses her own relatively recent experiences to describe how identity is shaped in the crucible of experience from graduate school to beyond. While many students have faced the challenge of moving beyond the student role, not many have analyzed the process and gone on to offer "keys to success" to those coming after. Shaina has now done this service which should be of help to professionals in formation now going through the process.

The flexible tailoring of identity in middle adulthood may be enhanced by engaging in freely chosen "play" activities. For example, individuals might achieve self-differentiation and social integration through leisure play, freely chosen. Kevin Rathunde and Russell Isabella discuss this intriguing issue in their chapter entitled "Play, Flow, and Tailoring Identity in Middle Adulthood." The authors use rich interview materials to illustrate their theoretical ideas. In the absence of events that force change upon the self, identity development often depends upon the willingness of a person to intentionally engage in challenges significant enough to require reordering priorities and goals.

In his chapter, Grant J. Rich considers "Optimizing Challenges: Eminent Elders Meet Adversity with Identity Flexibility." Rich performed deep analysis on two case studies of eminent elders who achieved great success and international reputation in their chosen fields. The case studies show how eminent creators, by making good use of flow, utilized identity flexibility in pursuit of their goals despite tremendous life challenges. This type of study seems worth pursuing to develop new interventions and therapies for those facing life adversity.

"Identity Flexibility and Buddhism" is the title of the chapter by Jeff Rosenberg. Our recent Western explosion of interest in Buddhism stems from many motivations and does not always focus on exploring Buddhist definitions of identity. Here, this self-definition includes the concept of "no self." In his masterful chapter, Rosenberg uses his own personal explorations, the teachings of key Buddhist teachers, and the experiences of his clients in therapy to learn more about what flexible identity means in that tradition. Is there such a thing as "identity"? Is "flexible identity" a contradiction in terms?

Another clinician, Vedat Şar, a specialist in dissociative identity disorders (or, by a former name, multiple personality disorders), contributed the chapter entitled "Identity Revised: A Clinician's Perspective on What an Identity-Based Model of Mind Looks Like." Identity is challenged by traumatic stress, and such challenges may lead to a disruption in psychological functions and, possibly, the emergence of clinical symptoms. Timely resolution seems to be associated with a capacity to be open to implement newly learned principles while keeping a basic level of continuity.

The next chapter focuses on the identity development of caregivers and includes discussion of the importance of flexibility being a part of caregiver identity. Those of us who have been caregivers for, perhaps, a parent or spouse know that experience can make us question who we are and what skills we actually possess. Kim Shifren, in her chapter on "Caregiving Identity and Flexibility," discusses identity development, followed by work on, specifically, *caregiver* identity development. Assessment tools for the study of caregiver identity development do exist, and the chapter concludes with ideas for future research.

First person stories of identity flexibility told from the individual's own history and perspective are important to our understanding of identity flexibility. Valerie Smith shares with us her personal evolution into the complex identity she now holds as an artist. Her chapter, "Dual Identities and the Artist," gives us a glimpse into how complicated and confusing this lifelong process can be. It may take a lifetime for someone to truly identify as an artist, but with that belief, identity and art can continue to grow. How do we combine our artist/nonartist selves? Again, the strongly personal and emotional language helps the reader to share Smith's experiences creating this complex identity. She also offers a glimpse at how the role of being a parent influences that complex identity creation.

Our sense of who we are can be challenged when we become seriously ill and life takes a different turn. Betsy Stellhorn talks about her personal experience of becoming a cancer patient in her first person chapter entitled "The Sick Self." Going from seeing herself as strong and healthy to suddenly seeing herself as a cancer patient with its attendant expectations quickly led her thru an understanding of the nature of impermanence. How to integrate the former healthy self with the current sick self? She says she still thinks wistfully of the "healthy, active grey-haired grandmother in her 80s" she thought she would be, but she no longer takes it for granted.

The last chapter, by Alan Waterman, is entitled "'Just When I Knew All of Life's Answers, They Changed the Questions': A Eudaimonist Perspective on Identity Flexibility During the Adult Years." Previously, research on identity development has focused primarily on the stages of adolescence and emerging adulthood. The focus of this chapter is on identity development between the ages of 35 and 50, when challenges to contentment can come from job or family or many other domains. Eudaemonic happiness is contentment or well-being, expressing virtue. The predictors of this successful, virtuous use of identity flexibility are also discussed.

Although these chapter authors discuss a wide variety of aspects of identity as it flexibly changes during adulthood in the face of numerous experiences, they are really addressing one key question. How adaptive and fluid is identity and how can we know ourselves as *both* continuing and changing? Exploring these ideas will raise the possibility of future research on adult identity.

Baltimore, MD, USA Jan D. Sinnott

Contents

Part I Concepts of Identity

1 **On the Stability of Identity Interacting with the Impermanence of Time** 3
Evangeline A. Wheeler

2 **Cognitive Underpinnings of Identity Flexibility in Adulthood** 19
Jan D. Sinnott

Part II Research, Theory, Personal Experiences

3 **Identity Flexibility and Wisdom in Adulthood: The Roles of a Growth-Oriented Identity Style and Contemplative Processes** 53
Sherry L. Beaumont

4 **An Experiential Exploration of Identity During Emerging Adulthood: The Impact of Growth Experiences on Emerging Adulthood Characteristics** 71
Luke Boardman

5 **Bridging the Gap: Black Immigrant Identities and Dreams of Home** 83
Leonie J. Brooks

6 **Flexibility in Persons with Dementia** 99
Cameron J. Camp

7 **Spirituality as a Framework for Confronting Life's Existential Questions in Later Adulthood** 115
John C. Cavanaugh

8 **Rural-to-Urban Migration, Identity, and Life Quality of the Badaga People in South India** 129
Gareth Davey

9 **The Concurrent Paths of Parental Identity and Child Development** 151
Maria P. Fracasso

10 **"Like a Constantly Flowing River": Gender Identity Flexibility Among Nonbinary Transgender Individuals** 163
M. Paz Galupo, Lex Pulice-Farrow, and Johanna L. Ramirez

11 **Identity Stories to Jettison** 179
Louise Green

12 **Work and Identity Flexibility** 183
Carol Hoare

13 **From Student to Professional: Thoughts on Roadblocks and Keys to Success** 197
Shaina A. Kumar

14 **Play, Flow, and Tailoring Identity in Middle Adulthood** 211
Kevin Rathunde and Russell Isabella

15 **Optimizing Challenges: Eminent Elders Meet Adversity with Identity Flexibility** 233
Grant J. Rich

16 **Identity Flexibility and Buddhism** 247
Jeff Rosenberg

17 **Identity Revised: A Clinician's Perspective on What an Identity-Based Model of Mind Looks Like** 265
Vedat Şar

18 **Caregiving Identity and Flexibility** 289
Kim Shifren

19 **Dual Identities and the Artist: A Personal Reflection** 303
Valerie A. Smith

20 **The Sick Self: A Personal Reflection** 309
Elizabeth Stellhorn

21 **"Just When I Knew All of Life's Answers, They Changed the Questions": A Eudaimonist Perspective on Identity Flexibility During the Adult Years** 313
Alan S. Waterman

Index 333

Contributors

Sherry L. Beaumont Department of Psychology, University of Northern British Columbia, Prince George, BC, Canada

Luke Boardman Loyola University Maryland, Baltimore, MD, USA

Leonie J. Brooks Psychology Department, Towson University, Towson, MD, USA

Cameron J. Camp Center for Applied Research in Dementia, Solon, OH, USA

John C. Cavanaugh Consortium of Universities of the Washington Metropolitan Area, Washington, DC, USA

Gareth Davey Research Centre for Languages and Cultures, School of Foreign Languages and Literature, Yunnan Normal University, Kunming, Yunnan Province, China

School of Anthropology and Conservation, University of Kent, Canterbury, Kent, UK

Maria P. Fracasso Psychology Department, Towson University, Baltimore County, MD, USA

M. Paz Galupo Psychology Department, Towson University, Towson, MD, USA

Louise Green River Road UU Congregation, Bethesda, MD, USA

Carol Hoare The George Washington University, Washington, DC, USA

Russell Isabella Department of Family and Consumer Studies, University of Utah, Salt Lake City, UT, USA

Shaina A. Kumar Psychology Department, Towson University, Towson, MD, USA

Lex Pulice-Farrow Psychology Department, Towson University, Towson, MD, USA

Johanna L. Ramirez Psychology Department, Towson University, Towson, MD, USA

Kevin Rathunde Department of Family and Consumer Studies, University of Utah, Salt Lake City, UT, USA

Grant J. Rich Consulting Psychologist, Juneau, Alaska, India

Rebecca N. Rochowiak Psychology Department, Towson University, Towson, USA

Jeff Rosenberg Clinical Psychologist and Executive Coach, Washington, DC, USA

Vedat Şar Koc University School of Medicine (KUSOM), Istanbul, Turkey

Kim Shifren Psychology Department, Towson University, Towson, MD, USA

Valerie A. Smith Utopian Dreamer, Artist's Closet, Baltimore, MD, USA

Jan D. Sinnott Towson University, Baltimore, MD, USA

Elizabeth Stellhorn LCSW-C, Silver Spring, MD, USA

Alan S. Waterman Department of Psychology, The College of New Jersey, Ewing Township, NJ, USA

Evangeline A. Wheeler Department of Psychology, Towson University, Towson, MD, USA

Part I
Concepts of Identity

Chapter 1
On the Stability of Identity Interacting with the Impermanence of Time

Evangeline A. Wheeler

Each of us has a sense of unique independence from other human beings. Though we are connected through family and community, you are independently *you* and I am independently *me*. The question of "Who are you?" or "Who am I?" is deceptively complicated. Immediately we might say that the answer depends on a particular life stage, or a certain period of psychological development, a specific social group, or even a unique physiological state. Because we might say that who we are depends on any number of variables, we intimate that who we are changes from time to time. Whether and how one's identity changes throughout a lifetime is a matter not agreed upon by the psychologists, sociologists, philosophers, or literary giants who study it. Many can find agreement, though, on the idea that malleability of identity can be both adaptive and damaging.

Interestingly, among psychologists who study identity, most theorizing has supported the correlation of a stable identity with a healthy mental status and even that one's identity is firmly formed by adolescence. In accord with that idea, most of what is written in the sociological literature about life in our 70s, 80s, and 90s suggests that who we are when we are old remains pretty close to who we were when we were young. But, in the novel *Love in the Time of Cholera* (Marquez, 1985) Gabriel Garcia Marquez writes: "He allowed himself to be swayed by his conviction that human beings are not born once and for all on the day their mothers give birth to them, but that life obliges them over and over again to give birth to themselves," suggesting we have different selves at various life stages and circumstances. Introduced decades ago, identity theory is a social psychological theory that attempts to understand identities, their processes of operation, and their consequences for interaction and society. Outside of academic psychology, identity is one of the most hotly debated topics in literary theory and cultural studies and is one of the most extensively studied constructs in other social sciences.

E.A. Wheeler (✉)
Department of Psychology, Towson University, Towson, MD, USA
e-mail: ewheeler@towson.edu

J.D. Sinnott (ed.), *Identity Flexibility During Adulthood*,
DOI 10.1007/978-3-319-55658-1_1

Sometimes the terms get confused, but identity is not equal to self-esteem. Self-esteem functions as a subjective indicator or gauge of other people's evaluations. An increase in self-esteem signals an increase in the degree to which one is socially included and accepted by others. A loss of self-esteem follows from a downward shift in the degree to which one is included and accepted by others, nor is identity equal to self-concept. Self-concept is more general, with identity a subset. What identity is, on an internal cognitive level, involves self-knowledge and stories about one's self. In research labs it can be measured with scales that focus on self-trait knowledge like the *Self-Concept Scale* and the *Twenty Statements Test* developed by Kuhn and McPartland in 1954.

In this discussion I will explore the intellectual debate over whether identity can be considered more stable versus more flexible and interject thoughts on how memory can be the mechanism to settle the debate. As a cognitive psychologist interested in issues of cognitive effects of mindfulness and meditation, I wonder often about the truthfulness of the idea that clinging to a sense of oneself as separate is the source of existential angst and much mental disorder. I hope to conceptualize a way for thinking about stable/flexible identity – what I will refer to as external and internal levels of identity. At the end I will posit that internal identity feels stable because it is held together in time by memory.

The Making of Identity

Typically, identity development purportedly begins with very young children's awareness that they are separate and unique individuals with first indications of this awareness being evident when children begin to recognize themselves, as when looking in a mirror, or when realizing that other people are not feeling their skinned knees. But even before that, in infancy, separation-individuation is a development phase where a baby slowly sees herself as different from the mother and is aware of her own identity (Mahler, Pine, & Bergman, 2000). *Separation* refers to the development of limits and to the differentiation in the infant's mind between itself and the mother, whereas *individuation* refers to the development of the infant's ego, sense of identity, and cognitive abilities. Mahler believed that disruptions in the fundamental process of separation-individuation could result later in life in a disturbance in the ability to maintain a reliable sense of individual identity. Then, in the case of toddlers, as when researchers place a dot of rouge on a child's nose, two-year-olds who see themselves in a mirror will touch their noses (Bullock & Lütkenhaus, 1989). Apparently, they recognize the reflected image as themselves. Further evidence for an early sense of identity awareness is the fact that the words "me," "I," and "mine" emerge very early in children's language. Elements of "Who am I?" get established rather early in life.

A concept of stable identity can be described as the subjective feeling of a person that they remain the same across situations and across time and that one's actions and experiences in these differing contexts can be related to the same core self.

Thus, from this perspective, developing a self that is unified and consistent is essential, and, in its absence, individuals are likely to experience continual uncertainty and anxiety. In fact, theories of self that are derived from Erikson's work argue that the maintenance of a stable, continuous, unified, core identity is necessary for healthy psychological functioning and well-being. In developing a theory, Erikson (1980) studied native cultures in the American west, impoverished children, upper middle class children, and emotionally disturbed children. Although Erikson's theory of identity development is widely cited, he was best known for the theory that each stage of life, from infancy on, is associated with a specific psychological struggle born of interaction with others that contributes to a major aspect of personality. That represented a quantum leap in Freudian thought by suggesting that the ego and the sense of identity are shaped over the entire life-span and that experiences later in life might help assuage the emotional damage of early childhood. A significant contribution was the concept of a malleable ego in adults, a departure from traditional theories of an ego fixed early in life and persisting to its end. Erikson's concepts, moreover, opened a door to the idea that adults, despite poor childhoods, could compensate for their deprivations. Empirical evidence for identity transitions beyond adolescence into early and middle adulthood has been growing within recent years, yet still much work remains to be done regarding delineation of the precursors to and mechanisms of changes in adult identity. Some longitudinal studies of the precursors to changes in adult identity find that various stressful life events are associated with different patterns of change in both identity exploration and identity commitment over time (see Anthis & LaVoie, 2006).

According to Erikson's highly influential theory, human beings develop identity by moving through a series of psychosocial crises that, ideally, culminate in a coherent, consistent identity, a central feature of which is continuity. A crisis period in infancy ends, for instance, with a resolution of the existential question of whether the world can be trusted. The period ends well if the infant has learned trust that she will be fed and loved. The crises of psychosocial development that lead to a stable identity are most apparent in the turbulent period of adolescence, when having an identity comes to mean seeing how your childhood experiences mesh into the experiences of the adulthood yet to come, or in other words, having a sense of your life story. Identity is forged by the interaction of a crisis period and a firm resolution about the crisis. Crisis mode is inherently unstable, and sustained failure to progress to a stable, coherent identity is viewed as maladaptive and pathological. If these crises are not resolved with respect to one's identity, and closure is not achieved, a problematic identity state of so-called diffusion or moratorium prevails (see Marcia, 2002) because the static constructions that form an individual's identity serve as a bulwark against the existential assaults of risk, tragedy, and meaninglessness that threaten the self with dissolution, chaos, and terror. But even mature adults, when subjected to conditions of uncertainty and rapid change, will experience identity crises and a resultant change, in spite of identity being largely cemented during the teenage years.

Each of the crises ascends at a particular point in life and must be resolved successfully to ensure a smooth progression to the next of the eight stages. Across years of growth, people gradually acquire a sense of continuity, social worth, and integration. The conscious sense of self that forms through the outcomes of myriad social interactions Erikson termed "ego identity." Even though identity is relatively stable when formed in this way, it changes as we go through life's challenges. Each new crisis affords the opportunity to further develop or to hinder the development of identity. Erikson's belief is that throughout each person's lifetime, different crises or conflicts are encountered unavoidably. Unlike Freud, Erikson argued that significant personality changes could occur in adulthood when psychosocial crises occur, as when intimate relationships are newly established, when middle age offers the decline of the physical body, when professional life is stagnated and when death nears.

Identity formation depends on additional factors beyond psychosocial crises. Consider olfaction. In one line of research (Low, 2013), the focus is on how olfactive-memory recollections become imbued with emotional qualities which also contribute to the reconstruction of one's identity. Given that odors are usually appraised in either positive or negative ways, scents are therefore not merely physiological but moral phenomena. When people are olfactorily perceived as pungent, the implication is that they are not only physically transgressive but morally questionable as well. In this manner, the odor becomes a symbol of the self where it concurrently represents the self as both a physical and a moral being. The narratives that research participants offer in their scent-based recollections indicate that one's identity and that of others are built in part upon olfactive recounts, thereby reiterating how moral identities may be explained vis-à-vis olfactory associations.

Also consider the role of food in identity formation. A systematic review of qualitative and quantitative research that answers the question about the relationship between food activities and the maintenance of identities in old age found that food activities contribute to the maintenance of women's gendered identities, the ethnic identities of men and women, and community identities (Plastow, Atwal, & Gilhooly, 2015). There was moderate evidence that a change in food choice and deteriorating health changed food activity participation, and these changes threatened identities. Further research is needed to develop understanding of how identity and mental well-being are maintained, despite changes in everyday activities like cooking and eating.

Or, is moral capacity more central to identity? Evidence for this idea comes from social cognition research finding that impression formation is largely dependent on the moral dimension. In other words, how we see people – whether they are positive or negative, to be approached or avoided – is mostly determined by our assessment of their moral character and not their intellect, knowledge, or other personality traits. In this way identity encompasses one's value system as well as one's view of knowledge and oneself as a learner and an agent in the world. Interestingly, their study (Addis & Tippet, 2004) was designed to test what types of cognitive damage cause people to no longer appear to be themselves to *others*. A crucial element of the design was testing for changes in identity from the perspective of a third-person observer rather than the individual herself. In addition to sidestepping many of the reliability problems intrinsic to first-person accounts, focusing on perceived identity allowed the investigators to assess the effects of memory and moral changes on the patient's relationship with others. This is an extremely important facet because when someone appears to be "not the same person," the social bonds between patients and loved ones or caregivers quickly deteriorate, and these bonds are critical to one's well-being and health. Specifically, the researchers recruited 248 volunteers with family members who suffered from one of three types of neurodegenerative diseases. Patients had either Alzheimer's disease (which affects cognition), frontotemporal dementia (which also affects cognition), or amyotrophic lateral sclerosis (ALS, which does not affect cognition). However, where Alzheimer's strongly affects things like memory and IQ, those with frontotemporal dementia tend to undergo changes in moral traits, that is, things like honesty, compassion, decency, and integrity.

It is interesting to examine this study in more detail. The participants, most of whom were married to or romantically involved with the patients, were instructed to rate how much the patient had changed in morality and personality since the disease began. To evaluate the degree of change in the perceived identity, participants gave information regarding any differences in their relationship with the patient that had occurred over the course of the disease's progression. For example, they were asked questions like, "Does the patient ever seem like a stranger to you?" and "Do you feel like you still know who the patient is?" Analysis of the data revealed that participants perceived the greatest disruptions in patients' identity when they observed changes in moral traits. Other cognitive deficits had no measurable effect on the perception of identity. Consequently, those with frontotemporal dementia showed the greatest changes in perceived identity, since it specifically affects the frontal lobe functions underlying moral reasoning and behavior. Interestingly, those with ALS showed no significant change in perceived identity despite the greatly distorted physical appearance that results from the widespread deterioration of motor function. Although there was minor change in identity perception in those with Alzheimer's, this was associated with changes in moral traits and not memory loss.

So this means that in cases of neurodegenerative diseases, efforts aimed at helping sufferers to understand themselves in terms of their moral traits (e.g., characteristics like altruism, mercy, and generosity) might restore their sense of identity and control as memory fades or cognition declines. Knowing that other people continue to perceive us as the same person, even when we feel that our own identity is changing, can allow us to securely protect a sense of self. Importantly, there should be clinical therapies that specifically focus on maintaining those cognitive processes that are involved in moral function.

Consider then that it is not our intelligence or our knowledge of the past or our passage through crises that defines us, but instead our moral behavior. Essentially, maybe identity is not what we know, but what we stand for. However, the trouble with this model of identity is that modes of moral behavior are not sufficiently nuanced to discriminate between persons. Let's say I have two women with memory loss and neither one remembers who they are in terms of distinct episodic memories but they both lived lives of moral virtue. Let's put them in a room where their intimate partners cannot see them, but they can email each other. Would the women be distinguishable by their intimate partners? Without a nuanced scale of what it means to be moral, morality will not discriminate between them. This introduces the notion that individuation is best done with memory. In the thought experiment here, the partners cannot tell with whom they are emailing unless either of the women can remember something of her previous life, like her partner's name, or a personal detail, or the time she hiked alone for days on the Appalachian Trail.

External Identity: Ourselves with Others

So identity formation begins early in life, but despite the wealth of findings across many disciplines, researchers remain divided over such enduring fundamental issues as what exactly identity is, and how identity processes function, especially in a social context. The questions are crucial: From a cultural standpoint, is identity individually or collectively oriented? Is it personally or socially constructed? Are the same primary factors involved in all identity formation (cognitions, culture, social milieu, parenting, health)? Can all identities be changed? Is the idea of different adult identities an imperative driven by technological advances? After all, the prior view of self that emphasizes stability and continuity may not any longer apply as well to contemporary technological society, since individuals' relationships to cultural symbols and core institutions increasingly are unstable, weakened, or broken. Do some people change and some don't? Is the change evident in the brain, or just in behavior, or just in self-report? External identity involves these questions of social interactions, while internal identity concerns cognitive and phenomenological processes: national identity, sexual identity, identity theft, and changing identity. There are several ways a researcher could frame the question of external identity by focusing in on a single important social aspect.

On the level of an external identity, having to do with our place as social beings, we claim particular identities based on our recognized roles (parent, professor, police officer), the social groups we belong to (club member, dance partner), and the personal characteristics that describe ourselves (taciturn, organized, optimistic). Your outer identity, your persona, is the result of the interaction, or friction, between your inner and outer experiences. It includes an array of qualities that you present to others as being you. It's how you want others to see you – as friendly, intimidating, modest, competent, helpless, nice, honest, powerful, sexy, or wounded. You select, organize, and present a certain package of these characteristics to others as though they were a *you* that is solid, consistent, and unchanging. Humans evolved in social groups and needed others to survive and reproduce. This prompted the evolution of motivation to seek the company of others, form social bonds, and curry favor of others in the group. Failure to have a social identity and to be thus accepted by others would have resulted in isolation and premature death, since survival without the protective covering of the group was limited. Given that social acceptance would be critical to survival, selection would have favored a mechanism that enabled a person to insure, via a social identity, a degree of acceptance by others.

However, your external identity is not entirely within your conscious control. It is a combination of those traits deemed appropriate and those that have been conditioned by your environment to have. In so far as you are able, you choose the identity you want to reveal to the world from the thousands of thoughts, impulses, and bodily sensations you experience daily. This filtering process never stops; therefore, your identity is constantly changing, unaware as we may be that it is. As an adult, you do much of this filtering automatically, although occasionally you may experience a conflict within your identity when an unwanted emotion surfaces and gets acted out in the world. Since there may be certain traits in your identity that you abhor, it speaks strongly to conditioning that you cannot prevent them from being part of who you present to the world. A social, external identity is a social and psychological necessity that develops automatically from childhood through adulthood. Everyone needs a public face in order to function.

This seems a somewhat different conception of identity than that referenced by the notion of flexibility of adult identity. Given that economically prosperous people in Western societies have high life expectancies, living decades longer than ever in the adulthood stage of life, the post-parenting years are filled with new life experiences, new social identities, and new complex cognitions. Scholars now examine how our identities can change when there are so many years left in which to do it, and life becomes replete with opportunities when we have time and health and money to spare. Because of the apparent necessity of having an identity that changes as we grow appreciably older, several social theorists have offered implicit and explicit critiques of the crisis model of identity formation suggested by conventional psychological theories. For example, maybe there is a progressive shift away from a predominance of self-concepts embedded in structured role relationships and toward a predominance of self-concepts defined in terms of characteristic ways of acting, feeling, or responding in social interaction. This can be taken as indicative of an identity increasingly composed of several separate identities that are relatively situation free rather than identities that draw upon the stability of institutional norms and roles.

Yet, people have the sense that, fundamentally, who they are remains constant over time. Even when memory is discontinuous, we feel we are the same person. For instance, suppose as a young woman I commit some embarrassing social indiscretion. Decades later, in middle age with a career as a professor, I can recall the incident. Later still, in my dotage, I remember my years as a college professor, but I've forgotten entirely not only the indiscretion but everything else I did in my youth. According to a memory criterion the young student is the same person as the professor, the professor is the elderly woman, but the elderly woman is not the young student. This is an impossible result: if x and y are one and y and z are one, x and z cannot be *two*. Instead, perhaps identity is comprised of a set of perceptions at any given reference point. The bundle of perceptions changes with each experience; therefore, there is no one enduring self that persists through each experience. The self, then, when perceived as something fixed through time, is an illusion. The persistence question can be understood as the attempt to find evidence for the same person existing at two different times. The most common formulation is something like this: If a person x exists at one time and a person y exists at another time, under what possible circumstances is it the case that x is y? Mainstream psychological theories of identity formation argue that normal developmental processes result in a consolidated, stable, core identity. Instability or confusion with respect to one's identity is thought to have a detrimental effect on emotional well-being. In contrast, constructionist theories of identity argue that, in recent decades, there has been a dramatic and sustained shift away from fixed, stable self-concepts and toward more fluid, fragmented ones. These theories argue that flexible identities are better adapted to the institutional instability, the rapid social change, and the evolving nature of social relations that characterize contemporary society. It follows that individuals who have more fluid identities will have higher levels of emotional well-being than individuals who have more stable identities.

Whereas prior to the late 1960s, a high percentage of respondents in research studies possessed a solid, static, socially anchored sense of self, identities that are relatively fluid have since become predominant. The mutable self is a self-concept that is sufficiently flexible to allow for variations in the locus of self across time and that is adaptive to broader cultural and structural changes in society. This is a counterargument to the notion that stable and consistent identities are necessary for healthy functioning. The contemporary social and technological world is inimical to the maintenance of a limited, self-contained, stable identity. We are becoming fluid and many-sided. Through largely unconscious processes, contemporary humans have evolved a sense of self-appropriate to the restlessness and flux of our time; the self increasingly is pulled in many directions as technology changes the quantity, variety, and intensity of our daily interactions with others. This mode of being differs radically from the fixed-identity view and enables us to engage in continuous exploration and personal experiment. Rapid social and technological change has contributed to a self that is malleable, a self of many possibilities. The stable identity of the past is replaced with the protean self, which is instead more flexible in the face of change, and which experiences many metamorphoses in the course of a life, trading in one personal style, personality, role, or belief system for another. Commensurate with these social changes, the self adapts and evolves, acquiring multiple and disparate potentials for being. If we think that lives and persons are unified, much as stories are said to be unified, how will our thinking about old age differ from that of someone who thinks that lives or persons can be strongly discontinuous? As Small (2007) writes in her study of the literature and philosophy of old age, declining to describe our lives as unified stories is the only way we can hope to live out our long lives. But, there are still exceptions to the notion that fragmented and fluid identities are adaptive to the rapid social change and instability of contemporary social life. Some versions of identity have continued to view identity consistency and verification as requisite to personal well-being. Examples of such research include Burke's (2004) identity control theory and Thoits' (1995) work on identity theory and stress.

An external identity is crucial to survive as a social being. But, as is suggested next, perhaps having an external locus of identity, identifying one's self based on factors that are external such as physical attributes, wealth, possessions, careers, and fame, leads to individual suffering and unhappiness. Everyone who has identified based on something external may become easily disequilibrated when these things are removed.

Internal Identity: Within Ourselves

On an internal level, identity deals with philosophical questions that arise about ourselves by virtue of our simply being human (in contrast with questions about ourselves that arise by virtue of our being living things, conscious beings, or material objects). Perhaps the root of human conflict and personal suffering is our fundamental misunderstanding of who we are, misled as we are by the possible illusion that we are isolated social identities, unconnected to the rest of the universe. The concept of homeostasis is helpful here. It is a kind of stability created by making adjustments any time changes occur. For instance, the human body is always working toward stable and constant conditions. It adapts to changing external circumstances by making internal adjustments. Homeostasis is essential for all biological processes. For example, body temperature in homoiothermic organisms has to be regulated in order to guarantee the maintenance of life. So, in basic terms homeostasis can be described as the way the body maintains and returns to stability. There seems necessary a unifying principle that conceptually binds together the ongoing avalanche of change and adaptation. "Identity" might be the unifying concept (Zhou, Pöppel, & Bao, 2014). That is, identity is the defining characteristics by which a person is recognized as a persisting entity over time.

Therefore, despite being multidimensional, internal identity has an overall coherence which gives a sense of unity rather than the subjective perception that one's identity is fragmented. Adding to the sense of coherence is the quality of continuity over time. People perceive themselves as essentially the same person over time, despite changing roles and life situations that are a part of external identity. As argued later in this essay, autobiographical memory has a clear role in the constitution of internal identity, enabling connections and coherence between discrete moments in consciousness that if lost would threaten one's sense of identity. Memory is at the heart of the way most people think about personal, internal identity. It is because I remember my first thrilling roller coaster ride that I think I am the same person as that scared, brave little girl 40 years ago. Taking this biological perspective as a framework, every organism including every human being has to establish and maintain a homeostatic state throughout time. This necessarily implies a "self," i.e., the identity of the organism to achieve this individual goal. As the homeostatic state may be violated because of perturbations by unexpected stimuli or changes of the metabolic state expressed for instance in the feeling of hunger, thirst, or sexual desire, the organism constantly monitors its internal state in order to maintain homeostasis. Identity might be the operating mechanism for maintaining equilibrium.

Indeed, it seems as though the most natural way to think about personal identity is in terms of some essential core self which does not change, even as all of one's inessential qualities (physical and mental) arise and pass away. What Buddhism-oriented scholars seem to be targeting is the sense of robust identity which underlies such discursive concepts as self or soul. And undermining this sense of robust selfhood requires far more than reasoning; it requires mental and behavioral training. This is why the cultivation of mindfulness and other meditation practices are so strongly recommended. A Buddhism-oriented view is that all that exists are fleeting physical events, feelings, conceptualizations, conative dispositions, and consciousness, though we mostly think of ourselves as a robust, unchanging self. If Buddhist philosophy denies a permanent internal identity, then identity is understood instead in terms of these five aggregates, the sum of which must not be taken for a permanent entity, since beings are nothing but an amalgam of ever-changing phenomena. Identity and individuality should be understood in terms of a combination of phenomena which appear to form the physical and mental continuum of an individual life.

Deep mindfulness practice can reveal the misperception in identity. Suppose I project an externalized identity that can be characterized as "someone who is competent." Over the years, I unconsciously come to believe that I am in fact highly competent, even though sometimes my inner experience is just the opposite, and I do not always actually feel so competent. Maybe I repeatedly suppress or control those parts of my emotional experience that do not fit this aspect of my outer identity. So then, if I am not the exemplar of competency, who am I? If I rely on my external identity to inform how I speak and act and to determine what my priorities should be, this is not in accord with a philosophy of no-self. In Buddhism the phenomenon of identity is created moment by moment in the mind when several factors come together – bodily sensations, feelings of pleasantness and unpleasantness, perceptions of whatever is stimulating the experience, mental formations around the stimulus, and consciousness. The stimulus may come from outside the body, from within the body, or from the mind. Regardless of its origin, you are aware of the stimulus and respond to it as either pleasant or unpleasant. This is natural, but when you identify with wanting the feeling to continue or to go away and start to grasp at the desire, you give birth to a separate, solid self. Really all that is happening is that you are reacting to something that is either pleasant or unpleasant. Let me explain more deeply with this example. In daily life we desire to win arguments with our partners, receive recognition from colleagues, or fulfill the desire to buy a new car, the attainment of which fails to lead to lasting satisfaction since each desire is always replaced by yet another one. Desires change and contradict one another, and many times what we say, think, or feel does not seem like the real us at all. When faced with the reality that the "you" with whom you identify gets physically sick, mentally feeble, and finally dies, it is a relief to believe that sense of identity is part of the not self, or what in Buddhist philosophy is called *anatta*.

So, according to academic researchers, identity accounts for what gives people their sense of personal continuity across time. Embedded in the conceptualization is the assumption of the reality of identity. To scholars who approach the study of identity with this assumption already accepted the possibility of no such thing as personal identity is scarcely conceived, and consequently, the fundamental question of whether personal identity exists in the first place remains unasked, and the no-self theory, that is, the rejection of the notion of personal identity altogether, is never fully considered. One of the reasons for not accepting a no-self theory seems to be a failure in distinguishing between reductionism and the no-self view. The reason for this error is understandable because, in a sense, the two theories agree. Both theories, for example, reject the notion of a substantive self which somehow exists beyond the bounds of experience. The difference, however, is that while the reductionist accounts (which explains the bundle of changing sensations we experience as somehow related to each other) then go on to resurrect the self and, consequently, its identity, in terms of putative psychological relations or various theories of the body, the no-self theory has no use for that. This is because the no-self theory is not a theory about the self at all. It is rather a rejection of all such theories as inherently untenable. And since reductionism is just one more theory about the self, it, too, must be untenable. Even philosophers like Hume, who reject the idea that there is an enduring self, still typically acknowledge the force of memorial experience in giving the impression of identity across time. Indeed, it is incumbent on theorists who deny persistence of self to prove that memory presents us with an illusion of identity.

Identity When the Brain Disrupts Memory

A past or a future person might be you if and only if you can now remember an experience from that past, or the future person can remember the moment that is now. If a person remembers an event, then she, the very person who remembers it, must have been present at the event. That is, a past or future person is you just in the case that you can now remember an experience she had then or she can then remember an experience you are having now. Call this the *memory criterion*. According to John Locke's memory theory of identity (Lännström, 2007), a person's identity only reaches as far as their memory extends into the past. This account of personal identity holds that memories are part of what make me the same as the person I was in the past. Memories of past actions go toward constituting personal identity. Even if one rejects the view that memory constitutes personal identity, memory nonetheless provides compelling evidence that "I" am the very person who did the action. But, simply remembering an experience is not enough to make you the person who had that experience. Obviously, if a neurosurgeon somehow implanted her grandmother's memory into my brain, that would not make me her grandmother.

It follows, then, that not yet having developed language with which to store memories, we have no episodic (autobiographical) memories of events that occurred before two years of age. Arguably, memories for personal experiences are not possible until the advent of language and the cognitive self, around 18–24 months old (Howe, 2003). So it is reasonable to extrapolate that very young humans have no sense of identity, contrary to what was stated above. But we can salvage that although language may be an important concomitant of memory more generally, it is perhaps not key to the beginning of autobiographical memory. The cognitive self has been measured using mirror self-recognition tasks in which, for example, infants show full self-recognition by touching their own nose rather than pointing to the mirror following the surreptitious application of a spot of rouge to their nose. It is at this point in their development that children also start to show signs of self-consciousness (e.g., shy smiling, gaze aversion, self-touching) when confronted with their images. Collectively, these behaviors provide a consistent picture of very young children who recognize themselves as independent beings with unique features, an achievement that most people agree is a developmental milestone indicating the ability to represent oneself as an object of knowledge and imagination but no sense of internal identity.

Internal psychological factors, physiological factors, and external life events all combine to affect identity. As one of the psychological factors, some identity scholars posit that memories of one's own past are crucial, especially for maintaining identity as we reach the opposite end of life's continuum and become elders. So much important change happens then to the nervous system: the brain and spinal cord lose nerve cells, and the remaining ones pass messages more slowly; waste products collect in the brain tissue as nerve cells break down causing abnormal formation of plaques and tangles. Breakdown of nerves can affect the senses in the form of reduced or lost reflexes or sensation. This leads to problems with movement and safety. Bones and teeth soften, and the rest of the body hardens. Blood vessels, joints, the muscle, and valves of the heart and even the lungs pick up substantial deposits of calcium and turn stiff. The heart becomes thicker-walled from having to pump against increased pressure and less able to respond to the demands of exertion. I catalogue these deteriorations to make the point that because of profound deleterious changes to cognitive and physical states in old age, and because many of us will live for decades in this condition, who we are must adapt to limitations that are always in flux. Our attitudes toward the aging process say something about what we consider essential to our identities, as individuals and as a member of the human species. As the body becomes old and our social lives – the external identity – transform in radical ways, we define ourselves differently. As a faltering nervous system affects cognition, our internal identity shifts as well.

Since a dominant philosophical view is that the answer to "Who am I?" depends critically on what one remembers about their personal history, then as a person's memory begins to disappear by dint of old age or by damage to the brain, so does her identity. This notion of identity as memory has received experimental support from psychology research, particularly by Addis and Tippett (2004) with Alzheimer's patients that found those exhibiting impairments in autobiographical memory (one's knowledge of their own past experiences and events from about ages 16 to 25) on standard psychological tests showed changes in the strength and quality of identity. Autobiographical memory decline was associated with cognitive decline but also with an experienced loss of personhood. The strength of identity was measured by the number of unique statements given by the patient in response to the question,

"Who am I?" (assessed by the validated *Twenty Statements Test*), while the quality of identity was measured by the abstractness of their answers, that is, by the lack of any specific details. It seems that autobiographical memories create a continuous first-person narrative that helps form a sense of self and identity. Such a narrative view of life is like each of our lives being an unfolding story in which we, its authors, strive to make sense of ourselves.

If identity is the sum of our thoughts and sensations and memories, then the first inescapable fact is that these depend on our brains. Some of the most compelling evidence that the self depends on the brain comes from studies of people who have suffered brain damage. Memory of past personal life episodes provides a sense of personal identity, the sense that I am the same person as someone in the past. But there exists at least one neurological case study of a patient who has accurate memories of scenes from his past, but for whom the memories lack the sense of "mineness." On the basis of this case study, it is proposed that the sense of identity derives from two components, one delivering the content of the memory and the other generating the sense that the memories belong to self. Although self-trait memory provides a critical sense of self, it is not sufficient for a sense of personal identity across time. This is illustrated by a number of patients, but the patient known in the literature as D.B. provides what is perhaps the most dramatic case (Klein & Nichols, 2012). Following cardiac arrest and presumed hypoxic brain damage, D.B. had knowledge of his own traits, and yet he was unaware that he had a past and was unable to imagine his future. This presumably is because the patient had severe damage to episodic memory rendering him incapable of recollecting a single event or experience from any point in his past and explains his lack of a sense that he existed in the past. From this example it seems that episodic memory is essential for the sense of personal identity across time. Strikingly, when episodic memory is partially intact, people retain a sense of identity even if there has been dramatic loss of other types of memory.

Finally, consider H.M., one of the most famous subjects of psychological investigation, who in 1953 had a large portion of his medial temporal lobes surgically removed to alleviate severe epileptic seizures. To see where the temporal lobes are, put a finger above your ear. If you were able to push that finger two inches into your head you would be in the area called the medial temporal lobe. In trying to alleviate H.M.'s seizures, most of the medial temporal lobes were excised bilaterally, including much of a structure called the hippocampus, the site of memory consolidation. After the surgery, there was an unanticipated side effect in that H.M. could not form any new episodic memories. However, he reveled in telling a few old stories about his childhood. He could not remember whether his parents were alive or dead, and he did not know where he was living, but he seemed to believe he was the same young man of his stories.

Yet, along with the episodic criterion for psychological continuity (i.e., the requirement that we have memories of events that happened to us) discussed above, what might provide for this personally felt and unwavering sense of personal continuity? One possibility is that there is a sense of personal continuity that derives from trait self-knowledge, a subsystem within semantic memory. An extensive review of the available research (Klein & Lax, 2010) shows that knowledge of one's traits is immune to loss in the face of multiple, often severe, neurological, and cognitive insult (including total retrograde and anterograde amnesia, autism, Alzheimer's dementia, and prosopagnosia); is empirically dissociable from trait knowledge of others (even well-known others such as the patient's family members) as well as from purely factual, non-dispositional self-knowledge; and can serve as a firmly entrenched foundation for one's sense that one "is, was, and will be." In short, the surprising and unanticipated resilience of trait self-knowledge may serve as the bedrock for one's sense that one is a continuing, experiencing self even when one's memory-based personal narrative has succumbed to the ravages of episodic amnesia.

Conclusion

Rather than positing the question of "Who am I?" to address identity, I reframed it as a consideration of how we maintain a sense of internal consistency across time. Identity is somewhat stable, somewhat flexible, and tied closely to what we remember of our lives. The literature on personal identity is vast, and it incorporates a grab bag of varying approaches, theses, and conceptual understandings. It is very loosely unified by investigations into the "identities" of "persons," but these are concepts with multiple senses. The argument between whether identity is stable or flexible, upon examination, seems a false one. The answer is both. We change identities according to social and physical experiences, yet our memories give us a story of self that is consistent.

"Do I contradict myself? Very well, then, I contradict myself; I am large. I contain multitudes" (Whitman, 1855). It seems to this cognitive psychologist that the most generous answer to what we mean when we talk about identity allows for the undeniable role of selected, episodic memories as a function of age, social milieu, and health status. Said another way: memory must be the thing holding identity together. The self is anchored upon past experiences where selective distillation of one's memory results in the reformulation of self and identity. Identity is constructed from the narrative of memory. Memory provides the evidence for a strict identity of self across time.

References

Addis, R., & Tippett, L. (2004). Memory of myself: Autobiographical memory and identity in Alzheimer's disease. *Memory, 12*(1), 56–74.

Anthis, K., & LaVoie, J. C. (2006). Readiness to change: A longitudinal study of changes in adult identity. *Journal of Research in Personality, 40*(2), 209–219.

Bullock, M., & Lütkenhaus, P. (1989). The development of volitional behavior in the toddler years. *Annual Progress in Child Psychiatry & Child Development*, 75–91.

Burke, P. J. (2004). Extending identity control theory: Insights from classifier systems. *Sociological Theory, 4*, 574–594.
Erikson, E. H. (1980). *Identity and the life cycle: A reissue*. New York: Norton.
Howe, M. L. (2003). Memories from the cradle. *Current Directions in Psychological Science (Wiley-Blackwell), 12*(2), 62–65.
Klein, S. B., & Lax, M. L. (2010). The unanticipated resilience of trait self-knowledge in the face of neural damage. *Memory, 18*(8), 918–948.
Klein, S. B., & Nichols, S. (2012). Memory and the sense of personal identity. *Mind: A Quarterly Review of Philosophy, 121*(483), 677–702.
Kuhn, M. H., & McPartland, T. S. (1954). An empirical investigation of self-attitudes. *American Sociological Review, 19*(1), 68–76.
Lännström, A. (2007). Locke's account of personal identity: Memory as fallible evidence. *History of Philosophy Quarterly, 24*(1), 39–56.
Low, K. Y. (2013). Olfactive frames of remembering: Theorizing self, senses and society. *The Sociological Review, 61*(4), 688–708.
Mahler, M. S., Pine, F., & Bergman, A. (2000). *The psychological birth of the human infant: Symbiosis and individuation*. New York: Basic Books.
Marcia, J. E. (2002). Identity and psychosocial development in adulthood. *Identity: An International Journal of Theory and Research, 2*(1), 7–28.
Marquez, G. G. (1985). *Love in the time of cholera*.
Plastow, N. A., Atwal, A., & Gilhooly, M. (2015). Food activities and identity maintenance in old age: A systematic review and meta-synthesis. *Aging & Mental Health, 19*(8), 667–678.
Small, H. (2007). *The long life*. Oxford, UK: Oxford University Press.
Thoits, P. A. (1995). Identity-relevant events and psychological symptoms: A cautionary tale. *Journal of Health and Social Behavior, 1*, 72–82.
Whitman, W. (1855). *Song of myself*.
Zhou, B., Pöppel, E., & Bao, Y. (2014). In the jungle of time: The concept of identity as a way out. *Frontiers in Psychology, 5*, 844.

Chapter 2
Cognitive Underpinnings of Identity Flexibility in Adulthood

Jan D. Sinnott

Ring the bells that still can ring
There is no perfect offering
There is a crack in everything
That's where the light comes in. (Leonard Cohen)

The main question I hope to address in this chapter is this: how can I create and hold a unified concept of my self and my identity at the same time I hold a concept of my self and my identity as growing, evolving, and changing? My answer will be that I use complex postformal thought and problem solving, a theory of adult cognitive development that rests on complex conceptual processes also seen in sciences such as quantum physics and self-constructing systems. Now that you have the short answer to my question, you, the reader, can read on for a deeper analysis, critique the ideas, or go on to another chapter. Your choice.

That main question addressed in this chapter arose in part from my own struggle with my sense of self, developing over my life time, one that I knew as a unified "me" but also knew as changing and evolving. There is one fantasy that I had as a younger person that I would love to keep forever: that I can not only "find my self" but can forever after keep the self that I find, keep that "real me." I imagined finding my "real" self can only happen through really hard work. I imagined that it would take years of adult life to find that real me, recognize her, and embrace her. To do this would demand that I could accept that real self, as she is.

But this truly is a fantasy because it ignores the reality about cognition that we have learned about through years of psychological research. To remember something or to think about it in a different context changes it, distorts the memory, if you will, over time. To illustrate, think of one simple psychological process: memories are changed as we remember them, by the mere act of remembering them in a new context and by subsequent experience. Just try to remember who you were as

J.D. Sinnott (✉)
Towson University, Baltimore, MD, USA
e-mail: jsinnott@towson.edu

J.D. Sinnott (ed.), *Identity Flexibility During Adulthood*,
DOI 10.1007/978-3-319-55658-1_2

a 20 year old. Do you see your self as a 20-something now in the same way as you saw yourself then? And more important, do friends agree with your memory of you as a 20 year old? Class reunions offer lots of chances to surprise people (and your self) as you accidently meet your selves from the past and are confused by somewhat new selves of friends attending.

Suggestions of healthy identity flexing come to us from many experiences like those of artists and mystics and individuals living in more than one culture. The "reentry shock" experienced by returning Peace Corps volunteers and veterans returning home from wars is another example, "healthy" when experiences are eventually resolved. Until the resolution we experience a kind of double bookkeeping where it is necessary to decide which of the competing selves to be.

We now have the provocative insights of the latest neuroscience explorations of the alternative-self/dissolved-self experiences of individuals who suffer from schizophrenia, autism, Alzheimer's disease, ecstatic epilepsy, Cotard's syndrome (individuals who think they are already dead), body integrity disorder (individuals' feelings that parts of their bodies do not belong to them), and other disorders (Ananthaswamy, 2015). Certain regions of the brain, when they misfire, can, for example, cause the self to leave the body entirely or to move back and forth between the ordinary self and a double of that self. Neuroscientists see self as residing both everywhere and nowhere in the human brains of these patients. However, neurological disorders do not represent *flexibility* of identity as much as *disordered* identity that does not allow for flexibility and is not especially adaptive. The suffering of these patients sometimes includes suicidality and almost complete withdrawal from life as typical adults experience it. The neuropsychological insights confirm the importance of body-mind connections to ideas of adult identity flexibility. Added to these insights is the fascinating work of psychologists like Kramer and Bressan (2015) who summarized data that we are not even unitary individuals (much less unchanging selves) but rather superorganisms, built out of both human and nonhuman elements whose *interaction* affects who we are. These "fellow travelers" include microbes in our brains and guts capable of altering our behavior, viral DNA incorporated into our cells, cells belonging to another human in our brains, and inherited copies of genes that have opposite behavioral effects.

In this present book and in this chapter, the emphasis is on the more ordinary adaptively evolving adult identity of individuals without a diagnosable condition. (One exception is the clinically focused chapter on dissociative disorders which directly addresses identity.) We seek understanding of our everyday sense of the unified "I" (the synchronic self) that philosophers, poets, and religious figures have found intriguing throughout recorded history, as well as understanding of our everyday sense of the evolving "I" (the diachronic self). But neuroscience findings offer some hint of what is going on at a *reductionist* level when various states of awareness of self occur, and this is what makes those findings new and interesting. We've never been able to observe at this level before, to see that certain regions of the brain such as the insular cortex, the temporoparietal junction, and the medial frontal cortex are more important than others for the sense of self as we normally know it.

How do we "know" ourselves, cognitively, with both a unified adult identity and an identity that keeps evolving?

To find perfect composure in the midst of change
Is to find ourselves in nirvana. (Suzuki Roshi)

The purpose of this chapter is to discuss a different way of conceptualizing the adult self and identity, namely, as a phenomenon in adults that is constantly created and re-created, but is known as a unity in spite of its constant change and flexibility. This concept of identity involves no permanent fixed quality; yet it is *felt* to be stable in an ongoing way.

This chapter addresses the question of how I can *think about* or *know* who "I" am when "I" constantly change. It addresses the processes by which I can know my ever-evolving self and not be confused by its ongoing evolution. The issues discussed in this chapter partly arise from the challenging fact that we human individuals know that we, ourselves, will change, age, and die. This is a chapter about the evolving, flexible self as a point at the center of events and experiences that surround us during our lives. Who are we as we change? Current models of identity and the self are good, but a wider model may be needed to accommodate the evolution of identity during adulthood, an evolution that exists concomitant with the feeling of an enduring self. In earlier work I have explored to some extent the construction of the self in the face of aging and death (Sinnott, 2011), the supremely important act of creativity in personally conceptualizing and making meaningful the later stages of life (Sinnott, 1998a, 1998b), and the cognitive underpinnings of the dance of adaptive transformation during adulthood (Sinnott, 2005). In this chapter I want to extend these ideas.

To ask deeper questions about the nature of evolving yet subjectively stable adult identity, I will use a number of models including complex postformal problem solving, physics, chaotic self-organizing systems, general systems theory, and creativity. What processes and destabilizing factors form (and reform) identity for an adult? What processes might maintain known continuity in the face of identity evolution? More specifically, what *cognitive processes* are underpinnings for the adult identity flexibility we experience and see all around us?

In Fig. 2.1 is a model for the construction of the flexible self and of one's flexible identity. This Figure provides a model for complex structural equation models that can be used to relate several factors in the underlying latent processes that may be involved in adult identity flexibility, as described, for example, by Caskie (2011). Figure 2.2 summarizes the multiple complex emotionally involving relationships that adults experience, relationships that are part of the construction of a flexible and evolving self and identity.

We begin model building by examining quantum physics ideas, living systems theory, and chaos theory. Then we go on to the most important cognitive model for this paper, the model of complex postformal thought.

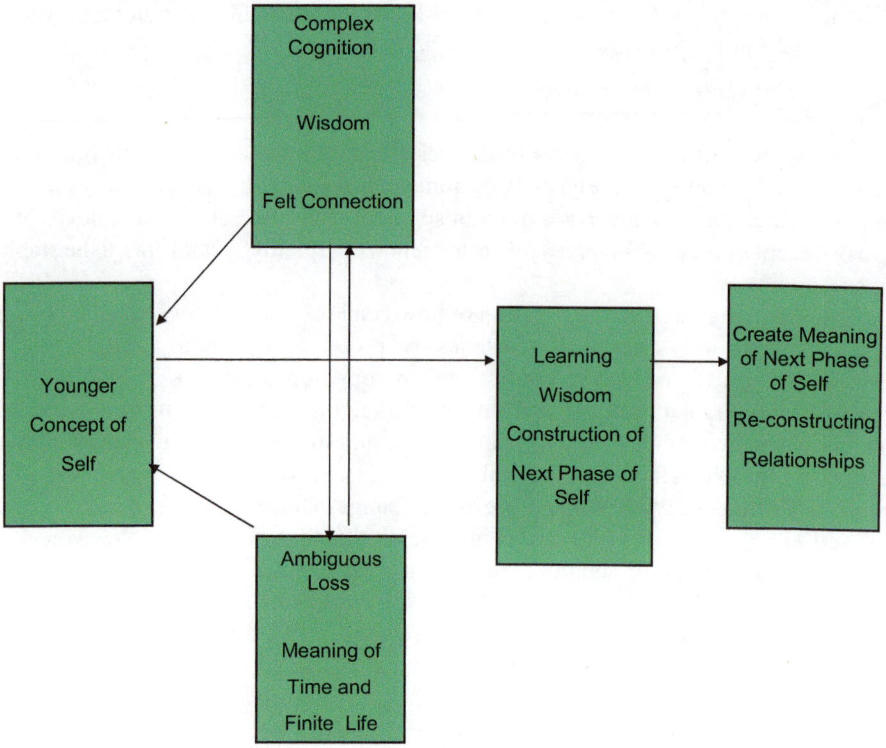

Fig. 2.1 Model for flexible construction of the self during the adult years of life

The Models of Quantum Weirdness, Living Systems, and Chaos Speak to Evolving Identity

The Universe is not only queerer than we imagine,
but it is queerer than we can imagine. (J.B.S. Haldane)

With the advent of quantum mechanics, physicists had to give up their preconceived ideas about the physical world. As Wolf (1981) described it so well in lay language, the quantum world holds surprises. For example, every observation of an atom made by physicists disrupts the atom. So how do we know the "real" atom? We can't get the atom to not be disturbed by our observation. We cannot ignore the fact that the origins of scientific ideas lie in the human imagination (Jones, 1992). Even Einstein acknowledged the fundamental role played by the imagination, in addition to the data, in the development of scientific theory, a creation of the human mind that more or less fits our observations of the natural world. In the new physics world, everything is interwoven with everything else. Knowing this "weirdness" is a complex cognitive act.

New physics quantum weirdness leads to three major paradoxes that have a strong relevance to our thoughts about knowing flexible adult identity in this chapter. First, things do not move in a continuous motion but jump or change in unpredictable, discontinuous ways. Second, what one observes depends upon what one

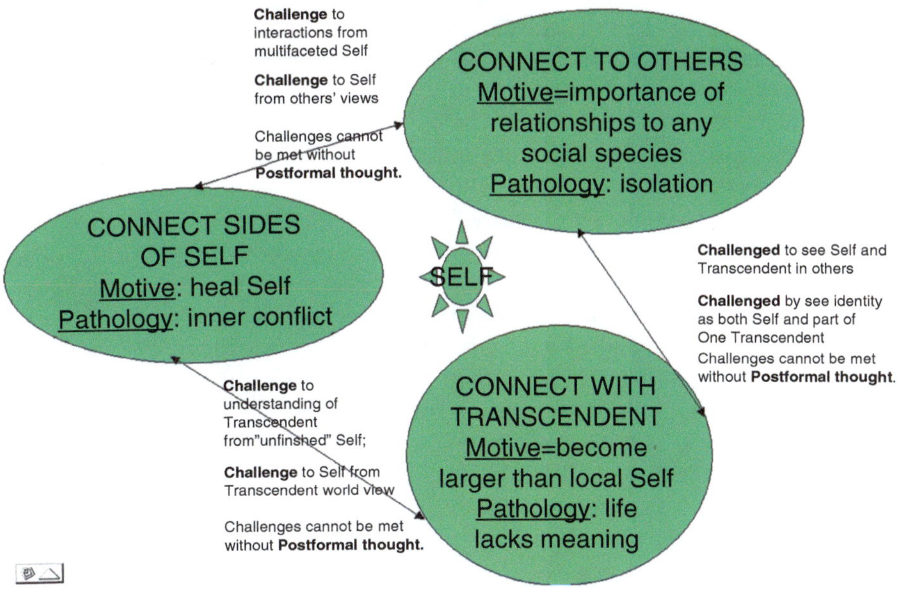

Fig. 2.2 Theory of felt connections and the construction of the concept of self

chooses to observe. Third, quantum mechanics describes an order in the world that includes us, such that the order in the universe may reflect order in our own minds. Atoms may not exist without observers of atoms.

How does this thinking relate to thinking about, and knowing, flexible adult identity? First, during adult development, identity, or the sense of self, does not consistently move in a predictable path to a completion point, but seems to "jump around" in what looks like unpredictable ways. Second, how an adult decides to examine the events of life in relation to the self determines the identity, or the self that seems to "be there." Third, the order (or disorder) we see in our identity over time seems to reflect the order (or disorder) and ongoing alteration in our own conceptualization of self or identity.

New Physics Models Underlying Identity Flexibility

The purpose of this part of our discussion is to review some important original ideas basic to the new physics as it was first articulated in relativity theory and quantum physics. Of course physics has evolved immensely since the origins of the new physics. But my purpose is to show how useful even the basic new physics ideas are as meta-theories for adult identity flexibility. Other post-Newtonian physics paradigms, especially general systems theory, chaos theory, and complexity theories of self-regulating systems, also will be discussed in later sections.

Far from being frightening or difficult, new physics ideas are extremely practical when they are applied. These advanced models are being considered in realms as different as spirituality and organization management, and some forms of many of the ideas are apparent in Native American and other indigenous traditions. After all, those concepts must be understandable to us at some level if they can, metaphorically speaking, keep us cognitively dancing in balance on the moving, rotating planet of our reality! These ideas are integral to the universe that is our home. Historically we have been accustomed to thinking that our home consists of one room, the layout of which is defined by "old" Newtonian physics which describes local small-scale reality. New physics simply opens the door to the rest of the rooms of the house and provides us with the larger floor plan of our home in nonlocal universal reality. Like so many moving adventures, once we get accustomed to the new living space, we can't imagine living without it. We move into the postformal larger reality home and think of it as our natural habitat. We become like the child who reaches teen years and can no longer think within the limits of a 6-year-old mind.

Let's review some of these basic original new physics concepts to see how they might be used as metaphors to help us understand adult identity flexibility. New and old physics give us two different ways to describe the "same" reality. Postformal thought permits us to cognitively process both realities at the same time, a cognitive structure that is useful for adaptive lifespan identity development.

Since they are more inclusive, probabilistic, and complex, new physics ideas are difficult to articulate in a verbal system dominated by more rigid functional relations. New physics ideas would be expected to occur later in the history of any idea development than the simpler and more readily demonstrated earlier ideas. This would be expected in all sciences in spite of the independence of these scientific fields. Scientific advances, whatever the science, take place in a particular historical period and are influenced by the overall tone, predominant thought patterns, and the cultural rules about reality current during that period (Kuhn, 1962; Riegel, 1977). If past history is any guide, new physics ideas will increase in any period as a function of the number of scientists dissatisfied with any paradigm, the developmental history of the science itself, and the capability of individual scientists to think in such inclusive and probabilistic ways. In sciences or in individuals, new physics thinking seems to occur because it is adaptive. Interested readers may want to peruse physics textbooks, tap into the huge array of technical books and articles, and read the recent edited compilations of ideas (e.g., Davies' *The New Physics*, 1989) or scan the very lay-reader-friendly work of writers such as Wolf (1981). In Newtonian pre-Einsteinian physics, classical mechanics developed as an outgrowth of everyday physical experience with the environment. This experience was first summarized in intuitive and anthropomorphic generalizations and then in abstract laws. New physics has been developed over a period of years in response to contradictions found while working with the theories of classical mechanics (Russell, 1969). The space of classical mechanics is Euclidian; all transformations in space are describable by Cartesian fixed coordinates and consist of either rotations or translations. Time is an absolute concept, and calculus, presuming continuity of matter and space, is an adequate mathematical tool.

The new physics realizes that measuring standards which appeared to be rigid and absolute were not. To use Einstein's famous example, it was as if the observer were on a speeding train but unaware of its movement. After carefully measuring and describing the environment and relations of objects found while sitting on the train and looking outside the window, the observer would have a certain amount of data. Some of the data would prove shockingly incorrect if the train came to a full stop and the observer were suddenly able to take into account the consequences of motion biases. None of the observer's measures had been wrong for the observer's specific time and place conditions; they simply were not the entire picture of reality. What the observer saw was real data carefully controlled by scientific methodology, but colored by the fact that measurement was not done with a fixed measure but with a changing one (Einstein, 1961).

The scientific or cognitive world of the pre-Einsteinian is like that of the traveler who is still unaware of his or her motion on the train. As we'll see later, developing minds are brought to awareness of their own "motion bias" by interpersonal interactions. The event that brought the awareness of motion bias to the scientist was work in electromagnetism. As a result of discoveries in that field, phenomena which are at variance with Newtonian physics were discovered. Newton, for example, held that only the distance between two objects determined the strength of forces they exerted upon one another. This was contradicted by Oersted's work, demonstrating that relative motion is also important in determining object interaction, and by Maxwell, who demonstrated field effects' importance in the strength of forces between bodies. Attempts to deal with these contradictions led to the new mathematical tools of vector analysis and tensor analysis, to Einstein's elaborations on relativity theory and to quantum mechanics. Contradictions led to a new physics.

The postulates of relativity theory in new physics are simple to express but difficult to conceptualize. Observers fail to recognize that their standards of measurement of events are *not* truly rigid (i.e., consistent or absolute) ones *unless* they deal with small-scale, isolated limiting case events. The *first postulate of relativity* is valid only for such limiting cases: If, relative to K, K′ is a uniformly moving system of coordinates devoid of rotations, K and K′ share the same natural laws (Einstein, 1961). In other words when two persons are both on the train, their scientific, objective findings agree with one another. The problem, as might be expected, comes when K and K′ are not uniformly moving systems of coordinates devoid of rotation, that is, when both observers are not on the same train. When one goes beyond the somewhat reductionist small-scale descriptions of nature, not every observer can be on the train.

The *second postulate, or the special theory of relativity*, was formulated in response to this type of problem and contradiction in data. In the second postulate, certain formerly rigid concepts such as time and space are made dependent on the motion (or non-motion) of the reference body. The Lorentz transform (Einstein, 1961) was developed as a mathematical tool for moving from one system of positional coordinates to another, to allow for the effect of shifting vantage points. According to this postulate, general laws of nature may still be deduced from such idiosyncratic experiences, *if* their coordinate systems are related by the Lorentz transform. In other words, if the space/time position on the train can be related to the space/time on the road, a general law which applies to both locations can be determined.

The *general theory of relativity or the third postulate* was formulated to replace Newton's theory of gravity, which would be impossible under this new set of assumptions, with an explanation consistent with the new set of assumptions. The inseparable space/time dimension of one body was coordinated with the dimension of nearness to another body. The result was that a graphic description of space/time took on a curvature. In other words, when two bodies approach one another, the closer they get, the more their paths in space/time deviate from a straight line. The closer a moving train approaches the top of a mountain, the slower and more circular its path. The mathematics of moving a vector like the train from place to place without changing its size or orientation (i.e., the mathematics of "parallel transport") was developed to deal with movement in space/time across a curved surface. Assuming that objects travel the most efficient route from point to point, this new tool allows one to describe space/time movement in spite of the gravitational field. It therefore allows transformation of coordinate systems even when such transforms are multidimensional and continuous. The general theory of relativity demands that a natural law be applicable to multidimensional, continuous transforms of coordinate systems, if it is to be a *general* law (Einstein, 1961).

Pre-Einsteinian theories include laws of nature which appear general, but which are general only under certain specific reductionist space/time conditions. Einstein's laws of nature include Newton's as special cases. Many assumptions characterize old physics and differ from those in new physics. We will consider just a few of these. Notice that both sets of assumptions have been verified with experimental evidence, so *both contradictory sets of assumptions are true*. Newtonian physics assumptions have been found to be true in small-scale, everyday systems, except for minor inconsistencies; new physics assumptions are true for the general case and include the others as special limiting conditions.

The nature of space differs between the two sets of assumptions (Kaufman, 1973). Space can be described as Euclidean when the measuring standard is at rest, the limiting case. Space must be described as non-Euclidean in the general case. In the former situation, the shortest distance between two points is a straight line, while in the latter, it is a geodesic (i.e., a curved path describing the shortest distance between two points located on a curved surface). Aristotelian logic appears challenged by the destabilization of concepts such as space and time and by the allowance of logical contradiction in terms of limiting case postulates vs. general-case postulates.

An assumption under Newtonian physics and the calculus which it utilized is the continuity of phenomena – time, place, and events – which are assumed to be isolated, measured against rigid standards, and ordered in an unchanging manner. Under the new set of assumptions, phenomena are continuous only in the limiting case, but discontinuous in general (Robertson & Noonan, 1968).

The absolute nature of time and space in the Pre-Einstein perspective is replaced by the space/time interval (Einstein, 1961). The interval allows the effect of time on space, or of space on time, to be taken into account when locating an event or reasoning about it. As events approach the speed of light, time slows down. An event which is simultaneous with another event (in one view) also precedes that event (in a second view) and is subsequent to it (in a third view). On the other hand, if the time element is variously measured, the position of the event in space may assume several contradictory sets of coordinates for the same event.

The conceptualization of the uniformity of space also changes (Russell, 1969). In the former metatheory, space is uniform throughout; in the latter, space appears filled with hills and valleys which offer greater and lesser resistances to moving bodies. These gravitational fields, i.e., the hills encountered, slow the moving body and make its path more circular, allowing it to approach but never attain the center of the field.

Two observers can never reach valid conclusions about the same event if they fail to take their own movement into account (Brillouin, 1970). What the two observers see at a given time would be determined by their motion relative to one another and to the event. Using the train example, if one person on the road and a second on the moving train see a star, the reality of their physical relation to the star can only be ascertained after the effect of the motion of the earth, the motion of the train, and the motion of the star are taken into account. The formulation of a scientific hypothesis, i.e., an epistemology or a knowing of the relations between oneself and the star, is incomplete if it does not develop beyond pre-Einsteinian notions. In other words, if one attempts to know the star in terms of physical experience in Newtonian physics terms, one will lack a complete understanding of the star in a larger sense. The lesser knowledge may be sufficient for some situations, but not for all situations. An additional abstraction from abstractions must be made, one which permits egocentrism in a sophisticated sense in which one always takes one's biases into account. Both the small-scale principles of physical relations, which are useful every day, and the general-scale multiple vantage points principles of physical relations, which are the more inclusive assessment, must coexist in thinking, contradictory as they seem to be, to know reality in all its forms and to adapt to different situations. Postformal thought gives us the cognitive framework for doing so. Conceptions of causality are broadened in new physics thought (Toulmin, 1970). The deterministic causality of Newtonian physics is enlarged by the deterministic probabilistic causality of quantum mechanics (Heisenberg, 1958; Schlick, 1970). Simple Newtonian deterministic physical causality would pertain in limited situations and would assume contiguity (i.e., cause and effect necessarily in contact). A new physics definition of causality, in contrast, could be "a timeless relation of dependency between two events" or "a center around which events (i.e., effects) are grouped." The relatedness of two specific events in a limited fixed space/time can be predicted on a simple, deterministic basis, but the general relatedness of two events only can be predicted on a complex, probabilistic basis. The implications of this for the scientific method have been vast. While the new student of science may still look for simple experimental "cause and effect relations," the advanced investigator is now more likely to focus on chaos and complexity theory, self-organizing systems, and the implicate order as he or she thinks about causes.

Causality is determinable within a relativistic system, but the limits bounding those determinants are much wider than they are in simpler systems. Ideas of nonlocal causation and the paradox of Shroedinger's cat certainly intrigue us. Relativistic thinking seems more ecologically valid for explaining effects and causes in a naturalistic setting where many variables are in constant interplay. Looking at the Newtonian micro-universe of the developing fetus, for example, one chemical change does determine a specific limiting case reaction. More important, though, is the overall general new physics reaction of the fetus which is determined not only by the chemical but probabilistically also by the prevailing fetal milieu and history. The chemical, in the general case, is simply the center of a complex but predictable response. Later writers examine such concepts as "nonlocal causality" in physics in general (e.g., Bohm, 1980), as well as in biology (e.g., Sheldrake, 1981, 1989, 1990) and medicine (e.g., Dossey, 1982, 1989). The concept of egocentrism comes full circle through transition from the prescientific ego-boundedness of the child, through supposed objectivity of the young adult, to the new physics notion that the data and the observer are in an ongoing necessary interaction. In the third stage, the person who attempts to be decentered and objective learns that subjectivity must be made part of the measure of the phenomenon itself and that objective reality is better defined as the sum of observational invariants, even though each of those invariants is known to be necessarily partly subjective (Born, 1962, 1964).

But there is a catch. The logic and laws of nature have been formulated within verbal conventions which make it difficult to understand this new physics objectivity in a non-polarized way. For example, present-tense declarative verbal statements fit Aristotelian logic but would not fit new physics general-case ideas well (Freedle, 1977). The "either A or non-A" forms in language usage are also basically old physics, making expressions of new physics ideas (e.g., "both A and non-A") seem contradictory. No wonder mathematicians or lovers sometimes avoid words.

How might developing individuals mutually affect one another in terms of analogs of the third postulate? In relativistic terms, they might change the shape and the dimensions of each other's developmental space/time and affect the direction of each other's movement. Development may fairly be visualized as a straight-line function in a small-scale event. But, over the life course, it is not fair to do so. We notice that the direction and speed of lifespan development is often changed by encounters with persons and events that the individual later perceives as important. The first others encountered have stronger deflecting action than later ones, just as planets caught in each other's gravitational fields remain influenced by that first encounter, unless changes within the planet itself or the passing of a stronger third body are the occasion for changing relationships. The interaction with developing others encountered during one's own development probably, in natural science terms, describes a geodesic. One continually approaches, circles, and is repelled by the other, but one has been permanently deflected and is constantly affected by the other's nearness. The impact is also mutual. Interpersonal space during development can then be described as a hilly surface with each individual as the top of a hill and all the hills in motion through space/time. As each gets nearer to knowing or influencing the other, resistance increases, so that a slowing circular motion carries the approaching ones around each other. If one were to step close to the surface of one of those hills, one body actually making giant circles around another would seem to move straight ahead; local small-scale events appear nonrelativistic and separable into individual developments and social developments.

General Systems Theory (GST) of Living Systems Underlies Identity Flexibility

Developed hand in hand with the new physics, GST is useful for students of adult development, especially those who want to understand the evolving yet stable self. It offers ways to think about complex system interactions, not only interactions among supposedly inert physical systems (the focus of physics) but also among *living* systems.

The reasons we are discussing these views of the world at all in this particular chapter are twofold. First, they are the ancestors or underpinnings of the theory of postformal thought which I contend allows us to know and understand our own identity flexibility. Second, scientists, philosophers, and humanists are turning more and more often to world views such as these to describe how twentieth-century humans construct their world and give their lives meaning. The physicist Wigner, in a lecture, once said that theories can be "interesting" or "amusing." An interesting theory may have merit, but often such theories are quickly forgotten; an amusing theory is a theory that makes one *think* and *play with the possibilities*. GST is an amusing theory.

GST is an attempt to unify science by finding structures and processes common to many "living" entities. Of greatest interest are entities which are complex organizations that have boundaries, have some continuity over time, and are able to change in orderly ways over time. Such entities may be called living systems (Miller, 1978), whether they are cells or societies or identities, of some other type of entity. GST included among its earlier theorists such luminaries as Norbert Wiener (1961) and Ludwig von Bertalanfy (1968). Today it is expressed in the language of quantum physics, chemistry, the many family systems approaches in clinical psychology, game theory (von Neumann & Morgenstern, 1947), biofeedback, sociology (Lock Land, 1973), and many other disciplines (Mahoney, 1991).

What are some of the core themes of GST? The first is the concept of a *system*, that is, a network of related components and processes that work as a whole. *Linkage* and *interaction* are key themes, because whatever influences one part or process influences all of the parts and processes, that is, influences the entire system. Systems coordinate their activities by means of *feedback*, either from within or without. Feedback from within leads to homeostasis or equilibrium within; feedback from without leads to balance between two or more systems. *Equilibrium* is a balance between or among system parts. Given a state of disequilibrium, there will be an energy flow from one part to another. Any number of systems can have common mechanisms (*isomorphic processes*) for doing some task. For example, getting energy from one point to another may occur by means of chemical transmission or glucose metabolism or by moving commuters via subways in a "city system." Because systems do interact and trade things such as energy, GST recognizes that scientists need to make deliberate decisions to specify system limits or parameters and levels of description. We have not always done this in the past. Thus, there is an awareness of the observer's input on the "reality" observed, an emphasis reminiscent of the new physics. For example, if I draw living system boundaries at the person level, I may correctly say that a middle-aged woman's depression is due to poor coping strategies; if I draw the boundaries at the societal living system level, I may argue with equal correctness that the depression is caused by social stigmas attached to women aging. I would be correct in both cases but would investigate different things.

Systems theory examines multiple causal variables, or at least considers that they may be present, and focuses most on the processes used to go from one state to another. This makes GST a "natural" for developmental psychologists studying flexible identity who are interested in the multi-determined processes behind changes over time as much as in the states of persons at various time points. GST as a world view is interested in both the melody and the chords of any life song.

What are some systems functions that are commonly present in all systems? First a "living" (in the broad sense used before) system operates so as to *maintain some continuity over time*, some structured wholeness, even while continuing, if appropriate, to grow. Second, systems function to *contain and transfer energy and information* from one point to another, within or between them. All systems have some means of *boundary creation* and maintenance, as well as means of *interaction with other systems*. This implies that the boundary must be permeable, to some extent, but not so permeable that the system will merge with other systems. Other systems functions are to *control processes, run circular processes, and give feedback*. The overall goal is to provide optimum input for continuity and growth while avoiding pathological abnormalities and *maintaining flexibility*. These functions apply to identity flexibility as well.

Systems do change over time. How does this happen? The only way systems can change over time is if some entropy or disorder is present. If this is counter-intuitive, consider for a moment what would happen if no disorder were present and all elements were structured into some form: there would be no space available and no raw material to use to make new forms. For example, if a child used all available blocks to make a toy city (i.e., all the blocks were "ordered"), some disorder would have to be introduced (e.g., push the blocks into a pile on the side) to make room for the next orderly structure (perhaps a large house) to be built. If my mind is made up about an issue, I must introduce doubt before a change of mind is possible. So disorder (entropy) not only is the catastrophic final state predicted by the second law of thermodynamics but also the beneficial means to a flexible reordering and growth to a larger order. When systems change over time, they usually move from complete disorder or potential through increasing order and bounding to a relative balance between order and potential, a state that may last most of the system's "lifetime." As systems "die" they move toward rigidity which is a state of very low potential and overwhelming order. All the system's decisions have been made already, so to speak; all its choices are over. The overly ordered, overly structured rigid state admits no change and will be shattered by any input from outside. An analogy is what happens to a rigid crystal goblet that breaks under high-frequency vibrations, whereas the even thinner skin on the hand holding it does not. Prigogene (1980) notes that it is always possible to create a better structure by shattering a rigid state. From that shattering and the availability it creates will come a more flexible, more complex form. This means the death of the old system or its reemergence in very altered form.

Imagine a situation in which two systems (e.g., societies or identities) come up against each other and try to influence each other, that is, they intrude on each others' boundaries. If the first system is not too rigid and too ordered, the influence and energy of the second will have an impact and alter the first. The reciprocal will also be true. But if the first system is rigid, the second will not influence it easily. It will have to try harder, if it can. Let's say the intruder system does try harder still. If it cannot influence the rigid first system subtly, the more violent influence it may resort to may result in a complete shattering of the first system. The first system did not "go with the flow," "co-opt the opposition," or "make a deal." For a rigid system where compromise is out of the question, every fight with a worthy opponent is a fight to the death. What a high price to pay for necessary and ordinary adaptations! The gentler dynamic – mutual influence of semi-ordered systems – occurs, for example, during non-loaded discussions by members of a couple.

System change over time therefore demands a significant degree of entropy. But systems resist disorder on any large scale, and change means the temporary elimination of much order. The resistance to disorder in the psychological system is evident in the sometimes painful reorganizations during personal change, e.g., change during psychotherapy or during crises. Any system tries to monitor and control the extent of disorder, but hopes not to need to resist absolutely, because that would take too much energy. Surviving systems balance their potentials and actualizations, have boundaries but are not closed entirely, try to fit many contexts flexibly, and attempt to interface with other systems without being engulfed or engulfing. Non-surviving systems may have the same structures (e.g., a boundary), but may have different processes (e.g., rigidity in a boundary) that are less adaptive. In the case of the evolving self or identity, flexible self-systems that find their boundaries challenged potentially evolving identity forces need to enlarge and reconfigure, or shatter.

Chaos, Complexity, Self-Regulating Systems, and Identity Flexibility

The ideas of chaos theory, complexity theory, and self-regulating systems are another way to describe complex interactions that relate to identity evolution with stability. These also arise from physics to some extent, but are grounded even more strongly in computer science and biology. They are all useful as world views or methods for the study of lifespan cognitive postformal development of identity and self.

The processes described by new physics, GST, chaos, complexity, and self-regulating systems can be deeply understood only by the postformal logical thinker because they often violate the core linear logic of the formal operational hypothetico-deductive scientific thinker. This is one reason these new sciences seem hard to grasp and hard to teach in the average high school or college physics class. Granted, a student can repeat back axioms of a science even if he or she does not understand them, but that is not deep understanding. The individual with deep understanding can use the concepts to creatively solve problems like that of evolving identity.

Chaos theory is a newer mathematical model that has been used in the last two decades to describe phenomena as different as leadership and management styles, weather, the structure of coastlines, brain wave patterns, adult learning, normal or abnormal heartbeat patterns, family transitions, the behavior of the mentally ill, intractable conflicts, and much, much more (Alper, 1989; Cavanaugh, 1989; Cavanaugh & McGuire, 1994; Crutchfield, Farmer, Packard & Shaw, 1986; Gleick, 1987; Gottman, 1991; Pool, 1989; Sinnott, 1990; Vallacher, Coleman, Nowak, & Bui-Wrzosinska, 2010; Wheatley, 2006). General and more lengthy descriptions of chaos theory are available in Abraham (1985), Barton (1994), Devaney (1989), Gleick (1987), Goerner (1994), Levine and Fitzgerald (1992), and Smith and Thelan (1993). Chaos theory describes the orderly and flexible nature of apparent disorder. It mathematically describes complex systems with nonlinear equations. It describes commonalities of *processes* over time which would otherwise appear *dis*orderly if viewed at one time point.

Chaos theory works with dynamical systems which are systems where the contents of the system and the processes of the system mutually influence each other. In such systems the current state of the system is fed back to it before it makes another iteration or goes through another round of changes. The system then repeats its process, each time with updated information. Such systems tend to begin to appear stable over time, although they are in a constant state of change.

But such systems are deterministic, as well as unpredictable with only the *appearance* of stability. The behavior at each iteration is not predictable, but the limits built into the system confine it in predictable ways. So there is a "hidden" order that also gradually emerges from beneath the disorder. Chaotic systems somewhat resemble the rambling pattern of footprints made by a curious dog on a very long leash; at first there seems to be no pattern, but soon, after enough walking, a pattern emerges. Part of that emergent pattern is centered on the leash and on what or whoever is holding it; that part is truly deterministic. Part of what emerges is specific to the next part of the dog's rambling walk; that part is unpredictable.

One striking feature of chaotic systems is the way in which they explain why a tiny disturbance or "perturbation" can lead to complete rescaling of the entire pattern of the system due to structural instability. This has been termed the butterfly effect (Lorenz, 1963, 1979) because weather forecasters using computer models have seen the "breeze" from a butterfly moving its wings (the idiosyncratic perturbation) eventually lead to a whole new direction of wind movement, even though the overall pattern of the actual wind was not changed by the creators of the computer model. Dynamical systems are generally structurally unstable, demonstrating these large impacts from small changes. However it is possible for them to be stable. We humans certainly prefer to think of things as structurally stable, especially identity, and therefore "find" stability even where little exists.

Another feature of chaotic systems is the way a seemingly random set of events, after many repetitive interactions, can coalesce around a point in an apparently orderly way. The impression is of a dominant feature of some sort, analogous to a dominant personality trait or a hurricane eye. This phenomenon is termed a *strange attractor* because the point looks like it pulls in the events around it.

It sometimes helps to think of chaos as organized disorder, as opposed to sheer randomness, or *dis*organized disorder. In orderly disorder a flexible structure is hidden in events that only seem to be driven by change when examined in linear or one-time slices. The hidden order unfolds gradually to make itself known when the longer-term nonlinear pattern is observed. In true randomness, or *dis*orderly disorder, there is no hidden underlying structure. Without some chaotic flexibility, some orderly readiness to fluctuate built into the system, a system (especially one like the heart or brain) is too rigid to adapt and live. For example, a rigid heartbeat pattern (no chaos) cannot effectively and efficiently correct for a small perturbing error like a skipped beat, so a heart attack occurs. A rigid brain wave pattern cannot respond effectively to an intellectual challenge, so poor performance results.

Chaotic disorder is nonrandom and has a kind of potential to correct for errors by the use of the underlying, hidden corrective mechanism of the basic, deeper pattern. Chaos is an order enfolded into apparent disorder; it is the pattern in the hologram, akin to the "implicate order" described by Prigogene and Stengers (1984). Implicate order means that an orderly message is encoded within the surface and the apparent disorder, so that the implied message can be unfolded and read. Genetic material is another example of this implied message which is unpacked, decoded, and read by the organism as the organism develops from its first cells to its full hereditary potential. But the unfolding makes even a very minor element powerful enough to create major effects.

Chaos theory gives a rationale for synchronous effects, those apparently unrelated events that seem to mysteriously occur together. The synchronous systems demonstrate entrainment in which one system locks on to the mode and pattern of another nearby system. The minor event in one system then can move the other system with it.

Chaos models have interesting ways of describing the mechanisms of abrupt or qualitative change. For example, a thinker can move from seeing the world with Piagetian concrete logic to somewhat suddenly (an "aha!" reaction) seeing the world with formal logic. When a thinker suddenly begins to see the world in Piagetian formal operational terms (whereas before the world was framed in concrete operational terms), many kinds of behavior are affected. Bifurcation models within chaos theory seem to describe this kind of sudden shift event. In a bifurcation model, at first possibilities (actually possible equation solutions) emerge from one point, like branches on a young sapling tree. But later in the tree's progression through time, the newest branches seem to cluster around several source points, not just one, with young branches coming off two or three more major limbs, going in different directions. This shift from one group of possibilities to several groups of possibilities is analogous to bifurcation. Before the new branching becomes clear, there seems to be considerable chaos; after it becomes clear, there seems to be more complex order. Another way to think about transition and bifurcation is to think about before having a first baby to postpartum family development. In this example, in the "before" state life seems to have a stable set of family relations configurations. Then, fairly quickly something happens, and after a period of greater disorder, several new configurations within the new three-person family branch off on their own tracks. Earlier we had variations on a parent-parent relational theme; later we have three possible centers of relations (the original one and parent no. 1 to child and parent no. 2 to child). In the example of the birth of a first child, we know what the proximate cause was that got the system to transform. In some bifurcating systems, the push to transformation is not so well known.

What might such a theory as chaos imply about reality and knowing the evolving self? First, it suggests that there is more than one sort of disorder. Useful, chaotic disorder provides fresh options and room to correct for past errors; useless disorder provides nothing that seems meaningful, now or later. Second, chaos theory suggests and implies the immense importance of each element in the system for the final outcome of the system as well as for the individual. Remember, a perturbation caused by one butterfly's wing can alter the weather pattern, besides allowing the butterfly to fly. And in our own personal histories, we all remember those small chance remarks or experiences that led to major identity changes. Chaos principles help validate our phenomenological experience. Third, chaos theory suggests the importance of openness to innovation to provide natural corrective devices for ongoing complex events like identity evolution, events where outcomes and goals are not totally clear to us. In that kind of event, a good process is our only safeguard against a manipulation that could cause unimagined damage when it has unforeseen consequences for a dynamical system. For example, we now understand the dangers we face by severely limiting the types of food crops we cultivate. Hundreds of variations on any given food crop species have been lost when we selected for the single species with the high yield. But in the event that a disease attacks that one species (as in the famous Irish potato famine of the last century), we would have lost the chance to recover because our process of dealing with multiple types of plant species was flawed. Retaining a non-evolving identity deprives us of growing in some newer useful way. We might begin to conceptualize lifespan identity evolution as a potentially chaotic system. If we do so, we would not expect to find many simple deterministic relationships. We would expect that some deterministic basic elements might be found, but that they will likely be the underlying, hidden order beneath the apparent disorder.

The system of lifespan identity development may be a structurally unstable system, subject to the large effects of tiny perturbations. As Cavanaugh and McGuire (1994) note, though, the whole idea in developmental research is to show how states change over time in a variety of individualized ways. Predicting factors that lead to bifurcations of systems, for example, predictions about the events that trigger a bifurcation between aspects of knowing the self, can be made and tested empirically. The new center of identity events might then appear to be a strange attractor.

Self-Organizing Systems

Self-organizing systems theory carries the ideas of chaotic nonlinear systems one step further by examining what happens when such systems reach conditions that are very far from their state of equilibrium. At that point systems reorganize themselves in unpredictable ways that are sometimes so dramatic (even if they *are* just computer models) that the term "artificial life" has been used to describe them (Waldrop, 1992).

The Santa Fe Institute was created to explore phenomena related to self-organizing systems and has become a kind of Mecca for complexity theorists. Interested readers may wish to explore this field in several books including those by Goldstein (1994) (on organizational change), Kauffman (1993) (on evolution), Kelly (1994), Maturana and Varela (1988) (on adaptive cognition), Nicholis and Prigogene (1989), and Waldrop (1992).

We tend to think of collective behavior as simply the accumulation of individual behavior, but it is more than that. Collective behavior tends to be nonlinear and tends toward self-organization. One molecule or one person (ignoring for the moment that persons are systems) may respond in a particular way to being pushed past its limits, while a collection of those molecules or persons will respond very differently and somewhat unpredictably. Self-organizing systems studies work with the unique properties of such collectives. Self-organization has the following features when it occurs, according to Goldstein (1994): system structure is radically reorganized; novel patterns emerge; random events are amplified and utilized; and a new coordination of parts is attained. These changes are not imposed on the system but emerge from it. Collective systems do not simply resist change or face destruction, but have the potential to ride the change to create a different organization within. The changes are self-orchestrated as this system reconfigures its own resources in the face of a far-from-equilibrium challenge.

Goldstein (1994) describes some characteristics of self-organization: a spontaneous and radical reorganizing occurs; equilibrium-seeking tendencies are interrupted; the system utilizes the disorganization as a chance for change within some limits; and unpredictable outcomes occur which leave the system more optimally organized. Self-organization can be used for systems of self and identity.

Complexity theory goes beyond qualitative descriptions of the kind of systems it deals with, namely, complex *adaptive* systems, by making complexity a quantity that is measurable. Complex systems also have similar qualities in whatever context they occur. The implications of this theory are simply too vast to be outlined yet. Imagine a unified theory of adaptive system change being applied to everything and this will give the scope of possibilities. Few topics are off limits! Possibilities include prediction of trends in evolving identity during adulthood and aging as multiple adaptive systems interact over time. Quantum theory is joined with these three other new theoretical models that help us understand the process of adult identity flexibility and stability: general systems theory, chaos theory, and the theory of self-organizing systems. These new models provide us with more useful ways to address questions of identity stability and change.

Postformal Cognition as a Cognitive Tool to Construct Flexible Adult Identity

We must care for the truth in front of us more than consistency. (Mohandas K. Gandhi)

In struggling to understand how adult identity could be *known* to be and felt to be both *evolving* and *stable*, we are looking for a model for identity that can comfortably be both (in abstract terms) "A" and "non-A." At a *concrete* logical level, this is a logical impossibility. In terms of *formal scientific logic*, this is impossible in the everyday scientific world of Newtonian physics. But in the world of *postformal* problem solving logic and the world of quantum physics, this is indeed possible. Together they describe the thinking of *mature adult* thinkers and take the step beyond "formal operational (scientific) logic" developed in adolescence according to Inhelder and Piaget (1958). The field of quantum cognition is now being explored to utilize new models to provide coherent explanations for many divergent and puzzling phenomena in psychology (Busemeyer & Wang, 2015).

Postformal complex thought and the research underlying it are described in my 1998 book, entitled *The Development of Logic in Adulthood: Postformal Thought and Its Applications*. The book outlines the theory and applications of postformal thought in an overview. Some references that explain this work further and speak to reliability and validity of the scale are as follows: Benovenli, Fuller, Sinnott & Waterman, 2011; Cartwright, Galupo, Tyree, and Jennings (2009), Galupo, Cartwright, and Savage (2010), Gavin, Galupo, and Cartwright (2009), Hilton, Tobin, Chrzanowska, and Sinnott (under review), Jennings, Galupo, and Cartwright (2009), Johnson (1991,1994, 2004), Riegel (1973, 1975, 1976), Rogers (1989), Rogers, Sinnott, and van Dusen (1991), Sinnott (1981, 1984, 1989a, 1989b, 1989c, 1989d, 1991a, 1991b, 1993a, 1993b, Sinnott, 1993c, 1994a, 1994b, 1996, 1997, 1998a, 1998b, 2000, 2002, 2003, 2004a, 2004b, 2005, 2006, 2008, 2009, 2010, 2011, 2013, 2014); Sinnott and Berlanstein (2006); Sinnott and Cavanaugh (1991); Sinnott and Johnson (1996); Yan (1995); and Yan and Arlin (1995). These references describe the nature and applications of the individual thinking operations that together make up postformal thought.

Much of this work was based on the years of research I performed with the support of the National Institute on Aging (NIA) of the National Institutes of Health (NIH), beginning with my postdoctoral training there. I am grateful to the Gerontology

Research Center (GRC) there, and the volunteers of the Baltimore Longitudinal Study of Aging (BLSA) and others who were my research respondents.

Postformal thought is a type of complex logical thinking that develops in adulthood when we interact with other people whose views about some aspect of reality are different from ours. It allows a person to deal with everyday logical contradictions by letting that person understand that "reality" and the "meaning" of events are *co*-created in an ongoing way. Both objectivity and a necessary subjectivity are useful in our epistemological understanding of the world. Postformal thought lets adults bridge two contradictory "scientifically" logical positions and reach an adaptive synthesis of them through a higher-order logic. The adult then goes on to live the larger reality. So the larger reality eventually *becomes* "true" and noncontradictory with the passage of time. Postformal thought includes a *necessary subjectivity*, which means that the knower understands that "truth" is partially a creation of the one who makes those choices. Postformal operations presume somewhat necessarily subjective selection among logically contradictory formal operational systems each of which is internally consistent and absolute. So it allows us to *organize multiple mutually contradictory systems of (scientific) logical thought.* These are the two main principles of this complex logical problem solving.

Postformal thought as a system of thinking uses all the mechanisms identified by cognitive psychology, mechanisms such as memory and attention. It develops after a certain amount of intellectual and interpersonal experience, according to my earlier research work. For example, only after experiencing intimate relationships, with their shared, mutually constructed logics about the reality of intimate life together, can a person be experienced enough to know (at a complex logical level) that the following is true. "If I think of you as an untrustworthy partner OR as a trustworthy partner, then treat you that way, you are likely to truly become that kind of partner." In other words, to know that both "A" and "non-A" are simultaneously true. Here is another example of postformal thought. When I begin teaching a college class, the class and I begin to structure the reality or truth of our relationship. Who are we? We decide on the nature of our relationship, act on our view of it, and mutually continue to create it in the days that follow. These various views, held by class members and by me, form several contradictory logical systems about the reality of our identities and therefore the reality of our relationships in the class. One student may see me as a surrogate parent and act within the formal logic inherent in that vision, to which I might respond by becoming more and more parental. Another student may logically construct me as a buddy and act within that logical system, to which I might respond by being a buddy too, or by being even more parental to compensate. I might view the class as stimulating or not and teach in such a way as to make them either! The result over the time of a semester will be an organized "truth" about my identity and my relationship with this class that is co-created by the class and me. When I finally come to *understand* that this is how truth works, that it is both "A" and "non-A," I am consciously thinking in a postformal way.

While postformal complex thought is *stimulated* by interpersonal interactions, once it becomes a thinking tool for a person, it may be *applied* to any kind of knowing situation, not just interpersonal ones. I may learn to use the tool of complex postformal thought through interactions with my spouse and go on to use it to think about Newtonian vs quantum physics which are also contradictory but simultaneously both true. Just as the tool of scientific logic can be used in any context, so the tool of complex postformal thought can be used in any context. This includes the context of thoughts about the nature of the self and identity.

Nine thinking operations make up postformal thought. Rationale for inclusion of these operations is given in my summary book about the theory (Sinnott, 1998b). The operations include metatheory shift, problem definition, process/product shift, parameter setting, multiple solutions, pragmatism, multiple causality, multiple methods, and paradox. You can go to the references above to read more about the meaning of each operation term, the ways these operations have been tested, and the research that provides an underpinning for these assertions. I will briefly describe each operation here, giving a simple example of each. Notice that the operations will relate to one another, but will describe different aspects of the complex thinking process. Notice too that all the operations relate to problem solving, in the broadest sense, and the "problem" of evolving identity.

Metatheory shift is the ability to view reality from more than one overarching logical perspective (e.g., from both an abstract and a practical perspective or from a phenomenological and an experimental perspective) when thinking about it. For example, do I think of my identity at work as one who is open to new areas of knowledge, or as one who is collecting a paycheck, or as both?

Problem definition is the realization that there is always more than one way to define a problem and that one *must* define a problem, for example, the problem of identity, to solve it, since we all see things like problems through our own unique current identity lenses. For example, I decide as an employee that my "problem" is to choose one or more identities: "how to be someone who does what my supervisor wants," or "how to be someone who serves the public," or is "how to exercise my creativity." Defining the problem of my identity in different ways usually leads to different ways to create my next nuanced version of it.

Process/product shift is realizing that I can reach a "content-related" solution to a given problem, as opposed to a solution that gives me a heuristic or a process that solves *many* such problems. For example, do I live out one identity and then "flip" to another, *only*, or do I learn a set of *general* skills for working with my several aspects of identity as a complicated whole? Can I use both approaches as desired?

Parameter setting is the realization that one must *choose* aspects of the problem in this case, identity, which must be considered or ignored for this particular solution. For example, I ask the question "How am I deciding which identity face to put forward among the several I know I have available? Is there a better way?" All these decisions and questions set limits for my activity (i.e., for my "solution to the problem of how to present myself in this case").

Multiple solutions mean that I can generate several solutions, in this case, ways to present myself, based on several ways to view the problem. For example, I can solve the "problem" of how to present myself as a spiritual person in three ways: identify as a member of a church, identify as a daily meditator, or identify as someone who does good deeds in the world.

Pragmatism in this case means that I am able to evaluate the solutions that I create for this problem of identity and then select on that is "best" by some definition. For example, knowing there are several ways to solve the problem of how to have the identity of a spiritual person, I can look at the appropriateness and practical utility of each. *Then* I am able, by some criterion, to pick the one that is "best."

Multiple causality is the realization that an event can be the result of several causes. For example, if a friendship fails, and my identity includes being a friendly person, I can be aware that it might be due to bad timing, lack of common interests, *and* my inability to think of what my friend might want.

Multiple methods are the realization that there are several ways to get to the same solution of a problem, in this case, how to see myself at a given time. For example, the solution to my personal problem of interpreting my stubbornness may be reached by multiple methods of attack. I can *accept* that I am a stubborn person as well as a kind person. Or I can *try to modify* my stubborn traits. Or I can simply see my self as kind and the other person as unworthy of my attention (*polarized position*).

Paradox is realizing that contradictions are inherent in reality and realizing that the broader view of an event can eliminate contradictions. For example, I see that, paradoxically, starting a family to avoid "being a lonely person" may leave me a lonelier self than before. In this paradoxical situation, I can only resolve my dilemma by reasoning about it at a more complex level. Only I can decide (self-referential thought) to "jump" to a new cognitive level, or not, to address the question and resolve the paradox within my identity. At that new postformal level, I can see that my self really can be lonely both with and without others and that I am the kind of person who both likes and hates being alone.

These cognitive operations are then applied as a whole, consciously or unconsciously, to solving the dilemma of stability and change in identity over time.

Creating the Flexible Adult Self: Complex Postformal Adult Cognition About Felt Connections

Do I contradict myself?
Very well then, I contradict myself,
I am large, I contain multitudes. (Walt Whitman)

As we know our flexible adult selves we see that complex postformal cognition is necessarily related to several emotionally salient or *felt* connections – connection among aspects of the identity or self of special interest to us in this chapter. When we speak of identity, we need to honor both the cognitive and the emotional parts of that concept (e.g., Miller, 2011). These types of emotionally salient connections include connections among the sides of the self, between self and another (an ongoing source of evolution of self), and between self and a transcendent (an additional source of evolution of self). Felt connection can be defined as conscious awareness of relatedness with an emotional attachment component. Adult cognitive development and the development of complex *felt* connection are motivated by *each other* and ultimately influence each other. That interrelationship is summarized in Fig. 2.2 (Sinnott, 2005, 2006, 2008, 2014; Sinnott & Berlanstein, 2006). Seven aspects of ideas in the Figure are outlined below.

The first part of the Figure to notice is that there are *three types of feeling connected.* These three elements are labeled "connect the sides of the self," "connect with others," and "connect with the transcendent." *Connecting the sides of the self* involves being in touch with and relating to the various aspects of our personalities, including disowned parts like the Shadow (Jung, 1931/1971). How we connect the sides of ourselves (and the *existence* of "sides" of the self) partly depends on early relationships in the family of origin. *Connecting with others* involves interactions between or among persons, the conscious or unconscious interpersonal relationship pattern we exhibit today. *Connecting with the transcendent* involves having an ongoing relationship with something or someone that is larger than the individual self, for example, The Great Spirit, the Universe, or God.

In the Figure each of these three types of feeling connected is united with the other two by lines and arrows going in both directions, indicating that each of the three elements influences and is influenced by the others in a circular fashion. Therefore, there are *three dynamic processes*, the dynamic of which we can discuss and study. The first process is the dynamic interplay between "connecting the sides of the self" and "connecting with others." The second process is the dynamic interplay between "connecting with others" and "connecting with the transcendent." The third process is the dynamic interplay between "connecting with the transcendent" and "connecting the sides of the self." Interventions and applications, described later, may make use of one or more of these three dynamic processes.

As humans we paradoxically desire both continuity and change. The dynamic interaction processes (those two arrows uniting any two elements in Fig. 2.2) also are described in terms of the *challenges to the self,* challenges posed by the simultaneous experience of any two types of connected feelings. The two types of connected feelings may not agree with each other.

Remember, when I speak of self here, I refer to a dynamic, changing center of events with which a person identifies at a human, ego level, even as it may be constantly transforming. An adaptive characteristic of the human cognitive process is to form concepts and label them as distinct from other concepts. At the same time, the same human thinker might also understand that on the level of physics or mysticism, this seemingly concrete thing, the self, is an illusion. (Self as an illusion is discussed in other chapters in this book.)

In the dynamic interaction between "connecting the sides of the self" and "connecting with others," two challenges occur. The self that exists at any one time is called into question by experiencing the reality of others; and the manner in which we perceive and relate to others is transformed as more sides of the self are accepted.

In the dynamic interaction between "connecting with others" and "connecting with the transcendent," two challenges occur. The manner in which we perceive and relate to others may be changed by our growing awareness of the transcendent. And the self connection with the transcendent might change when challenged by the behavior of others close to us.

The three sets of processes are also labeled with *a motivation factor* in Fig. 2.2. That factor suggests *why* a person might want to do the difficult work of rising to the challenge of constructing and maintaining the self when new contradictory information emerges during the dynamic interactions. When the dynamic interaction process involves "connecting the sides of the self" (coupled with some other element), motivation comes from the desire to be more complete or whole, to heal. When the dynamic interaction process involves the element of "connecting with others" (coupled with some other element), motivation comes from our desires to maintain and improve ties with people important to us. When the dynamic interaction process involves "connecting with the transcendent" (coupled with some other element), motivation comes from the desire to increase our participation in something spiritual, something larger than our local selves. Motivations, therefore, can be both practical and existential.

Failure to Feel Connected in Any One Dimension

There can be a failure to feel connected *within* any single one of the three types of felt connections mentioned above: within the self; between the self and other persons; and with the transcendent. These particular failures are labeled *pathology* in Fig. 2.2. They have implications for identity and emotional well-being.

First, if there are failures in the development of the felt connections within the self, the person might experience inner conflicts, surprisingly conflicted or self-sabotaging decisions, and a feeling of fragility. The person tends to lose the self upon interacting with others. The person rigidly judges to be "bad" those persons who seem to represent the sides of the self that have not been accepted and integrated. The person is stuck at "either A or non-A, but not both."

Failure to establish felt connections with others might lead to different problems. For example, the person might feel isolated or abandoned, as if no one can understand him or her. Intimacy and generativity (Erikson, 1982) might not be possible, then, for that person. The person is stuck in "A" with no "non-A" possible. These are not unresolved contradictions for the self, but a lonely outcome for the individual.

Failure to establish connections with something or someone larger than the self, i.e., with some transcendent meaning for life, may carry yet another set of problems. There may be an existential crisis. The person may be driven by anxiety about death or may find life tragic and meaningless. For the person there is nothing that gives a larger platform from which to view current problems or setbacks. There is no larger platform of cognition from which to view the contradictory "A" "non-A" situation.

These failures to feel connected, and the resulting difficulties, leave the person with sadness and a yearning to re-weave the web of life, to take part in the dance of life, and construct the self in some more coherent way. Metaphorically speaking, for the circle folk dance of construction of self to go well, we need three things. We need to feel mastery of many steps (connections within the contradictions in the self), to feel connected to other dancers in the circle (interpersonal connection with the personal self), and to be in connection with the overall pattern the dance represents (connection with the transpersonal or transcendent, larger view that rises above the lower-level contradictions experienced by the self). We need to feel the three types of connection or relationship.

What Happens to Adult Identity Flexibility When Adults Lack Postformal Thought?

The figure also refers to *complex postformal thought* in relation to each challenge. To successfully integrate the types of connections and their sometimes disparate or conflicting ideas in an ongoing way, yet preserve a concept of a self that is whole, postformal complex cognitive operations must be used. The conflicting ideas, and the person's high motivation to work out the conflict, provide an occasion for the initial and continuing learning of this complex thinking ability. Possession of this thinking ability provides the means for more easily handling the challenge of conflicting relational structures. The ability leads to the continuing construction of the self during the lifetime.

However, a person may suffer from what might be called a *cognitive pathology*. Failure to develop complex postformal cognitive representations and some integration of the reality of the several types of felt connections, whatever the reason for that failure, leaves the self in a fragmented and conflicted state with few conscious cognitive tools to become whole. The person in such a state may never consciously conceptualize and grasp a way to be able to live with multiple strongly felt but contradictory connections. Learning is needed. Some examples may clarify this point.

For example, on a cognitive level it may seem impossible to such a person to integrate his or his connections with many other persons of all different types into a unified self that feels whole or connected inside. It will seem like either the whole, integrated self or the deep connections with other persons will have to be sacrificed. The problem is that the person cannot conceive of a way of connecting with others without losing the self, a very unsatisfactory "borderline" life outcome. Learning the integration can only occur with the learning and use of postformal complex thought.

In a second example of a cognitive failure, the person without complex cognitive representations may be faced with integrating felt connection with others and a felt connection to the transcendent. The person may conceive of no alternatives but to give up a spiritual search (connection with the transcendent) in favor of keeping connections with loved ones or to break connections with the loved ones in order to continue a spiritual search. Again, the person's "solution" leads to a less than satisfactory adult development outcome due to (unnecessary) either/or choices and loss of felt connection of some type. Only a postformal cognitive representation of self would integrate both aspects of felt connection. Learning can foster this (Sinnott & Berlanstein, 2006).

A final example might add additional light. The person who cannot cognitively represent the complex process of integrating two types of felt connection may have a third type of problem. That person may not be able to conceive of knowing and accepting the multiple sides of the self (some sides of self considered "good," some considered "less than good") *and* feeling (guiltlessly) connected with a God figure. A resolution could only occur if one set of felt connections is sacrificed (e.g., surrender of self to the Divine Will or give up religion/spiritual self). Again, the *non-*resolution, based on the inability to conceptualize in postformal terms at a more complex level, closes off life options for growth of self and identity. It closes off options for flexibly feeling connected and whole in multiple ways simultaneously.

As a person tries to balance or be *cognitively consistent* about connections in all these areas of relationship, similarity in the existential story of the relationships will be sought because it would make thinking about them easier. If, for example, parts of my self cannot be trusted, *and* others cannot be trusted *and* God cannot be trusted, my thinking about life is simplified in one coherent pattern of distrust.

This theoretical approach suggests a way to sustain a unified, coherent self that tolerates the ongoing changes and contradictions that are part of the evolving self. With postformal thought and problem solving, the identity and the self can be known as a seemingly coherent center around which the events of the person's evolving, sometimes contradictory evolving self and identity, are experienced.

Cavanaugh and McGuire (1994) suggest that chaos theory can help us frame and answer several questions about adult cognitive development which, since it underlies felt connection, would naturally suggest important questions about identity. Chaos theory with its concept of attractors, expressed through postformal theory, could help explain why identity shows a few "spurts" at certain times (based on the pull of a new, stronger attractor) but smooth progression most of the time. See, for example, Bleidorn's 2015 article discussing "What Accounts for Personality Maturation in Early Adulthood?" Chaos theory, expressed through postformal thought, could address why flexibility in felt connection (i.e., moving easily among attractors so as to relate in many ways) is so hard to maintain in a static way (our feelings of strong connectedness ebb and flow). It could show how modes of self-concept develop. And it could resolve the persistent question of why relational activities and feelings in one area of life (e.g., identity as related to the transcendent) do not necessarily generalize to other areas of identity (e.g., connection among the sides of the self).

Applications and Research Strategies

The ideas expressed in this chapter can be observed in numerous everyday situations, can suggest ways to help therapists and clients, and can form the basis of research that empirically supports these theories. Space limitations prevent elaborating on all these applications here in this chapter. Entire books and articles related to these topics have been cited in other parts of this chapter. Consider especially the summaries in Sinnott (1998). There we see postformal thought related to numerous applications of identity flexibility in everyday life. For example, the identity flexibility of the therapist and the therapy client is discussed (Armstrong, 1991). Another chapter focuses on adults creating themselves over time with the aid of postformal thinking. There are several reports on research with successful administrators and master teachers using postformal thought to increase their flexibility on the job, and couples using postformal thought to become identity-flexible mates to their intimate partners to experience more satisfying close relationships. The book also suggests ways to teach adults to use postformal thought and to increase their own identity flexibility in family and workplace contexts. Identity flexibility that involves thinking of myself as part of the flow of life, as a citizen of the Universe, as well as an individual life is the demand of those who want to see us as a part of all living things,

Three basic approaches will be useful in future research on identity flexibility in adults. We can test for postformal thinking and then compare groups with a little or much postformal ability in an identity-challenging situation to see how they perform and then describe their identity. A second approach would be to interview respondents in a sudden natural experiment (e.g., job loss, divorce, graduation, birth of first child, military attack) exploring their identity narratives (see Kroger & McLean, 2011) to see if a more complex identity can be achieved and used in adaptive ways during the situation by those knowing their worlds in a more postformal way. A third approach could include qualitative studies of the thinking processes of individuals who do demonstrate identity flexibility as they encounter the challenges of the later stages of life.

There is much work that remains to be done to more fully answer the questions raised in the first paragraph of this chapter. We need to explore our identity as a constantly elaborating work in progress during the course of adult development. The "problem" of the evolving self can be solved if we begin to see self as a unified process, an experienced center of events that belongs to us, and do not focus on self simply as an object in its own right. We can then wrestle more effectively with the psychological koan: who am I if I am an evolving self?

"And it does not hurt to have a sense of humor!"
Elderly Buddhist priest discussing how the wise person
thinks of the impermanence of identity in the face of life challenges and death

References

Abraham, R. (1985). Is there chaos without noise? In P. Fisher & W. Smith (Eds.), *Chaos, fractals, and dynamics* (pp. 117–121). New York: Marcel Dekker.

Alper, J. (1989). The chaotic brain: New models of behavior. *Psychology Today, 23*, 21.

Ananthaswamy, A. (2015). *The man who wasn't there: Investigations into the strange new science of the self.* New York: Dutton.

Armstrong, J. (1991). Keeping one's balance in a moving system: The effects of the multiple personality disordered patient on the cognitive development of the therapist. In J. D. Sinnott

& J. Cavanaugh (Eds.), *Bridging paradigms: Positive development in adulthood and cognitive aging* (pp. 11–18). New York: Praeger.

Barton, S. (1994). Chaos, self organization, and psychology. *American Psychologist, 49*, 5–14.

Benovenli, L., Fuller, E., Sinnott, J., & Waterman, S. (2011). Three applications of the theory of postformal thought: Wisdom, concepts of god, and success in college. *Research in the Social Scientific Study of Religion, 22*, 141–154.

Bleidorn, W. (2015). What accounts for personality maturation in early adulthood? *Psychological Science, 24*, 245–252.

Bohm, D. (1980). *Wholeness and the implicate order*. London: Routledge and Kegan Paul.

Born, M. (1962). *Einstein's theory of relativity*. New York: Dover.

Born, M. (1964). *Natural philosophy of cause and chance*. New York: Dover.

Brillouin, L. (1970). *Relativity reexamined*. New York: Academic Press.

Busemeyer, J. R., & Wang, Z. (2015). What is quantum cognition and how is it applied to psychology? *Psychological Science, 24*, 165–169.

Cartwright, K. B., Galupo, M. P., Tyree, S. D., & Jennings, J. (2009). Reliability and validity of the complex postformal thought questionnaire. *Journal of Adult Development, 16*, 183–189.

Caskie, G. I. L. (2011). Latent growth models: A quantitative method for studying adult development and learning. In C. Hoare (Ed.), *The Oxford handbook of reciprocal adult development and learning* (2nd ed., pp. 61–79). New York: Oxford University Press.

Cavanaugh, J.C. (1989). *The utility of concepts in chaos theory for psychological theory and research*. Paper presented at the Fourth Adult Development Conference at Harvard University, Cambridge MA.

Cavanaugh, J. C., & McGuire, L. (1994). The chaos of lifespan learning. In J. Sinnott (Ed.), *Interdisciplinary handbook of adult lifespan learning* (pp. 3–21). Westport, CT: Greenwood.

Crutchfield, J. P., Farmer, J. D., Packard, N. H., & Shaw, R. S. (1986). Chaos. *Scientific American, 255*, 46–57.

Davies. (1989). *The new physics*. London: Cambridge University Press.

Devaney, R. (1989). *An introduction to chaotic dynamical systems*. Redwood City, CA: Addison-Wesley.

Dossey, L. (1982). *Space, time and medicine*. Boston: Shambhala.

Dossey, L. (1989). *Recovering the soul: A scientific and spiritual search*. New York: Bantam.

Einstein, A. (1961). *Relativity: The special and general theory*. New York: Crown.

Erikson, E. (1982). *The lifecycle completed*. New York: Norton.

Freedle, R. (1977). Psychology, Thomian topologies, deviant logics, and human development. In N. Datan & H. Reese (Eds.), *Lifespan developmental psychology: Postformal perspectives on experimental research* (pp. 317–342). New York: Academic Press.

Galupo, M. P., Cartwright, K. B., & Savage, L. S. (2010). Cross-social category friendships as a context for postformal cognitive development. *Journal of Adult Development, 17*, 208–214.

Gavin, J. L., Galupo, M. P., & Cartwright, K. B. (2009). The role of postformal cognitive development in death acceptance. *Journal of Adult Development, 16*, 166–172.

Gleick, J. (1987). *Chaos: Making a new science*. New York: Penguin Books.

Goerner, S. (1994). *Chaos and the evolving psychological universe*. Langhorne, PA: Gordon & Breach Scientific Publishers, S.A..

Goldstein, J. (1994). *The unshackled organization*. Portland, OR: Productivity Press.

Gottman, J. (1991). Chaos and regulated change in families: A metaphor for the study of transitions. In P. A. Cohen & M. Hetherington (Eds.), *Family transitions* (pp. 247–272). Hillsdale, NJ: Erlbaum.

Heisenberg, W. (1958). *Physics and philosophy*. New York: Harper and Row.

Hilton, S., Tobin, E., Chrzanowska E., & Sinnott, J. (under review). Measuring postformal thought consistently with three types of scales: Agreement between short form objective items, long form objective items, and open-ended responses to a dilemma. *Journal of Adult Development*.

Inhelder, B., & Piaget, J. (1958). *The growth of logical thinking from childhood to adolescence*. New York: Basic Books.

Jennings, J., Galupo, M., & Cartwright, K. (2009). The role of postformal cognitive development in death acceptance. *Journal of Adult Development, 16*, 166–172.
Johnson, L. (1991). Briding paradigms: The role of a change agent in an international technical transfer project. In J. Sinnott & J. Cavanaugh (Eds.), *Bridging paradigms: Positive development in adulthood and cognitive aging* (pp. 59–72). New York: Praeger.
Johnson, L. (1994). Nonformal adult learning in international development projects. In J. D. Sinnott (Ed.), *Interdisciplinary handbook of adult lifespan learning* (pp. 203–217). Westport, CT: Greenwood.
Johnson, L. (2004). *Postformal thinking in the workplace*. Stockholm: University of Stockholm Press.
Jones, R. S. (1992). *Physics for the rest of us: Ten basic ideas of 20th century physics*. New York: Fall River Press.
Jung, C. (1930/1971). The stages of life. In J. Campbell (Ed.), *The portable Jung*. New York: Viking Library.
Kaufman, W. (1973). *Relativity and cosmology*. New York: Harper and Row.
Kelly, K. (1994). *Out of control: The new biology of machines, social systems and the economic world*. Reading, MA: Addison-Wesley.
Kramer, P., & Bresson, P. (2015). Humans as superorganisms: How microbes, viruses, imprinted genes, and other selfish entities shape our behavior. *Psychological Science, 10*, 464–481.
Kroger, J., & McLean, K. C. (2011). Identity narratives during the adult years. In C. Hoare (Ed.), *Oxford handbook of reciprocal adult development and learning* (pp. 173–185). New York: Oxford University Press.
Kuhn, T. (1962). *The structure of scientific revolutions*. Chicago: University of Chicago Press.
Levine, R. L., & Fitzgerald, H. E. (Eds.). (1992). *Analysis of dynamic psychological systems, Vols. 1 & 2*. New York: Plenum.
Lock Land, G. T. (1973). *Grow or die*. New York: Random House.
Lorenz, E. (1963). Deterministic non-periodic flow. *Journal of Atmospheric Science, 20*, 130–141.
Lorenz, E. (1979). *Predictability: Does the flap of a butterfly's wings in Brazil set off a tornado in Texas?* Paper presented at the annual meeting of the American Association for the Advancement of Science, Washington, DC.
Mahoney, M. J. (1991). *Human change processes*. New York: Basic Books.
Maturana, H., & Varela, F. (1988). *The tree of knowledge*. Boston: New Science Library.
Miller, J. (1978). *Living systems*. New York: McGraw Hill.
Miller, M. E. (2011). Mature transformations in adulthood facilitated by psychotherapy and spiritual practice. In C. Hoare (Ed.), *The Oxford handbook of reciprocal adult development and learning* (2nd ed., pp. 265–283). New York: Oxford University Press.
Nicholis, G., & Prigogene, I. (1989). *Exploring complexity*. New York: Freeman.
Prigogene, I. (1980). *From being to becoming*. San Francisco: Freeman.
Prigogene, I., & Stengers, I. (1984). *Order out of chaos: Man's new dialogue with nature*. New York: Bantam.
Riegel, K. (1975). Adult life crises: A postformal interpretation of development. In N. Datan & L. Ginsberg (Eds.), *Lifespan developmental psychology: Normative life crises* (pp. 99–129). New York: Academic Press.
Riegel, K. F. (1973). Postformal operations: The final period of cognitive development. *Human Development, 16*, 346–370.
Riegel, K. F. (1976). Toward a postformal theory of development. *American Psychologist, 31*, 679–700.
Riegel, K. F. (1977). Past and future trends in gerontology. *The Gerontologist, 17*, 105–113.
Robertson, H. P., & Noonan, T. W. (1968). *Relativity and cosmology*. Philedelphia: Saunders.
Rogers, D., Sinnott, J., & Van Dusen, L. (1991, July). *Marital adjustment and social cognitive performance in everyday logical problem solving*. Paper presented at the 6th Adult Development Conference, Boston, MA.

Rogers, D. R. B. (1989). *The effect of dyad interaction and marital adjustment on cognitive performance in everyday logical problem solving* (Doctoral dissertation, Utah State University, Logan, Utah.)

Russell, B. (1969). *The A B C of relativity*. New York: Mentor Books.

Schlick, M. (1970). Causality in contemporary physics. In J. Toulmin (Ed.), *Physical reality: Philosophical essays on 20th century physics* (pp. 83–121). New York: Harper and Row.

Sheldrake, R. (1981). *A new science of life*. Los Angeles: Tarcher.

Sheldrake, R. (1989). *The presence of the past: Morphic resonance and the habits of nature*. New York: Viking.

Sheldrake, R. (1990). *The rebirth of nature*. London: Century.

Sinnott, J. D. (1981). The theory of relativity: A metatheory for development? *Human Development, 24*, 293–311.

Sinnott, J. D. (1984). Postformal reasoning: The relativistic stage. In M. Commons, F. Richards, & C. Armon (Eds.), *Beyond formal operations* (pp. 298–325). New York: Praeger.

Sinnott, J. D. (1989a). Changing the known, knowing the changing. In D. Kramer & M. Bopp (Eds.), *Transformation in clinical and developmental psychology* (pp. 51–69). New York: Springer.

Sinnott, J. D. (1989b). *Everyday problem solving: Theory and applications*. New York: Praeger.

Sinnott, J. D. (1989c). General systems theory: A rationale for the study of everyday memory. In L. Poon, D. Rubin, & B. Wilson (Eds.), *Everyday cognition in adulthood and old age* (pp. 59–70). New Rochelle, NY: Cambridge University Press.

Sinnott, J. D. (1989d). Lifespan relativistic postformal thought. In M. Commons, J. Sinnott, F. Richards, & C. Armon (Eds.), *Beyond formal operations I* (pp. 239–278). New York: Praeger.

Sinnott, J. D. (1991a). Limits to problem solving: Emotion, intention, goal clarity, health, and other factors in postformal thought. In J. D. Sinnott & J. Cavanaugh (Eds.), *Bridging paradigms: Positive development in adulthood and cognitive aging*. New York: Praeger.

Sinnott, J. D. (1991b). What do we do to help John? A case study of everyday problem solving in a family making decisions about an acutely psychotic member. In J. D. Sinnott & J. Cavanaugh (Eds.), *Bridging paradigms: Positive development in adulthood and cognitive aging* (pp. 203–220). New York: Praeger.

Sinnott, J. D. (1993a). Use of complex thought and resolving intragroup conflicts: A means to conscious adult development in the workplace. In J. Demick & P. M. Miller (Eds.), *Development in the workplace* (pp. 155–175). Hillsdale, NJ: Erlbaum.

Sinnott, J. D. (1993b). Teaching in a chaotic new physics world: Teaching as a dialogue with reality. In P. Kahaney, J. Janangelo, & L. Perry (Eds.), *Theoretical and critical perspectives on teacher change* (pp. 91–108). Norwood, NJ: Ablex.

Sinnott, J. D. (1993c). Yes, it's worth the trouble! Unique contributions from *everyday* cognition studies. In H. Reese & J. Puckett (Eds.), *Lifespan developmental psychology: Mechanisms of everyday cognition* (pp. 73–94). NJ: Erlbaum.

Sinnott, J. D. (1994a). *Interdisciplinary handbook of adult lifespan learning*. Westport, CT: Greenwood.

Sinnott, J. D. (1994b). New science models for teaching adults: Teaching as a dialogue with reality. In J. D. Sinnott (Ed.), *Interdisciplinary handbook of adult lifespan learning* (pp. 90–104). Westport, CT: Greenwood.

Sinnott, J. D. (1996). The developmental approach: Postformal thought as adaptive intelligence. In F. Blanchard-Fields & T. Hess (Eds.), *Perspectives on cognitive change in adulthood and aging* (pp. 358–383). New York: McGraw-Hill.

Sinnott, J. D. (1997). Brief report: Complex postformal thought in skilled research administrators. *Journal of Adult Development, 4*(1), 45–53.

Sinnott, J. D. (1998a). Creativity and postformal thought. In C. Adams-Price (Ed.), *Creativity and aging: Theoretical and empirical approaches*. New York: Springer.

Sinnott, J. D. (1998b). The development of logic in adulthood: Postformal thought and its applications. In J. Demick (Ed.), *Plenum series on adult development*. New York: Plenum.

Sinnott, J. D. (2000). Cognitive aspects of unitative states: Spiritual self-realization, intimacy, and knowing the unknowable. In M. E. Miller & A. N. West (Eds.), *Spirituality, ethics, and relationship in adulthood: Clinical and theoretical explorations* (pp. 177–198). Madison, CN: Psychosocial Press.

Sinnott, J. D. (2002). Postformal thought and adult development: Living in balance. In J. Demick & C. Andreoletti (Eds.), *Handbook of adult development*. New York: Plenum.

Sinnott, J. D. (2003). Teaching as nourishment for complex thought. In N. L. Diekelmann (Ed.), *Teaching the practitioners of care: New pedagogies for the health professions, Interpretive studies in healthcare and the human services series* (pp. 232–271). Madison, WI: University of Wisconsin Press.

Sinnott, J. D. (2004a). Learning as a humanistic dialogue with reality; new theories that help us teach the whole person: Context of learning and complex thought: Implications for modern life. In T. Hagestrom (Ed.), *Stockholm lectures: Adult development and working life* (pp. 78–108). Stockholm: University of Stockholm Press.

Sinnott, J. D. (2004b). Learning as a humanistic dialogue with reality; new theories that help us teach the whole person: Complex postformal thought and its relation to adult learning, life span development, and the new sciences. In T. Hagestrom (Ed.), *Stockholm lectures: Adult development and working life* (pp. 109–152). Stockholm: University of Stockholm Press.

Sinnott, J. D. (2005). The dance of the transforming self: Both feelings of connection and complex thought are needed for learning. In M. A. Wolf (Ed.), *Adulthood, new terrain, new directions* (pp. 27–38). San Francisco: Jossey Bass.

Sinnott, J. D. (2006). Spirituality as "feeling connected with the transcendent": Outline of a transpersonal psychology of adult development of self. *Religion, Spirituality, and the Scientific Study of Religion, 16*, 287–308.

Sinnott, J. D. (2008). Neo-Piagetian concepts of cognitive development in adults. In M. Cecil Smith & N. DeFratis-Densch (Eds.), *Handbook of research on adult learning and development*. New York: Erlbaum.

Sinnott, J. D. (2009). Complex thought and construction of the self in the face of aging and death. *Journal of Adult Development, 16*(3), 155–165.

Sinnott, J. D. (2010). Coherent themes: Individuals' relationships with God, and their early childhood experiences, bonds with significant others, and relational delusions during psychotic episodes have common existential and relational themes. *Journal of Adult Development, 17*(4), 230–244.

Sinnott, J. D. (2011). Constructing the self in the face of aging and death: Complex thought and learning. In C. Hoare (Ed.), *Oxford handbook of adult development and learning* (2nd ed., pp. 248–264). New York: Oxford University Press.

Sinnott, J. D. (Ed.). (2013). *Positive psychology: Advances in understanding adult motivation*. New York: Springer Publishing.

Sinnott, J. D. (2014). *Adult development: Cognitive aspects of thriving close relationships*. New York: Oxford University Press.

Sinnott, J. D., & Berlanstein, D. (2006). The importance of feeling whole: Learning to "feel connected", community, and adult development. In C. H. Hoare (Ed.), *Oxford handbook of adult development and learning* (pp. 381–406). New York: Oxford U. Press.

Sinnott, J. D., & Cavanaugh, J. (Eds.). (1991). *Bridging paradigms: Positive development in adulthood and cognitive aging*. New York: Praeger.

Sinnott, J. D., & Johnson, L. (1996). *Reinventing the university: A radical proposal for a problem focused university*. Norwood, NJ: Ablex.

Smith, L. B., & Thelan, E. (Eds.). (1993). *A dynamic systems approach to development*. Cambridge, MA: MIT Press.

Toulmin, J. (1970). *Physical reality: Philosophical essays on 20th century physics*. New York: Harper and Row.

Vallacher, R. R., Coleman, P. T., Nowack, A., & Bui-Wrzosinska, L. (2010). Rethinking intractable conflict. *American Psychologist, 65*, 262–278.

Von Bertalanfy, L. (1968). *General systems theory*. New York: Braziller.
Von Neumann, J., & Morgenstern, O. (1947). *Theory of games and economic behavior*. Princeton, NJ: Princeton University Press.
Waldrop, M. (1992). *Complexity: The emerging science at the edge of order and chaos*. New York: Simon and Schuster.
Weiner, N. (1961). *Cybernetics*. Cambridge, MA: MIT Press.
Wheatley, M. J. (2006). *Leadership and the new science: Discovering order in a chaotic world*. San Francisco: Barrett-Koehler Publishers.
Wolf, F. A. (1981). *Taking the quantum leap*. New York: Harper & Row.
Yan, B. (1995). *Nonabsolute/relativistic (N/R) thinking: A possible unifying commonality underlying models of postformal reasoning*. Unpublished Ph.D. dissertation, University of British Columbia, Vancouver.
Yan, B., & Arlin, P. K. (1995). Non-absolute/relativistic thinking: A common factor underlying models of postformal reasoning? *Journal of Adult Development, 2*, 223–240.

Part II
Research, Theory, Personal Experiences

Chapter 3
Identity Flexibility and Wisdom in Adulthood: The Roles of a Growth-Oriented Identity Style and Contemplative Processes

Sherry L. Beaumont

Introduction

Knowing yourself is the beginning of all wisdom. (Aristotle)

Based on Erikson's (1994) theory of lifespan psychosocial development, considerable research has investigated how individuals develop and maintain an ego-identity. Identity has been defined as "a self-structure – an internal, self-constructed, dynamic organization of drives, abilities, beliefs, and individual history" (Marcia, 1980, p. 159). Erikson proposed that developing a clear and coherent sense of identity by late adolescence is necessary for the future development of intimacy/love in early adulthood, generativity/care in middle adulthood, and integrity/wisdom in late adulthood. That supposition has been supported by research demonstrating that identity clarity/balance positively predicts intimacy during early adulthood (e.g., Orlofsky, Marcia, & Lesser, 1973) and generativity in middle adulthood (e.g., Stewart, Ostrove, & Helson, 2001). However, considerably less research has focused on the predictive link between identity and wisdom. To address this gap in the literature, my research has focused on examining whether a particular identity processing style provides a pathway for wisdom.

Grounded in Erikson's (1994) theory, much identity research has focused on the benefits of having achieved a clear, consistent, and strong sense of identity for positive adjustment and socio-emotional functioning. Even when identity is studied in adults beyond the 20s, which is relatively infrequent, researchers still seem to hold onto the assumption that what is important for predicting positive adjustment and character is having a firm, almost unshakable, commitment to who one is (i.e., having "achieved" a sense of identity). Although Erikson proposed that identity is not

S.L. Beaumont (✉)
Department of Psychology, University of Northern British Columbia,
3333 University Way, Prince George, BC V2N 4Z9, Canada
e-mail: Sherry.Beaumont@unbc.ca

J.D. Sinnott (ed.), *Identity Flexibility During Adulthood*,
DOI 10.1007/978-3-319-55658-1_3

necessarily static, there is much less credence paid to the idea that having an identity that is evolving rather than fixed or permanent provides the underlying flexibility that is necessary for healthy adaptation to challenges that are experienced across the lifespan. Perhaps this oversight is due in part to Erikson's description of ego-identity as including the felt sense of continuity and sameness over time. Yet, it is worth considering that one may experience a felt sense of inner sameness while also experiencing evolution in one's sense of self. Individuals who are able to do so must possess a flexible identity that includes particular ways of processing new information about themselves and the world that ultimately leads to greater self-knowledge and wisdom.

In this chapter, I will argue that at any age in adulthood, identity flexibility, or a sense of self-identity that evolves in the face of congruent or incongruent self-knowledge attained from experiencing life's joys and challenges, is what provides the basis for developing wisdom. I present an argument and supporting evidence that flexibility in one's identity is afforded by the use of a *growth-oriented identity style* or a style of identity processing that is oriented "toward the growth of integrated (wise) self-knowledge" (Beaumont, 2011, p. 177). Additionally, I will argue that the growth-oriented identity style predicts wisdom byway of identity processes that are contemplative in nature.

Identity Development and Flexibility

Erikson (1994) described identity as "the style of one's individuality" (p. 50), and the development of identity depends upon the dynamic processes of self-exploration and meaning in life, the goal of which is increasing differentiation and connection to others. The initial phase of dealing with identity issues and concerns takes place during adolescence and early adulthood, although identity issues may arise at other points in the lifespan (Erikson, 1994). When early identity development is not optimal, as in the case of identity diffusion, the individual will have difficulty with future psychosocial developments and general well-being because the ego lacks a coherent synthesis around a core identity (Erikson, 1994).

Erikson's concept of identity was operationally defined by Marcia (1966) who developed a measurement paradigm that served to empirically investigate individuals' progression toward achieving a clear and balance sense of identity (Berzonsky & Adams, 1999). Marcia's Identity Status Interview resulted in groups of individuals who could be classified into one of four identity "statuses": diffusion, foreclosure, moratorium, and achievement. Categorization into each of these identity status groups is based on one's advancement toward identity achievement in two domains (occupation and ideology) via two processes (exploration and commitment; Marcia, 1993). Findings of 40 years of research have shown patterns of characteristics for individuals in the four identity status groups, with the most favorable outcomes and adaptive qualities associated with individuals who have gone through an identifiable period of identity exploration ending in a firm commitment to his/her identity (referred to as "identity achievement"; Marcia, 1980, 1993).

Marcia (1976) originally proposed and found early support for the supposition that identity formation occurs during late adolescence and early adulthood and is reflected in progressive growth through the various identity statuses. However, other longitudinal research showed that the identity statuses of some individuals remain stable throughout adulthood. For example, Adams and Montemayor (1987) found that only about 50% of their sample showed progressive growth in identity formation (as reflected by movement from diffusion or foreclosure to moratorium or achievement) during late adolescence and early adulthood; the remaining 50% of their sample showed patterns of stable, regressive, or unstable patterns of identity formation. Thus, research, based on the identity status paradigm, supports the idea that some adults experience stability in their identities across adulthood, whereas others experience patterns of flexibility and change.

The identity status paradigm has been criticized on conceptual grounds that directly or indirectly address the issue of flexibility in one's identity. Although Marcia (1966) proposed that the identity statuses reflect differences in "individual styles of coping" (p. 558), researchers have tended to describe the identity statuses merely as "static or outcome variables" (Clancy Dollinger, 1995, p. 476) with the implication that stable identity achievement is what provides the greatest predictor for psychological well-being. This approach, of treating identity as a static entity, fails to address the question of how an individual maintains a healthy identity that is capable of evolution when faced with life challenges that make identity changes necessary.

Identity Processing

Although most identity theories and research in some way link back to Marcia's conceptualization of Erikson's theory (Schwartz, 2001), those that focus on the processes through which individuals develop, maintain, or change their identities provide the most promise for addressing the question of flexibility in identity during adulthood. If referring to identity development, "the term *process* concerns the general course of change over time in some variable. This general course can be described as a *developmental trajectory or pathway*" (Bosma & Kunnen, 2001, p. 40). However, in the identity literature, more short-term processes tend to be studied; those "processes involved in real-time situations in which identity is at stake" (Bosma & Kunnen, 2001, p. 41). *Identity process* is defined as "the means by which identity content is encoded, elaborated, and integrated" (Berzonsky, 1988, p. 256). These processes have been described as microlevel because they can occur over shorter periods of time (e.g., seconds, minutes, hours); however, long-term pathways in the development of identity across the lifespan are made up of sequences of these more real-time, microlevel processes (Bosma & Kunnen, 2001). Thus, relatively few researchers focus on long-term identity development; rather, most (including me) tend to focus on the micro-processes that support or hinder identity adjustment, with the assumption that these micro-processes are related to pathways of identity development across the lifespan.

Over the years, there have been various perspectives posited that focus on the importance of the processes that underlie the formation, maintenance, or change in identity. The most common identity processes posited as important for identity balance/adjustment are processes related to identity exploration, experiential openness, and individual differences in the cognitive processes of assimilation and accommodation. For example, in his work on identity formation during adolescence, Grotevant (1987) emphasized the importance of openness to experience for the propensity to engage in identity exploration, or "problem-solving behavior aimed at eliciting information about oneself or one's environment," which is seen as critical for healthy identity formation (p. 204). Other researchers have similarly emphasized the roles of identity exploration and experiential openness as necessary conditions for experiencing the internal processes that elicit revisions or changes in identity statuses in adulthood (Kroger & Green, 1996).

The other processes most often discussed in reference to explanatory models of individual differences in identity are those that rely upon Piaget's concepts of cognitive assimilation and accommodation. For example, identity assimilation and accommodation have been used to explain meaning-making processes in identity by Kunnen and Bosma (2000) as well as identity processing styles by both Whitbourne (e.g., Sneed & Whitbourne, 2003; Whitbourne, Sneed, & Skultety, 2002) and Berzonsky (1990, 2011). Generally speaking, "identity assimilation is a process that individuals use to maintain a sense of self-consistency," whereas "identity accommodation is a process of changing identity in response to experiences" (Sneed & Whitbourne, 2003, p. 313–314). In all approaches to identity that use assimilation and accommodation as explanatory processes, it is argued that a balance in the use of both processes results in the most adaptive and flexible identity (e.g., Sneed & Whitbourne, 2003).

An example of the important roles of both exploration/openness and assimilation/accommodation can be seen in Berzonsky's (1990, 2011) identity style theory. Berzonsky posits a constructivist account of identity formation and maintenance in which one constructs a sense of self-identity through interaction with one's inner and outer worlds. He defined identity as "a self-constructed cognitive representation of oneself that is used to interpret self-relevant information and to cope with personal problems and life events" (Berzonsky, 1990, p. 156).

Three *identity styles* can be used to construct, maintain, or modify one's identity, with individual differences in style use based on preferences determined by personality, motivation, and lifestyle choices/habits (Berzonsky, 1990, 2011). Early in the development of his theory, Berzonsky (1990) described the styles in terms of differences in the social-cognitive processes of openness/exploration and assimilation/accommodation (among other qualities). More recently, the three styles have been described primarily in terms of two cognitive systems, rational/analytical and intuitive/experiential, borrowed from Epstein (1990) and which Berzonsky(2011) refers to as a dual-process model of identity processing. The intuitive/experiential system is quick and automatic but is prone to distortions and biases, whereas the rational/analytical system requires more mental effort but is less prone to subjective distortion (Berzonsky, 2008, 2011). "Both rational and intuitive processes are postulated to play a role in self-construction and adaptive behavior and people can shift between them... However, individual differences in the use of the two cognitive systems have been found" (Berzonsky, 2008, p. 645).

Individuals who prefer to use an *informational identity style* "actively seek out, evaluate, and use self-relevant information" (Berzonsky & Kuk, 2000, p. 83), and they tend to be skeptical of their self-views, question their assumptions and beliefs, and explore and evaluate information that is relevant to their self-constructs (Berzonsky, 1992a; Berzonsky & Sullivan, 1992). The use of this style is positively associated with experiential openness and introspectiveness (Berzonsky, 2003) and is hypothesized to be based in balanced use of assimilation and accommodation processes resulting in a flexible self-identity (Berzonsky, 1990). Two specific cognitive strategies are used by these individuals, both intuitive/automatic and rational/analytical processes (Berzonsky, 2008), which result in vigilant decision-making (Berzonsky & Ferrari, 1996) and problem-focused coping (Beaumont & Seaton, 2011; Berzonsky, 1992a).

Individuals who prefer to use a *normative identity style* "deal with identity questions and decisional situations by conforming to the prescriptions and expectations of significant others" (Berzonsky & Kuk, 2000, p. 83). The use of a normative style is negatively related to openness and introspectiveness (Berzonsky & Sullivan, 1992) and positively related to avoidant coping (Berzonsky, 1992a), the need for closure, and conservative, authoritarian, and racist sociocultural views (Soenens, Duriez, & Goossens, 2005). These tendencies toward rigidity may be due to the use of more assimilation than accommodation processes (Berzonsky, 1990), as well as an overuse of automatic/intuitive processing, which results in premature cognitive commitments, cognitive biases, and efforts to preserve pre-existing beliefs about themselves and the world (Berzonsky, 2008).

Individuals who prefer to use a *diffuse-avoidant identity style* are "reluctant to face up to and confront personal problems and decisions" (Berzonsky & Kuk, 2000, p. 83), and they are believed to form an unstable or empty self-identity through excessive cognitive accommodation (Berzonsky, 1990). Diffuse-avoidant style users report low introspectiveness and openness (Berzonsky & Sullivan, 1992) and high neuroticism (Clancy Dollinger, 1995), and they use maladaptive cognitive and behavioral strategies, such as intuitive reasoning (Berzonsky, 2008), avoidant coping (Berzonsky, 1992a), and cognitive and behavioral disengagement (Beaumont & Seaton, 2011).

According to Berzonsky (2011), by late adolescence, all individuals should be capable of using all three identity styles, but each individual will tend to favor a particular style. That hypothesis is supported by results showing that individual differences in identity styles are evident in similar percentages in early, middle, and late adulthood age periods (Beaumont & Pratt, 2011; Beaumont & Zukanovic, 2005). Nevertheless, in samples of emerging and young adults, age was positively correlated with the informational style (Beaumont, 2011; Beaumont & Pryor, 2013) and negatively correlated with the normative and diffuse-avoidant styles (Beaumont, 2009, 2011; Seaton & Beaumont, 2011b). Thus, it is possible that particular growth experiences during the periods of emerging and early adulthood may provide the opportunity for the development of a more balanced, yet flexible, identity style.

The Growth-Oriented Identity Style and Wisdom

The primary objective of the research conducted by me and my students has been to determine if there is a particular identity processing style that is most conducive to the development of character strengths, personal growth, and wisdom in adulthood. Using Berzonsky's (1990, 1992b) theory and measure of identity styles as a starting point, this program of research has revealed that the use of an informational style, among emerging and young adults, uniquely and positively predicts measures of strength and maturity of character (e.g., mature defenses, Seaton & Beaumont, 2011a; ego resilience, Seaton & Beaumont, 2014; emotional intelligence, Seaton & Beaumont, 2011b; generativity, Beaumont & Pratt, 2011), as well as the desire to grow and develop (e.g., curiosity/exploration, Seaton & Beaumont, 2008; personal growth, Beaumont & Seaton, 2008).

To further uncover the unique identity processing style associated with personal growth toward maturity and strength of character, additional studies focused specifically on the prediction of wisdom. Although Erikson (1998) believed that the maturity required for the development of wisdom requires aging, he also stressed that wisdom is grounded in identity synthesis developed much earlier in development. In fact, research has shown that aspects of wisdom, such as self-reflectiveness, begin to develop in late adolescence and can then stabilize by the mid-twenties (Pasupathi, Staudinger, & Baltes, 2001). Thus, I became curious about whether certain flexible and adaptive identity processes (i.e., those based in self-reflection and experiential openness) in emerging adults make this particular developmental period important for initiating evolution toward wisdom.

Researchers consider wisdom as a multidimensional construct involving a balanced perspective that includes mature understanding, judgment, and general social-cognitive competence (e.g., Baltes, Glück, & Kunzmann, 2005; Baltes & Staudinger, 2000). Generally speaking, wisdom has been considered in three ways in the literature: (1) *general wisdom* involves insights about life in general based primarily on knowledge- or intelligence-related facets (Staudinger, Dörner, & Mickler, 2005), (2) *personal wisdom* encompasses a person's insight or perspective into his or her own life that involves a particular pattern of dispositional characteristics (Staudinger et al., 2005), and (3) *integrated wisdom* is based on an integration of Eastern and Western philosophical and spiritual traditions, which combine aspects of the other two wisdom perspectives (Ardelt, 2003) and deep self-knowledge, acceptance, and compassion for self and others (Germer, 2013).

Following from Orwoll and Perlmutter's (1990) argument that mature adjustment in the form of wisdom involves advanced self-development and self-transcendence, I examined predictive relationships between Berzonsky's (1990) identity styles, self-actualization, and self-transcendence in 18–35-year-olds (Beaumont, 2009). The informational style was the only identity style that positively predicted both aspects of personal wisdom, which in turn positively predicted the presence of meaning in life and subjective happiness. In fact, the informational style uniquely predicted personal wisdom even after controlling for the overlapping variance accounted for by the strength of respondents' commitment to their identities.

In a second study focused specifically on emerging adults (ages 18–29), I investigated the relationships between identity styles and wisdom based on Ardelt's (2003) East-West integrative model and measure (the Three-Dimensional Wisdom Scale or 3DWS). This approach is based on Clayton and Birren's (1980) concept of wisdom as "a multidimensional attribute involving the integration of general cognitive, affective, and reflective components" (p. 130). *Cognitive wisdom* is a complex understanding of life involving a comprehension of "the significance and deeper meaning of phenomena and events, particularly with regard to intrapersonal and interpersonal matters" (Ardelt, 2003, p. 278). Critical for cognitive wisdom is *reflective wisdom* which involves the ability to look at others and the world beyond oneself by considering multiple perspectives (Ardelt, 2003, 2009). This capacity for perspective-taking provides a basis for developing the self-awareness that allows one to perceive reality without distortions, defenses, or preoccupations (Ardelt, 2003). This reduction in self-centeredness allows for a sympathetic and compassionate love for others, which is the hallmark of *affective wisdom*.

The informational style was the only identity style that positively predicted all three aspects of wisdom, which in turn predicted mindfulness (open and receptive awareness and attention) and savoring (regulating and prolonging the positive aspects of experiences; Beaumont, 2011). These findings, which the informational style positively predicts reflective, affective, and cognitive wisdom (as measured by the 3DWS), have been replicated in our other research with different samples of emerging adults (Beaumont, Dimler, & Pryor 2015; Beaumont & Pryor, 2013). In two of those studies, age was positively correlated with both the informational style and wisdom, which suggests that even in the relatively short age span of 18–29, advances in both wisdom and identity flexibility (the use of the informational style) are evident. In fact, it is possible that emerging and early adulthood are sensitive or optimal periods for establishing the use of this flexible identity style which provides a basis for possible wisdom development.

Following the precedent set by Ardelt (2003, 2009), in all three identity and integrated wisdom studies, additional analyses were included to capture the qualities associated with the wisest individuals by comparing those who scored in the upper wisdom quartile with those who scored in the middle and lowest quartiles on wisdom. The findings revealed that compared to the lowest or middle quartiles of wisdom scorers, the emerging adults who scored in the highest quartile on total wisdom scores reported significantly lower scores on the diffuse-avoidant style and higher scores on the informational identity style, identity commitment (Beaumont, 2011; Beaumont et al., 2015; Beaumont & Pryor, 2013), mindfulness (Beaumont, 2011;

Beaumont & Pryor, 2013), self-reflection, self-insight (Beaumont & Pryor, 2013), self-compassion (Beaumont & Pryor, 2015), savoring (Beaumont, 2011), purposeful meaning in life, and eudaimonic well-being (Beaumont et al., 2015).

Together the results of those studies suggest that the informational style provides a pathway for the development of wisdom. Based on that supposition, I argued that

> Berzonsky's (1990) description of the informational identity style should be expanded to include the pursuit of wisdom and personal growth (Beaumont, 2011). As a start, I suggested that the complexity of this style would be better captured by the descriptive label, growth-oriented identity style or *growth style*, which can be defined as a style of identity processing that is oriented "toward the growth of integrated (wise) self-knowledge". (Beaumont, 2011, p. 177)

Although to the best of my knowledge, the descriptive phrase of "growth-oriented" has not previously been used to describe an identity processing style, it has been used to refer to the personality characteristics or behaviors that promote eudaimonic well-being (Kashdan & Steger, 2007) and wisdom (Csikszentmihalyi & Rathunde, 1990; Staudinger et al., 2005). Staudinger et al. claim that it is the desire for personal growth inherent in the "growth-related personality" that is important for the development of wisdom. Similarly, Csikszentmihalyi and Rathunde argue that it is the pursuit of wisdom itself that is personally meaningful for those who engage in growth-oriented behaviors:

> One might claim that the pursuit of wisdom is intrinsically rewarding based on the fact that the reflective dimension of wisdom belongs to a class of autonomy or growth-oriented behaviors that do not provide a direct and immediate benefit for the individual in any technical or practical way. Such autotelic (auto = self, telos = goal) behaviors produce an optimal state of enjoyment in consciousness and are perceived as rewarding in themselves. (p. 39)

Below, I offer arguments and supporting evidence that the growth-oriented identity style involves various contemplative processes. Inherent in these arguments is the idea that it is these contemplative processes that provide the basis for the identity flexibility necessary for the development of wisdom during adulthood.

The Role of Contemplative Processes

The evidence showing a predictive link between a growth-oriented identity style and wisdom cannot be accounted for solely by balanced assimilation and accommodation processes, which, as was reviewed earlier, are often used to explain healthy identity achievement. What is not elaborated in those previous perspectives is a fuller explanation of the internal change processes that occur *between* assimilation and accommodation processes. Internal change processes, such as an "altered perspective or new awareness through introspection," occur when there is an internal "discontent or coming to terms with oneself" at a time of no strong external source or influence for change (Kroger & Green, 1996). What is needed in identity theory/research is a greater explanation of the internal change processes that precede accommodative changes in one's identity (Kunnen & Wassink, 2003). In fact, I would argue that it is these pre-accommodation processes which foster the identity flexibility necessary for adaptive maturity, such as resilience or wisdom.

The links between the growth-oriented identity style and wisdom also cannot be fully accounted for by the cognitive processes described by Berzonsky (2008, 2011). Specifically, although the gross-level cognitive processing associated with this style might include both rational and intuitive processes, as was found by Berzonsky (2008) for the informational style, these processes cannot, by themselves, explain how the growth-oriented identity style can be linked to the complex reflective and affective processes inherent in integrated wisdom. In support of that statement, Ardelt (2010) has argued that the development of wisdom requires more than just cognitive processes: "It appears that growth in wisdom requires a combination of cognition, self-reflection, openness to all kinds of experiences, and the recognition and acceptance of uncertainty" (p. 195).

My argument is that what better accounts for the link between the growth-oriented identity style and wisdom is the use of more complex and integrative *contemplative processes*. The term *contemplation* is typically used in the educational and research literatures to refer to contemplative epistemology, pedagogy, or specific practices geared toward introspection, mindfulness, and personal growth. In all cases, "... the contemplative approach is one of inquiry into the nature of things, a scientific suspension of disbelief (and belief) in an attempt to 'know' reality through direct observation by being fully present in the moment" (Barzebat & Bush, 2014, p. xiii). All contemplative practices or modes of inquiry have in common an inward personal focus that allows the individual to develop both self-insight and greater connections beyond oneself (Barzebat & Bush, 2014, p. 5). As Hart (2004) has so eloquently said, "...they share in common a distinct nonlinear consciousness that invites an inner opening of awareness. This opening within us in turn enables a corresponding opening toward the world before us" (p. 29).

As they relate to identity and wisdom, I define contemplative processes as *ways of understanding and accepting the nature of one's inner and outer reality through direct experience and observation in the present moment*. Because these processes are moment-to-moment direct experiences, they can be described as the micro-processes linking the growth style and wisdom by fostering pre-accommodative change in one's self-identity. Such processes should deepen one's self-understanding, build mindfulness and self-compassion, and generate acceptance, appreciation, and compassion (Barzebat & Bush, 2014, p. 6). This conception of contemplative processes is grounded in the Buddhist psychology perspective on wisdom, in which importance is placed on detachment from self, acceptance of suffering, mindful awareness, and compassion for self and others (Germer, 2013).

As summarized in Table 3.1, I argue for two broad types of contemplative processes, depth processes and breadth processes, which underlie the connection between the growth-oriented identity style and wisdom. *Depth processes* are those forms of contemplation that foster a deeper development of self-awareness and self-acceptance, including self-reflection, self-insight, and self-compassion. Ardelt (2003) argues that engaging in self-reflection is necessary for the development of

Table 3.1 Heuristic model of the contemplative processes of the growth-oriented identity style

Contemplative processes
I. Depth processes: foster a deeper development of self-awareness and self-acceptance
Self-reflection:
"The inspection and evaluation of one's thoughts, feelings, and behaviors" (Grant, Franklin, & Langford, 2002, p. 821)
Self-insight:
"The clarity of understanding of one's thoughts, feelings, and behaviors" (Grant et al., 2002, p. 821)
Self-compassion:
"Being caring and compassionate towards oneself in the face of hardship or perceived inadequacy" (Neff, Kirkpatrick, & Rude, 2007, p. 140)
II. Breadth processes: develop self-expansion or transcendence by fostering a broader awareness, acceptance, appreciation, and compassion for connections beyond oneself (with others or life/existence itself)
Mindfulness:
"The awareness that emerges through paying attention on purpose, in the present moment, and nonjudgmentally to the unfolding experience moment to moment" (Kabat-Zinn, 2003, p. 145)
Acceptance:
"A willingness to let things be just as they are the moment we become aware of them" (Germer, 2013, p. 7)
Meaning in life (MIL):
"The sense made of, and significance felt regarding, the nature of one's being and existence" (Steger, Frazier, Oishi, & Kaler, 2006)
Appreciation/gratitude:
"The appreciation of what is valuable and meaningful to oneself" (Sansone & Sansone, 2010, p. 18)
Compassion:
The ability to open oneself up to the suffering experienced by others "along with the wish to alleviate it" (Germer, 2013, p. 10)

self-awareness and self-insight, and both foster greater acceptance of oneself through self-compassion (Neff, 2003).

Breadth processes go beyond deep self-knowledge, providing a detachment or transcendence from one's self-concept, through mindfulness, acceptance, a sense of meaning and appreciation for life, and compassion for others. These combined contemplative processes provide direct observation of oneself and one's experiences in the present moment with the autotelic goals of deepening one's self-awareness and self-acceptance while also broadening one's awareness of connections to existence beyond oneself. The outcome of these experiences should be the development of wisdom and compassion through self-realization (the goal of depth processes) and self-transcendence (the goal of breadth processes). Ardelt (2003) offers an explanation for how these depth and breadth processes may be connected:

> … through the practice of (self-) reflection, people on the path to wisdom learn not to react to unpleasant sensations, to accept the reality of the present moment, and to understand

> their own and other persons' motives and behavior... genuine feelings of sympathy and compassion for others will emerge only after a decrease in self-centeredness through transcendence of subjectivity and projections.... (p. 279)

Table 3.2 provides research evidence in support of this proposed model of contemplative identity processes. Specifically, the growth-oriented identity style is positively related to all of the depth and breadth processes, and it is the only identity style (of Berzonsky's three styles) that is positively related to measures of these processes. In summary, the higher one's use of the growth-oriented style, the higher is the reported self-reflection, insight (Beaumont & Pryor, 2013), self-compassion (Beaumont & Pryor, 2015), mindfulness (Beaumont, 2011; Beaumont & Pryor, 2013), coping through acceptance (Beaumont & Seaton, 2011), presence of meaning in life (Beaumont, 2009; Beaumont & Scammell, 2012), counting one's blessings (Beaumont, 2011), and compassionate love for humanity (Bruser & Beaumont, 2010). All but two of the measures listed in Table 3.2 (because they have not yet been researched) have also been found to be positively related to wisdom (total, reflective, cognitive, and affective, as measured by the 3DWS).

Concluding Comments

The goal of this chapter was to argue that identity flexibility may be afforded by the use of a growth-oriented identity style. This style of identity processing is oriented toward the development of personal growth and wisdom through the use of processes that are contemplative in nature. Contemplative processes are ways of understanding and accepting the nature of one's inner and outer reality through direct experience and observation in the present moment. The specific contemplative processes of self-reflection, insight, self-compassion, mindfulness, acceptance, appreciation, meaning in life, and compassion have all been found to be significantly associated with a growth-oriented identity style (Beaumont, 2009, 2011; Beaumont & Pryor, 2013, 2015; Beaumont & Scammell, 2012; Beaumont & Seaton, 2011; Bruser & Beaumont, 2010).

Citing Grotevant, Thorbecke, and Meyers (1982), who apparently first used the term "identity flexibility," Whitbourne (1986) described it as "the process of deliberate and informed comparison of one's present identity commitments with other possibilities; that is, the adult's readiness to initiate a life change that temporally precedes the process of making that change" (p. 164). I would argue that there is sufficient evidence that the use of a growth-oriented identity style, along with the associated contemplative processes, may provide the capacities that create a readiness to change at any point in adulthood. Although support for this model is provided by previous research on the growth-oriented style, wisdom, and the various

Table 3.2 Relationships between the contemplative processes and the growth-oriented identity style or wisdom

Contemplative processes	Construct measured	*r* (growth style)	*r* (wisdom)	References
I. Depth processes				
Self-reflection	Self-reflection (Grant et al., 2002)	0.51	0.42	Beaumont and Pryor (2013)
Self-insight	Insight (Grant et al., 2002)	0.25	0.53	Beaumont and Pryor (2013)
Self-compassion	Self-compassion (Neff, 2003)	0.15	0.46	Beaumont and Pryor (2015)
II. Breadth processes				
Mindfulness	Dispositional mindfulness (Brown & Ryan, 2003)	0.14	0.52	Beaumont (2011)
	Facets of mindfulness (Baer, Smith, Hopkins, Krietemeyer, & Toney, 2006)	0.33	0.61	Beaumont and Pryor (2013)
Acceptance	Acceptance coping (Carver, Scheier, & Weintraub, 1989)	0.30	–	Beaumont and Seaton (2011)
Meaning in life (MIL)	Presence MIL (Steger et al., 2006)	0.21	0.55 (self-actualization)	Beaumont (2009)
			0.40 (self-transcendence)	
Appreciation/gratitude	Counting one's blessings (Bryant & Veroff, 2007)	0.25	0.20	Beaumont (2011)
Compassion	Compassionate love for humanity (Sprecher & Fehr, 2005)	0.49	–	Bruser and Beaumont (2010)

Unless otherwise indicated, the measure of wisdom was Ardelt's (2003) 3DWS. All Pearson correlations (*r*) are significant at least at the $p < 0.05$ level. Blanks in the fourth column are due to no research having yet been conducted to confirm contemplative processes, further questions remain about the more complex interconnections between these contemplative processes, the relevant importance of each of these processes, the short-term or long-term progression of these processes, and whether the proposed model might be expanded to include other contemplative processes. Future research should be directed at addressing these and other related questions.

As Buddhist psychology, with its emphasis on contemplation and meditation for the development of compassionate wisdom, becomes more popular, both in contemporary society and in academic fields such as positive psychology, I believe that identity researchers will be called upon to consider more complex and integrated processes to better account for identity flexibility. As argued here, I believe that at least a beginning answer lies in the area of contemplative pedagogy and psychology. It is in contemplative processes and practices that we find the context for creating a flexible self-identity that brings deep self-refection, insight, acceptance, and, ultimately, compassion and wisdom.

In conclusion, I offer Thomas Merton's (1972) passionate declaration on the beauty of contemplation:

> Contemplation is the highest expression of man's intellectual and spiritual life. It is that life itself, fully awake, fully active, fully aware that it is alive. It is spiritual wonder. It is spontaneous awe at the sacredness of life, of being. It is gratitude for life, for awareness and for being. It is a vivid realization of the fact that life and being in us proceed from an invisible, transcendent, and infinitely abundant Source. (p. 1)

References

Adams, G. R., & Montemayor, R. (1987). *Patterns of identity development during late adolescence: A descriptive study of stability, progression and regression*. Unpublished manuscript. Logan, UT: Utah State University.

Ardelt, M. (2003). Empirical assessment of a three-dimensional wisdom scale. *Research on Aging, 25*, 275–324. doi:10.1177/0164027503025003004.

Ardelt, M. (2009). How similar are wise men and women? A comparison across two age cohorts. *Research in Human Development, 6*, 9–26. doi:10.1080/15427600902779354.

Ardelt, M. (2010). Are older adults wiser than college students? A comparison of two age cohorts. *Journal of Adult Development, 17*, 193–207. doi:10.1007/s10804-009-9088-5.

Baer, R. A., Smith, G. T., Hopkins, J., Krietemeyer, J., & Toney, L. (2006). Using self-report assessment methods to explore facets of mindfulness. *Assessment, 13*, 24–45. doi:10.1177/1073191105283504.

Baltes, P. B., Glück, J., & Kunzmann, U. (2005). Wisdom: Its structure and function in regulating successful life span development. In C. R. Snyder & S. J. Lopez (Eds.), *Handbook of positive psychology* (pp. 327–347). New York: Oxford University Press.

Baltes, P. B., & Staudinger, U. M. (2000). Wisdom: A metaheuristic (pragmatic) to orchestrate mind and virtue toward excellence. *American Psychologist, 55*, 122–136. doi:10.1037//0003-066X.55.1.122.

Barzebat, D., & Bush, M. (2014). *Contemplative practices in higher education: Powerful methods to transform teaching and learning*. San Francisco: Jossey-Bass.

Beaumont, S. L. (2009). Identity processing styles and personal wisdom: An informational identity style predicts self-actualization and self-transcendence. *Identity: An International Journal of Theory and Research, 9*, 95–115. doi:10.1080/15283480802669101.

Beaumont, S. L. (2011). Identity styles and wisdom during emerging adulthood: Relationships with mindfulness and savoring. *Identity: An International Journal of Theory and Research, 11*, 155–180. doi:10.1080/15283488.2011.557298.

Beaumont, S. L., Dimler, A., & Pryor, T. (2015). *Passion, life meaning, and eudaimonic well-being in the growth-oriented identity processing style*. Unpublished manuscript. Prince George, Canada: University of Northern British Columbia.

Beaumont, S. L., & Pratt, M. M. (2011). Identity processing styles and psychosocial balance during early and middle adulthood: The role of identity in intimacy and generativity. *Journal of Adult Development, 18*, 172–183. doi:10.1007/s10804-011-9125-z.

Beaumont, S. L., & Pryor, T. (2013). *The role of mindfulness in identity and wisdom among emerging adults*. Poster presented at the First International Mindfulness Conference, Rome, Italy.

Beaumont, S. L., & Pryor, T. (2015). *Contemplative processes in identity and wisdom: Examining a growth-oriented identity style*. Unpublished manuscript. Prince George, Canada: University of Northern British Columbia.

Beaumont, S. L., & Scammell, J. (2012). Patterns of spirituality and meaning in life related to identity. *Identity: An International Journal of Theory and Research, 12*(4), 345–367. doi:10.1080/15283488.2012.716380

Beaumont, S. L., & Seaton, C. L. (2008). *Identity processing styles predict patterns of coping: The role of an informational identity style in positive reinterpretation and growth*. Poster presented at the Fifteenth Annual Conference of the Society for Research on Identity Formation, Chicago.

Beaumont, S. L., & Seaton, C. L. (2011). Patterns of coping associated with identity processing styles. *Identity: An International Journal of Theory and Research, 11*, 348–336. doi:10.1080/15283488.2011.613590.

Beaumont, S. L., & Zukanovic, R. (2005). Identity development in men and its relationship to psychological distress and self-worth. *Canadian Journal of Behavioural Science, 37*(1), 70–81. doi:10.1037/h0087246.

Berzonsky, M. D. (1988). Self-theorists, identity status, and social cognition. In D. K. Lapsley & F. C. Power (Eds.), *Self, ego, and identity: Integrative approaches* (pp. 243–262). New York: Springer.

Berzonsky, M. D. (1990). Self-construction over the life span: A process perspective on identity formation. In G. J. Neimeyer & R. A. Neimeyer (Eds.), *Advances in personal construct theory* (Vol. 1, pp. 155–186). Greenwich, CT: JAI Press.

Berzonsky, M. D. (1992a). Identity style and coping strategies. *Journal of Personality, 60*(4), 771–788. doi:10.1111/j.1467-6494.1992.tb00273.x.

Berzonsky, M. D. (1992b). *Identity Style Inventory (ISI3): Revised version*. Unpublished measure.

Berzonsky, M. D. (2003). Identity style and well-being: Does commitment matter? *Identity: An International Journal of Theory and Research, 3*, 131–142. doi:10.1207/S1532706XID030203.

Berzonsky, M. D. (2008). Identity formation: The role of identity processing style and cognitive processes. *Personality and Individual Differences, 44*, 643–653. doi:10.1016/j.paid.2007.09.024.

Berzonsky, M. D. (2011). A social-cognitive perspective on identity construction. In S. J. Schwartz, K. Luyckx, & V. L. Vignoles (Eds.), *Handbook of identity theory and research* (pp. 55–76). New York: Springer.

Berzonsky, M. D., & Adams, G. R. (1999). Reevaluating the identity status paradigm: Still useful after 35 years. *Developmental Review, 19*, 557–590. doi:10.1006/drev.1999.0495.

Berzonsky, M. D., & Ferrari, J. R. (1996). Identity orientation and decisional strategies. *Personality and Individual Differences, 20*, 597–606. doi:10.1016/0191-8869(96)00001-3.

Berzonsky, M. D., & Kuk, L. S. (2000). Identity status, identity processing style, and the transition to university. *Journal of Adolescent Research, 15*, 81–98. doi:10.1177/0743558400151005.

Berzonsky, M. D., & Sullivan, C. (1992). Social-cognitive aspects of identity style: Need for cognition, experiential openness, and introspection. *Journal of Adolescent Research, 7*(2), 140–155. doi:10.1177/074355489272002.

Bosma, H. A., & Kunnen, E. S. (2001). Determinants and mechanisms in ego identity development: A review and synthesis. *Developmental Review, 21*, 39–66. doi:10.1006/drev.2000.0514.

Brown, K. W., & Ryan, R. M. (2003). The benefits of being present: Mindfulness and its role in psychological well-being. *Journal of Personality and Social Psychology, 84*, 882–848. doi:10.1037/0022-3514.84.4.822.

Bruser, R., & Beaumont, S. L. (2010). *The link between identity processing style and compassionate love: Are mindfulness and self-compassion key components?* Poster presented at the 6th Biennial International Meaning Conference, Vancouver, BC.

Bryant, F. B., & Veroff, J. (2007). *Savoring: A new model of positive experience*. Mahwah, NJ: Erlbaum.

Carver, C. S., Scheier, M. F., & Weintraub, J. K. (1989). Assessing coping strategies: A theoretically based approach. *Journal of Personality and Social Psychology, 56*, 267–283. doi:10.1037/0022-3514.56.2.267.

Clancy Dollinger, S. M. (1995). Identity styles and the five-factor model of personality. *Journal of Research in Personality, 29*, 475–479. doi:10.1006/jrpe.1995.1028.

Clayton, V. P., & Birren, J. E. (1980). The development of wisdom across the lifespan: A reexamination of an ancient topic. In P. B. Baltes & O. G. Brim Jr. (Eds.), *Life-span development and behavior* (Vol. 3, pp. 103–135). New York: Academic.

Csikszentmihalyi, M., & Rathunde, K. (1990). The psychology of wisdom: An evolutionary interpretation. In R. J. Sternberg (Ed.), *Wisdom: Its nature, origins, and development* (pp. 25–51). New York: Cambridge University Press.

Epstein, S. (1990). Cognitive-experiential theory. In L. Previn (Ed.), *Handbook of personality theory and research* (pp. 165–192). New York: Guilford Press.

Erikson, E. H. (1994). *Identity: Youth and crisis*. New York: W. W. Norton. (Original work published in 1968).

Erikson, E. H. (1998). *The life cycle completed (extended version)*. New York: Norton. (Original work published in 1982).

Germer, C. K. (2013). Mindfulness: What is it? What does it matter? In C. K. Germer, R. D. Siegel, & P. R. Fulton (Eds.), *Mindfulness and psychotherapy* (2nd ed., pp. 3–35). New York: Guildford.

Grant, A. M., Franklin, J., & Langford, G. (2002). The self-reflection and insight scale: A new measure of private self-consciousness. *Social Behavior and Personality: An International Journal, 30*, 821–829. doi:10.2224/sbp.2002.30.8.821.

Grotevant, H. D. (1987). Toward a process model of identity formation. *Journal of Adolescent Research, 3*, 203–222. doi:10.1177/074355488723003.

Grotevant, H. D., Thorbecke, W., & Meyers, M. L. (1982). An extension of Marcia's identity status interview into the interpersonal domain. *Journal of Youth and Adolescence, 11*, 33–47. doi:10.1007/BF01537815.

Hart, T. (2004). Opening the contemplative mind in the classroom. *Journal of Transformative Education, 2*, 28–46. doi:10.1177/1541344603259311.

Kabat-Zinn, J. (2003). Mindfulness-based interventions in context: Past, present, and future. *Clinical Psychology: Science and Practice, 10*, 144–156. doi:10.1093/clipsy/bpg016.

Kashdan, T. B., & Steger, M. F. (2007). Curiosity and pathways to well-being and meaning in life: Traits, states, and everyday behaviors. *Motivation and Emotion, 31*, 159–173. doi:10.1007/s11031-007-9068-7.

Kroger, J., & Green, K. E. (1996). Events associated with identity status change. *Journal of Adolescence, 19*, 477–490. doi:10.1006/jado.1996.0045.

Kunnen, E. S., & Bosma, H. A. (2000). Development of meaning making: A dynamic systems conceptualization. *New Ideas in Psychology, 18*, 57–82. doi:10.1016/S0732-118X(99)00037-9.

Kunnen, E. S., & Wassink, M. E. K. (2003). An analysis of identity change in adulthood. *Identity: An International Journal of Theory and Research, 3*, 347–366. doi:10.1207/S1532706XID0304_03.

Marcia, J. E. (1966). Development and validation of the ego identity status. *Journal of Personality and Social Psychology, 3*, 551–558. doi:10.1037/h0023281.

Marcia, J. E. (1976). Identity six years after: A follow-up study. *Journal of Youth and Adolescence, 5*, 145–150. doi:10.1007/BF01537490.

Marcia, J. E. (1980). Identity in adolescence. In J. Adelson (Ed.), *Handbook of adolescent psychology* (pp. 102–138). New York: Wiley.

Marcia, J. E. (1993). The ego identity status approach to ego identity. In J. E. Marcia, A. S. Waterman, D. R. Matteson, S. L. Archer, & J. L. Orlofsky (Eds.), *Ego identity: A handbook for psychosocial research* (pp. 3–21). New York: Springer.

Merton, T. (1972). *New seeds of contemplation*. New York: New Directions. Original work published in 1961).

Neff, K. (2003). The development and validation of a scale to measure self-compassion. *Self and Identity, 2*, 223–250. doi:10.1080/15298860309027.

Neff, K. D., Kirkpatrick, K. L., & Rude, S. S. (2007). Self-compassion and adaptive psychological functioning. *Journal of Research in Personality, 41*, 139–154. doi:10.1016/j.jrp.2006.03.004.

Orlofsky, J. L., Marcia, J. E., & Lesser, I. M. (1973). Ego identity status and the intimacy versus isolation crisis of young adulthood. *Journal of Personality and Social Psychology, 27*, 211–219. doi:10.1037/h0034787.

Orwoll, L., & Perlmutter, M. (1990). The study of wise persons: Integrating a personality perspective. In R. J. Sternberg (Ed.), *Wisdom: Its nature, origins, and development* (pp. 160–177). Cambridge, UK: Cambridge University Press.

Pasupathi, M., Staudinger, U. M., & Baltes, P. B. (2001). Seeds of wisdom: Adolescents' knowledge and judgment about difficult life problems. *Developmental Psychology, 37*, 351–361. doi:10.1037/0012-1649.37.3.351.

Sansone, R. A., & Sansone, L. A. (2010). Gratitude and well being: The benefits of appreciation. *Psychiatry (Edgmont), 7*(11), 18–22.

Schwartz, S. J. (2001). The evolution of Eriksonian and neo-Eriksonian identity theory and research: A review and integration. *Identity: An International Journal of Theory and Research, 1*, 7–58. doi:10.1207/S1532706XSCHWARTZ.

Seaton, C. L., & Beaumont, S. L. (2008). Individual differences in identity styles predict proactive forms of positive adjustment. *Identity: An International Journal of Theory and Research, 8*, 249–268. doi:1010.1080/15283480802181891.

Seaton, C. L., & Beaumont, S. L. (2011a). Identity processing styles predict the use of mature, neurotic and immature defense styles. *Identity: An International Journal of Theory and Research, 11*, 1–24. doi:10.1080/15283488.2011.540736.

Seaton, C. L., & Beaumont, S. L. (2011b). The link between identity style and intimacy: Does emotional intelligence provide the key? *Identity: An International Journal of Theory and Research, 11*, 311–332. doi:10.1080/15283488.2011.613586.

Seaton, C. L., & Beaumont, S. L. (2014). Exploring the links between identity styles and forgiveness in university students. *Canadian Journal of Behavioural Science, 46*, 366–374. doi:10.1037/a0032009.

Sneed, R., & Whitbourne, S. K. (2003). Identity processing and self-consciousness in middle and late adulthood. *Journal of Gerontology: Psychological Sciences, 58B*, 313–319. doi:10.1093/geronb/58.6.P313.

Soenens, B., Duriez, B., & Goossens, L. (2005). Social-psychological profiles of identity styles: Attitudinal and social-cognitive correlates in late adolescence. *Journal of Adolescence, 28*, 107–125. doi:10.1016/j.adolescence.2004.07.001.

Sprecher, S., & Fehr, B. (2005). Compassionate love for close others and humanity. *Journal of Social and Personal Relationships, 22*, 629–651. doi:10.1177/0265407505056439.

Staudinger, U. M., Dörner, J., & Mickler, C. (2005). Wisdom and personality. In R. J. Sternberg & J. Jordan (Eds.), *A handbook of wisdom: Psychological perspectives* (pp. 191–219). New York: Cambridge University Press.

Steger, M. F., Frazier, P., Oishi, S., & Kaler, M. (2006). The meaning in life questionnaire: Assessing the presence of and search for meaning in life. *Journal of Counseling Psychology, 53*, 80–93. doi:10.1037/0022-0167.53.1.80.

Stewart, A. J., Ostrove, J. M., & Helson, R. (2001). Middle aging in women: Patterns of personality change the 30s to the 50s. *Journal of Adult Development, 8*, 23–37. doi:10.1023/A:1026445704288.

Whitbourne, S. K. (1986). Personality development in adulthood and old age: Relationships among identity style, health, and well-being. *Annual Review of Gerontology & Geriatrics, 7*, 189–216.

Whitbourne, S. K., Sneed, J. R., & Skultety, K. M. (2002). Identity processes in adulthood: Theoretical and methodological challenges. *Identity: An International Journal of Theory and Research, 2*, 29–45. doi:10.1207/S1532706XID0201_03.

Chapter 4
An Experiential Exploration of Identity During Emerging Adulthood: The Impact of Growth Experiences on Emerging Adulthood Characteristics

Luke Boardman

Emerging adulthood provides an interesting inquiry into identity flexibility because it is a period of opaque identity metamorphosis. The emerging adult's identity is a complex system of dichotomies: adolescent vs. adult, freedom vs. responsibility, expectations vs. exploration, and the overall sense of bouncing between all of these. The simple explanation of this phenomenon is contingent upon the answer to the following question: "what is an adult?" If one knows this answer, then one knows his or her level of identification within the adolescent-adult continuum.

However that answer is hard to come by, an answer as elusive as the definition of emerging adulthood itself. Dr. Jeffery Jensen Arnett, the scholar who brought the term "emerging adult" to the fore and developed its credibility as a developmental phase, defines emerging adulthood as "a new theory of development from the late teens through the twenties, with a focus of ages 18–25. I argue that this period, emerging adulthood is neither adolescence nor young adulthood but is theoretically and empirically distinct from them both (Arnett, 2000)."

This definition is thorough in its establishing of the distinct developmental phase of emerging adulthood but also leaves a lot more to be discovered. Most importantly the question remains of what is happening within the emerging adult during this phase? Is it easier to distinguish two emerging adults from each other than two adults or two adolescents? There of course are physiological developmental differences between a person of age 15, 25, and 45, but the experiential difference is subjective and cannot be seen with the categorizing eye.

Per Dr. Arnett's definition, we know definitively what an emerging adult is not: an adolescent or an adult. We also know that in general, the emerging is developing skills that will set up a future career and life path. We know an emerging adult exists in industrialized countries where this individual is afforded the choice to make decisions that further his or her life in way that corresponds with established life goals.

L. Boardman (✉)
Loyola University Maryland, 4501 N. Charles St., Baltimore, MD 21212, USA
e-mail: lboardman@loyola.edu

J.D. Sinnott (ed.), *Identity Flexibility During Adulthood*,
DOI 10.1007/978-3-319-55658-1_4

Dr. Arnett describes this period as the "volitional years" (Arnett, 2000), meaning a period of choice for the emerging adult, given this option is provided to the individual.

Choice is a defining characteristic of emerging adulthood. In in the context of adolescence and adulthood, choice seems to be less of an option. An adolescent faces the authority structures of family, school, social circles, and society. An adolescent's opinions are not taken as seriously due to lack of experience and autonomy. On the other hand, an adult's choice is also less available than an emerging adult's. This individual is locked into the responsibility of a job/career in addition to supporting himself or herself and family members. In between these two stages of life is the emerging adult, an individual that could be experiencing an incredibly variant level of choice depending on the individual's situation.

With the importance of choice brought to the fore, it can be said that this current study was designed to explore the experiential insight that leads to choice in an emerging adult. It is a study of life experience and existential awareness as it is applied to the flexibility of identity during the emerging adulthood period. Furthermore it focuses on emerging adults that make meaning out of life-changing experiences and how choice plays into the lives of these individuals. The summation of these variables is the construct of self-determination, which seeks to understand why some emerging adults are more self-determined, more willing to make choices, and more willing to take control of their lives than others.

Existential Lens

> *And there were always choices to make. Every day, every hour, offered the opportunity to make a decision, a decision which determined whether you would or would not submit to those powers which threatened to rob you of your very self, your inner freedom; which determined whether or not you would become the plaything of circumstance, renouncing freedom and dignity to become molded into the form of the typical inmate.* (Frankl, 1984)

Choice and freedom are symbiotic, and one cannot exist truly without the other. A choice requires some level of autonomy, however minute, because the choice-maker must be the agent in deciding, thus demonstrating freedom. The above passage from Victor Frankl's *Man's Search for Meaning* is a very extreme example of freedom and choice in an environment where there virtually was none. During his time as a concentration camp prisoner, Frankl's family, life's work, and identity were destroyed, but as expressed in this passage, he was still left with a choice to make, one that determined the validity of his authentic self as a human being rather than a de-identified inmate.

The decision Frankl speaks of is one of autonomy versus total control. His view was one from a place of devastation, but the inner freedom he spoke of is the autonomy that exists opposite of circumstance. According to Frankl, having this inner freedom is the only way to not become a plaything of circumstance, a controlled entity that lacks the inner freedom to make choices that coincide with its life goals.

Although Frankl's experience as a concentration camp prisoner cannot be directly applied to the contemporary emerging adult in an industrialized western country, the principle of the message is that autonomy is necessary to seek out and implement the life that is desired.

Through this existential lens, we can conceptualize emerging adulthood not only as a period of transition, uncertainty, and exploration but also one of prime importance in existential development. The existential issue of freedom is the primary component of choice in the emerging adult and is one that sets apart the autonomous from the controlled. Paralleling Frankl, the controlled emerging adult becomes the plaything of circumstance. This individual is one that is moved like a pawn on another's chessboard, following the expectations of others and subduing inner desires. The choice of identity that characterizes emerging adulthood requires an individual to be comfortable with the uncertainty of exploring different aspects of the self. One must choose to do this and choose to endure the uncertainty, ideally finding solid footing in an identity that is congruent with the authentic self.

In order to hone in on the specific components of choice, this study utilized a focus on the variable of agency. Agency is defined as an "action or intervention, especially such as to produce a particular effect" (Oxford Dictionaries, 2015). For the purposes of this study, this definition demonstrates a crucial application of agency to the emerging adult and the individual's determination to take action by making choices with intended consequences that are consistent with life goals. Agency has been studied in the emerging adulthood literature, showing to be a variable that is representative of the transition-nature of emerging adulthood.

One study (Schwartz, Côté, & Arnett, 2005) found agency to be positively correlated to identity exploration and flexible commitment. This implies that a certain level of agency allows the individual to take charge of his or her life in a way that influences his or her decision-making by affording the individual a comfort in the uncertainty of the emerging adulthood period. In other words, an emerging adult with a significant level of agency is determined to strive toward choices and try things on along the way. Also, a certain level of agency in an individual would make them more apt to explore different aspects of his or her identity as well as more apt to make commitments to life decisions, as is seen by the correlations in the study (Schwartz et al. 2005).

With agency in the context of emerging adulthood, we have a portrait of a person who understands that his or her actions can result in consequences that are harmonious with the individual's life goals. This individual understands that taking charge of his or her life could involve exploring different interests, relationships, career choices, and passions in general, all of which contribute to the transient nature of identity during this stage. But the courage to put oneself fully into these "self-experiments" requires an awareness of consequential control.

This control is conceptualized by the construct of the causality orientation (Deci & Ryan, 1985), a construct that takes agency one step further to the intersection of self-awareness, life goals, and decision-making. A causality orientation is the level at which an individual understands the cause of the events in his or her life, and according to the founders of the theory Edward Deci and Richard Ryan, an individual has different levels of the autonomy, controlled, and impersonal orientation. The autonomy orientation portrays the individual who is highly aware that his or her actions are the cause of the events in his or her life and is motivated by his or her own goals. This concept is parallel to intrinsic motivation (Coon & Mitterer, 2010). The controlled orientation portrays the individual who is controlled by external stimuli, like accolades and the expectations of others, while the impersonal orientation portrays the individual who feels as if he or she cannot control the events in his or her life at all, which is characterized by a state of inactivity (Deci & Ryan).

For the purposes of this study of the transient identity components of the emerging adult, it is clear that the autonomy causality orientation best represents our highly agent emerging adult, one who is determined and aware enough to make the decisions he or she needs to make to get the desired life outcome. Furthermore, this individual is powered by his or her own drive and is not significantly swayed by external rewards. Rather, the awareness of living consistently with one's own goals provides a self-validation that makes the unstable nature of the emerging adulthood period both fruitful and tolerable. And consistent with the findings of Arnett (2000), one with an autonomous causality orientation should have a level of self-responsibility that would render the individual more apt to make goal-consistent life decisions and therefore emerge from the emerging adulthood stage as an explored, experienced, and self-aware individual with regard to life goals and identity.

Narrative Identity

Emerging adulthood naturally lends itself to a narrative framework. The individual is between the stages of adolescence and adulthood while exhibiting the behaviors of each. Much of this stage can be thought of in the traditional sense of "coming of age," a character in a story gathering experiences that incrementally contribute pieces to the bridge to adulthood. With these new experiences, the character's identity splinters and grows into different areas on the self, all while holding a self-centric perspective on the awareness of this development.

Simply put, the emerging adult individual is the star of his or her own feature film, the agent of action toward self-awareness. This reaffirms agency as a primary construct that differentiates one emerging adult from the other. Agency in this context is a life-story construct which represents the degree to which individuals are able to affect change in their lives or influence others in their environment (McAdams & McClean, 2013). With a narrative lens, the emerging adult individual can be put clearly in a developmental context, providing a personalized take on the growth during this period.

This current study emphasized the focus on the growth experiences of emerging adults with the intention of discovering the impact of these experiences on the development of increased self-awareness. In other words, the individual is able to see how the experience plays into the narrative by learning what changed between point A and point B. Therefore these growth experiences function as catalysts:

crucial turning points in emerging adulthood. They have implications on this development because of their impact on self-awareness and identity. To have this self-awareness, identity flexibility is inherently required, because to understand the effect of a significant event on one's life requires a reflexive identity concept that updates with these significant experiences.

This current study approaches identity as a self-regulating system of life experience, self-awareness, and meaning making that puts the individual in his or her own context. The study's focus on emerging adulthood narrows the scope to its specific identity characteristics, identity exploration, experimentation/possibilities, negativity/instability, other-focus, self-focus, and feeling "in-between" (Reifman, Arnett & Colwell, 2007). To richen this investigation, the study also sought to understand how causality orientations (autonomous, controlled, and impersonal) and existential thinking work during this period. Therefore the study seeks to support the following hypothesis: emerging adult-aged individuals who reported one or multiple growth experiences will report significantly different data regarding emerging adult identity, causality orientation, and existential thinking.

Method

Participants

Recruitment was based on convenience, and since data was collected entirely online, participants responded to the survey from many areas of the world. Almost all of the participants were college students, most were of the typical emerging adult age, while a few were older than the typical age ($M = 21.34$, $SD = 3.38$). To allow the exploration of emerging adult characteristics in higher ages while also eliminating extreme outliers, the maximum age analyzed was 33. The study included 108 females, 41 males, and 2 participants who described themselves as cisgender and gender-neutral, respectively. Every participant was a student at a university, which is how they were able to gain access to the survey. Recruitment was based on convenience. Extra course credit was given by professors in three separate classes at large universities in the United States as a means for recruitment. Other participants were recruited through two national social science research websites: Socialpsychology.org and Psychological Research on the Net.

Procedure

This study was approved by the Towson University Institutional Review Board. The data collection took place through SurveyMonkey. Participants were given the measurements in the following order: general causality orientation scale (GCOS), life event measurement, inventory of the dimensions of emerging adulthood (IDEA), and scale of existential thinking (SET). The study took approximately 15 min to complete, but the amount of time taken to complete the study varied because it depended on the amount of time the participant spent writing his or her life event(s).

Measures

The measurement of life event narrative was assessed qualitatively. For this measurement, the participant received the following prompt:

> Has a particular event occurred in your life that made a significant impact on who you are today? This could be a positive or a negative event, and is one that stands out in your memory. If so, please describe the event in the text box below. Be sure to include your age when the event took place, and as much detail as you would like to include. There is no limit to how much you can write. After you finish writing, please answer the questions below the text box. If more than one event stands out, there are additional text boxes where you can write about other events, each of which are followed by the same questions that follow the first text box.

Following this prompt, the participant was presented with a text field in which they could write about their event. There was no limit to how much they could write. Three additional text fields and corresponding sets of questions were available to the participant if they wanted to write about an additional life event. It was made clear to the participant that reporting these additional life events, as well as the initial life event, was not required to complete the study.

Emerging adulthood identification was measured by the IDEA (Reifman, et al., 2007). The scale consisted of a master question, "Is this period of your life a…," and 31 items that functioned as responses to this master question. Some examples of the responses items are "…time of confusion," "…time of instability," "…time of independence," and "…time of separating from parents."

Participants responded to the items on a scale of one (strongly disagree) to four (strongly agree). Scores were calculated for six subscales, each of which reflected aspects of emerging adulthood. The subscales were identity exploration, experimentation/possibilities, negativity/instability, other-focus, self-focus, and feeling "in-between." The convergent validity of the IDEA was tested. This was done by testing the scale against measurements with a similar aim. These other measurements include measurements of life satisfaction ($r = 0.86$), self-mastery ($r = 0.76$), novelty seeking ($r = 0.69$), future orientation ($r = 0.78$), and parental control which was analyzed with two factors ($r = 0.79$ and $r = 0.62$). Reliability analysis for this current study yielded an internal consistency of $\alpha = 0.88$.

Causality orientation was measured by the GCOS (Deci & Ryan, 1985). The scale featured 12 vignettes that proposed a scenario, to which the participant responded to three questions for each scenario, assessing the three outcome causality orientations: autonomy, controlled, and impersonal. For each vignette, the participant read a hypothetical situation and was presented with three reactions to the situation which corresponded to the three types of causality orientations.

The following is an example of a vignette: "You had a job interview several weeks ago. In the mail you received a form letter which states that the position has been filled. It is likely that you might think: a) It's not what you know, but who you know; b) I'm probably not good enough for the job; c) Somehow they didn't see my qualifications as matching their needs." These three responses represented the control, impersonal, and autonomy causality orientations, respectively.

The participants responded to each of the three responses on a Likert scale from one (very unlikely response to the situation) to seven (very likely responses to the situation). Reliability analysis of the measurement from previous research yielded internal consistencies of $\alpha = 0.74$ for autonomy, $\alpha = 0.69$ for control, and $\alpha = 0.74$ for impersonal (Deci & Ryan, 1985). Reliability analysis for this current study yielded internal consistencies of $\alpha = 0.80$ for autonomy, $\alpha = 0.69$ for control, and $\alpha = 0.81$ for impersonal.

The level of existential thinking was measured by the SET (Allan and Shearer, 2012). The measure consisted of 11 items that required the participant to rate the level in which they engage with the listed questions on the following scale: 1 = no, 2 = sometimes, 3 = often, 4 = almost all the time, and 5 = all the time. Some examples of the questions include, "Do you spend time in meditation, prayer, or reflecting on the mysteries of life?", "Do you think about ideas such as eternity, truth, justice and goodness?", and "Have you ever reflected on the nature of reality or the universe?"

Scores of the SET can range from 11 to 55. Investigations into the reliability and validity of this measure were made by Allan and Shearer by conducting the test in three different populations. It was found that the scale had a test-retest reliability of 0.91. It was also found that the scale had internal consistencies ranging from $\alpha = 0.88$ to $\alpha = 0.94$. Convergent validity was also assessed by correlating the scale to a number of theoretically related variables, including intrinsic religiousness, life satisfaction, search for meaning in life, and the presence of meaning in life. Of these, the scale correlated highly with both search for and presence of meaning in life, pointing out the scale's convergence of these related ideas and how the scale successfully measures them. Reliability analysis for this current study yielded an internal consistency of $\alpha = 0.87$.

Results and Discussion

To analyze the results, the scores on the measures were isolated into two categories: growth experience and nongrowth experience. This was done by analyzing the narrative responses in a way that looked for elements of a growth experience. In total, there were 151 completed narrative responses of which 58 were growth experiences (38.41%). The participants were not asked to provide any insight gained from the experiences that they share; however, some did on their own accord and this element was used to dictate a growth experience. For example, one 18-year-old male participant shared the following narrative:

> A particular event that was a negative but then turned out to be a positive event was when I tore my ACL playing soccer. It was my junior year in high school, so I was 17 years old at the time. I was in Sacramento playing in the state cup and in the last game, a kid hit me from behind when the ball was coming to me and my right leg that was already planted in the ground, buckled. I heard a pop and then couldn't move my knee. A couple weeks went by and the MRI results came in telling me that my ACL was torn in half and required surgery to play soccer again. After surgery, 7 months went by of constant physical therapy and I was able to play my senior year. It showed me that through hard work and dedication, I could accomplish anything that I set my mind to. Although I didn't play a lot due to my injury, at least I was able to go out there and play the game that I have loved for so long.

This participant's narrative exhibited elements of a growth experience, even explicitly saying that the tearing of the ACL went from a negative event to a positive one because it reestablished the participant's love for soccer despite the setback. This is a clear example of the type of unprompted shared insight that was found in many of these narratives.

Another clear example of a growth experience can be found in the following narrative by a 23-year-old female participant:

> Throughout high school and my first year of college, due to personal emotional and situational struggles I had little motivation for school. Most of the teachers I had during these years acknowledge my intellect and were frustrated with my lack of motivation and effort towards my studies, and therefore I was often dismissed as a slacker. Then, when I was 19, I took my first course in adolescent development and had my first experienced with the professor who would soon become my mentor. I remember her coming up to me after class one day and saying to me "What do you want to do with your life? You are really good at this stuff." We sat and spoke for a good 20 minutes, and she offered to waiver certain requirements for an advanced seminar that she teaches so that I could take the class the following semester. This woman grew to be my mentor, the first person to believe in me when I didn't even believe in myself. Today, I am two years out of college and have obtained a position as a Study Coordinator at a lab affiliated with an IV league university. I look forward to going back to graduate school to pursue my career. I often wonder how different my life would be now if I hadn't met my mentor.

This participant provided another example of a growth experience as an emerging adult. This narrative is different from the first in that it did not involve a direct negative setback like the injury, but rather featured an overall lack of motivation. That motivation was started by an awareness of her potential and lack of direction, and through the mentorship she received, she was able to apply her intellect to something she is passionate about, stabilizing her identity and putting her on a path on which she has achieved success and further goals to pursue.

A final example of a growth experience comes from a 30-year-old male. This participant is outside of the typical emerging adulthood age range, but his narrative regards an experience as an emerging adult and provides a unique insight into the developmental period and its aftermath years later:

> My early twenties consisted of heavy partying and very few responsible actions. I managed to get arrested for DUI twice at the age of twenty one and a third time at the age of twenty six. I was sentenced to one full year in prison. This event was like living in an alternate reality where time stood still and change was forced. The culture shock alone was enough to scare me into adulthood, but the violence and corruption really sealed the deal. Getting

> beat up in prison was the true turning point. That helpless feeling was devastating to any confidence I might have had. It has been three years and three days since my release but I remember all of it so clearly; like it was yesterday.

What is unique about this narrative is that the participant explicitly mentioned the world "adulthood." For this participant, his experience of three DUI arrests and a year in prison, which was described as a surreal alternative reality in where he experienced an intense lifestyle change among a culture of violence and corruption that he experienced directly, was a clear catalyst that propelled him into adulthood. A life of minimal responsibilities had been transformed for him into a hole that he needed to crawl out of, requiring autonomy, decision-making ability, and responsibility for his actions to do so. This narrative provides a fruitful before and after look at one experience of emerging adulthood that sheds light on an extreme carefree stage and an outcome of adulthood, requiring an autonomous takeover of his life upon his release from prison.

This study also employed quantitative techniques to gain a closer look at the effects of growth experiences on emerging adult characteristics. The scores of the GCOS, IDEA, and SES were isolated into a growth experience and nongrowth experience group. To see if there were any significant distinctions between the two groups, descriptive statistics were gathered as shown in Tables 4.1 and 4.2.

There were certain outcome variables that resulted in higher means for the growth experience group compared to the nongrowth experience group. These variables were identity exploration, experimentation, other-focus, self-focus, and feeling "in-between" from the IDEA and the level of existential thinking from the SET. An independent samples t-test was conducted for the outcome variables and no difference between the means of the two groups was found to be statistically significant. For the sake of this study however, the differences in means suggest a possible experiential difference between these individuals that requires further investigation.

The variables of identity exploration and experimentation imply a salient characteristic of identity flexibility. The emerging adult period requires an investigation of different identity aspects and a testing of those aspects, giving both of these variables

Table 4.1 Descriptive statistics for nongrowth experience group

	N	M (SD)	Range	Minimum	Maximum	Variance
Autonomy	96	53.46 (8.88)	50.00	24.00	74.00	78. 86
Controlled	96	54.34 (7.72)	50.00	27.00	77.00	59.64
Impersonal	96	52.24 (7.89)	44.00	32.00	76.00	62.29
Identity exploration	92	3.34 (0.54)	3.00	1.00	4.00	0.29
Experimentation	92	3.38 (0.53)	3.00	1.00	4.00	0.28
Negativity	92	2.98 (0.59)	3.00	1.00	4.00	0.35
Other-focus	92	2.47 (0.72)	3.00	1.00	4.00	0.51
Self-focus	92	3.28 (0.48)	3.00	1.00	4.00	0.23
Feeling "in-between"	92	3.20 (0.76)	3.00	1.00	4.00	0.57
Existential thinking	92	30.43 (8.56)	39.00	11.00	50.00	73.35

Table 4.2 Descriptive statistics for growth experience group

	N	M (SD)	Range	Minimum	Maximum	Variance
Autonomy	55	53.13 (5.51)	29.00	34.00	63.00	30.37
Controlled	55	53.16 (6.40)	27.00	40.00	37.00	40.95
Impersonal	55	51.84 (6.90)	30.00	34.00	64.00	47.62
Identity exploration	55	3.44 (0.50)	1.86	2.14	4.00	0.24
Experimentation	55	3.47 (0.44)	1.60	2.40	4.00	0.19
Negativity	55	2.94 (0.50)	2.00	1.71	3.71	0.25
Other-focus	55	2.53 (0.76)	3.00	1.00	4.00	0.58
Self-focus	55	3.41 (0.43)	2.00	2.00	4.00	0.18
Feeling "in-between"	55	3.30 (0.70)	3.00	1.00	4.00	0.48
Existential thinking	55	31.85 (9.43)	38.00	17.00	55.00	88.94

a valid home in the emerging adulthood discussion. Other-focus and self-focus, although seemingly contradictory, require the emerging adult to evaluate relationships with others as well as a relationship with the self. The two are reflexive in that an affirmed self-identity must be achieved to successfully relate authentically to others. In addition, identity exploration and experimentation manifest with the other-focus and self-focus dyad by the means of exploring different lifestyles and relationships and experiencing different levels of dissonance with each, eventually narrowing down to a more syntonic way of life that befits the individual, like wearing different hats and seeing which fits the best.

Feeling "in-between" is the most stage-like characteristic of these. The emerging adult straddles adolescence and pure adulthood, exhibiting characteristics of both. As an obvious characteristic of emerging adult development, this variable would be most utilized qualitatively to investigate which aspects of feeling "in-between" are most salient. The variable of existential thinking suggests that this stage, already ripe with questioning, stretches into the existential realm. In addition to questions about identity, the emerging adult is likely faced with more universally existential issues. Most obvious are self-determination and decision-making, but also loneliness and death comprehension could also be salient. A study could look at this variable in isolation and would likely find more of the negative aspects of this developmental stage, growing pains, if you will. The IDEA variable of negativity captures this aspect well and provides the perspective that emerging adulthood can be a turbulent stage as these developmental experiments could often result in uncertainty.

The variables of the GCOS were not found to be statistically significant between growth experience groups but they play important roles in the understanding of self-determination in emerging adulthood. Taking control of the events of one's life is a strong characteristic of positive emerging adult development, closely aligned with the autonomy causality orientation. Succumbing to the pressures of external rewards and not understanding the causes of life events, characterized by the controlled and impersonal causality orientation, respectively, are the more compromised orientations. Within emerging adulthood, these would represent a foreclosure and lack of awareness of personal ambitions which would inhibit the positive self-awareness required to align one's life with one's ambition.

Conclusion

Emerging adulthood is still a relatively new field of social science research and therefore it is still a new frontier of exploration. To describe emerging adulthood as a stage that is dense with the requirement of identity flexibility would be an understatement. This stage requires the guessing and testing of one's self in reference to the world, and to land successfully as a responsible adult, an ability to make decisions has to be achieved. Though emerging adulthood exists as a phenomenon of industrialized countries, it represents the space between responsibilities, and within that space is a world of decisions and uncertainty working simultaneously. Research should expand on the focus of this study by looking at the experiential factors of the emerging adult in a variable-specific way in order to separate the personalized experiences of the individual and overall characteristics of the emerging adulthood period. This study was just the beginning, and it provides the stories of growth of a select few regarding emerging adulthood, but there are more stories out there and more information that will elucidate the necessary reflexive nature of identity during emerging adulthood.

References

Agency [Def. 3]. (n.d.) *Oxford Dictionaries*. Retrieved August 29, 2015, from http://www.oxforddictionaries.com/us/definition/american_english/agency

Allan, B. A., & Shearer, C. B. (2012). The scale for existential thinking. *International Journal of Transpersonal Studies, 31*(1), 21–37.

Arnett, J. J. (2000). Emerging adulthood: A theory of development from the late teens through the twenties. *American Psychologist, 55*(5), 469–480.

Coon, D., & Mitterer, J. O. (2010). *Introduction to psychology: Gateways to mind and behavior with concept maps*. Belmont, CA: Wadsworth.

Deci, E. L., & Ryan, R. M. (1985). The general causality orientations scale: Self-determination in personality. *Journal of Research in Personality, 19*, 109–134.

Frankl, V. E. (1984). *Man's search for meaning: An introduction to logotherapy*. New York: Simon & Schuster.

McAdams, D. P., & McLean, K. C. (2013). Narrative identity. *Current Directions in Psychological Science, 22*(3), 233–238.

Reifman, A., Arnett, J. J., & Colwell, M. J. (2007). Emerging adulthood: Theory, assessment, and application. *Journal of Youth Development, 2*(1), 40–50.

Schwartz, S. J., Côté, J. E., & Arnett, J. J. (2005). Identity and agency in emerging adulthood: Two developmental routes in the individualisation process. *Youth and Society, 37*(2), 201–229.

Chapter 5
Bridging the Gap: Black Immigrant Identities and Dreams of Home

Leonie J. Brooks

Bridging the Gap: Black Immigrant Identities and Dreams of Home

> "Since leaving Guyana at the age of 3, I've never really felt like I fully belong anywhere. Due to the British school system and being a kid who wanted to blend in, I sacrificed my native tongue. Only to find out that I was still an outsider. To the kids at school I was an African booty scratcher. When I got around my family and only replied back to them in English, I was a sellout and an Akata. Outside I was embarrassed and fearful to show my 'Africanness'. Then at the same time, fearful to show too much of my Black British and African American side at home. Then I came across Nkrumah, Fela, Sankara, Dubois and many other Pan-Africanist leaders and then I understood that my burden was a blessing and that I had a mission. I'm stuck in this limbo and I know now that I'm here to bridge the gap…I believe that no black, African, Moor or what ever you may call yourself, will gain any respect around the world, unless Africa is respected first. We children of the "gap" shouldn't take our position lightly. So when I say "I'm not Black enough for Brooklyn and not African enough for Accra". I say it with pride, because I understand my mission and I see my position as a strength and not a weakness" (K Abbensetts, personal communication, November 7, 2015).

The preceding quote personifies the experience of many Black immigrants, particularly those who move from predominantly Black home countries to majority White domiciles. For numerous Black immigrants, the challenge to redefine themselves and figure out their identities in a new racial and ethnic context can be quite daunting. Who am I? Where do I belong? Where do I call home? These are new questions several Black immigrants grapple with, which can have multifaceted answers depending on a variety of factors. These factors can include age at the time of migration, reasons for migration, push factors (circumstances in the home country that contribute to the decision to leave) (Holder, 2007), and pull factors (the host

L.J. Brooks, Ph.D. (✉)
Psychology Department, Towson University, 8000 York Rd, Towson, MD 21252, USA
e-mail: LaBrooks@towson.edu

J.D. Sinnott (ed.), *Identity Flexibility During Adulthood*,
DOI 10.1007/978-3-319-55658-1_5

country's attitude toward migrants, opportunities in the host country) to name a few. In addition, the salience of one's national identity is prone to shift depending on context. Nationality is just one of various identities that Black immigrants hold. Other important identities could include race, ethnicity, gender, sexual orientation, religion, and disability status that intersect and influence how the immigrants might view themselves, as well as their engagement in interpersonal relationships with members of the host country and other immigrant groups. Deaux (2011) suggests that the American experience is a diverse one particularly for immigrants. She observes, "and certainly, the immigrant, who has begun life in a different country with its own unique history and cultural practices, experiences the United States in quite different ways (p. 70). While modern-day immigrants have similar aspirations of creating better lives for themselves and their families as their predecessors, they 'are not always accepted as being part of the American purpose, even if they become naturalized citizens or if their children are born here and are legally citizens from birth'" (Deaux, 2011, p. 71). What does it mean then for the Black immigrant who may identify as a naturalized American or hyphenated American, but who is not recognized as such by his or her fellow citizens? Is developing a flexible identity that can adapt to shifting cultural dynamics the most effective strategy for Black immigrants to adopt?

This chapter will highlight the multidimensional experiences of Black immigrants in the United States as it relates to the complex process of establishing and maintaining their continuously evolving national, racial, and ethnic identities in a predominantly White context. A brief overview of relevant identity and acculturation theories will be presented. Descriptions of the experiences of Black immigrants in the United States as depicted in the literature, as well as anecdotal data from individual interviews from an ongoing study of first- and second-generation Black Caribbean immigrants, will be integrated throughout the chapter. Seventy-four Caribbean immigrants and second-generation Caribbean Americans, including 46 women and 28 men, shared information about their racial identities, encounters with discrimination, and unique acculturation experiences as part of a sabbatical research project which began in 2007 and continued with follow-up interviews of some participants in September 2011. Participants were recruited from Caribbean organizations in Washington DC, Maryland, Connecticut, New York, New Jersey, Florida, and Georgia. They migrated from Jamaica, Trinidad and Tobago, Guyana, Grenada, Haiti, Montserrat, St. Croix, Barbados, Dominica, St. Lucia and St. Vincent and the Grenadines. Ranging in age from 19 to 73, they shared their migration stories, coping strategies, and cultural traditions as part of the research project. An additional ten participants (six women and four men), ranging in age from 36 to 75, were recruited in a similar fashion to the process described earlier during the summer of 2015, to answer similar questions about their acculturation experiences and cultural identities. Finally, whether and how Black immigrants attempt to cultivate assimilationist, traditionalist, bicultural or flexible, and transnational identities as an adaptive survival strategy while living in the United States is explored.

Identity Development

Questioning one's identity and place in the world is a natural phenomenon experienced by adolescents and emerging adults as they navigate the terrain of identity development proposed by Erikson (1968). One's identity consists of all "beliefs, ideals, and values that help shape and guide a person's behavior" (Cherry, 2005). Erikson's stage theory of psychosocial development examined the impact of social influences on the development of personality across a person's life span. Erikson proposed that all people go through a series of eight stages of development throughout their lives and that at each stage an essential conflict or crisis must be resolved in order to fully master and integrate the key quality of that stage. Erikson believed that the formation of a coherent identity was one of the key tasks in one's life. The identity conflict emerges most significantly during adolescence, though Erikson did not believe that establishment of one's identity was restricted to adolescence. Rather, one's identity is modified and develops throughout the life span, as individuals face new challenges and encounter various experiences (Cherry, 2005). According to Erikson, identity is "...a subjective sense as well as an observable quality of personal sameness and continuity, paired with some belief in the sameness and continuity of some shared world image. As a quality of unself-conscious living, this can be gloriously obvious in a young person who has found himself as he has found his communality. In him we see emerge a unique unification of what is irreversibly given – that is, body type and temperament, giftedness and vulnerability, infantile models and acquired ideals – with the open choices provided in available roles, occupational possibilities, values offered, mentors met, friendships made, and first sexual encounters" (1970). Identity crises occur more often with the advancements and increased cross-cultural contacts that ensue frequently across the world. These conflicts happen throughout the life span, especially during moments of significant change including starting a new job, the beginning of a new relationship, the end of a marriage, or the birth of a child. These changes facilitate the opportunity to investigate diverse parts of oneself (roles, values, beliefs, attitudes, and behaviors) in distinct areas of one's life (work, family, and other interpersonal relationships) (Cherry, 2005). The transitions and challenges that accompany migration from one country and culture to another are particularly salient opportunities for identity crises to emerge. Black immigrants from the Caribbean and Africa must negotiate the various aspects of their social/cultural identities which include national origin, race, and ethnicity among many others (i.e., religious affiliation, sexual orientation, etc.). For many Black immigrants whose heritage culture was predominantly Black (i.e., they were born and raised in majority Black countries), race was a less salient part of their identity than other aspects (i.e., nationality, socioeconomic status, professional affiliation, etc.). One immigrant from the Caribbean island of St. Vincent, who participated in a study of acculturation experiences among Black Caribbean immigrants, stated "here in the US it's more about color…it is more class based in St. Vincents, the divisions are more class-based…we are mostly Black and non-Blacks are not seen as white…they are Vincentian first" (U. Mars, personal communication, October, 2007). This statement is a common example of the primary salience of nationality and class in terms of cultural identities, as compared to race which is considered the more significant identity in the United States. Migrating to a country where they are now part of a visible racial minority that is often viewed with suspicion or associated with negative attributes can be quite jarring. Race becomes much more prominent in terms of how these migrants are viewed and defined by others in the host country and thus becomes more significant for many Black immigrants' identities (Benson, 2006). Contending with what it means to be "Black" in a sometimes hostile host country climate while also navigating how (if any) you are distinct from traditional African-Americans because of your migrant status is a complex endeavor (Roopnarine & Krishnakumar, 2006). An examination of the process of racial identity development is an important aspect of understanding the Black immigrant experience.

Black Racial Identity Development Theories

Racial identity can be defined as the degree to which a person recognizes and appreciates himself or herself as a racial being within a hierarchical social structure (Neville & Walters, 2004). There are a number of Black racial identity development models, the most prominent and well documented being the Cross model of psychological Nigrescence first proposed by William Cross in 1971. This model was established during the Civil Rights Movement in the United States during the 1960s and outlines a five-stage process during which Black people in America progress from espousing a White frame of reference to a positive Black frame of reference (Sue & Sue, 2013). African-Americans begin at the *preencounter stage* where they "consciously or unconsciously devalue their own Blackness and concurrently value White values and ways" (Sue & Sue, 2013, p. 291). Black individuals in this stage typically experience "self-hate, low self-esteem and poor mental health" (Vandiver in Sue & Sue, 2013, p. 291). During the *encounter stage*, the individual first experiences a significant crisis or incident that contests previously held beliefs and behaviors (i.e., the murder of Martin Luther King Jr. was a profound and earth-shattering event for African-Americans in 1968). As a result, a modification in worldviews transpires, and individuals often feel guilt and anger at being "brainwashed by White society" (Sue & Sue, 2013 p. 291). In the *immersion-emersion stage*, individuals retreat from White society and immerse themselves in Black culture resulting in the emergence of Black pride and the eventual reduction of guilt and anger. During the *internalization stage*, general anti-White sentiments dissipate, and an increased sense of inner security, tolerance, and flexibility appears, as conflicts between old and new identities are settled. Finally, in the *internalization-commitment stage*, African-Americans embrace a solid commitment to civil rights, social justice, and social change.

Cross updated his theory in 1991 to include the concept of *race salience* during the initial *pre-encounter* stage to capture "the degree to which race is an important and integral part of a person's approach to life" (Sue & Sue, 2013, p. 292). Therefore, an individual's race can play a major or minimal role in his or her identity, and one can have a positive, pro-Black or negative, anti-Black frame of reference. *Race salience* replaced the term "pro-White," and an individual in the *pre-encounter* stage can have a *pre-encounter assimilation* identity (an individual with low race salience and neutral feelings toward Blackness), a *pre-encounter miseducation* identity (an individual who accepts the negative and stereotypical misinformation about Black people from the wider culture and compartmentalizes this information in order to protect himself or herself from these negative images and to preserve a positive personal self-image), or a *pre-encounter anti-Black* identity (an individual who has high race salience and strong negative feelings about Blackness). Someone with a *pre-encounter assimilation identity* would not consider race as an important part of his or her identity and would embrace an "American" framework that would not necessarily include low self-esteem or self-hate. Vincent A. (2016), a Nigerian immigrant, posted in MIT Admissions Blog on July 8, 2016: "I moved to the United States of America three years ago…And in Nigeria, virtually everyone has the same dark skin. Sure, there's a substantial number of white people and Asians and a tapestry of races, but mostly, we're black, and because we're mostly black, 'being black' was never a term that was part of my daily vocabulary. You were tall or short or fat or skinny or intelligent or a complete and utter idiot, but you weren't black. It was as weird as saying 'you're human'…mostly I didn't know if I had the 'right' to consider myself black. The word referred to African-Americans right." This is an example of the experience of low race salience without necessarily having a negative view of one's racial identity. Cross does contend, however, that someone with a *pre-encounter anti-Black* identity would have low self-esteem and self-hate as a result of being exposed to a racist society where negative images of Blacks are commonplace in the media and larger society. These negative images are integrated into the racial self-concept, resulting in self-loathing (Cross & Vandiver, 2001).

Vincent A. (2016) continues in his blog post to describe a harrowing encounter experience that dramatically increases his race salience and ignites further exploration and development of his Black identity. "A few months here, and I decided to go to the post office…after I'm done at the post office, I'm walking down Central Square feeling pretty good…I'm almost at my dorm when I hear someone screaming 'Hey? HEY!' I turn around to see a heavyset, middle-ages white man racing towards me. I start to panic. I'm clumsy as hell so I probably dropped my ID card or my debit card on the sidewalk and he spotted it. I reach into my pockets, but even as I'm tapping around feeling both cards secure and in place, I start to realize something is wrong because his face is contorted in rage…Next thing I know, his arms are around my shirt, and he's shaking me telling me to confess. 'I saw you?' he says. 'I saw you grab her wallet. Where is it? Where is it?'. He's screaming in my face…I notice one of the MBTA buses parked on the side of the road, but only vaguely, because my head is somewhere else, adrift in confusion, and as it sinks in what he's accusing me of, and as he begins to say 'why can't you niggers – ' I completely lose it. I start to scream at him…I start to yell about calling the police. 'Call the police!' he tells me. 'Call them right now'. We're interrupted by someone hanging out the bus, yelling at us to get our attention. It's another man and he's saying, 'You got the wrong guy! You got the wrong guy!' For whatever reason the man holding me chooses to believe him. He lets me go. Without saying a word – a single word – he turns around and beings to walk towards the bus. I stand there…stunned, waiting to see if he'll say anything, but he keeps walking…I've been in America for 3 years and I feel wholly unqualified to speak about matters like this. In Nigeria, they floated past my radar, so why take them on now? I don't know. I can't hide under some fancy little idea that there's a barrier between black and African…because what matters to these people – you know who these people are – is that they can take one look at the color of your skin, and populate their minds with the entire backstory of you."

Additionally, in his updated model, Cross created two distinct identities during the *immersion-emersion* stage, *anti-White and pro-Black*, resulting in three potential combinations of identities *anti-White*, *pro-Black*, *and anti-White/pro-Black combined.* Finally, Cross combined his previous fourth (*internalization*) and fifth stages *(internalization-commitment*) into one stage *internalization* with the accompanying three possible identities *internalization* (*Black*) *nationalist* (an individual with high Black positive race salience), *biculturalist* (an integration and valuing of both Black and American identities), and *multiculturalist* (high salience of multiple identities including race, gender, sexual orientation, etc.) (Cross & Vandiver, 2001). Cross' model of psychological Nigrescence has been widely studied (Cross, Smith & Payne, 2002). He developed the Cross Racial Identity Scale (CRIS) to assess his revised model, which has demonstrated high predictive validity (Vandiver, Fhagen-Smith, Cokley, Cross, & Worrell, 2002; Worrell, Cross & Vandiver, 2001). For example, greater endorsement of pre-encounter self-hatred attitudes has been associated with decreased self-esteem (Vandiver et al., 2002).

Building on Cross' Nigrescence model, Janet Helms created a racial identity development model for Black Americans (Helms, 1990), which was expanded to apply more widely to all racial minorities or people of color (Helms, 1995). Helms also developed a parallel theory of racial identity development for White Americans. In the expanded model, Helms revised Cross' five racial identity stages into "ego statuses" that outline the various beliefs, attitudes, and behaviors African-Americans (and other people of color) utilize to form a positive racial identity within the context of a hierarchical racial system that oppresses racial minorities. The term status was used instead of stages to highlight "dynamic evolution rather than static personality structures or types" (Helms & Cook, 1999). In the initial status *conformity*, an individual has internalized overall White middle-class ideology of what it means to be Black in society with images associated with being Black are typically negative and White are usually positive. Race is also considered inconsequential. In the *dissonance* status, a major shift in the individual's worldview regarding race occurs as an increased awareness of race and racism emerges. Individuals contend with disputing previously internalized negative perceptions of Blackness while also attempting to determine what it means to be Black on a personal level. In the *immersion/emersion* status, one fully immerses oneself in the Black experience and ultimately emerges from this experience with more nuanced and flexible beliefs about race. At this stage, all associations with Blackness are considered good, while Whiteness are perceived as bad. Additionally, meanings of Blackness are externally driven. In the *internalization* status, meanings of Blackness are now internally defined and other relevant social identities (e.g., sexual orientation, gender) are beginning to be considered. In the *internationalization commitment* status, there is an incorporation of a positive racial identity as well as the utilization of a multicultural framework that fosters coalition building with others from historically oppressed groups (Neville & Walters, 2004). A post by Michelle Denise Jackson in September 2014 on the *For Harriet* blog exemplifies the internationalization commitment status: "To my dear white folks, I want you to know that I sincerely love you. Really, I do. But I love social justice too. And my love for social justice does not mean that I hate you... Social justice is not meant to exclude you. Indeed, I believe actually engaging white people to be anti-racist allies is necessary for social progress...my belief in social justice means I believe in equality, in the dignity and value of all human lives. It means that sometimes not everything is about you."

The Racial Identity Attitudes Scale (RIAS) was developed by Helms and Parham (Helms, 1990), to assess the first four statuses in the model, which has generally received some strong empirical support. In particular, relationships between Black identity development and psychological adjustment as well as counseling process and outcome have been supported (Atkinson, 2004), though there have been some questions regarding the internal consistency of the scale (Fischer & Moradi, 2001), subscale compositions and scoring procedures (Ponterotto, Fuertes & Chen, 2000), range restrictions for pre-encounter and internalization items, and social desirability for the pre-encounter items (Fischer & Moradi, 2001). In terms of empirical support, an association between racial identity attitude and mental health has been demonstrated, suggesting that increased internalization of a positive racial identity is related to increased psychological well-being and better coping skills among African-Americans (Neville & Walters, 2004). More psychological distress and lower psychological well-being have been associated with less comfort and awareness of one's racial identity. "*Conformity* attitudes have been found to be related to greater perceived stress, self-derogation, and suppressed anger, while *internalization* attitudes have been found to be related to greater problem-solving efficacy, increased self-esteem and positive identification with one's ethnic origin" (Neville & Walters, 2004, p. 93). Black racial identity development has also been positively associated with self-concept (Wilson & Constantine, 1999) and self-esteem (Phelps, Taylor, & Gerard, 2001).

If the aforementioned Black racial identity development models are useful for understanding the experience of race as part of one's identity for African-Americans, what implications do these Black racial identity development theories have for Black immigrants living in the United States? Do Black immigrants develop their racial identities in similar ways to African-Americans? Or are there differences in how Black immigrants develop and view their racial identity, particularly those who are born and raised in majority Black countries? In a study of racial identity (measured by Helms and Parham RIAS), experiences of perceived discrimination and racism, and coping style among African-Americans ($n = 40$) and English-speaking

Black Caribbean immigrants ($n = 64$) conducted by this author, African-Americans were more likely to idealize their Black/African-American racial identity and immerse themselves in stereotypical behaviors reflecting Black identity than Caribbean immigrants as indicated by a significant difference in their average scores on the immersion subscale (Brooks, James & Mogard, 2008). Interestingly, within this same sample, African-Americans reported higher scores on the integration subscale than Caribbean immigrants, suggesting that they were also more likely to take a less reactive stance and incorporate positive aspects of White culture into their own cultural identity while maintaining positive pro-Black attitudes than Caribbean immigrants. The Caribbean immigrants' scores on the encounter (related to the aforementioned *dissonance status*) and immersion racial identity subscales were significant predictors of depression and anxiety, which is consistent with previous research that has found immersion attitudes in particular to be associated with poor self-esteem, high anxiety, and high levels of anger or hostility (Parham & Helms, 1985).

Researchers who have studied racial and ethnic identification among Black immigrants have arrived at a variety of conclusions. Mary C. Waters, a sociologist who has studied Black Caribbean immigrants (first and second generation) over several years, highlights a fluidity in the salience of race for some Black Caribbean immigrants that is determined by context (Waters, 1999; Kasinitz, Mollenkoph, Waters, & Holdaway, 2008). "The situation determines the identity chosen by most people, and there is a great deal of ease in moving back and forth between different identities. This interchangeability of identity labels also extends for many people for whom their racial identity as black is foremost in their consciousness. Many respondents stated they thought of themselves as black when they felt threatened by whites" (Waters, 1999, p. 62–63). One of Waters' interviewees from a study of West Indian immigrants and their children in New York City, a 36-year-old Guyanese man who had been living in the United States for 2 years, stated "When I am in the situation in which blacks are threatened as such by whites generally, I assume a position of a black man. Whenever you have general problems at work, for example it may not be against a Guyanese or a West Indian, it may be against a black American, and in that context therefore I assume a black posture. And whenever the conflict relates mainly to Guyana, of if I am discussing an issue in the Caribbean of which there is a particular feature of Guyana which would play an important part in the discussion, then in those circumstances I am Guyanese" (Waters, 1999, p. 63). Another interviewee, a 38-year-old Jamaican women, shared that in situations when she could be a distinct minority, such as when she entered an unfamiliar neighborhood, she would seek out a Black face: "It's good to identify a face that's you know, looks like yours, but Black is Black, it's not Jamaican" (Waters, 1999, p. 63). It did not matter if the individual was Jamaican to this respondent; the fact that the person was Black was what would provide her with a sense of comfort and safety. In the previously mentioned study of experiences of perceived discrimination and racism among African-Americans and English-speaking Black Caribbean immigrants conducted by this author, both African-Americans and Caribbean immigrants selected their primary racial identification as "Black," but when Caribbean immigrants were given the option to choose between West Indian and African-American as their primary *cultural* identification, they chose West Indian (Brooks, James & Mogard, 2008). Several of these respondents also indicated in follow-up structured interviews that they disliked having to choose Black/African-American on demographic forms because they did not consider themselves to be African-American per se but rather Caribbean born Black or West Indian, suggesting a preference for ethnic or national identity or at least a desire to distinguish themselves from African-Americans. A respondent from St. Lucia answered the question "do you feel pressured to consider yourself African American?" by saying "Not really, I make it clear that I'm not. I get slightly upset when I fill out forms and there is not space for Black, only African American. I shouldn't be forced to choose African American" (C. Augustine, personal communication, October, 2011). As Waters suggests, Black Caribbean immigrants are not necessarily "choosing *between* race and ethnicity" when faced with situations that determined whether their race or national identity was more important. Many respondents in her study and in my own research have expressed a great deal of pride in their racial identity as Black people and did not see a conflict between having strong national or ethnic identity (i.e., Jamaican, Trinidadian, West Indian) and being Black. They resented the idea of not having both their national and racial identities acknowledged (in demographic forms) or in encounters with Americans who make assumptions about their ethnic identity based on their race. This phenomenon of distancing on the part of some Black Caribbean immigrants from African-Americans has been explained in models of immigrant incorporation. It is a strategy by which becoming American and utilizing one's social capital as an immigrant while achieving success requires a complex negotiation between maintaining a strong ethnic and cultural identity (as an immigrant), and assimilating into American culture and losing one's immigrant cultural distinctiveness (Habacker, 2012). The challenge for Black Caribbean immigrants is that if they choose the latter option and attempt to assimilate, they become not just Americans, but African-American, which, according to some, results in downward mobility, given the historical and present-day levels of discrimination and prejudice against racial and ethnic minorities in general and Black Americans in particular within American society (Waters, 1999). A Trinidadian respondent from my study of Black Caribbean immigrants shared "I think I've had the best of both worlds as a Black person representing a different kind of Black person…I've been given better opportunities than people who are African American…I also feel that white people have dealt differently with me because I am a different kind of Black person…I wonder if they don't know that I am Black….Even though white folks have been accepting, some of them make assumptions…(being) Black from a 'third world country' (I) couldn't have had certain experiences, they are shocked that you do have these experiences" (C, Francis, September 6, 2011, personal communication). While the maintenance of one's distinct ethnic identification may seem advantageous to Black Caribbean immigrants, Showers (2015) argues that the same advantage may not hold up for Black African immigrants. Black African immigrants who migrate with high levels of education, obtain Canadian citizenship, and already have English-speaking ability still experience downward social and economic mobility, racism, and exclusion (Creese, 2011). In one study of a group of West African immigrant women working in the healthcare sector in Washington DC, entrenched perceptions of the African continent as "backward and inferior" served as barriers for professional advancement and upward mobility, despite their robust educational backgrounds, professional experience, and English proficiency (Showers, 2015). The nuanced responses to the issue of racial and ethnic identification and how Black immigrants select, amplify, and integrate their multiple identities within their new cultural context make an examination of acculturation important for understanding their experiences.

Immigrant Incorporation/Acculturation and Identities

The pervasive climate and the degree of support for and openness toward immigrants that is present in the host/receiving culture have a significant impact on how immigrants behave and view themselves in the new society (Phinney, Horenczyk, Liebkind & Vedder, 2001). "Policies toward immigration in immigrant-receiving societies, provide a context that supports or hinders in varying degrees immigrant parents' transmission of systems of beliefs and values" (Dion, 2006, p. 305), which influences the degree to which immigrants will maintain heritage beliefs and customs that shape their self-concepts. An example of this was reflected in Canada's policy of multiculturalism that existed since the early 1970s, which emphasized respect for heritage cultures, intergroup tolerance, and respect for different groups within Canada. In this climate, one would expect immigrants to have support for preserving connections to their original culture while adapting to their host culture, including the upholding of a strong national identity to some degree. In receiving countries where there is a strong anti-immigrant sentiment that is also reflected in official policies including legislation, the pressure to assimilate is much stronger. However, for visible racial minority immigrants who face prejudice and discrimination at various levels, the opportunity to assimilate within a predominantly White context is often difficult and for some impossible, as race and racism become barriers to progress. So how do non-White immigrant groups, specifically, Black immigrants, become incorporated into America's racial structures?

Scholars who have studied this phenomenon have various perspectives. Some present an assimilation approach, stating that all immigrant groups must lose their ethnic culture in order to gain acceptance in mainstream White American society (Gordon, 1964). Others argue that due to the intractable nature of racism and discrimination in the social structure of the United States, a segmented assimilation approach was more applicable and realistic (Portes and Zhou, 1993). Black immigrants and their children face daunting odds and must develop multifaceted strategies to successfully acclimate within the culture. These strategies are heavily influenced by whether or not immigrants enter the country with significant educational and economic advantages. Those with these exceptional advantages can often make a relatively smooth transition, while those without these assets end up on a downward trajectory and become part of impoverished, urban, predominantly Black enclaves leading to racial exclusion from the mainstream. There are others who suggest that because more recent immigrants have intermarriage patterns and linguistic assimilation similar to the first generations of Southern European and Irish immigrants in the early twentieth century, this is evidence that the racial categories in the United States are more adaptable and flexible (Alba & Nee, 2003). "This makes it possible for at least some non-white immigrants to eventually blend into mainstream America…much the same way that Irish, Italian and Jewish immigrants did" (Habacker, 2012). Habacker contends that the process is much more complex, at least for some Ethiopian and Eritrean immigrants who consider themselves to be Habasha, a separate, non-Black ethno-racial category that highlights their Semitic roots. In her ethnographic field study of first-generation African immigrants in Washington DC, she found that many were not assimilating into African-American communities or relating to African-American experiences of racism and exclusion. Rather, they were either situating themselves exclusively within their own ethnic Habasha community in Washington DC, or "strategically assimilating" if they were financially well-off, curtailing their experiences with racism by remaining connected to their ethnic community and engaging with Whites as members of the upper and middle class.

Other research suggests that more immigrants are adopting a transnational identity (Glick-Schiller, Basch & Blanc, 1995 ; Upegui-Hernandez, 2012) which allows for the maintenance of ethnic identification with the home culture, adopting particular attributes from the new culture with attempts for strategic assimilation, and, within this framework, engaging in combinations of "plural civic and political memberships, economic involvements, social networks and cultural identities that link people and institutions in two or more nation-states in diverse, multi-layered patterns" (Morawska, 2007, p. 149). This approach allows for even greater flexibility in identity that can be both internally and contextually driven. (Ferguson, Bornstein & Pottinger, 2012)

Because racial categories are more complex and fluid in many countries in Africa, the Caribbean, and South, Central, and Latin America, the ways in which one defines one's race could be quite different than how race is defined in the United States with discrete categories for Black and White. For example in Jamaica, with a motto reflecting racial tolerance "Out of Many One People," rigid Black and White racial categorization is rejected and "a more complex system in which a multiplicity of factors (e.g., ancestry, complexion, social standing, and education) determine "race." Consequently, "Jamaicans hardly think about race…especially since all their role models both social failures and society's leaders are black" (Vickerman, 2007, p. 485), and race essentially becomes detached from achievement. More recent immigrants from Jamaica are apt to adopt an ethnic identity that is semi-independent from African Americans with the ability to uphold a strong national identity, while at the same time express a racial identity that is in solidarity with African-Americans, particularly as they still face anti-Black racism and discrimination as African-Americans do (Vickerman, 2007).

In a recent edited book about the experiences of immigrant professors, Hutchison (2016) posits that immigrant professors (IPs) strive to become a "good fit" in both their professional and broader social contexts and that this pursuit for acceptance necessitates "a shift in one's psychological landscape, creating a new identity" (p. 13). He describes identity as fluid and suggests that in their interactions with individuals in the new host culture, IPs must reconcile their original identities from their homelands, with new identities imposed upon them in their new environments, creating a third hybridized identity which is more expansive. Hutchison indicates that his Ghanaian identity became African, and a Lithuanian professor's identity became Eastern European, "because it is easier for locals to remember broader regions people come from, as opposed to specific, unfamiliar countries" (p. 14). Mfum-Mensah (2016), another Ghanaian-born professor teaching in the United States, describes the daunting task of remaining a "rooted African," trying to preserve his associations with relatives back home while making a life in America (p. 151). Hutchison likens the process of identity development that IPs experience to that of an adolescent's process of psychosocial development, mentioned earlier in the chapter.

In this author's own experience of adjusting to living in the United States after migrating from Jamaica as a preteen, the challenges I encountered because of differences in spelling words in "British English" versus "American English" and the constant ridicule from peers because of my distinctive Jamaican accent resulted in feelings of humiliation and isolation that became unbearable (Brooks, 2016). Hutchison, Quach, and Wiggan (2006) note that there is frequently a devaluing of an immigrant's communication and experience if there are differences in spelling, meaning of words, expression, or accents, regardless of how well one communicates in English. As I struggled to develop my own sense of self within this new culture, I decided to "become American" and adopted an "American accent" at school while retaining my Jamaican identity at home. Another Jamaican immigrant describes utilizing the strategy of creating a "corporate accent" at work after finding himself having to repeat what he said constantly to his colleagues. He recognized he needed to present himself in a particular way, and "I somehow developed a 'professional accent', closer to what I call a mainstream corporate American accent…I had to then learn how to switch how I spoke between buying food at the Jamaican store down the street, to saying excuse me to the (American) lady right next to me at the cashier in the same store. I got tongue tied a couple of times" (O. Thompson, personal communication, August, 9, 2015). Scholars suggest that second-generation Black Caribbean immigrants undergo a similar process of defining, forming, and reshaping their racial and ethnic identities and that they struggle with how to define place, identity, and citizenship just as much as their immigrant predecessors (Lorick-Wilmont, 2014). They create fluid racial and ethnic identities that reflect an "'in-between-ness' of experience of being both 'black in America' and 'a child of a black immigrant in America'" (Lorick-Wilmont, 2014, p. 93). They also try to "bridge the gap" while navigating multiple identities that include race, nationality, sexual orientation, gender, and religion. A second-generation immigrant from the author's study describes her primary national identity as Jamaican-American, her most salient identity as American, and attends a church constituted mainly of Caribbean-born individuals (P. Williams, personal communication, August, 2, 2015).

As poignantly expressed in the quote at the beginning of the chapter, I have found myself bridging the gap between my home and adopted homelands, creating a more fluid, adaptable identity in order to navigate the multiple cultural environments I encounter personally and professionally. Another respondent who was born in New York, lived in the Caribbean country of Suriname from ages 4 to 14, and then migrated back to Florida identifies as Caribbean-American and finds this identity as most salient. Although in professional settings her identity as a Black woman becomes more significant. Black immigrants, like many other migrants, are continuously negotiating their identities in multiple cultural contexts, and it appears that the ability to be flexible in one's perceptions and interactions is advantageous, whether it is bicultural or transnational in emphasis (Fuligni & Tsai, 2015). Like many of my immigrant peers, my own identity has evolved and reflects a more complex, multifaceted, and global frame.

Recent studies suggest that racial categories within the United States are becoming less immobile (Bean & Lee, 2009), as reflected in gradual changes in the race question on the US Census to include the opportunity to report more than one race or other races (particularly among Hispanic/Latino categories) and the growing possibility of recognizing varied racial and ethnic diversity within the Black racial category. How this emergent recognition of diversity among Black immigrants translates into how they are treated and their opportunities for full acceptance, success, and upward mobility within a majority White culture is still an open question. What is certain is that Black immigrants will continue to bridge the gap, utilizing various strategies, unique strengths, and resilience in order to thrive in their new homelands while remaining connected to their native countries. A Jamaican respondent in this author's ongoing study of Caribbean immigrant experiences said it best: "My national identity has not and will not change. However, my assimilation and adoption of North American cultural norms has impacted my life, and I have adapted to some of these norms as a Jamaican/American…The Caribbean and its people (at home and abroad) constitute an important and productive part of the world…generations of our people have made great contributions to mankind and we will continue to do so…to know us is to love us. Get to know our heritage, our cultural norms, our rich history…with no love lost for my homeland, I love being in the US" (K. Haughton, personal communication, September, 2015).

References

Alba, R., & Nee, V. (2003). *Remaking the American mainstream: Assimilation and contemporary immigration*. Cambridge, MA: Harvard University Press.

Atkinson, D. R. (2004). *Counseling American minorities* (6th ed.). New York: McGraw Hill.

Bean, F. D., & Lee, J. (2009). Plus ca change…? Multiraciality and the dynamics of race relations in the United States. *Journal of Social Issues, 65*(1), 205–219.

Benson, J. E. (2006). Exploring the racial identities of Black immigrants in the United States. *Sociological Forum, 21*(3), 219–247.

Brooks, L. J. (2016). Not an easy road: Journey of a Jamaican academic. In C. Hutchison (Ed.), *Experiences of immigrant professors: Cross-cultural differences, challenges, and lessons for success* (pp. 177–187). New York: Routledge.

Brooks, L.J., James, S., & Mogard, K. (2008). *The struggle continues: The experiences of perceived discrimination and racism amongst African American and English Speaking Caribbean Black immigrants*. Paper presented at the Eighth Annual Institute for the Promotion and Study of Race and Culture Diversity Challenge Conference, Boston College, Chestnut Hill, MA.

Cherry, K. A. (2005). *Erikson's stages of psychosocial development*. Retrieved from http://psychology.about.com/od/psychosocialtheories/a/psychosocial.htm

Creese, G. (2011). *The new African diaspora in Vancouver: Immigration, exclusion and belonging*. Toronto, ON: University of Toronto Press.

Cross, W. E., Smith, L., & Payne, Y. (2002). Black identity. In P. B. Pedersen, J. G. Dragnus, W. J. Lonner, & J. Trimble (Eds.), *Counseling across cultures* (pp. 93–108). Thousand Oaks, CA: Sage.

Cross, W. E., & Vandiver, B. J. (2001). Nigrescence theory and measurement. In J. G. Ponterotto, J. M. Casas, L. A. Suzuki, & C. M. Alexander (Eds.), *Handbook of multicultural counseling* (2nd ed., pp. 371–393). Thousand Oaks, CA: Sage.

Deaux, K. (2011). An immigrant frame for an American identity. *Applied Developmental Science, 15*(2), 70–72.

Dion, K. K. (2006). On the development of identity: Perspectives from immigrant families. In R. Mahalingam (Ed.), *Cultural psychology of immigrants* (pp. 299–314). Mahway, NJ: Lawrence Erlbaum Associates.

Erikson, E. H. (1968). *Identity: Youth and crisis*. New York: Norton.

Erikson, E. H. (1970). Reflections on the dissent on contemporary youth. *International Journal of Psychoanalysis, 51*, 11–22.

Ferguson, G. M., Bronstein, M., & Pottinger, A. M. (2012). Tridimensional acculturation and adaptation among Jamaican Adolescent-Mother Dyads in the United States.

Fischer, A. R., & Moradi, B. (2001). Racial and ethnic identity: Recent developments and needed directions. In J. G. Ponterotto, J. M. Casas, L. A. Suzuki, & C. M. Alexander (Eds.), *Handbook of multicultural counseling* (2nd ed., pp. 341–370). Thousand Oaks, CA: Sage.

Fuligni, A., & Tsai, K. M. (2015). Developmental flexibility in the age of globalization: Autonomy and identity development among immigrant adolescents. *Annual Review of Psychology, 66*, 411–431.

Glick-Schiller, N., Basch, L., & Blanc, C. S. (1995). From immigrant to transmigrant: Theorizing transnational imigration. *Anthropological Quarterly, 68*(1), 48–63.

Gordon, M. (1964). *Assimilation in American life: The role of race, religion and national origins*. New York: Oxford University Press.

Habacker, S. (2012). Not Black but Habasha: Ethiopian and Eritrean immigrants in American Society. *Ethnic and Racial Studies, 35*(7), 5–26.

Helms, J. E. (1990). An overview of Black racial identity theory. In J. E. Helms (Ed.), *Black and white racial identity. Theory, research and practice* (pp. 9–47). New York: Greenwood.

Helms, J. E. (1995). An update of the Helms's White and people of color racial identity models. In J. G. Ponterotto, J. M. Casas, L. A. Suzuki, & C. M. Alexander (Eds.), *Handbook of multicultural counseling* (pp. 181–198). Thousand Oaks, CA: Sage.

Helms, J. E., & Cook, D. A. (1999). *Using race and culture in counseling and psychotherapy: Theory and process*. Boston: Allyn and Bacon.

Holder, C. B. (2007). West Indies. In M. C. Waters & R. Udea (Eds.), *The new Americans: A guide to immigration since 1965* (pp. 674–686). Cambridge, MA: Harvard University Press.

Hutchison, C. (2016). *Experiences of immigrant professors: Cross-cultural differences, challenges, and lessons for success*. New York: Routledge.

Hutchison, C.B., Quach, L., & Wiggan, (2006). The interface of global migrations, ESL teaching and learning, and academic cosmopolitan identity development. *Forum on Public Policy Online*. 2006 Edition. Retrieved from http://www.forumonpublicpolicy.com/archive06/hutichson.pdf

Jackson, M. D. (2014). My commitment to social justice does not mean I hate white people. *For Harriet*. Retrieved from http://www.forharriet.com/2014/09/my-commitment-to-social-justice-does.html#axzz4EnaHxEgf

Kasinitz, P., Mollenkopf, J. H., Waters, M. C., & Holdaway, J. (2008). *Inheriting the city: The children of immigrants come of age*. New York: Russell Sage Foundation.

Lorick-Wilmont, Y. S. (2014). Narrating negotiations of racial-ethnic identity and belonging among second-generation Black Caribbean immigrants in the United States. In L. Way (Ed.), *Representations of internarrative identity* (pp. 93–114). Hampshire, Great Britain: Palgrave Macmillan.

Mfum-Mesah, O. (2016). Negotiating the trilogy of Blackness, "Africanness," and "Accentness": A "Native-Alien" professor's tale. In C. Hutchison (Ed.), *Experiences of immigrant professors: Cross-cultural differences, challenges, and lessons for success* (pp. 144–154). New York: Routledge.

Morawska, E. (2007). Transnationalism. In M. C. Waters & R. Ueda (Eds.), *The new Americans: A guide to immigration since 1965* (pp. 149–163). Cambridge, Massachusetts: Harvard University Press.

Neville, H. A., & Walters, J. M. (2004). Contextualizing Black America's health. In D. R. Atkinson (Ed.), *Counseling American minorities* (6th ed., pp. 83–103). Boston: McGraw-Hill.

Parham, T. A., & Helms, J. E. (1985). The relationship of racial identity attitudes to self-actualization and affective states of Black students. *Journal of Counseling Psychology, 32*, 431–440.

Phelps, R. E., Taylor, J. D., & Gerard, P. A. (2001). Cultural mistrust, ethnic identity, racial identity, and self-esteem among ethnically diverse Black students. *Journal of Counseling and Development, 79*, 209–216.

Phinney, J. S., Horenczyk, G., Liebkind, K., & Vedder, P. (2001). Ethnic identity, immigration and well-being: An interactional perspective. *Journal of Social Issues, 57*(3), 493–510.

Ponterroto, J. G., Fuertes, J. N., & Chen, E. C. (2000). Models of multicultural counseling. In S. D. Brown & R. W. Lent (Eds.), *Handbook of counseling psychology* (3rd ed., pp. 639–669). New York: Wiley.

Portes, A., & Zhou, M. (1993). The new second generation: Segmented assimilation and its variants. *The Annals of the American Academy of Political and Social Science, 530*(1), 74–96.

Roopnarine, J. L., & Krishnakumar, A. (2006). Conceptual and research considerations in the determinants of child outcomes among English-speaking Caribbean immigrants in the United States: A cultural-ecological approach. In R. Mahalingam (Ed.), *Cultural psychology of immigrants* (pp. 277–298). Mahway, NJ: Lawrence Erlbaum Associates.

Showers, F. (2015). Being black, foreign and women: African immigrant identities in the United States. *Ethnic and Racial Studies, 38*(10), 1815–1830.

Sue, D. W., & Sue, D. S. (2013). *Counseling the culturally diverse* (6th ed.). Hoboken, New Jersey, Wiley.

Upegui-Hernandez, D. (2012). "Because I'm neither Gringa nor Latina". Conceptualizing multiple identities within transnational social fields. In R. Josselson & M. Harway (Eds.), *Navigating multiple identities: Race, gender, culture, nationality and roles* (pp. 227–253). New York: Oxford University Press.

Vandiver, B., Cross, W. E., Jr., Worrell, F., & Fhagen-Smith, P. E. (2002). Validating the cross racial identity scale. *Journal of Counseling Psychology, 49*, 71–85.

Vickerman, M. (2007). Jamaica. In M. C. Waters & R. Ueda (Eds.), *The new Americans: A guide to immigration since 1965* (pp. 479–490). Cambridge, MA: Harvard University Press.

Vincent, A. (2016). *Black lives matter*. MIT Admissions. Retrieved from http://mitadmissions.org/blogs/entry/black-lives-matter

Waters, M. C. (1999). *Black identities. West Indian immigrant dreams and American realities*. New York: Russell Sage Foundation.

Wilson, J. W., & Constantine, M. G. (1999). Racial identity attitudes, self-concept and perceived family cohesion in Black college students. *Journal of Black Studies, 29*, 354–366.

Worrell, F. C., Cross, W. E., & Vandiver, B. (2001). Nigrescence theory: Current status and challenges for the future. *Journal of Multicultural Counseling and Development, 29*, 201–211.

Chapter 6
Flexibility in Persons with Dementia

Cameron J. Camp

The focus of this chapter is on the capacity of persons diagnosed with dementia to exhibit flexibility in their actions, thinking, attitudes, and creative capacities. The overall intent of this focus is both to provide evidence of flexibility in these persons and simultaneously to combat negative stereotypes about persons with dementia and the way we think about dementia in general.

How Did It Ever Come to This?

Dementia is generally thought of as a condition in which persons show continuingly diminished physical and cognitive capacity, reduced flexibility, and the inability to acquire new information or interests. It is characterized as a continuing spiral of decline, resulting in death – a characterization fostered both by the popular media and even by some groups that purportedly serve as advocates for persons with dementia and their relatives. In the USA, this process stems from the "medicalization" of dementia, in which "Alzheimer's disease" became a medical condition in search of a medical cure (Hollister, Fox, & Chaufan, 2009). While this process has served to funnel research funding into the efforts of medical model researchers, a case can be made that a subsequent effect has been the disempowerment of persons with dementia and their family members. For the past 30 years, "the cure" has been touted as being "5 years away." With the passage of the National Alzheimer's Project Act, the USA has officially declared that our government's top priority and goal for dealing with dementia is to "Prevent and Effectively Treat Alzheimer's Disease by 2025." While other goals of the act address support for caregivers, funding is disproportionate regarding allocations for research versus caregiver support. For example,

C.J. Camp, Ph.D. (✉)
Center for Applied Research in Dementia, 34194 Aurora Road #182, Solon, OH 44139, USA
e-mail: Cameron@cen4ard.com

J.D. Sinnott (ed.), *Identity Flexibility During Adulthood*,
DOI 10.1007/978-3-319-55658-1_6

in January of 2014, new federal funding allocated for Alzheimer's disease included a $100 million increase for the National Institute on Aging for Alzheimer's research, which was added to the National Institutes of Health's approximately $484 million in Alzheimer's research funding for fiscal year 2013. A further $3.3 million was provided to support Alzheimer's caregivers.

The consequences of the search for "the cure" thus have led to the de-emphasis of finding support and providing a better quality of life for persons with dementia. In addition, the voices of persons with dementia and their caregivers have been muted, and the "story" of dementia has been taken over by "professionals" who describe disease and loss as what dementia "is." The medicalization of dementia has created a self-fulfilling prophecy, in which persons with dementia are assigned a "sick person role," are treated as children, and then are medicated when they "act out" in rebellion to this treatment.

What often occurs in western societies is that a diagnosis of dementia is given to a person, and the person and their caregivers are told the usual scenario described in the first sentences of this chapter. This is seen in the case of a Christine Bryden, who had been a successful researcher and scientist in Australia with a job in the Department of the Australian Prime Minister. She was a single mother when she received a diagnosis of dementia. She relayed to my wife and I over dinner that that when this diagnosis was given to her, "the neurologist basically wrote me a prescription for disengagement" from life. In this case, however, she did not follow the physician's advice. Afterward, she remarried and is now an international spokesperson for the rights of persons with dementia. We remember distinctly when she handed us her business card which listed her occupation as "advocate." She has been fulfilling the role of advocate for persons with dementia successfully and forcefully for 20 years (Bryden, 2016).

In this chapter, cases in which flexibility is shown even in persons who are supposedly incapable of demonstrating this capacity (i.e., persons with dementia) will be presented. It is hoped that in doing so we will contest existing attitudes and assumptions and create greater opportunities for challenge and change for persons with dementia and related cognitive disorders. The focus of this chapter is on the capacity for flexibility and renewal even among older adults who have received a diagnosis of dementia. The purpose for writing this chapter is to reframe how we think about persons with dementia. This is necessary to both improve the quality of life of persons who now have dementia and to insure that those who receive this diagnosis in the future will not be trapped in a negative, self-fulfilling prophecy. In other words, we must save ourselves.

This is not to simplistically ignore the losses that occur as a result of dementia, but we must also remember to avoid the "excess disability" generated by "toxic social environment" to use the words of Tom Kitwood (1996, 1997a, 1997b). We must begin to consider dementia as a disability or chronic condition and to emphasize the goal of living well with dementia, just as we try to live well with diabetes, to live well with Down Syndrome, to live well with traumatic brain injury, or to live well with cancer.

Using the Capacities of Persons with Dementia

Regardless of what you might have read in the past, persons with dementia can learn (e.g., Camp, 2006b; de Werd, Boelen, Rikkert, & Kessels, 2013; Zanetti et al., 2001). They also have capacities and abilities that are retained, often far into the course of dementia. Each of these classes of competencies, especially when used in concert, provides possibilities for the display of flexibility in thought and behavior in persons with dementia. Persons with dementia learn by doing, a process that often goes by the rubric of "procedural learning and memory." These include habits, skills, motor learning, conditioning, location learning, and priming, to mention a few (e.g., Squire, 1992, 1994). For example, if a person with dementia starts to attend a day center or is admitted to a skilled nursing residence, it does not take long for the person to learn that a particular chair is "their" seat for meals. If another resident sits or is placed in "their" seat, the resident who has been sitting there becomes upset. Thus, learning has taken place after the onset of dementia and after the diagnosis of dementia has been pronounced and after such a pronouncement has led to the person being placed in a day center or residential setting. Persons with dementia are learning things every day, but the dominant paradigm for considering what dementia "is" has woefully neglected observing these phenomena, much less worked to emphasize them.

Thus, while these capacities have been studied and research for decades (e.g., Squire, 1992, 1994), the application of this knowledge to the treatment of dementia has been lagging. An exception to this has been the development of Montessori-Based Dementia Programming™ and Spaced Retrieval as interventions for dementia (Camp, 2006a, 2006b). In essence, work in this area has demonstrated conclusively that persons with dementia can learn new behaviors, strategies, habits, etc. Many examples of this will be provided next.

Examples of Flexibility in Persons with Dementia

What starts to happen when persons with dementia are viewed in terms of their remaining capacities rather than as "patients?" What possibilities become available? In this chapter you will find a series of examples in answer to these questions, in the hopes of demonstrating the flexibility available to persons who have dementia when given the opportunity to explore their potentials and to express themselves.

Beer Making

At a long-term care community in Oregon, the executive director previously served as an activity director for a memory unit serving persons with dementia. She had been trained in the use of the Montessori method as a way to provide "treatment" to residents with dementia – a treatment based on the values of respect and dignity and an approach that involves providing meaningful activity and social roles to such residents (e.g., Camp, Zeisel, & Antenucci, 2011). In other words, in this paradigm the "treatment" for dementia involves providing a better quality of life and creating a model in which persons with dementia live in a home, embedded within a community, with strong connections to "outer" community and the world at large (Camp, 2013).

Upon beginning her job as executive director, one of her first actions was to hire a woman aged 70 years to serve as director of activities. This older woman accepted the position on the condition that "her residents would not be asked to take part in 'old people' activities." One of the first activities begun at this residence was the formation of a beer making club. This involved residents being given the opportunity to engage in home brewing beer under the direction of a volunteer who was familiar with the process.

Brewing beer requires many steps along with patience. In this case, it required a community of older adults with cognitive impairment working together, then waiting for the beer to be ready for bottling, etc. Rather than the "busy work" often given to persons with dementia to "occupy their time," beer making resulted in a tangible product in which the residents could take pride, especially when their beer won prizes in beer making competitions. Residents had to learn new skills, acquire new habits, and learn to wait to see the results of their labors. Brewing beer gave these persons a chance to create a sense of community, of shared accomplishment, and to give them a reason to look forward to the future. Outings to beer brewing events created the opportunity for these persons to interact with much younger beer brewers who shared a common interest with them. Imagine the scene of older adults with dementia discussing the use of different varieties of hops with persons in their 20s with tattoos and body piercings. Oddly enough, for many of these older adults, this opportunity might not have occurred in their lives if they had not received the diagnosis of dementia and if they had not been in a residence in which staff emphasized a capacity for flexibility in these persons.

Afterward, beer club members began to explore making a wide variety of different types of beers, created their own label ("Old Tarts" beer), and commandeered a storage area to turn it into a bistro where they could serve their beers to visitors. Note that over time the self-confidence and willingness to try new endeavors continued to increase in these persons. As is always with case with the Montessori approach, learning and extensions of initial work are open-ended and can lead wherever individuals want to go.

Residents who did not want to make alcoholic beverages formed a jam and jelly making club, with similar results. The products of their labors were entered into fairs and began to win prize ribbons. Coffee roasting became a new activity available for these residents. Again, these activities may not have been available to these individuals with dementia under "normal" circumstances.

Training Dogs

In this same residence, another activity program was developed – training dogs. Many dog commands are manual signals, such as for "stay," "sit," "roll over," etc. A dictum of Maria Montessori was "they will learn through their hands." She understood that procedural learning emphasizing motor actions was an effective way to teach, and this proved true for these residents with dementia. They enjoyed the activity so much that the activity director began to ask a rescue shelter to provide puppies for training, since older dogs were getting worn out from the frequency of practice provided. Puppies that can be said to have been trained are more "adoptable," and so these residents were able to increase the odds of puppies being given a better quality of life. In addition, residents who had learned the training commands began to teach them to new residents. This illustrates another "hidden" flexibility in persons with dementia – the capacity to teach others what they have (recently) learned, as well as to learn from one's peers.

Finally, we see the capacity for groups of older adults who did not know one another in the past to learn how to live together, work cooperatively, and form supportive communities – after receiving the diagnosis of dementia.

Learning a New Language

If persons with dementia have the capacity for new learning, what happens when they are empowered and asked what they would like to learn? When touring a nursing home in Switzerland, my wife and I were given a speech of welcome by two residents with dementia. The speech was written down and spoken in English. What was remarkable was that these women had been asked what they would like to learn, and their answer had been that they wanted to learn the English language. More remarkable still was the fact that their teacher was another resident of the nursing home who spoke and wrote English, along with other languages. We left with the suggestion that probably there were other nursing homes in the area with residents who had a similar interest and that an internet course on learning English could connect these residents and give them persons to practice and correspond with. We will never forget the last words of their speech to us "Thank you for giving us back our liberty."

One reason we made this suggestion was that another resident at this Swiss nursing home had learned to go to the internet each morning and select news stories that he thought would be of interest to residents. This was a procedure and skill which he acquired after becoming a resident in the nursing home (i.e., after receiving the diagnosis of dementia). His activity was so successful that the director of the residence began uploading this newspaper and sending it out to other nursing homes in the area, even though they were "competitors." Later that day, we saw a copy of that day's "newspaper" at another residence for persons with dementia in that town.

Thus, there already was a collaboration among residences for persons with dementia in the area, which could be drawn upon to set up interactive internet courses among these habitations. In addition, there was enough cooperation and flexibility among different residences within this area to support such an undertaking.

Creating Companies

At the residence where persons with dementia make beer, the residents also began a company. They would make soaps and lotions by hand, using natural local ingredients. The residents have their own company logo and business cards. Proceeds from sales of the products are donated to a charity selected by the company workers. Similarly, a group of residents in an assisted living residence for persons with dementia started a company making dishwasher detergent by hand from all natural ingredients. They decided to use funds from sales of their products to help acquire a therapeutic pet for their home. Here is an example of groups of persons with dementia joining together to form enterprises. Many were not "business people" before undertaking these endeavors, but they saw a way to contribute to the welfare of others or to the welfare of their community and so launched into a new career.

Given that persons with dementia can learn new procedures, another interesting exercise is to examine what procedures staff members of residential settings for persons with dementia are performing and to examine whether persons with dementia can be trained to perform those functions. This produces the benefits of creating meaningful activities and social roles for residents, creating a cadre of volunteers from among residents who can relieve the burden of staff members, and creating a sense of community among residents in which they are enabled to have the capacity to care for each other. This manifests itself in many ways.

Resident-Led Activity Programming

In a number of research projects (Camp & Skrajner, 2004; Skrajner & Camp, 2007; Skrajner et al., 2012, 2014), persons with dementia have been trained to become leaders of small group activities for other persons with dementia. In these programs, resident leaders were able to obtain greater engagement during these Montessori-based activities than were obtained by regular staff during standard activity programming. Staff members in nursing homes also have been trained to be able to create such programming (Skrajner et al., 2014). The author has observed a person with dementia in a nursing home lead a group activity for 1 h involving 30 residents with dementia without assistance from staff. Thus, it is possible for residents to take leadership roles and to assist other residents in their efforts to take part in engaging activities.

The author was visiting a residence for persons with dementia in which a music program for residents was being held. The "typical" songs were being sung, such as "You Are My Sunshine" and "Daisy, Daisy." Another resident, sitting outside of the room and looking in, called the first author over and said, "I want you to do me a favor. If you ever see me inside of that room doing what they are doing and enjoying myself, please hit me in the head with a brick." This gentleman had been a radio personality, author, lecturer, and a general man of letters. He found the music and the activity he was watching demeaning and degrading. Staff member, working with the first author, assisted in enabling this man to create and lead a short story reading and discussion group for the same residents he had been observing. The man of letters would select short stories, along with music and other props, to enable residents to discuss topics in the stories and to share stories from their lives with each other. He continued to lead this group until shortly before his death.

A nursing home resident with Huntington's disease (a form of dementia that impairs both cognition and motor control) wanted to help fellow residents with Alzheimer's disease. She could read and had good social skills. A large screen television set was connected to a touch screen computer for her, and reading/discussion stories developed for persons with dementia were put onto a slide presentation, with one page per slide. This woman would gather residents with Alzheimer's disease into the room with the screen and could advance slides (e.g., pages of the story along with discussion questions) just by touching the computer screen. She would ask various members of the group to read a page on the screen aloud while the other members of the group read the screen silently and then ask for discussion. Thus, by focusing on her capacities rather than her disabilities, she was able to fill the role of reading group leader very effectively and acquired this capacity after her diagnosis had been given (Mattern & Kane, 2007).

Staff members of the Cleveland Chapter of the Alzheimer's Association were trained to train clients with early-stage dementia to fill the role of small group activity leader (Camp, Skrajner, & Kelly, 2005). One gentleman with early stage dementia in particular took this training to heart. Twice a week for 18 months he took a taxi to an assisted living residence to lead a reading and discussion group for residents with dementia. He would work to come up with discussion topics and themes to explore on his "days off." Over the course of this time his dementia progressed, but the reading and discussion group members helped compensate for this by giving him more and more assistance. At the end of this time, he was admitted to an advanced dementia unit and died shortly afterward. While he was serving as a volunteer for the assisted living residence, he confided that he had been an accountant for most of his adult life, but the work he was doing with "his group" was the most meaningful work he had ever accomplished. A physician who knew the man remarked to the first author, "Yes, but this only lasted 18 months." This incident is provided as an example of what can be provided by a medical model of treatment, focused on "the cure," versus an alternative way of treating dementia focused on improving life.

Remembering Those Close to Us

At another assisted living residence for persons with dementia, residents were taking part in a novel learning program for persons with dementia (Camp, 2011). When one of their number had to go to the hospital, a group of his friends decided to visit him in the hospital for their "outing." When a member of their group would die, they would plant a rose bush with that member's name on it in their community garden.

At a nursing home in Switzerland, their community garden has an area that resembles a Zen garden, with sand and rocks. However, each rock has the name of a resident who has passed away along with the date of the resident's death. After a resident has died, a rock to commemorate the resident is placed in that part of their garden and a ceremony, created by the residents for this purpose, is performed. In that place, when a person dies, an announcement is made and residents as well as staff gather at the front door to view the coffin containing their friend and to say good-bye. This is different that the "typical" way that persons who die leave a nursing home – at midnight through the back door. While this may be done to "spare" residents the sight of a coffin or dead person leaving, the result is that when a person dies there is no chance to bid farewell, and staff often try to deflect questions about the dead resident.

When an executive involved with dementia care was informed of this rock garden, his response was "How can you have residents involved with such a thing? Won't that make them cry?" The answer given was "Of course. This is what persons do when they have lost a loved one. Denying them the opportunity to grieve is cruel. How would you feel if you lost a loved one? Would you want other people to tell you not to cry? Would you want to know if someone you loved had died? This is about treating persons as you want to be treated."

At a nursing home in Australia, staff asked residents to let them know what residents wanted which was not being provided now. After the residents' council surveyed their peers, the answer was that residents wanted to attend the funerals of residents who had died. Now, going to funerals is a standard resident outing for that residence.

Altruism in Persons with Dementia

Persons with dementia living in an assisted living residence, having Haitian staff, started a fund-raising drive for earthquake victims in Haiti. At another assisted living residence for persons with dementia, residents decided to collect donations for a charity they wanted to support. They asked the manager of a local grocery store for permission to set up a collection table outside of his store. They did this, collected the donations, and presented the manager with a gift as thanks for allowing them to do this. Then they sent in their donation to the charity in the name of their residence.

At the residence described earlier regarding beer making and dog training, a resident with less advanced dementia was complaining about and confronting another resident who had more advanced dementia. The latter resident had considerable difficulty feeding herself, and the former resident had no sympathy for someone who "shouldn't be allowed to eat with the rest of us." Interestingly, when staff began to ask the less impaired resident to assist the other resident (e.g., to help feed her at meals), empathy toward the resident with impairments developed and their relationship changed. In a similar way, we have seen residents who were antagonistic and in which one member of the dyad was visually impaired begin to have very positive relationships when the person with unimpaired vision was asked to and began to read to the resident with visual impairments.

Residents with dementia in nursing homes have created visiting groups whose members visit other residents who are ill (but not contagious). They work in shifts so that the resident who is sick can have extended contact with another person. Sometimes, if the resident who is not well is unable to communicate, the visitor may simply hold the other person's hand. That is all that is needed, and it is an important contribution to the life and spirit of the community.

Intergenerational Programming

A number of programs have been developed to enable persons with dementia to serve in the role of mentor for children. Rather than the standard intergenerational programming which involves children coming to perform in a group while older adults passively watch, this approach involves one-to-one interactions between a child and an older adult with dementia in which the older adult teaches the child (Camp & Lee, 2011; Camp, Orsulic-Jeras, Lee, & Judge, 2004; George, Whitehouse, & Whitehouse, 2011; Gigliotti, Morris, Smock, Jarrott, & Graham, 2005; Jarrott & Bruno, 2003; Lee, Camp, & Malone, 2007). In our work with dyads of persons with dementia and preschool children, persons with dementia have taught children: academics (such as teaching phonics or counting), activities of everyday living (such as how to put clothes on a hanger, how to use tools such as a screwdriver, how to set a table), motor skills (e.g., putting together puzzles), and grace and courtesy (e.g., how to use a handkerchief to blow your nose).

At the Montessori International School of the Plains in Omaha, Nebraska, upper elementary and high school students 1 day a week have their classes in an assisted living residence for persons with dementia and are joined by residents of the memory care neighborhood as well as by clients with dementia from an adult day program at that site. Persons with dementia and student from the school interact in one to one and in small group activities and enjoy the opportunities that become available to learn together and to learn from each other.

Creative Arts

In a nursing home with a memory neighborhood for persons with dementia in Avignon, France, staff assisted residents in creating a movie called "The Threads of Life." Staff asked residents to dictate stories and events from different periods of their lives (e.g., childhood, school years, the time of Nazi occupation, liberation, etc.). Then, the residents dressed in appropriate costumes and narrated their stories into microphones in front of an audience of family members, friends, and staff. Music was played and sung which was appropriate for each of these life periods. For example, the song sung by residents when the era of Nazi occupation was described was the song of the French resistance fighters. This performance was video recorded (https://www.youtube.com/watch?v=CXq1Ck1PMNs).

When the author visited this nursing home and memory neighborhood afterward, he was invited to a showing of the movie of the performance. All residents involved in the movie, as well as staff and family members of the residents, came to see the movie. It lasted for over an hour. No one left, and at the end of the movie, a resident over the age of 90 years who had been in the movie stood and said "When I came here I did not have much energy, and did not see much reason for going on. But being here with you, and doing these things, gives me new energy to continue living." His daughter and all of us in the audience were in tears, of course. His daughter then said, "You brought my father back. I believed he was definitely lost. This is what was told to me." Then the medical director of the nursing home stood up and said "This is a revolution. This is how we must treat dementia." Afterward we all went out into the courtyard – residents, family members, and staff – and drank wine and sang songs until 1 o'clock in the morning. We were a community.

What is interesting is that this story does not end. Residents and staff of the memory care community decided to create another performance – a play called "tell me about love." This was performed early the next year and was open to the public. Once persons with dementia and their caregivers begin to shift their beliefs in what is possible, and see what can be accomplished, they acquire the flexibility and confidence to continue onward. This is an open-ended process. The limits are those of our imaginations.

A woman living in the memory neighborhood of this nursing home, having taken part in the first movie and hearing about the musical to be performed, decided that she wanted to learn to play the piano so that she could contribute to the new entertainment program. A volunteer who played piano began to work with her. The volunteer would play cords and the woman would play melody. At first she played melody with one hand, and then she progressed to playing melody with two hands. While doing this, a physician who knows her entered the room. When he saw the woman, the doctor asked "How is this possible? She cannot use her right hand!" After seeing this, the physician had to revise his thinking (becoming more flexible in his own thinking).

In Melbourne, Australia, an assisted living residence for persons with dementia was opened. One resident with dementia decided that she wanted to try painting using a paint-by-numbers kit. She did this with several kits and enjoyed it. Then her family gave the woman a book on how to draw. She read this and began following the instructions of the book and getting better and better at drawing. Next, she began to draw her own design and proceeded from there to painting original works of art. At the one-year anniversary of the opening of the residence, an exhibit of her works was shown, placed in chronological order. It served as an impressive testament to the capacity of this person to display competence and the flexibility to engage and progress in the creative process – after receiving the diagnosis of dementia.

Persons with dementia have been shown to successfully engage in a wide variety of artistic endeavors, including writing poetry, photography, taking part in improvisational theatre, dance, learning to appreciate fine art, story writing, forming choirs, and leaning to play musical instruments. The evidence for this is both abundant and relatively easy to access, but often these accomplishments are viewed as isolated events rather than as a demonstration of the capacity of persons with dementia to express themselves creatively. Again, these are all examples of the flexibility inherent in persons with dementia if their physical and social environments support it.

Travel

At a nursing home in Switzerland, residents with dementia and staff decided that they would go together on a trip to the annual Lemon Festival in Menton on the Côte d'Azur. They liked it so much that five to ten residents now go back there every year. Of course, the choice to go or not comes from the residents. At another nursing home in Switzerland, staff members began to ask residents what they would like to do. Three residents said they were dreaming about going back skiing which they had not done for many years. A video of the outing is at this site: https://www.youtube.com/watch?v=TPHc-Ge0tZM.

At a nursing home in Crémines, Switzerland, residents and staff members together leave campus each summer to go a large house in the mountains for the holidays – a period of several weeks. The house is well adapted for motor and sensory deficits. What is interesting, regarding flexibility, is that the staff members relate that the residents behave very differently during those days. In fact, they acted *normally*. For example, staff saw some residents with swallowing deficits (who under the usual circumstances would only be able to eat pureed food) being able to eat ordinary food (even steak with French fries) without any problem.

Resident-Led Communities

At an adult day center in New South Wales, Australia, the Montessori approach to dementia treatment was implemented over the course of a year. After that, clients with dementia would come to the center, set up their own activities, and run their own activities. Staff members' roles were to assist if assistance was requested and otherwise to observe. In fact, staff began to ask if they could be allowed to be part of activities. These clients with dementia also decided to hold a surprise birthday party for the manager of the center and did so. One client with advanced dementia had the role of wrapping crepe paper along a handrail. Though it took him most of the morning, he did this task independently and was able to take pride in the completion of this task – his contribution to the celebration.

In Beachwood, Ohio, a memory neighborhood was developed within an assisted living community (Stone Gardens). The neighborhood was named "Helen's Place," in honor of a former resident of the assisted living community. It was designed from its inception as a "resident-led community," and a model of care known as "The Social Life Template®" was created to guide in its creation and development. In this model, choice is given throughout the day to residents, and residents control their lives and are encouraged to be as independent as possible. For example, residents' committees decide on outings for the community, entertainment, and scheduling of activities. A group of residents is responsible for greeting new residents to the community. Residents decided on the rules for visitors, such as "No tours during meals, but tours during programs are ok." (This rule was created because the residents said that no one likes to be watched by strangers while they are eating.)

In the memory neighborhood in Avignon, mentioned earlier, committees make all life decisions. When the type of sandwiches that were to be created by residents to be served to residents for snack was to be decided, the choices were picked by a "sandwich committee." When the 1 year anniversary of Helen's Place was to be celebrated, residents decided not to have the party in their neighborhood because it was too small to hold all of their friend and family members whom they wished to invite. The celebration instead was held in a large room within the Stone Gardens assisted living residence. The member of the neighborhood selected the food to be served and the entertainment presented, read testimonials they had composed about what it was like to live in Helen's Place, and made certain that both wine and beer options were available for themselves and their guests.

When told they were to be visited by a state legislator and a state senator, the community of Helen's Place met to decide how best to meet with these visitors and to exhibit the special qualities of their community. After a lively debate, the group voted on a resolution to simply keep doing what they would normally do. The majority favoring this approach advanced the argument that this was the best way to demonstrate what it was like to live there. When the visitors came, they observed the residents reading and discussing a story about Abraham Lincoln. Whether this was ironic or not is open to debate.

Helen's Place residents also created rules for resolving conflicts among neighborhood members. These involved items such as rules will be decided by a majority vote and in case of a tie a coin flip will determine the outcome; no one may insult another resident, and if this takes place, the person giving the insult must leave (if there is a disagreement about whether an insult was given, both persons must refrain from speaking to one another); etc. It is important to realize that if a truly person-centered neighborhood is created as a model for living together for individuals with dementia, then conflict will inevitably arise on occasion. This is the consequence of providing independence and empowerment to these individuals. It is a similar situation to what occurs in a college dormitory when individuals are put together and must live together when they did not know one another in the past. In an environment where persons with dementia either stay in their rooms or are placed in chairs along the walls of a room and sit with their chins on their chests, there is no conflict among residents. Of course, this situation is devoid of respect, dignity, and a life worth living.

The Price of Flexibility: Giving Up Control

The key element that becomes apparent in these examples is that flexibility can be obtained in the systems which promote flexibility in the provision of care to persons with dementia. Rigid systems exercise a great deal of control over the lives of persons with dementia, in essence robbing residents or clients with dementia of their autonomy and freedom in the name of providing safety and a calm environment. A good example to think of is a meal in which a number of persons sit at tables in a dining room. In a community model, where persons at the table know one another and are interested in each other's lives, such meals can be noisy due to the multiple conversations being carried on simultaneously. A research team from Latrobe University investigating the effects of providing training in Montessori approaches to dementia care within a day center environment in Melbourne noted that the first change they observed from baseline observations to observations taken after staff training was that the environment was decidedly noisier due to clients with dementia speaking to each other during activities, due to clients becoming responsible for preparing and serving morning tea, etc. Initial results found significant increases in engagement in these clients after introduction of this training to staff members (Developing purposeful activities, 2015), and a video resource and manual based on this training is available from Alzheimer's Australia Victoria.

In a nursing home in Neuchatel, Switzerland, on April 1, 2014, inspectors arrived from the Canton in which the nursing home was located. In this residence, only persons with moderate to advanced dementia were admitted. On that day, residents who had been previously trained met the inspectors and led the tour and inspection of the nursing home. At the end of the inspection, the official visitors gathered in the parking lot and found that on each of their backs there was a piece of paper with a drawing of a fish. This is the Swiss equivalent of having a "Kick Me" sign attached to one's back (note the date of the inspection). The nursing home received its first perfect score for an inspection and also was awarded a prize for excellence in dementia care. The point is that we must demand that the standard for dementia care should be the creation of a place where we ourselves would want to live.

The Audacity of Hope

This chapter has focused on emphasizing the flexibility that persons with dementia are capable of showing, but this capacity largely is determined by the environment surrounding these persons. Thus, another purpose of this chapter is to highlight barriers to flexibility that exist, primarily in systems which attempt to more or less rigidly control persons with dementia and those who provide care to them. This is done through controlling resources purportedly earmarked for persons with dementia, by emphasizing the "suffering" of persons with dementia, and by continually promoting a message of hopelessness to create learned helplessness on a systemic scale.

Our quality of life as human beings largely is defined by our emotional state. Persons in extreme poverty who are part of a caring, sharing community may have a better quality of life than a healthy, wealthy, angry, and lonely person with enormous wealth. Persons with dementia, even in its advanced stages, who feel loved, who feel needed, who have a sense of purpose, and who feel in control of their lives, – i.e., who are treated with respect, dignity, and equality – can live well. For "patients" or "sufferers" with a disease, who have these images kept front and center each day by caregivers and the prevailing culture, this is not the case. We must acknowledge the capacity for flexibility in persons with dementia, we must encourage and support flexibility in how we think about dementia, and we must demand flexibility in the care systems and regulations governing care systems for persons with dementia. We must demand more resources for psychosocial programs to support persons with dementia and their families. We must "treat" dementia through providing a good quality of life for persons with (and without) dementia. We also must emphasize the need to empower persons with dementia. (The title of Christine Bryden's new book (2016) speaks this sentiment eloquently: "Nothing about us, without us!"). Where dementia is concerned, we must continually and relentlessly support the audacity of hope. This is how we fight dementia.

> At first I reacted to the trauma of diagnosis by believing the lie of dementia – that I would decline and that there was no hope. I was able to cast this lie aside and challenge accepted wisdom. I fought off depression, to live for today and tomorrow with dignity and cheerfulness. (Bryden, 2016, p. 167)

Acknowledgment I wish to thank the many persons with dementia, their family members, their friends, and their professional caregivers for providing us with these examples of hope and flexibility. They are, quite literally, too numerous to mention but we believe that their stories will live on, inspiring those who read this to build upon their achievements. Thanks also to the many colleagues who have worked with me over the years and who also provided so many examples and inspiration. A merely partial list includes friends and partners with AG&D in France (Veronique Durand and Jerome Erkes, especially), Mallory Jenkins, Vince Antenucci, Michelle Bourgeois, Alice Roberts, Tim Fickenscher, Ross Wilkoff, and Marina Sanchez. This chapter is dedicated to Mary Crist, who has Alzheimer's disease and is the mother of Linda Camp.

References

Bryden, C. (2016). *Nothing about us, without us! 20 years of dementia advocacy*. London: Jessica Kingsley Publishers.

Camp, C. J. (2006a). Montessori-based dementia programming™ in long-term care: A case study of disseminating an intervention for persons with dementia. In R. C. Intrieri & L. Hyer (Eds.), *Clinical applied gerontological interventions in long-term care* (pp. 295–314). New York: Springer.

Camp, C. J. (2006b). Spaced retrieval: A case study in dissemination of a cognitive intervention for persons with dementia. In D. Koltai Attix & K. A. Welsch-Bohmner (Eds.), *Geriatric neuropsychological assessment and intervention* (pp. 275–292). New York: The Guilford Press.

Camp, C. J. (2011). *Psychological treatment of dementia*. Presidential address (Div. 20 – Adult Development and Aging), annual conference of the American Psychological Association. Washington, DC.

Camp, C. J. (2013). The Montessori approach to dementia care. *Australian Journal of Dementia Care, 2*(5), 10–11.

Camp, C. J., & Lee, M. M. (2011). Montessori-based activities as a trans-generational interface for persons with dementia and preschool children. *Journal of Intergenerational Relationships, 9*, 366–373.

Camp, C. J., Orsulic-Jeras, S., Lee, M. M., & Judge, K. S. (2004). Effects of a Montessori-based intergenerational program on engagement and affect for adult day care clients with dementia. In M. L. Wykle, P. J. Whitehouse, & D. L. Morris (Eds.), *Successful aging through the life span: Intergenerational issues in health* (pp. 159–176). New York: Springer.

Camp, C. J., & Skrajner, M. J. (2004). Resident-assisted Montessori programming (RAMP): Training persons with dementia to serve as group activity leaders. *The Gerontologist, 44*, 426–431.

Camp, C. J., Skrajner, M. J., & Kelly, M. (2005). Early stage dementia client as group leader. *Clinical Gerontologist, 28*(4), 81–85.

Camp, C. J., Zeisel, J., & Antenucci, V. (2011). Implementing the "I'm Still Here Approach": Montessori methods for engaging persons with dementia. In P. E. Hartman-Stein & A. La Rue (Eds.), *Enhancing cognitive fitness in adults* (pp. 401–417). New York: Springer.

Developing purposeful activities. (2015). *Australian Journal of Dementia Care, 4*(5), 25.

de Werd, M. M., Boelen, D., Rikkert, M. G. M. O., & Kessels, R. P. C. (2013). Errorless learning of everyday tasks in people with dementia. *Clinical Interventions in Aging, 8*, 1177–1190.

George, D., Whitehouse, C., & Whitehouse, P. (2011). A model of intergenerativity: How the intergenerational school is bringing the generations together to foster collective wisdom and community health. *Journal of Intergenerational Relationships, 9*, 389–404.

Gigliotti, C., Morris, M., Smock, S., Jarrott, S. E., & Graham, B. (2005). An intergenerational summer program involving persons with dementia and preschool children. *Educational Gerontology, 31*, 425–441.

Hollister, B. A., Fox, P., & Chaufan, C. (2009). The Alzheimer's disease movement and the debate between cure vs care: The repercussions of reliance on the biomedical model as a social movement resource. In *Gerontologist* (Vol. 49, pp. 228–228). Washington, DC: Gerontological Society of America.

Jarrott, S. E., & Bruno, K. (2003). Intergenerational activities involving persons with dementia: An observational assessment. *American Journal of Alzheimer's Disease and Other Dementias, 18*, 31–37.

Kitwood, T. (1996). A dialectical framework for dementia. In R. T. Woods (Ed.), *Handbook of the clinical psychology of aging* (pp. 267–282). Chichester, UK: Wiley.

Kitwood, T. (1997a). The experience of dementia. *Aging & Mental Health, 1*, 13–22.

Kitwood, T. (1997b). *Dementia reconsidered*. Buckingham, UK: Open University Press.

Lee, M. M., Camp, C. J., & Malone, M. L. (2007). Effects of intergenerational Montessori-based activities programming on engagement of nursing home residents with dementia. *Clinical Interventions in Aging, 2*(3), 1–7.

Mattern, J. M., & Kane, E. (2007). Huntington's disease client as activity leader. *Clinical Gerontologist, 30*(4), 93–100. doi:10.1300/J018v30n04_07.

Skrajner, M. J., & Camp, C. J. (2007). Resident-assisted Montessori programming (RAMP™): Use of a small group reading activity run by persons with dementia in adult day health care and long-term care settings. *The American Journal of Alzheimer's Disease & Other Dementias, 22*(1), 27–36.

Skrajner, M. J., Haberman, J. L., Camp, C. J., Tusick, M., Frentiu, C., & Gorzelle, G. (2014). Effects of using nursing home residents to serve as group activity leaders: Lessons learned from the RAP project. *Dementia, 13*(2), 274–285.

Skrajner, M. M., Haberman, J. L., Camp, C. J., Tusick, M., Frentiu, C., & Gorzelle, G. (2012). Training nursing home residents to serve as group activity leaders: Lessons learned and preliminary results from the RAP project. *Dementia, 11*, 263–274. doi:10.1177/1471301212437457.

Squire, L. R. (1992). Memory and the hippocampus: A synthesis from findings with rats, monkeys, and humans. *Psychological Review, 99*, 195–231.

Squire, L. R. (1994). Declarative and nondeclarative memory: Multiple brain system supporting learning and memory. In D. L. Schacter & E. Tulving (Eds.), *Memory systems 1994* (pp. 203–232). Cambridge, MA: The MIT Press.

Zanetti, O., Zanieri, G., Di Giovanni, G., De Vreese, L. C., Pezzini, A., Metitieri, T., et al. (2001). Effectiveness of procedural memory stimulation in mild Alzheimer's disease patients: A controlled study. *Neuropsychological Rehabilitation, 11*(3–4), 263–272.

Chapter 7
Spirituality as a Framework for Confronting Life's Existential Questions in Later Adulthood

John C. Cavanaugh

Humanity's oldest surviving literary work, the *Epic of Gilgamesh*, tells of the title character's search for the answer to one of life's great issues: the search for eternal life as an answer to the question "What happens next?" Ever since, we have struggled to find answers to life's great existential questions: What is the meaning of life? Why do bad things happen to good people? Is there anything more than this life? Why is there so much suffering? Why am I here? Attempts to answer these questions form the core of every major religion; have been continual themes in philosophy; have been the message of countless works of literature, poetry, music, art, and other forms of expression; motivated scores of heated debates over every conceivable beverage; and even served as the focal topic of a Monty Python film.

That we are still seeking definitive answers after more than 4000 years of documented attempts belies both the timeless nature of the issues and their seeming intractability. It may also be a reflection of the fact that whatever answers are achieved are individual ones, not generalizable ones that could apply to all. It is this latter perspective that is adopted in this chapter. My basic premise is that each person reaches an individual resolution of the great existential questions that is a result of the confluence of all of the usual developmental aspects (e.g., physical, cognitive, personality, emotional, sociocultural, interpersonal, etc.), operating within the broader sphere of accumulated knowledge and understanding of the underlying rules governing the universe as understood at any specific point in time (e.g., quantum theory, general relativity, string theory, chaos theory, etc.) (see also Wessels & Müller, 2013). As will become clear, the optimal point for the creation of individual resolutions is in later adulthood, when certain developmental processes and experience are best aligned to handle the inherent ambiguity of the issues and to place oneself in a larger context.

J.C. Cavanaugh, Ph.D. (✉)
Consortium of Universities of the Washington Metropolitan Area,
1100 H Street, NW Suite 500, Washington, DC 20005, USA
e-mail: jccphd@yahoo.com

J.D. Sinnott (ed.), *Identity Flexibility During Adulthood*,
DOI 10.1007/978-3-319-55658-1_7

Before delving into these matters, it is important to differentiate between what this chapter will (and will not) discuss. First, this chapter focuses on *spirituality*, as differentiated from *religion*, *religiosity*, or *religious involvement*. Spirituality in this context is viewed as the search for the sacred (Pargament, 2013) and the search for meaning (Park, 2013; Park, Edmondson, & Hale-Smith, 2013). Pargament (2007, 2013) and Pargament and Mahoney (2005) note that the sacred refers not just to traditional concepts of a higher power but also to any object or thing (e.g., a relationship) that takes on a sacredness or transcendence. Park and colleagues (Aldwin, Park, Jeong, & Nath, 2013; Park, 2013; Park et al., 2013) point to the centrality of spirituality in meaning making and "can inform all aspects of meaning, informing beliefs and providing ultimate motivation and primary goals for living and guidelines for achieving those goals, along with a deep sense of purpose and mattering" (Park, 2013, p. 42). In contrast, religion and related concepts are usually viewed as concerning organized belief structures that are most often institutionalized into formal groups (e.g., Oman, 2013; Pargament, Mahoney, Exline, Jones, & Shafranske, 2013). It is all too common for the various terms to be used interchangeably, with the unsurprising outcome of general confusion in the literature.

Second, the later adulthood developmental frame for this chapter focuses only on the potential interactions of the various components. Detailed discussions of the individual developmental trajectories of the components are beyond the scope of this chapter. Additionally, the emphasis here will be on the specific interactions among cognitive/intellectual and psychosocial development. While acknowledging that there are numerous other key influences on human development, in terms of later adulthood, these are the areas in which most of the relevant empirical research has been done.

Third, there are clear connections between this chapter and the field of transpersonal psychology in that I will discuss the integration of spiritual and transcendent aspects of people's experience and psychological theory; a thorough discussion of this field is beyond the scope here. The interested reader might consult Johnson (2005), Balaban (2006), Geary (2006), Humphrey (2015), or others for more detailed discussions.

Merton, Rohr, and an Approach to Spirituality in Later Adulthood

The idea that significant spiritual development occurs during adulthood has been embedded in writings on spirituality for centuries, largely grounded in the experience of mystics within various traditions. For our purposes, we will focus on the developmental shift initially developed by Thomas Merton, the twentieth-century Trappist monk whose writings on spirituality drew not only from the Judeo-Christian tradition but also extensively from the Buddhist and other eastern traditions. In his books *Seeds of Contemplation* (Merton, 1949) and its revision *New Seeds of Contemplation* (Merton, 1962), Merton draws an important distinction between the

False Self and the *True Self*. Essentially the distinction is between the superficial, external self that we mean when we use the first person singular pronoun "I," the self that Merton considers a prison from which we must escape, and the joy of dwelling in union with the essence of everything in the universe in the core of our soul, the self that Merton argues we must become. The False Self reflects egocentric desires; the True Self reflects oneness with the universe.

Richard Rohr, the Franciscan friar and founder of the Center for Action and Contemplation, takes this progression and further refines it (Rohr 2011, 2013). Rohr writes that spiritual development across adulthood consists of the movement from Merton's *False Self* (that Rohr defined as a focus on personal achievement grounded in the ego) to the *True Self* (that Rohr defined as a reference point that is both "utterly within you and utterly beyond you at the very same time").

Rohr (2011) writes that the False Self is rooted in a relative identity that each of us creates for ourselves, an identity that depends critically on external indicators of success (e.g., title, prestige, salary, status, etc.). The False Self is inherently fragile, tends to be dissatisfied because it depends on external definitions of achievement, and is felt as separate from others in the sense that we want to belong to the "in" group and define others selectively as members of the "out" group. Change is to be feared. Morality is defined in terms of adherence to rules. In short, the False Self is the result of building one's ego structure based on incorporating external messages regarding of "values" and "success." There is a heavy emphasis on doing things "correctly" according to the rules of the group or society.

In Rohr's (2013) view, achieving the True Self involves (re)discovering the universality and wholeness, an "authentic inner knowing," that has always been within, but has gone unrecognized or unacknowledged. The True Self does not see anything with absolute certainty, which is what Rohr means by mature faith. The True Self is the fulfillment of the search for answers to the core existential questions. It entails a letting go and an acceptance of what is.

Rohr, along with mystics such as Merton, Julian of Norwich, Hafiz, and Rumi, provides a parallel description to Erikson, Jung, and others, all of whom it could be said described the search for personal meaning in life to, in the end, be a search for becoming who we already are in a fully integrated way. Like Dorothy in the *Wizard of Oz*, we discover that we already had everything we need, so the apparently empty basket is given to us as an opportunity to fill in our own way.

A key characteristic of the True Self (or the integrated self as Erikson (1982) might have put it) is a holistic, universalist view of higher principles. There is a recognition that all things are connected, both within and without the individual. There is an understanding of a certain immutability to truth and that relationships are the real foundation on which all else is based. External standards and judgments no longer matter. It is not about personal achievement but personal integrity based on inner truths that does.

Merton (1955) argued that the True Self depends critically on the cognitive abilities to deal with paradoxes and contradictions and to tolerate ambiguity. For example, he points out that real love is only kept by giving it away, and it can only be given perfectly when it is also received. He also points to numerous examples of deep contradictions in the New Testament, such as the notion that those who attempt to save their lives will lose them, but those who lose their lives will save them. Such ability to hold and unpack both sides of a paradox or contradiction requires advanced cognitive developmental outcomes that unfold in adulthood.

For both Merton and Rohr, the True Self reflects the *soul*. By whatever label, it is an experience of the transcendent nature of the universe. It is a recognition that life in some sense (e.g., as energy) continues beyond personal death, which results in a different, less anxiety-ridden view of personal death.

The developmental transition described by Merton and Rohr (as well as others) from the False Self to the True Self has its genesis in the processes underlying adult development more generally. Now that the broad pattern of change in spiritual perspective has been briefly described, let us turn to these underlying processes before returning to consider how all of these coalesce into a coherent framework for understanding spirituality in later adulthood.

Setting the Stage: Cognitive Development in Adulthood

The development of thought and reasoning across adulthood has received a great deal of attention over the past few decades (Sinnott, 2009, 2010, 2014). Whereas formal-operational thinkers (a level first achieved by most people in adolescence but that extends into adulthood; Inhelder & Piaget, 1958; Siegler & Alibali, 2004) arrive at outcomes based on logic grounded in their own experience, and are quite confident that their reasoning is absolutely correct, adults tend to think differently. As a rule, adults are reluctant to draw conclusions based on the limited information explicitly provided in a problem or specific situation, especially when the problem can be interpreted in different ways (Sinnott, 1998). Rather, adults often point out that there is much about the problem or issue we don't know, making it much more ambiguous. Adults may eventually decide on a particular outcome or conclusion, but they do so only after considering aspects of the situation that go well beyond the information given or that is obvious. Such thinking shows a recognition that other people's experiences may be quite different from one's own and that other points of view are equally valid to their own, at least at the conceptual thought level.

Clearly, the thought processes adults use are different from formal operations (Kitchener, King, & DeLuca, 2006; Sinnott, 2009, 2010). Unlike formal-operational thinking, this approach involves considering situational constraints and circumstances, realizing that reality sometimes constrains solutions and knowing that feelings matter.

Based on numerous investigations, researchers concluded that this different type of thinking represents a qualitative change beyond formal operations that happens in identifiable steps across adulthood (King & Kitchener, 2004; Kitchener et al. 2006; Merriam & Bierema, 2014; Sinnott, 2009, 2010, 2014). Such thought, called **postformal thought,** *is characterized by a recognition that truth* (i.e., *the correct answer) may vary from situation to situation, that solutions must be realistic to be* *reasonable, that ambiguity and contradiction are the rule rather than the exception, and that emotion and subjective factors usually play a role in thinking.*

Several research-based descriptions of the development of thinking in adulthood have been offered. Two are most relevant for the present discussion.

One view concerns the development of reflective judgment, *a way in which adults reason through dilemmas involving current affairs, religion, science, personal relationships, and the like.* Based on decades of longitudinal and cross-sectional research, Kitchener and King (1989) and Kitchener et al. (2006) refined descriptions and identified a systematic progression of reflective judgment. The first three stages in the model represent prereflective thought, levels at which people do not acknowledge and may not even perceive that knowledge is uncertain. Consequently, they do not understand that some problems exist for which there are not clear and absolutely correct answers. About halfway through the developmental progression, people think very differently. In Stages 4 and 5, they are likely to say that nothing can be known for certain and to change their conclusions based on the situation and the evidence, representing an understanding of the subjective nature of knowledge. As adults continue their development into Stages 6 and 7, they begin to show true reflective judgment, understanding that people construct knowledge (and hold firm convictions) using evidence and argument that is situational and carefully analyzed from multiple perspectives.

A second approach is Sinnott's Complex Theory of Adult Cognitive Development, also premised on postformal thought (Sinnott, 1998, 2009, 2010, 2014). It is grounded in the premise that a key aspect of adult development is increased ability to be self-reflective, or mindful, about one's own thought process, a fundamental aspect of many spirituality traditions and approaches (e.g., Buddhism, mysticism). For Sinnott, the key developmental pathway is one of deeper understanding of alternative "logics" or ways of viewing and experiencing reality. The main characteristics of postformal thought in Sinnott's approach are as follows:

- *Metatheory shift* is the ability to view reality from more than one overarching logical perspective. Put simply, it is the ability to take another person's frame of reference and understand reality from their vantage point.
- *Problem definition* is the realization that there is always more than one way to define a problem, so each person may have a unique definition of the same problem.
- *Process/product shift* is the realization that one can reach both a "content-related" solution to one specific problem and a solution that gives a heuristic or a process that solves many such problems.
- *Parameter setting* is the realization that each person must choose those aspects of the problem context that must be considered or ignored in order to reach a solution.
- *Multiple solutions* means that each person can generate several solutions to the same problem, based on several different ways of viewing the problem.
- *Pragmatism* means that each person is able to evaluate the solutions created for the problem and then select one that is "best" by some criterion (criteria).

- *Multiple causality* is the realization that a situation can be the result of several causes.
- *Multiple methods* is the realization that there are several ways to get to the same solution of a problem.
- *Paradox* is the realization that contradictions are inherent in reality and that a broader view of a situation can resolve contradictions.

The main point in Sinnott's approach is that as people traverse adulthood, they become increasingly able to hold and bridge contradictory concepts or multiple points of view and create adaptive syntheses of them at a higher level of understanding. Sinnott argues that this developmental progression is most likely to be facilitated through interpersonal relationships.

In addition to an increased understanding that there is more than one "right" answer, adult thinking is characterized by the integration of emotion with logic (Diehl et al., 2014; Jain & Labouvie-Vief, 2010; Labouvie-Vief, 2006; Labouvie-Vief, Grühn, & Studer, 2010). As they mature, adults tend to make decisions and analyze problems not so much on logical grounds alone, as on pragmatic and emotional grounds. Externally prescribed rules and norms are viewed as relative, not absolute. Mature thinkers realize that thinking is an inherently social enterprise that demands making compromises with other people and tolerating contradiction and ambiguity. Such shifts mean that one's sense of self also undergoes a fundamental change.

Setting the Stage: Personality Development in Adulthood

To understand how personality is inextricably intertwined with key life outcomes such as well-being, health, longevity, and spirituality, let us base our approach in the definition of one of the founders of the filed, Gordon Allport (1961): "Personality is the dynamic organization within the individual of those psychophysical systems that determine [the person's] characteristic behavior and thought" (p. 28). For our discussion, the operative concepts here are that personality is dynamic and that it drives behavior and thought. From this view, people are best understood as both who they are and what they are attempting to accomplish or to be (Cantor, 1990).

The Six-Foci Model of Personality and Adult Development

A contemporary model of personality that integrates several conceptual threads and research lines is Hooker's (2002) and Hooker, Choun, and Hall (2010) six-foci model. This model integrates personality structures (traits, personal action constructs, and life stories) with personality processes (states, self-regulation, and self-narration). The structures and processes are paired into three levels of increasing individuality: traits and their accompanying states (Level I) are found universally; specific personal action constructs and their accompanying self-regulatory processes, often described as personal goals (Level II), can be shared but are more individualized than general traits-states. Finally, one's life story and its accompanying self-narration (Level III) are unique to each individual (Hooker & McAdams, 2003).

A full description of the six-foci model is beyond the scope of this chapter. For present purposes, it is the Level III pairing (life story and self-narration) that is most germane. Level III has been developed most completely through Erikson's life span theory of psychosocial development, the latter stage of which we turn to next.

Integrity Versus Despair

As people enter late life, they begin the struggle of *integrity versus despair*, which involves the process by which people try to make sense of their lives. According to Erikson (1982), this struggle comes about as older adults work to understand their lives in terms of the future of their family and community. Thoughts of a person's own mortality and death are balanced by the realization that they will live on through children, grandchildren, great-grandchildren, and the community as a whole through their life's work. This realization produces what Erikson calls a "life-affirming involvement" in the present.

The struggle of *integrity versus despair* requires people to engage in a *life review*, the process by which people reflect on the events and experiences of their lifetimes. To achieve integrity, a person must come to terms with the choices and events that have made his or her life unique. There must also be an acceptance of the fact that one's life is drawing to a close. Looking back on one's life may resolve some of the second-guessing of decisions made earlier in adulthood (Erikson, Erikson, & Kivnick, 1986), especially given that the longer-term (positive) consequences of those decisions may now be apparent. In contrast, others feel bitter about their choices, blame themselves or others for their misfortunes, see their lives as meaningless, and greatly fear death. These people end up in despair rather than integrity.

Research shows a connection between engaging in a life review and achieving integrity, so life review has become a basis for effective mental health interventions with older adults (Westerhof, Bohlmeijer, & Webster, 2010), especially for older individuals with depression (Hallford & Mellor, 2013). A therapeutic technique called "structured life review" (Haight & Haight, 2007, 2013) has been shown to be effective in helping people deal with stressful life events.

Reaching integrity is an individual journey. Erikson (1982) emphasizes that people who demonstrate integrity come from all backgrounds and cultures and arrive there having taken different paths. Such people have made many different choices and followed many different lifestyles; the point is that everyone has this opportunity to achieve integrity if they strive for it. Those who reach integrity become self-affirming and self-accepting; they judge their lives to have been worthwhile and good. In Erikson's view, integrity involves coming to terms with one's "one and only lifecycle" and, after integrating all the aspects of one's life, realizing that "death loses its sting" (1959, p. 98). This final stage in Erikson's theory brings the person face to face with the existential question: Did I lead a meaningful life?

Setting the Stage: The Development of Felt Connection

There is another key developmental process in adulthood that is central to understanding the development of spirituality—the development of how we feel connected to the various sides of the self, to others, and to the universe at large (i.e., transcendence). Sinnott (2004, 2006, 2010, 2014) calls this collection of connections Felt Connection. She proposes that the three aspects noted above are central to understanding the notion of self and comprise the origins of the developmental changes in the self noted in the previous section.

For Sinnott (e.g., 2010), connecting the sides of the self involves being in touch with and relating to the various aspects of our personalities, including those that constitute unacknowledged aspects such as the Shadow (Jung, 1930/1971). Connecting with others involves interactions between or among persons that we experience daily. Connecting with the transcendent involves having an ongoing relationship with a power that is larger than oneself, for example, the Great Spirit, the Universe, or God.

In Sinnott's view, each of the three arenas has a motive and pathology (or negative outcome), and the three sets of bilateral interactions each includes challenges and a common prerequisite. These can be understood as follows:

- *Connecting sides of the self:* The motive is to heal the self into one integrated whole. The negative outcome or pathology is inner conflict.
- *Connecting to others:* The motive is the importance of relationships for any species. The negative outcome or pathology is isolation.
- *Connecting with the transcendent:* The motive is to become larger than the local self. The negative outcome or pathology is living a meaningless life.
- *Challenges in the dynamic interplay between connecting with self and connecting with others:* The challenges are the interactions from a multifaceted self and the self viewed from the perspective of others.
- *Challenges in the dynamic interplay between connecting with others and connecting with the transcendent:* The challenges are to see the self and the transcendent in others and see one's identity as both self and transcendent.
- *Challenges in the dynamic interplay between connecting with the transcendent and with the self:* The challenges are to understand the transcendent from an "unfinished" self and to the understanding of the self taking transcendence into account.
- *Common prerequisite:* For development in all three arenas, postformal thought is a necessary requirement.

The common prerequisite of postformal thought underlying successful achievement of each of the three connections connects the developmental progressions apparent in personality, especially the self, and their respective roles in preparing the individual to face the ultimate existential questions. For example, one can easily see the inherent tension and contradiction between the concepts of "self" and "transcendent" as pitting a concept grounded in the importance of "me" being central to all things against a concept grounded in the importance of "all creation" being a unified whole and indivisible into separate "selves." As we will see in the next section, Sinnott's Felt Connection framework is especially useful in understanding the underlying adult developmental processes impelling (or inhibiting) the transition from the False Self to the True Self.

Existential Questions, Postformal Thought, Personality, and Connections: Spirituality in Later Adulthood

The integration of the aspects of spirituality and its underlying adult developmental processes discussed in this chapter results in what could be described as a more integrated notion of the self in service of meaning making (e.g., Kavar, 2015; Nelson-Becker & Gilbert, 2014; Park, 2013; Sinnott, 2009, 2010) as a way for the individual to resolve the core existential questions. This linkage with meaning making has a long history in psychology, most notably dating from Frankl (1946).[1] Lips-Wiersma (2002a, 2002b) extends this connection to the workplace and argues that people's resolution of existential questions in the workplace such as "What is the meaning of my work?" is resolved through a spirituality-based approach to meaning making. The present contribution to this tradition is to further ground meaning making with respect to the existential questions of life with core underlying adult developmental processes.

The dependence of the development of spirituality in later adulthood on the underlying developmental processes of cognitive and personality development, integrated through Sinnott's Felt Connection framework, gives a new and more thorough understanding to Merton's and Rohr's co-description of the developmental progression from the False Self to the True Self in spirituality. Common to both Merton and Rohr is a basis of False Self in what could be considered as thinking that is trapped in a single logical structure, unable to conceive of alternative points of view. For instance, Rohr (2011, 2013) frames the False Self as the basis for exclusionary practices, such as claiming that there is only one true faith (the believer's own) and that all others are heretical. From the earlier discussion in this chapter and the fuller descriptions in both Merton's and Rohr's writings, it is clear that this single logic, egocentric perspective of the False Self is incapable of understanding the

[1] Although Frankl does not explicitly use the concept spirituality, his notion of meaning making is based on "the self-transcendence of human existence," an idea very much in line with both Merton and Rohr, for example, who frame it within spirituality.

rich, deeper meanings of the inherent contradictions and paradoxes that form the core of the major religious traditions (e.g., Jesus' teachings in the New Testament, Zen kōans, Daoist teachings, etc.), instead focusing on the surface meanings alone. Research on the development of the self and on Felt Connections indicates that the False Self is incapable also of deeply understanding the challenges underlying truly reciprocal relationships, such as those exemplified by the Golden Rule. As Rohr notes, doing what is best for another often involves "hating" oneself in the sense that the action ("love") toward another means that in the specific situation at hand, the self "loses" so that the other may "gain."

In contrast, the True Self depends critically on postformal thought in order to resolve the contradictions and paradoxes that unlock the connection to the transcendent, which for Merton and Rohr is a cardinal characteristic of this higher spiritual experience. In particular, Merton and Rohr describe similar processes by which one integrates various aspects of the self, one's relationships with others, and one's relationship with the transcendent (which they both label as God), all of which, as Sinnott (2004, 2005, 2010) notes, depend on postformal thought. To read Merton's and Rohr's descriptions of the True Self is to sense the triumph of the full integration of thought with emotion and self, to have the corrective lenses necessary to see through the blurriness of paradox to a clarity never before experienced.

When in the fullness of time one faces the ultimate existential questions regarding life's meaning, how each individual resolves them (or not) depends entirely on whether the developmental processes underlying the movement from the False Self to the True Self have been nurtured and completed. Certainly, attempting to work through questions such as "What is the meaning of life?" or "Is there anything after this existence?" is approached fundamentally differently depending on developmental level. Just the difference between the compulsion for a single view, tolerating no others, and the realization that there are untold numbers of answers and this is the one I choose for me at this point in my life reflects a complex confluence of underlying developmental processes.

Concluding Thoughts

As understood through Merton's and Rohr's progression from the False Self to the True Self, the developmental trajectory of spirituality in later adulthood becomes a key example of the dynamic interplay among the underlying adult developmental processes of cognition, personality and the self, and the connections we establish within ourselves, with others, and with the transcendent. Taken a step further, it can be argued that personal spiritual development rests first on the deep understanding and resolution of the inherent contradictions and paradoxes that form the core beliefs within religious traditions, described as such by mystics in each of them. It is the fundamental cognitive capacity to hold both aspects of a paradox in mind simultaneously and to be at peace with that that provides the basis for beginning the transition from the False Self to the True Self.

It is this cognitive ability that powers our ability to integrate the various aspects of ourselves into the whole described by Erikson. This, too, involves resolving paradox via the integration of the Shadow (or other aspects of our self typically kept out of conscious reach). Both Merton and Rohr are clear that the transition they describe involves coming to peace with the understanding that the ultimate legacy issue is whether it is based in tangible "stuff" or intangible relationships and their ripple effects. As did the author of *Ecclesiastes*, Merton and Rohr argue that an integrated approach to relationships is what ultimately carries the day. This sets the stage for the last component—the integration of the contradictory aspects of ourselves that form the components of our connections with others and with the transcendent.

In his book *No Man Is an Island*, Merton (1955) makes the point of finding the "one thing necessary" in life, from which all meaning and happiness flows. But here's the kicker:

> Happiness consists in finding out precisely what the "one thing necessary" may be, in our lives, and in gladly relinquishing all the rest. For then, by a divine paradox, we find that everything else is given us together with the one thing we needed. (Merton, 1955)

Answering the ultimate existential question of whether one's life has had meaning in the affirmative depends critically on the ability to live in the paradox. That, in turn, depends on the ability to think at a deeply abstract level and to embrace and integrate all the parts of oneself into a single, paradoxical whole. Doing that will, assuredly, provide the "one thing necessary": the happiness of a meaningful life.

References

Aldwin, C. M., Park, C. L., Jeong, Y.-J., & Nath, R. (2013). Differing pathways between religiousness, spirituality, and health: A self-regulation perspective. *Psychology of Religion and Spirituality, 6*, 9–21. doi:10.1037/a0034416.

Allport, G. (1961). *Pattern and growth in personality*. New York: Holt, Rinehart, and Winston.

Balaban, E. (2006). Cognitive developmental biology. *Cognition, 101*, 298–332. doi:10.1016/j.cognition.2006.04.006.

Cantor, N. (1990). From thought to behavior: "Having" and "doing" in the study of personality and cognition. *American Psychologist, 45*, 735–750. doi:10.1037/0003-066X.45.6.735.

Diehl, M., Chui, H., Hay, E. L., Lumley, M. A., Grühn, D., & Labouvie-Vief, G. (2014). Change in coping and defense mechanisms across adulthood: Longitudinal findings in a European American sample. *Developmental Psychology, 50*, 634–648. doi:10.1037/a0033619.

Erikson, E. H. (1959). Identity and the life cycle: Selected papers. *Psychological Issues, 1*, 1–171.

Erikson, E. H. (1982). *The life cycle completed: Review*. New York: Norton.

Erikson, E. H., Erikson, J. M., & Kivnick, H. Q. (1986). *Vital involvement in old age*. New York: Norton.

Frankl, V. (1946). *Ein Psycholog erlebt das Konzentrationslager*. (trans as *Man's search for meaning*). Vienna: Verlag für Jugend und Volk, Gesellschaft m.b.H.

Geary, D. (2006). Evolutionary developmental psychology. *Developmental Review, 26*, 113–119. doi:10.1016/j.dr.2006.02.005.

Haight, B. K., & Haight, B. S. (2007). *The handbook of structured life review*. Baltimore: Health Professions Press.

Haight, B. K., & Haight, B. S. (2013). Confidentiality in the structured life review. *International Journal of Reminiscence and Life Review, 1*, 36–38. Retrieved from http://www.ijrlr.org/ojs/index.php/IJRLR/article/view/21/6

Hallford, D., & Mellor, D. (2013). Reminiscence-based therapies for depression: Should they be used only with older adults? *Clinical Psychology: Science and Practice, 20*, 452–468. doi:10.1111/cpsp.12043.

Hooker, K. (2002). New directions for research in personality and aging: A comprehensive model for linking levels, structures, and processes. *Journal of Research on Personality, 36*, 318–334. doi:10.1016/S0092-6566(02)00012-0.

Hooker, K., & McAdams, D. P. (2003). Personality reconsidered: A new agenda for aging research. *Journal of Gerontology: Psychological Sciences, 58B*, P296–P304. doi:10.1093/geronb/58.6.P296.

Hooker, K., Choun, S., & Hall, B. (2010). Personality and emotion in later life. In J. C. Cavanaugh & C. K. Cavanaugh (Eds.), *Aging in America (Vol.1): Psychological aspects* (pp. 102–134). Santa Barbara, CA: Praeger Perspectives.

Humphrey, C. (2015). Shadows along the spiritual pathway. *Journal of Religion and Health, 54*(6), 2376–2388. doi:10.1007/s10943-015-0037-2.

Inhelder, B., & Piaget, J. (1958). *The growth of logical thinking from childhood to adolescence*. New York: Basic Books.

Jain, E., & Labouvie-Vief, G. (2010). Compensatory effects of emotional avoidance in adult development. *Biological Psychology, 84*, 497–513. doi:10.1016/j.biopsycho.2010.03.008.

Johnson, M. (2005). *Developmental cognitive neuroscience*. Padstow, UK: Blackwell.

Jung, C. (1930/1971). The stages of life. In J. Campbell (Ed.), *The portable Jung* (pp. 3–23). New York: Viking Library. Retrieved from https://archive.org/stream/ThePortableJung/The%20Portable%20Jung_djvu.txt

Kavar, L. F. (2015). Spirituality and the sense of self: An indicative analysis. *The Qualitative Report, 20*, 697–711. Retrieved from http://www.nova.edu/ssss/QR/QR20/5/kavar8.pdf

King, P. M., & Kitchener, K. S. (2004). Reflective judgment: Theory and research on the development of epistemic assumptions through adulthood. *Educational Psychologist, 39*, 5–18. doi:10.1207/s15326985ep3901_2.

Kitchener, K. S., & King, P. M. (1989). The reflective judgment model: Ten years of research. In M. L. Commons, C. Armon, L. Kohlberg, F. A. Richards, T. A. Grotzer, & J. D. Sinnott (Eds.), *Adult development: Vol. 2. Models and methods in the study of adolescent and adult thought* (pp. 63–78). New York: Praeger.

Kitchener, K. S., King, P. M., & DeLuca, S. (2006). Development of reflective judgment in adulthood. In C. Hoare (Ed.), *Handbook of adult development and learning* (pp. 73–98). New York: Oxford University Press.

Labouvie-Vief, G. (2006). Emerging structures of adult thought. In J. J. Arnett & J. L. Tanner (Eds.), *Emerging adults in America: Coming of age in the 21st century* (pp. 59–84). Washington, DC: American Psychological Association.

Labouvie-Vief, G., Grühn, D., & Studer, J. (2010). Dynamic integration of emotion and cognition: Equilibrium regulation in development and aging. In M. E. Lamb & A. M. Freund (Eds.), *The handbook of life-span development: Vol. 2. Social and emotional development* (pp. 79–115). Hoboken, NJ: Wiley.

Lips-Wiersma, M. (2002a). Analysing the career concerns of spiritually oriented people: Lessons from contemporary organisations. *Career Development International, 7*, 385–397. doi:10.1108/13620430210449911.

Lips-Wiersma, M. (2002b). The influence of spiritual "meaning-making" on career behavior. *The Journal of Management Development, 21*, 497–520. doi:10.1108/02621710210434638.

Merriam, S. B., & Bierema, L. L. (2014). *Adult learning: Linking theory and practice*. San Francisco: Jossey-Bass.

Merton, T. (1949). *Seeds of contemplation*. Norfolk, CT: New Directions.

Merton, T. (1955). *No man is an island*. San Diego, CA: Harvest Books.

Merton, T. (1962). *New seeds of contemplation*. New York: New Dimensions.

Nelson-Becker, H., & Gilbert, M. C. (2014). Spirituality and older women: The journey home to self. In *School of social work: Faculty publications and other works* (Paper 33). Retrieved from http://ecommons.luc.edu/socialwork_facpubs/33

Oman, D. (2013). Religious and spirituality: Evolving meanings. In R. F. Paloutzian & C. L. Park (Eds.), *Handbook of the psychology of religion and spirituality* (2nd ed., pp. 23–47). New York: Guilford Press.
Pargament, K. I. (2007). *Spiritually integrated psychotherapy: Understanding and addressing the sacred*. New York: Guilford Press.
Pargament, K. I. (2013). Searching for the sacred: Toward a nonreductionistic theory of spirituality. In K. I. Pargament, J. J. Exline, & J. W. Jones (Eds.), *APA handbook of psychology, religion, and spirituality: Vol. 1. Context, theory, and research* (pp. 257–273). Washington, DC: American Psychological Association.
Pargament, K. I., & Mahoney, A. (2005). Sacred matters: Sanctification as a vital topic for the psychology of religion. *The International Journal for the Psychology of Religion, 15*, 179–198. doi:10.1207/s15327582ijpr1503_1.
Pargament, K. I., Mahoney, A., Exline, J. J., Jones, J., & Shafranske, E. (2013). Envisioning an integrative paradigm for the psychology of religion and spirituality. In K. I. Pargament, J. J. Exline, & J. W. Jones (Eds.), *APA handbook of psychology, religion, and spirituality: Vol. 1. Context, theory, and research* (pp. 3–19). Washington, DC: American Psychological Association.
Park, C. L. (2013). The meaning making model: A framework for understanding meaning, spirituality, and stress-related growth in health psychology. *The European Health Psychologist, 15*, 40–47. Retrieved from http://openhealthpsychology.net/ehp/issues/2013/v15iss2_June2013/EHP_June_2013.pdf#page=13
Park, C. L., Edmondson, D., & Hale-Smith, A. (2013). Why religion? Meaning as motivation. In K. I. Pargament, J. J. Exline, & J. W. Jones (Eds.), *APA handbook of psychology, religion, and spirituality: Vol. 1. Context, theory, and research* (pp. 151–171). Washington, DC: American Psychological Association.
Rohr, R. (2011). *Falling upward: A spirituality for the two halves of life*. San Francisco: Jossey-Bass.
Rohr, R. (2013). *Immortal diamond: The search for our true self*. San Francisco: Jossey-Bass.
Siegler, R. S., & Alibali, M. W. (2004). Children's thinking (4th ed.). Upper Saddle River, NJ: Prentice-Hall.
Sinnott, J. D. (1998). *The development of logic in adulthood: Postformal thought and its applications*. New York: Plenum Press.
Sinnott, J. D. (2004). *Feeling connected, spirituality, and adult development: A new theory of their interrelationships*. Invited paper presented at the Annual Conference on Research and Spirituality, Loyola College, Columbia, MD.
Sinnott, J. D. (2005). Spirituality as "feeling connected with the transcendent": Outline of a transpersonal psychology of adult development of self. In R. L. Piedmont (Ed.), *Religion, spirituality, and the scientific study of religion* (pp. 287–308). Leiden, The Netherlands: Koninklijke Brill NV.
Sinnott, J. D. (2009). Complex thought and construction of the self in the face of aging and death. *Journal of Adult Development, 16*, 155–165. doi:10.1007/s10804-009-9057-z.
Sinnott, J. D. (2010). Coherent themes: Individuals' relationships with God, their early childhood experiences, their bonds with significant others, and their relational delusions during psychotic episodes all have the similar holistic, existential, and relational themes. *Journal of Adult Development, 17*, 230–244. doi:10.1007/s.10804-009-9090-y.
Sinnott, J. D. (2014). *Adult development: Cognitive aspects of thriving close relationships*. New York: Oxford University Press.
Wessels, F., & Müller, J. C. (2013). Spirituality in narratives of meaning. *HTS Theological Studies, 69*. Retrieved from http://www.scielo.org.za/scielo.php?pid=S0259-94222013000200003&script=sci_arttext
Westerhof, G. J., Bohlmeijer, E., & Webster, J. D. (2010). Reminiscence and mental health: A review of recent progress in theory, research, and interventions. *Ageing and Society, 30*, 697–721. doi:10.1017/S0144686X09990328.

Chapter 8
Rural-to-Urban Migration, Identity, and Life Quality of the Badaga People in South India

Gareth Davey

Introduction

Academic musing about social identity dates to the turn of the last century with early social scientists such as Charles Horton Cooley, William James and George Herbert Mead, to name a few (Cooley, 1902; Mead, 1934). Building on these early foundations, various ideas of social identity have since been advanced, including theories of internalized identity meanings such as balance theory (Heider 1946), role identity theory (McCall & Simmons 1966), identity theory (Stryker 1968, 1980), identity accumulation theory (Thoits, 1983) and identity control theory (Burke, 1991), and also situational-based perspectives which emphasise group affiliations, social milieu and associated behaviours, cognitions and emotions, for example, situated identity theory (Alexander & Knight, 1971), affect control theory (Heise, 1979), and social identity theory (Tajfel & Turner, 1979). There is also a burgeoning literature on collective identity which delineates identity-related dynamics of groups and their cultures, politics and social movements, grounded on classic sociological constructs like collective consciousness (Durkheim), class consciousness (Marx), Verstehen (Weber) and Gemeinscaft (Tonnies) (Melucci, 1989; Nagel, 1995; Prentice, Miller, & Lightdale, 1994; Taylor & Whittier, 1999).

While there has been a sizeable scholarly interest in social identity, most is about Western countries and numerically dominant ethnic groups in non-Western countries, and far less is about ethnic minority groups. In India, for example, there are many minority groups that might construct different notions of identity based on their distinct cultural and historical practices. This chapter is a qualitative inquiry of

G. Davey (✉)
Research Centre for Languages and Cultures, School of Foreign Languages and Literature, Yunnan Normal University, Kunming, Yunnan Province, China

School of Anthropology and Conservation, University of Kent, Canterbury, Kent, UK
e-mail: gjdavey@gmail.com

J.D. Sinnott (ed.), *Identity Flexibility During Adulthood*,
DOI 10.1007/978-3-319-55658-1_8

social identity and quality of life of the Badagas, a caste and rural community of more than 160,000 in several hundred hamlets in the Nilgiri Hills (Hockings, 2013), a locale in South India with a long history in academic literature since it became a strategic outpost for British colonists and writers in the mid-nineteenth century (Emeneau, 1938; Hockings, 1989, 2008; Mandelbaum, 1941; Rivers, 1906). The Badagas are officially designated by the Indian Government as a Backward Class which means they are regarded as socially disadvantaged and therefore eligible for government assistance with education and employment. They have long been associated with agriculture and still constitute a rural population, nowadays cash-crops such as tea and vegetables; the significance of agriculture in their culture is evidenced by a dozen or so annual festivals and life-cycle rituals. The majority of Badagas are followers of Shaivism, a popular sect of Hinduism, and their village Hinduism has unique features such as the worship of Badaga folk heroes as deities. They speak Badagu, a Dravidian language characterised by an oral tradition of ballads, folktales, myths, plays, poetry, proverbs and prayers (Hockings, 1988; Pilot-Raichoor, 1997; Hockings and Pilot-Raichoor, 1992). The organisation of Badaga society accords to the Dravidian kinship system, to some extent regarded now as a past time of Indian life, like the caste system generally. Prior to Western medicine, the Badagas practised folk medicine based on local health beliefs and treatments such as herbal remedies and spiritualism (Hockings, 1980). In recent decades, the Badagas have experienced substantial change, and alternative ways of thinking and living, amid the country's so-called development and globalisation. A notable means of change, and the focus of this chapter, concerns new forms of social identity and life quality as the Badagas migrate from the rural Nilgiri to cities in search of employment and higher education, a wave of the large-scale rural-to-urban migration and subsequent urbanisation sweeping across India.

The first aim of this chapter is to investigate the social identities of the Badagas, defined here as an individual's sense of self derived from belonging to their ethnic group, and the ways they distinguish themselves and others through perceived group membership with Badagas and non-Badagas—essentially an understanding of who they are and their place in the social world. Social identity is not the same as personal identity—an individual's self-understanding of their own unique and idiosyncratic attributes—as it is a shared identity which involves collectivity and sociality. There has been no empirical investigation of social identity among Badagas, although scholars have speculated on their differences and similarities with other peoples in the Nilgiri and South India, a starting point of the present study. As exemplified above, the Badagas are typically portrayed as a distinct and homogenous caste with fixed criteria such as birthplace, culture, language, locality and so forth. This representation of a fixed and static identity and community, the common sense and popular understanding of the Badagas, can be traced to the colonial era and early literature which reflects a strong positivist stance of straightforward and unproblematic relationships between peoples in the world and their representation, tied up with cultural relativism. The Nilgiri is also stereotyped in the literature as a cultural enclave of more than a dozen tribal groups, including the Badagas, isolated from the lower plains of Coimbatore by steep mountainous escapements and thick blankets of subtropical forest which until recently permitted only brief and sporadic contact with the outside. This perspective, still prevalent in academic writings (e.g. Hockings, 2013; Nielson & Pritchard, 2009), emphasises the antiquity, distinctiveness, and geographical isolation of the Nilgiri and its peoples (Mandelbaum, 1989). Alternatively, a minority of writers have emphasised similarities between the Badagas and others in the Nilgiri and beyond—for example, Dravidian languages, kinship systems, Saivite Hinduism and gift and commodity relationships in previous times—which paints a picture not of a unique and isolated locale but an integral piece of South India (Mandelbaum, 1989). Archaeological evidence also implies an open and accessible Nilgiri since ancient times (Fenicio, 1603; Zagarell, 1997). Another point to consider is the supposed migration of the ancestors of the Badagas to the Nilgiri several centuries ago, a key theme in their oral tradition which retells stories of ancient peoples fleeing the Mysore region and founding the Badaga community (Benbow, 1930; Dulles, 1855; Harkness, 1832; Hockings, 1999, 2013; Ouchterlony, 1868; Shortt, 1868; Thurston, 1909). While the accuracy of oral tradition should be treated with caution, the migration, if it really happened, means the Badagas might retain similarities with the plains folk they left only a few centuries ago.

Authors have also speculated on social identity change in the nineteenth and twentieth centuries amid the social upheaval of British India's societal reform, construction of infrastructure and transportation, demarcation of sovereignty, commercialisation of agriculture, population surveillance, taxes and so forth—a completely new way of life. Indian Civil Service officials settled in the Nilgiri in the 1820s. It later became the summer administrative headquarters and capital of the Madras Presidency and a military base and missionary station (Mandelbaum, 1989). As people in neighbouring areas settled in the Nilgiri for business and employment (Heidemann, 1997), it became a melting pot of cultures and identities. Hockings (1999) believes these changes, concentrated in the newly founded towns in the Nilgiri, initially had minimal influence on the social identity of the Badagas as they continued their way of life as subsistence farmers and exchanged goods and services with other local peoples in gift and commodity relationships. However, they gradually embraced change, for example, intensive cash crop cultivation, employment in local businesses and enrolment of children in schools run by missionaries (Hockings 1999; Mandelbaum 1989). Previous writers have also postulated the capacity of the Badagas to understand themselves as belonging to a cohesive and well-defined group was crucial for coping with the changing circumstances in modernising India (Hockings 1968, 1993). This speculation of social identity change is insightful but only scratches the surface of what it really means to be Badaga, and how such meanings have changed, a shortcoming addressed in this chapter with an empirical investigation of social identity.

The second aim is to explore the quality of life of the Badagas, defined here as their general wellbeing and circumstances which characterise their existence today—being well physically, psychologically and materially—and its linkage with social identity. Studies of the Badagas have focused on their economy and standard of living and paint a bleak picture. Since the late 1990s, the profitability of tea cultivation, the mainstay of the local economy, declined sharply, but operating and overhead costs increased. To reduce production costs to offset lost income, farmers abandoned some agricultural practises which had consequences for tea quality and consumer demand (Neilson & Pritchard, 2009). The annual income of Badaga tea growers decreased 82% between 1998 and 2001 based on a 50% decrease of average green leaf prices from Rs. 12/kg to Rs. 5.95/kg (Neilson & Pritchard, 2009). Reduced incomes and economic hardship impinged on their quality of life. A sizeable proportion of people switched from farming to other professions, as 50,329 tea smallholders were enumerated in the Nilgiri in 2006 compared to 60,389 in 2001 (Neilson & Pritchard, 2009). However, past commentary on their quality of life seems biased. Some writings come across as a nostalgic return to the colonial past, concerned with imperial history and Western culture to speak for the Badagas. An example is the usage of concepts such as 'development', 'modern' and 'success' to portray the colonial era and its influence on quality of life in positive terms. Mandelbaum (1982, p. 1460), for example, believed the Badagas 'flourished' and 'took advantage of' the changes taking place; and Hockings (1999) concluded the Badagas in the 1990s represented a 'successful', 'powerful' and 'wealthy' South Indian community as they had risen from humble beginnings as several hundred refugees, which he attributed to their 'progressive' attitudes of embracing British rule. These expressions, reminiscent of the cultural, economic and political aspirations of the West and its writers, position the way of life in the Nilgiri during British rule as superior, as authors tend to write as if colonialism, and its large-scale cultural diffusion, is what past and present is all about. However, the good life, subjective and culture-bound, does not mean the same for all people, and designations such as 'modern' and 'success' seem to be constructions of academics and not the Badagas. Also, negative aspects of colonialism have been glossed over in earlier writings on the Badagas to portray some kind of path to utopia. While I am not aware of a history of harsh mistreatment of the Nilgiri peoples in British India, which could be the case or an artefact of the literature, it is fair to conclude their way of life and social and natural environment were completely and irreversibly changed forever without their consent. Moreover, the policies of the British Raj were exploitative as the region was ruled with considerable power by relatively small numbers of British, and the longstanding way of life was replaced with capitalism and social inequality (Misra, 1999). However, it is important to put this criticism in to context by pointing out that studies of the Nilgiri began when anthropology was emerging as an academic discipline and derived many of its key notions from colonialism. Previous scholars espoused the conventional thinking of their day when modernisation emphasised an evolutionary trajectory of progress from the so-called 'traditional' (underdeveloped) societies, a short-hand way of referring to the experience of agrarian societies before the impact of the recent West, to 'modern' (industrial) societies, a way of referring to societies after the impact of the West in economic, political, social and technological terms. Discourses on modernity in Indian social science were initially concerned with application of this classical model to India, and the literature on the Nilgiri fits this consensus. However, anthropologists and sociologists have since moved away from neoclassical economics and structural determinism to focus instead on people's experiences and social constructions of reality, and recent scholarship has explored and interrogated the various cultural and social meanings of modernisation, now a highly contested topic in the social sciences (Mathews and Izquierdo, 2010;

Elder-Vass, 2012). Also, previous studies of Badagas emphasised objective quality of life, based on tangible criteria measured by experts (e.g. income), whereas the present study explores subjective quality of life, a more personal evaluation by people of the circumstances in which they live—a reflective appraisal of how life is going which encompasses their beliefs, emotions, feelings, opinions and life experiences and histories, essentially internal perceptions of external conditions (Cummins, 1995, 1996; Diener, 1984; Selin & Davey, 2012; Sirgy et al. 2006). This chapter acknowledges concepts such as social identity and quality of life are not simply a matter of economics and living standards determined only by academics but actively produced by the people under study as constructions and perceptions of reality and social practices important in the present. As there have been no studies of the subjective quality of life of the Badagas, the present study attempts to capture aspects of the good life that matter to them to allow for a better understanding.

In summary, the cultural heritage and current circumstances of the Badagas suggest they might have distinct experiences and understandings of social identity and life quality. Therefore, this chapter examines the human experience of being Badaga in contemporary India to gain an appreciation of the ways people make sense of themselves and their lives. Specifically, it focuses on rural-to-urban migrants in Bangalore and their sense of social identity and life quality in relation to migration and urban living. The study also sheds light on the process of identity change, and linkages between identity and quality of life, justified by an emerging literature on health and wellbeing (Haslam, Jetten, Postmes, & Haslam, 2009; Jetten, Haslam & Haslam, 2012). The migrants had left the Nilgiri—the social context in which they identified as Badaga—and moved to a new environment where they attempted to uphold a sense of autonomy while also becoming competent social members of the city where the supporting structures of their former identity no longer existed, changing notions of what it means to be a member of their caste as they engaged the local and global realities of the twenty-first century.

Method

Location

The study commenced in Bangalore in 2010 and continued with follow-up interviews in 2012 and 2013. Bangalore was chosen as the study location because it is the capital and largest city of Karnataka State, a major destination of rural-to-urban migrants.

Participants and Sampling

A sample of 24 interviewees was selected by convenience and purposive sampling. Sample size was determined by data saturation and ceased when dimensions and gaps in each theme in the thematic analysis had been explicated. The sample consisted of men only, as they represented the vast majority of rural-to-urban migrants encountered by the researcher. Each participant satisfied the following inclusion criteria: (1) identified himself as Badaga, (2) born in the Nilgiri and brought up in an agricultural background, (3) within the age-range 18–65 years, (4) able to converse verbally in English, and (5) gave informed consent. The average age of the sample was 35 years, and half was in the age category of 18–30 years as the majority of migrants were young men. Two-thirds of the sample had completed secondary school, and one-third tertiary education. The participants were employed in the city in a range of occupations in business, civil service, education, engineering and finance.

Data Collection and Analysis

The participants chose the location of their interviews (coffee shops, homes and public places), several hours in duration according to their preferences. To establish empathy and rapport, interviews commenced with an introduction and warm-up discussion, followed by guiding questions as a context for discussion: What is your background and current situation? How do you identify yourself, and how do others identify you? What sorts of things come to mind when you think of being Badaga? How do you see yourself as Badaga and other people in the city as similar or different? What personal and social factors influence you being Badaga? How is your life and quality of life in the city? What aspects of city life do you like and dislike? Interview questions were broached loosely to explore the men's own understandings without overly directing them along predetermined routes. Data were analysed by inductive thematic analysis to identify and sort salient consistencies, reoccurrences and essence-capturing elements in the data (codes), repeated patterns of meaning which captured something important to the overall research questions. Collections of codes with shared characteristics were grouped in core topics (categories) and then linked and integrated (themes) to consolidate meaning and explanation (codes→categories→themes). This coding process was recursive and involved concurrent data collection and analysis and recategorisation of coded data following reflection on emergent patterns. When completed, the analysis furnished a rich picture of the participants' collective experiences, discussed below. The research underwent ethical review and risk assessment in accordance with university research governance procedures. Manual (paper-and-pencil) coding by one coder was utilised to remain close to the data.

Findings

The migrants' accounts can be conceptualised as four broad themes: (a) Departing the Nilgiri: Social Mobility, (b) Living in Bangalore, (c) Being Badaga and (d) Becoming City Badaga: A Journey of Self-Discovery. Below is a description of each theme, which represents a consensus among the interviewees unless described otherwise, exemplified with interview quotes.

Departing the Nilgiri: Social Mobility

All of the men had grown up in the Nilgiri and relocated to Bangalore as adults; some had previously resided in other cities. Reasons for leaving the Nilgiri were discussed. Working in agriculture did not sustain a decent standard of living, and they complained of limited employment opportunities. Jobs were sparse and menial and unskilled, whereas the city offered more choice, especially for graduates, a key reason for their migration as they had sought career and personal development prospects in the city's booming business and financial sectors. Several interviewees were employed in the city by renowned Indian and international companies. Thus, their migration was styled as social mobility. An interviewee summarised his career progression in Bangalore:

> I got a job as a Customer Service Rep in a call centre. Six months later, I was in a training workshop to be a supervisor. After probation, I got promoted to be my team's manager; now, I am a middle manager. I am not stopping here! (Male, 26)

The above quote describes a Badaga man's career progression after he arrived in Bangalore and his ambitions for the future. Such opportunities—promotion from an entry-level to middle-management position and access to a management training programme—were said to be almost non-existent in the Nilgiri.

The interviewees had not encountered major difficulties finding work in Bangalore. They enjoyed a high income, as their monthly earnings ranged 20,000 (recent college graduate) to 100,000 Rupees (senior manager) at the time of the initial interviews in 2010; in comparison, farmers in the Nilgiri typically earned less than 5000. The current situation was compared to the past, as the 1980s and 1990s were labelled the 'The Good Old Days' when agriculture was profitable and the Badagas had a comparatively high standard of living in terms of income level, availability of employment and ease by which they were able to satisfy their needs and wants. Said an interviewee:

> My father graduated from a top university when few of us [Badagas] went to university. He declined a job offer from the city government to return to my grandfather's tea estate. Believe it or not, profits then were much higher than working in Bangalore! Back in his time he made so much money—as much as 10,000 [Rupees] a week—he didn't know what to do with it all! (Male, 22)

The above comment contrasts the interviewee's situation to the past when tea cultivation was profitable. The quote also suggests temporal change in rural-to-urban migration: While he had migrated to Bangalore for economic prosperity, his father, several decades previously, returned to the Nilgiri from the city for the same reason. It also shows rural-to-urban migration among the Badagas is not a recent phenomenon.

The interviewees also discussed positive aspects of life in the Nilgiri. They reasoned the Badagas were relatively well-off compared to many other rural communities in India, especially in states such as Bihar, Madhya Pradesh, Orissa and Uttar Pradesh. Smallholder farmers in other tea-growing communities in India were said to survive only with government hand-outs. Though many Badagas struggled to make ends meet, the vast majority were at least able to satisfy basic needs with sufficient resources for living—food, water, education, healthcare, and housing. Many families consumed home-grown vegetables, and rice was available throughout Tamil Nadu at low prices because of government subsidies, about one Rupee per kilogram at the time of the interviews; and utility bills such as electricity and water were inexpensive. A wide range of low-cost goods were available in nearby shops, markets, and towns. Also, many Badagas were home owners and landowners because they had inherited ancestral land and property. Quality of life in the Nilgiri was also captioned in terms of its beautiful natural scenery, fresh air, multiple sides of weather and abundant nature. The interviewees also described a strong sense of community in the Nilgiri, a feeling that everyone matters to one another—that by being a member of the Badaga community, they were contributing to something worthwhile. They considered themselves to be a big family as they knew and cared about everyone and felt engaged and connected. Being part of this close, caring community was conducive to enjoying life and enabled them to cope when things became difficult; the migrants missed these meaningful social relationships in the city, although they valued the freedom, independence and individualism of urban living.

Some of the men had moved to Bangalore for further and higher education opportunities and stayed in the city after graduation. In their view, the availability and quality of colleges in Bangalore was superior to the Nilgiri and surrounding areas and reputed throughout India. Coimbatore, a city 228 km from the Nilgiri with more than 150 colleges and universities, is another popular choice of Badaga students.

Living in Bangalore

The interviewees painted a picture of contentment with life in Bangalore. Positive talk about the city emphasised employment and career opportunities and convenient living with availability of amenities and products and leisure activities. They were financially independent, and material goods had become important. Disposable incomes and spending power, alongside the availability and diversity of consumer products, had led to their adoption of a consumer culture, a new notion of living characterised by new experiences and sites of consumption, a materialist orientation disconnected from their previous hold on frugality when they lived in the Nilgiri. Though their consumption habits had changed, they also made it clear the Badagas, including themselves, were not adherents of materialism and wealth; a hallmark of being Badaga was a simple way of life and disinterest in materialism. The Badagas in the Nilgiri were described as content and happy because they embraced simple lifestyles and were satisfied with what they had. Conditions in rural villages, although a world apart from the city, were said to be sufficient to uphold satisfaction with life. Their notion of the good life is not something one has, but something who one is, a perspective of looking spiritually inward and outward through contemplation and inner reflection rather than in material surroundings; this perspective was entwined with Hindu beliefs. When asked to clarify the contradiction apparent in this explanation—which is they had adopted a consumer culture in Banglore yet put the Badagas and themselves on a pedestal as detractors of materialism—they interpreted their consumption as different to others in the city, 'Badaga consumerism' underscored by strong views about the ownership of goods as necessities of living rather than symbols of wealth or social status.

There was, however, a downside to life in Bangalore. Cost of living constrained their choices. As exemplified in the comment below, their incomes were sufficient to financially support daily living, as everyday necessities were affordable, but many goods and activities were too expensive. Property prices and rents were expensive, and only three of the interviewees owned an apartment or house; the others rented accommodation, typically a single bedroom in a shared house at a cost of Rs. 5000–10,000 monthly. Even so, all of the interviewees acknowledged their standard of living was higher than in the Nilgiri, and about half of the sample remitted money to their families, typically several thousand Rupees monthly. Despite complaints of affordability, they did not consider themselves in poverty, and none lived in squatter settlements, shantytowns or slums, even though these types of housing existed in Bangalore.

> Things can be cheap, things can be costly. The price tag on imported items will blow your mind. Prices have gone up a lot. My salary is not low but I have to think twice when buying…I don't spend much [money] when with my friends, I just window shop. It's possible to live here cheaply, though…I have just enough to get by. (Male, 19)

Working in the city was challenging with long working hours, high-performance expectations such as meeting targets and deadlines and time-consuming commutes. The interviewees mentioned work-related pressure, burnout, insomnia, relationship issues with colleagues such as rivalry and clashes of personality and the impossibility of a work-life balance. About one-third of the sample said their job was exhausting; they spent all of their time either working or resting from work and had no energy or time for other activities.

At the time of the initial interviewees in 2010, Bangalore's economy was still affected by the global financial crisis, triggered by valuation and liquidity problems in the United States. A recession hit Bangalore in 2009 with financial and job losses. Two of the interviewees had lost their jobs, and several others had reduced salaries, working hours and perks. As a result of the recession, many of the interviewees feared job security and had cancelled or postponed financial plans such as a mortgage application and setting up a business. One man described his unemployment during this time:

> I was an engineer for G.E. It was a good job, but we were laid off at short notice in early 2009. I couldn't find another job for three-months. I tried my best, but few were recruiting. I was in a difficult position. I didn't return to the Nilgiri…I was too ashamed to tell my parents. Thank god my savings covered my rent. Now I work for Rolls Royce; it's okay, but not as good as before. (Male, 28)

Other challenges were described as typical frustrations of city life: inadequate services such as bad road conditions, frequent electricity outages, water shortages, construction work and noise, pollution, traffic jams, and limited greenery. Economic and population growth had put considerable pressure on urban infrastructure and resources. These issues impinged on the interviewees' enjoyment and quality of life, as shown in the complaint below, but were generally regarded as minor inconveniences:

> The power blacks out a few times a day. We've been without power for an hour today. It's a short time, but we can't do many things. I sometimes work from home, and can't do my work. My wife cannot prepare dinner. We can't even go out because the shops are left high and dry. (Male, 42)

Discrimination and inequality were not perceived to be major problems in Bangalore, and the migrants considered themselves to be socially accepted by others. Also, they held favourable attitudes of Bangaloreans and praised their acceptance of difference and cultural diversity.

Being Badaga

The interviewees discussed the meanings of being Badaga. It was conveyed as the essence of who they were and how they understood themselves and others, ultimately how they made their way through life. In this way, being Badaga was described as both an inner feeling of existing, thinking and state of mind, which imbued their lives with meaning and capacity to enjoy and live life, and an outward feeling of engaging with the world at large, as illustrated in the quotes below. Distinct lines ran between 'Badaga' and 'non-Badaga'. Being a native of the Nilgiri and belonging to the Badaga community were important, as they saw themselves as part of a collective—'the Badagas'. From this perspective, being Badaga was ascribed at birth, in virtue of being born in the community in the Nilgiri, and the inteviewees expressed a strong emotional accord with their 'motherland'. This connection with the Badaga community remained strong and central despite their residence in the city.

> I am a Badaga, and always will be a Badaga by heart. It's my true character, deep in the depths of my soul. It comes from God, my ancestors, my people. Us Badagas are a big family…and we are all on the same page, so-to-speak. (Male, 37)

> I love being a Badaga, it's really who I am…my mind, my thoughts, my essence, my life. But I want to state categorically that I am also proud [to be a Badaga] because I was born there [in the Nilgiri], it's my motherland, a special place where we are the same and love each other. (Male, 31)

Family was important to their understanding of identity and extended beyond immediate family members to include villagers and ancestors. Living the good life hinged on the collective (family, village, community), and they talked about 'collective happiness', construed as the general mood of the Badagas, and a collaboration among families and friends in which everyone worked together for the common good, a shared and combined sense of the wellbeing of the community as a whole. Individual happiness was said to stem from this social footing, as to be happy was grounded in the happiness of others; similarly, life's problems for an individual were interpreted as problems for the family and community. However, in Bangalore, individual autonomy—greater personal freedom to pursue one's own interests, goals and choice of lifestyle—now characterised their lives, as they tended to put themselves first, in contrast to their former lifestyles in the Nilgiri which were more cooperative and interdependent with others around them. The interviewees regretted separation from family and friends while in Bangalore, although they were able to visit the Nilgiri regularly, and trips were planned to coincide with family events and days of festivity.

Morals and principles were also important. 'Doing the right thing' was said to be the guiding principle of every Badaga, defined in the interviews as 'doing one's duty of being good', 'honesty and truthfulness', 'meeting responsibilities', 'friendliness and hospitality', 'going above and beyond the call of duty' and 'accountability to oneself', rules of thumb for how they lived. This Badaga philosophy of life imbued direction for the choices they made, and satisfaction with life, linked to doing good and being at peace with oneself.

Fluency in Badagu was put forward as another building block of being Badaga. As the principal means of communication in homes and villages, the language differentiated the Badagas and non-Badagas, enabled true expression of inner feelings and thoughts and nurtured common and social understanding, necessary for full participation in their culture and society. However, the Badagas are also literate in Tamil, and in Bangalore the interviewees only used English as the language of daily and work life. Whereas Badagu was regarded as the tool of communication among Badagas and participation in events such as ceremonies and festivals, English and Tamil served interaction with non-Badagas and life outside the community in the Nilgiri.

They elaborated on their experiences of being Badaga in Bangalore. Rural-to-urban migration and urban living were conveyed as a vehicle of personal growth. They still maintained a resolute foothold with the Nilgiri, but also had developed a sense of belongingness in the city, a place which had gradually become much more personal. From this perspective, they articulated identity as flexible and changing, as concurrent connections with both rural and urban had given rise to what some of the interviewees referred to as 'City Badaga', a collective of like-minded individuals with similarities in their backgrounds, changed circumstances, modes of doing and association with urban territory, grounded on assimilation of urban culture and lifestyle. Further discussions about the meanings of City Badaga revealed it was a minority subgroup with similarities and distinctions to the Badagas in the Nilgiri and non-Badagas in Bangalore; the migrants considered themselves subtly different to the Badagas in the Nilgiri by having an understanding of the customs, social norms, and world views of both rural and urban, and they considered themselves to be competent to navigate and maintain their lives and relationships in both without having to choose between them. Thus, being City Badaga was viewed positively as an enriched understanding of the world.

In Bangalore, they put on their City Badaga hat to embrace urban norms and way of life; in the Nilgiri, however, it was juxtaposed with the 'Nilgiri Badaga' identity commitment, a way of doing aligned more with the rural community and its social norms. Thus, identity flexibility was also explained as a strategy of self-presentation to others through regulating the type of person they thought they needed to be in each social context to address the relevant expectations and needs of others. Identity as City Badaga was also objectified in terms of material distinctions, notably geographical distance between Bangalore and the Nilgiri, alongside differential access to income and products and services. Below is an example of an interviewee who worked as a financial advisor in Bangalore that begins with a description of his City Badaga identity, which emphasised his urban life, profession and workplace, and then his Nilgiri Badaga identity when he visited the Nilgiri.

> I'm a City Badaga here all of my waking time, seven days a week, morning to night. My job is a financial advisor. I wear this suit, this name tag, and act like I am one! Most people just see me as another city guy, my clients just see me as 'the financial advisor'. But when I return to the Nilgiris, I put on my Badaga clothes, speak Badagu, and say the things they want to hear, do the things they expect. I return to my old ways, completely different to here. (Male, 28)

Although both identities were conveyed as either-or terms (either City Badaga or Nilgiri Badaga), differences between them were subtle. They were unified by similarities more than divided by differences, and continuities between Bangalore and the Nilgiri were also emphasised. This enabled adaption to city life and also legitamised the new identity coming to the fore, as reflected in the following comment:

> There is no written manifesto which tells us what we should do or believe in. Yes, we [City Badaga] have our quirks, our points of view, but I don't think we do things that unusually. You know, most of us Indians are Hindus, not much difference, just a little. Actually, this helped me to settle-in. (Male, 31)

But the differences, although subtle, were important. Being City Badaga meant the shedding of some long-standing practices. In Bangalore they continued morning prayers and listened to Badaga songs and music. Also, they returned to the Nilgiri as often as possible to visit family and participate in community events. However, most customs could not be performed easily, as the Badaga way of life was said to be interlocked with villages, society and the totality of the Nilgiri. For example, homes and villages have shrines and clearly demarcated places of worship, and religious events involve the entire family and community. Limited leisure time hindered the practice of time-consuming traditions such as preparation of Badaga dishes, unsuitable for their fast-paced city lifestyles. Discontinuing the Badaga precedent was described as a sense of loss, accompanied by feelings of anxiety, guilt and shame, as they regretted not being able to participate more often in Badaga customs and ceremonies. But even though they desired to uphold traditions considered important to being Badaga, they also made an effort to master the protocol necessary for successful living in the city, and residence in Bangalore enabled them to experiment with new experiences, challenge aspects of their former lives unsuitable in the city and sift through the past to uncover new ways of being in the present:

> I love living as a Badaga, but I also have to match Bangalore. Let me give you an example. Let's say you got a job here, in this coffee shop. As an employee, your opinions should match those of your company. Your work duties should be in line too, say to meet your targets. If not, you will be fired. It's either kill or be killed. Yes, you can have your own ways, but you have to do what you have to do. It's the same as my life here. You need to give-and-take to get on in life. (Male, 50)

Becoming City Badaga: A Journey of Self-Discovery

Becoming City Badaga was articulated as an ongoing process of personal growth, a new way of living and making sense of themselves and the world, and just as much about exploring awareness of who one is as it was about acquainting with the propositions of urban culture. It did not take place as a coercive effort to change but as a subtle shifting perspective of oneself. The process began before they had arrived in Bangalore by bringing into awareness that which was on the horizon, followed by the migration and exploration of the new environment by testing for comfort and safety, participating in city life, dealing with surprises they encountered and then honing life skills during the initial months in Bangalore. They gradually took hold of their changing way of being—a realisation that they were living and thinking in different ways to survive and succeed—as they moved from feeling out of place in the city to feeling comfortable. Gradually, the self, as they saw it, became enriched with a new awareness of oneself through changing relations with society, not a replacement of old with new but a reframing of previous experiences with novel perspectives, a new understanding of life; and, as they faced the reality of who they were and what they were becoming, they came to acknowledge and accept themselves as City Badaga.

As the city and its peoples gained a prominent hold, the migrants valued the chance to dig deeply in to their inner selves by questioning how they understood and went about life. Thus, becoming City Badaga was described as a journey through different perspectives of self-understanding—a journey of self-discovery that had changed their view of themselves and the world—and out of this came the emergence of a new sense of self invested in both their past and present. As fully fledged City Badaga, they felt grounded on a new understanding of life and were proud of achieving something valuable, not only new skills and confidence but an entirely new way of being. Therefore, the boundary between Nilgiri Badaga and City Badaga was constructed and surmounted by the interviewees as a process of changing self-definition as Badaga, an interface of reflection and negotiation with oneself in different social contexts:

> Man, I used to be a sleepwalker…on autopilot. Not good, uh? I shifted to B'lore, I was asking myself why I do things this way or that way. The more I understood, the more I got on with guys here. We are all from different places. What's made me misty-eyed is how my different thinking styles came together. The 'me' that has always been me is still there, but I have improved, I feel different, I feel like a new man. (Male, 25)

However, the interviewees mentioned challenges and frustrations when adjusting to the city. As the unfamiliar in Bangalore became familiar, they were in a situation of not being able to go back to their former selves, but also unsure of the outcome of going forward, as if one foot was on the gas pedal and another on the brakes. They realised becoming City Badaga was irreversible, which played on their conscience as they toyed with its moral convictions, even though they had no choice as non-involvement in the city was not an option. However, these concerns turned out to be unfounded, as only a few of the men had experienced a major struggle to come to terms with the change, partly because they maintained a foothold with their residual culture such as regular trips to the Nilgiri and socialising with other Badagas in Bangalore, and also because they came to see the new identity not as a threat but as normative, as if to say 'city living is the thing to do'. Moreover, the move to Bangalore was for good reasons, and their time in Bangalore was cherished as a chance to better themselves and experience new situations which counterbalanced the negative aspects.

The key to being comfortable with oneself in Bangalore was openness to new experiences and change. It was important to accept and relish different ways of being and living, even when they did not fully agree with them, and to work around difficulties which meant making compromises and reaching a common ground. Connecting with other Badagas in the city was said to be important for coping successfully with the transition from rural to urban. Each interviewee had a small circle of close Badaga friends in Bangalore and nearby cities who cared about them and whose company they enjoyed. Badagas who understood and related to their predicament, and whom the interviewees could also understand, afforded a sense of emotional comfort and reassurance, as well as support for being City Badaga, a shared sense of amity and belonging which validated it as a legitimate existence. Family support and reassurance was also important, interpreted as permission to do whatever was needed to make a life for themselves in the city. Whereas most interviewees had supportive family members, some were more traditional minded and indifferent to the demands imposed by modern living, interpreted by the interviewees as forbiddenness to fully partake in urban life. About a fifth of the interviewees had encountered hostility and negativity from parents or family members concerning some aspect of their new lives in the city. They criticised the older generation for a contradiction in their wants: On the one hand, they wanted to see their children succeed, but they also wanted things to remain the same. The quote below, for example, reveals a mismatch between the expectations and interests of an interviewee and his parents. Conservatism by family and others put the interviewees at the centre of a tug-of-war between trying to satisfy the expectations of both family and the city, and therefore Nilgiri Badaga and City Badaga as alternative identity commitments were considered as a way to balance these opposites, although it did not solve every issue.

> I love my family to pieces. But when I told them I wanted to study fashion design, they persuaded me to do something else. To please my father, I am doing a business course. But I really love fashion. Life there is simple and closed...my family is not in the 'real world'... they just don't understand...geez, my family has really screwed me up! (Male, 18)

They were also concerned the Badaga community in the Nilgiri might label them as over identified with the outside. Some elders were described as conservative and fierce defenders of the status quo by criticising modernity as a destabiliser of tradition. Some of the interviewees even worried they might be excluded from the Badagas at large, relegated to the fringe of society through stigmatisation and marginalisation, especially if they distanced themselves permanently from traditional beliefs and practices. Identity flexibility, which helped to maintain and showcase their continuing affiliation with the Nilgiri and desire to uphold its way of life, buffered this threat. However, rather than an illusion of harmony, they came to accept irreconcilable differences which involved treading a fine line. The interviewees referred to only a possible outcome and not an experience, as none of the men had experienced hostility or marginalisation as a result of their migration, although actual examples of moral condemnation and social exclusion by the community were recalled to support their concerns. A notable example was personal experiences of intercaste marriage among family and friends, a major conflict between tradition and modern. Badaga marriage practises, grounded in Hinduism, involve an elaborate set of religious customs, including substantive consultation with family and elders, that forbid a marriage of different castes which is taken to mean caste and spiritual contamination out of tune with the workings of Karma (the pollution impurity of intercaste marriage is thought to cause permanent misfortune and trouble for the bride and groom and their families for future generations). The interviewees described examples of intercaste marriage among family and friends, and the emotional toll:

> I have seen it with my own eyes. My brother married a Tamil [women] he met at work in Chennai. Folks in our village did not agree to it. Why? Because the marriage is a union joining us [Badagas] and them [other caste]. When my brother and his wife visit [the Nilgiri], they give him them the 'cold shoulder'. My parents have a tough time dealing with the gossip; when neighbours visit, it's the first thing they talk about, again and again. He asks for my help. But what can I do?". (Male, 36)

Discussion

The key finding of the study concerns the ways the Badagas made sense of identity. When the interviewees discussed the meanings of their identities, they said it was important to have been born in the Badaga community in the Nilgiri and to have Badaga ancestry. Speaking Badagu was regarded as vital to being Badaga, although its popularity was declining, as were folk beliefs and ideals which imbued direction for how people lived. Also, the meaning of 'Badaga' evoked feelings of pride, worthiness, and admiration of the efforts and achievements of ordinary men and women, yet humbled by the perceived failures of the Badagas. A thread tying these strands was a profound personal sense of being Badaga, the fundamental basis of their existence. However, on this common background rested diversity, as Badaga identities were in a state of flux. In an India more mobile and connected than ever before, the migrants questioned who they were, how they lived and what kinds of social groups they belonged to; and, in the midst of these changes, new forms of identity and sociality emerged. The migrants thought of themselves concurrently as Badagas and city residents, a sense of identity rooted on both an original and new social context, a changing notion of what it meant to be a member of their caste as they engaged novel milieu in contemporary India.

Another important finding was flexibility in the meaning and expression of Badaganess. In Bangalore, the rural-to-urban migrants identified as City Badaga, a social identity commitment and collective of people that embraced urban norms and way of life and shared experiences and similarities in their changed circumstances, an alternative to both the Badagas in the Nilgiri and Bangaloreans in the city. However, in the Nilgiri they regarded themselves as Nilgiri Badaga, a way of doing aligned more with the rural community and its norms. City Badaga and Nilgiri Badaga as identities and social groups constructed by the migrants were based on perceptions of the ideal person in Bangalore and the Nilgiri respectively, whereby urban and rural cultures and lifestyles were turned into a site of differentiation. However, rather than making a binary choice of identifying solely with either identity, which would have led to problematic trajectories in family relationships in the Nilgiri or adjustment to the city, the migrants engaged in identity flexibility to express an appropriate identity in either rural or urban context. While City Badaga and Nilgiri Badaga were constructed by the interviewees as opposites, based on beliefs about the sort of person one is and should be in Bangalore or the Nilgiri respectively, they were actually mutually constitutive, and therefore, it is important not to imply a false dichotomy that only plays out distinctiveness. For example, each identity orientation was acted out by the same person as a negotiation with his social context, the type of Badaga they thought they needed to be to fit in and to uphold social accord. Also, they professed fairly positive views of both identities and both heritage and host cultures rather than regarding one as superior or inferior, as being Badaga—City Badaga or Nilgiri Badaga—was a positive and powerful sense of belonging and connection. That identity flexibility rested on the continuity of existing identity elements compatible with new ones honed in the new setting, the migrants managed to maintain a strong sense of being Badaga while concurrently adjusting to and incorporating features of urban life, and so it was both persistent and changeable. While the Badagas who went to the city underwent cultural change, the all-encompassing Badaganess remained. Continuity was also evidenced by the notion that the signifier 'Badaga' alone, whatever its meaning, was sufficient to differentiate themselves and others.

The second aim of the chapter is to explore the quality of life of the Badagas. The interviewees in Bangalore revealed a rich array of information about their general wellbeing, a timely update as previous research was completed in the 1990s (Hockings, 1999, 2013). Importantly, the findings shed light on the meaning and key ingredients of the good life from the Badaga perspective interwoven into their unique cultural and historical background. At the core was self-understanding of being Badaga which imbued the capacity to enjoy and make their way through life. Also, the good life was embedded in the social: Meaningful social relationships with others, especially family and community, a key ingredient of a fulfilling and satisfying life. They emphasised 'collective happiness', a shared and combined sense of the wellbeing of the Badagas as a whole and the general mood of the community. The Badagas in the Nilgiri were also regarded as a content community because they were satisfied with simple lifestyles. Another major cord of the good life was a relationship with God and Hinduism, notably doing good in life according to morals and desirable ways of living, and set on the concept of Karma, as they believed a life of contentment and peace fitted into place for those who genuinely respected others and did good deeds. From this perspective, happiness was interpreted as something who one is rather than something one has, looking spiritually inward and outward through contemplation and reflection rather than in material surroundings regarded as illusionary and transient.

Unfortunately, a salient theme in the interviews was a negative quality of life in the Nilgiri which centred on the low profitability of agriculture. At the time of the study, Badaga farmers barely made enough money to survive, and some tea gardens were financially unviable; their livelihoods were characterised as low incomes and living standards, debt, unemployment, limited opportunities and out-migration to nearby cities. The interviewees' interpretation of quality of life in the Nilgiri involved temporal comparison with the 1990s when employment and high returns from tea cultivation supported a comparatively higher income and standard of living; and social comparison with rural peoples in other states perceived to be worse off, as well as socioeconomic inequalities between the Nilgiri and urban areas. However, these comparisons seem simple considering the wide range of relative standards past and present, and therefore a more thorough comparison is needed in follow-up research (Albert 1977; Diener and Biswas-Diener 2002; Diener and Lucas 2000; Diener, Lucas, Oishi, & Suh, 2002; Festinger 1954; Michalos 1985; Tajfel 1978). Regarding quality of life in Bangalore, the migrants painted a picture of contentment—particularly with employment, income, convenient living and access to education—grounded on notions of social mobility and personal growth, albiet balanced with a downside to city life such as cost of living, challenging work conditions, job insecurity and separation from family and friends. The wellbeing of the migrants did not appear to be compromised by any major issue; no tension with Bangaloreans was apparent, and there was no indication City Badaga was devalued by its members or others.

The research also explored the intersection of migration, social identity and quality of life. Migration and city residence were sometimes emotionally challenging, especially when the men relocated and adjusted to the new environment and changing perspectives of self, as they felt torn between the Nilgiri and Bangalore. However, only a minority experienced a major struggle, and their experiences of negativity are perhaps not surprising considering their sense of social identity changed, as it is well documented the loss of the familiar can be challenging.

Judging from the migrants' relatively healthy adjustment to the city, it could be argued identity flexibility served them well as a novel avenue to express autonomy in the city while maintaining connectedness to family and native culture in the Nilgiri, a buffer of potential hostility and negativity, although doing so was a careful balancing act and not risk-free. Indeed, rural-to-urban migration and subsequent identity change were viewed positively as a vehicle of personal transformation, a changed view of self and others which came out of experimenting with their Badaganess and new ways of thinking and making sense of themselves. Also, the novel identity affiliation with the city nurtured friendship among the migrants to support and be involved with each other, a common space they occupied as Badagas outside the Nilgiri. This was evident in the identity-promoting activities of the City Badagas such as friendship networks, crucial for people marginalised in the city such as the interviewees who experienced difficulties connecting with Badagas. Membership of the City Badaga group also reassured the migrants to experiment with the new ways of being in the city and therefore validated the legitimacy of their new identity. These linkages concur with previous research in a number of academic disciplines which position social identity as central to health and wellbeing, although the dynamics are complex and not elaborated here (Jetten, Haslam & Haslam, 2012). That the migrants reported enriching experiences of identity flexibility concurs with portrayals in the literature of identity change as a necessary cultural innovation for people to live together in difference in a globalised world (Ang, 2001). These findings are also a fertile ground for developing theoretical linkages of how identities are collectively reconstructed and contested. The notion of identity as malleable and not immutable is now widely accepted in the social sciences, yet the mechanisms through which it is shaped, especially among minority ethnic groups, is unclear, and the present study is a glimpse of the contextual determinants and specific processes of new identifications.

In conclusion, there is little doubt the Badagas are living in momentous times. Migration to urban areas, grounded on broader transformation of India, has shaped multifaceted changes to Badaga culture and society. At an empirical level, the study unpacked the ways the rural-to-urban migrants negotiated their Badaganess while navigating the realities of inevitable change taking place in society, and the circumstances in which they lived. At a theoretical level, however, it deconstructs and redefines the notion of 'Badaga' portrayed in the anthropological literature. The discovery of identity flexibility among the Badagas—documented for the first time in this chapter—dispels the orthodox standpoints in the literature of the Badagas as a homogeneous, spatially bound and static caste of more than 160,000 (Hockings, 2013) and of the Nilgiri as an isolated cultural enclave of indigenous peoples, characterised by stereotyped descriptions (Hockings, 1999; Mandelbaum 1989; Nielson & Pritchard, 2009). Instead, the present study shows identity among Badagas was varied and thoroughly in flux with the evolving local and global realities of the twenty-first century which elicited fundamental changes in its meaning and expression, not only ways of living and social mobility but alternative notions of self-understanding. In other words, the label 'Badaga' is fixed in name only, as it seems to be primarily a process of being and becoming, open to negotiation with the moment and context, and an expression of human experience in the many and varied ways it is lived—and not a fixed entity reduced to simple criteria. The significance of these findings is perhaps dampened by the stubbornness in the literature of the prevailing yet simplistic definition of the Badagas based on criteria such as birthplace, culture, locality, language and so forth—the popular understanding of the group as people who hail from a particular region of India, speak a particular language and behave a particular way. This simple representation and perpetuation of a rigid Badaga identity and community can be traced back to the colonial and early literature and its strong positivist stance of straightforward and unproblematic understandings of the world, tied up with cultural relativism, essentially an artefact of the othering process which evolved in the discourse of early foreign writers and that became inscribed as the standard identity, even by the Badagas themselves. This chapter's findings show identification as Badaga transcends the old Euro-American stereotype in the literature, a revisionist narrative of the former homogenisation approach. It should also be noted this chapter breaks new ground in the literature by locating social identity construction in a rich background and history which goes beyond the realm of experimental and quantitative laboratory-based designs which dominate social identity research.

While this chapter relates specifically to the Badagas, it also constructs a window through which to understand other minority peoples, and the extent to which change increasingly permeates understandings of self, a more intimate and complete understanding of the impact of India's social and economic transformation. The Badagas played an active role in unpacking the representations around which they organised identity and quality of life, a more personal evaluation of life than previous research which echoed the views of academics and their objective and stereotypical categories of description. The point here is the conditions of the Badagas, and what improvements are needed, if any, depend in part on what they think and not only the views of academics in previous research which emphasised objective aspects of life quality, notably economy and standard of living. Existing commentary on India's rise tends to concern economics and living standards while overlooking people's lived experiences, a weakness addressed in this chapter. Taking this a step further, the issue of what it means to be Badaga is ultimately about being Indian—City Badaga as a localised 'Indianness'—and how it is constantly in flux, a pertinent concern at the forefront of debate about the future, not only in India but the world at large. That City Badaga can be construed as part of a new Indianness shaped at the local level, it serves as a starting point for understanding other peoples, and focuses attention on the fact that in India today people are adopting flexible identities to survive and thrive. Finally, it is important to note the study's findings have limitations. As only one sample was interviewed in Bangalore, and only educated men, it does not represent all Badagas in urban areas. Alternative samples of interviewees (for instance, without a college education, and workers in low-paying jobs in factories, hotels, restaurants and shops) might reveal different findings, probably a multiplicity of identity flexibilities. Also, as migrants tend to represent a select group of people that leave their native place voluntarily to pursue opportunities in a new society, it is not certain the findings will generalise to nonmigrants in the Nilgiri.

References

Albert, S. (1977). Temporal comparison theory. *Psychological Review, 84*(6), 485–503.

Alexander, C., & Knight, G. (1971). Situated identities and social psychological experimentation. *Sociometry, 34*(1), 65–82.

Ang, I. (2001). *On not speaking Chinese: Living between Asia and the West.* London: Routledge.

Benbow, J. (1930). *The Badagas—beliefs and customs.* Bangalore: United Theological College.

Burke, P. (1991). Identity processes and social stress. *American Sociological Review, 56*(6), 836–849.

Cooley, C. H. (1902). *Human nature and the social order.* New York: Charles Scribner's Sons.

Cummins, R. A. (1995). On the trail of the gold standard for subjective well-being. *Social Indicators Research, 35*(2), 179–200.

Cummins, R. A. (1996). The domains of life satisfaction: An attempt to order chaos. *Social Indicators Research, 38*(3), 303–328.

Diener, E. (1984). Subjective well-being. *Psychological Bulletin, 95*(3), 542–575.

Diener, E., & Biswas-Diener, R. (2002). Will money increase subjective well-being? A literature review and guide to needed research. *Social Indicators Research, 57*, 119–169.

Diener, E., & Lucas, R. (2000). Explaining differences in societal levels of happiness: Relative standards, need fulfillment, culture, and evaluation theory. *Journal of Happiness Studies, 1*(1), 41–78.

Diener, E., Lucas, R. E., Oishi, S., & Suh, E. M. (2002). Looking up and looking down: Weighting good and bad information in life satisfaction judgments. *Personality and Social Psychology Bulletin, 28*(4), 437–445.

Dulles, J. W. (1855). *Life in India; or, Madras, the Neilgherries, and Calcutta.* Philadelphia: American Sunday-School Union.

Emeneau, M. (1938). Toda culture thirty-five years after: An acculturation study. *Annals of the Bhandarkar Oriental Research Institute, 19*(2), 101–121.

Elder-Vass, D. (2012). Towards a realist social constructionism. *Sociologia Problemas E Práticas, 70*, 9–24.

Fenicio, G. (1603). [Letter] dated 1 April, 1603. Missão de Sodramala [sic]; trans. by A. de Alberti in Rivers 1906 (pp. 719–730).

Festinger, L. (1954). A theory of social comparison processes. *Human Relations, 7*, 117–140.

Harkness, H. (1832). *A description of a singular aboriginal race inhabiting the summit of the Neilgherry Hills, or Blue Mountains of Coimbatoor, in the southern peninsula of India.* London: Smith, Elder and Company.

Haslam, S. A., Jetten, J., Postmes, T., & Haslam, C. (2009). Social identity, health and well-being: An emerging agenda for applied psychology. *Applied Psychology. An International Review, 58*(1), 1–23.

Heidemann, F. (1997). Immigrant labourers and local networks in the Nilgiri. In P. Hockings (Ed.), *Blue mountains revisited: Cultural studies on the Nilgiri Hills* (pp. 148–163). Delhi: Oxford University Press.

Heider, F. (1946). Attitudes and cognitive organization. *The Journal of Psychology, 21*(1), 107–112.

Heise, D. R. (1979). *Understanding events: Affect and the construction of social action.* Cambridge, UK: Cambridge University Press.

Hockings, P. (1968). Identity in complex societies: Are the Badagas caste or tribe? *Journal of African and Asian Studies, 2*, 29–35.

Hockings, P. (1980). *Sex and disease in a mountain community.* New Delhi: Vikas Publishing House.

Hockings, P. (1988). *Counsel from the ancients: A study of Badaga proverbs, prayers, omens and curses.* Berlin: Mouton de Gruyter.

Hockings, P. (1989). *Blue mountains: The ethnography and biogeography of a South Indian region.* Delhi: Oxford University Press.

Hockings, P. (1993). Ethnic identity in a complex society: The Badaga case. *Bulletin of the National Museum of Ethnology, 18*(2), 347–364.
Hockings, P. (1999). *Kindreds of the earth: Badaga household structure and demography*. New Delhi: SAGE Publications.
Hockings, P. (2008). All aboard the Nilgiri express! – sustained links between anthropology and a single Indian district. *History and Anthropology, 19*(1), 1–16.
Hockings, P. (2013). *So long a Saga: Four centuries of Badaga social history*. New Delhi: Manohar.
Hockings, P., & Pilot-Raichoor, C. (1992). *A Badaga-English dictionary*. Berlin: Mouton de Gruyter.
Jetten, J., Haslam, C., & Haslam, S. A. (Eds.). (2012). *The social cure: Identity, health and well-being*. London: Psychology Press.
Mandelbaum, D. (1941). Culture change among the Nilgiri tribes. *American Anthropologist, 43*(1), 19–26.
Mandelbaum, D. (1982). The Nilgiris as a region. *Economic and Political Weekly, 17*(36), 1459–1467.
Mandelbaum, D. (1989). The Nilgiris as a region. In P. Hockings (Ed.), *Blue mountains: The ethnography and biogeography of a South Indian Region* (pp. 1–19). Delhi: Oxford University Press.
McCall, G. J., & Simmons, J. L. (1966). *Identities and interactions*. New York: Free Press.
Mead, G. H. (1934). *Mind, self, and society from the standpoint of a social behaviorist*. Chicago: University of Chicago Press.
Mathews, G., & Izquierdo, C. (2010). *Pursuits of happiness: Well-Being in anthropological perspective*. New York: Berghahn Books.
Melucci, A. (1989). *Nomads of the present: Social movements and individual needs in contemporary society*. Philadelphia: Temple University Press.
Michalos, A. (1985). Multiple discrepancies theory (MDT). *Social Indicators Research, 16*(4), 347–413.
Misra, P. K. (1999). The Badaga way of life. *The Hindu*. 14/12/99.
Nagel, J. (1995). *American Indian ethnic renewal: Red power and the resurgence of identity and culture*. Oxford: Oxford University Press.
Neilson, J., & Pritchard, B. (2009). *Value chain struggles: Institutions and governance in the plantation districts of South India*. Chichester: Wiley-Blackwell.
Ouchterlony, J. (1868). *Geographical and statistical memoir of a survey of the Neilgherry Mountains*. Madras: Higginbotham.
Pilot-Raichoor, C. (1997). Badaga and its relations with neighbouring language. In P. Hockings (Ed.), *Blue mountains revisited: Cultural studies on the Nilgiri Hills* (pp. 136–147). Delhi: Oxford University Press.
Pilot-Raichoor, C., & Hockings, P. (1992). *A Badaga-English dictionary*. Berlin: Mouton de Gruyter.
Pilot-Raichoor, C. (1997). Badaga and its relations with neighbouring languages. In P. Hockings (Ed.), *Blue mountains revisited: Cultural studies on the Nilgiri Hills* (pp. 136–147). Delhi: Oxford University Press.
Prentice, D. A., Miller, D. T., & Lightdale, J. R. (1994). Asymmetries in attachments to groups and to their members: Distinguishing between common-identity and common-bond groups. *Personality and Social Psychology Bulletin, 20*(5), 484–493.
Rivers, W. H. R. (1906). *The Todas*. London: Macmillan and Co..
Selin, H., & Davey, G. (2012). *Happiness across cultures: Views of happiness and quality of life in Non-western cultures*. New York: Springer.
Sirgy, M., Michalos, A., Ferriss, A., Easterlin, R., Patrick, D., & Pavot, W. (2006). The quality-of-life (QOL) research movement: Past, present, and future. *Social Indicators Research, 76*(3), 343–466.
Shortt, J. (1868). *An account of the tribes on the Neilgherries*. Madras: Higginbotham & Co..
Stryker, S. (1968). Identity salience and role performance: The relevance of symbolic interaction theory for family research. *Journal of Marriage and the Family, 30*, 558–564.

Stryker, S. (1980). *Symbolic interactionism: A social structural version*. Menlo Park, CA: Benjamin Cummings.

Tajfel, H. (Ed.). (1978). *Differentiation between social groups: Studies in the social psychology of intergroup relations*. London: Academic Press.

Tajfel, H., & Turner, J. C. (1979). An integrative theory of intergroup conflict. In W. Austin & S. Worchel (Eds.), *The social psychology of intergroup relations* (pp. 33–47). Monterey, CA: Brooks Cole.

Taylor, V., & Whittier, N. (1999). Collective identity in social movement communities: Lesbian feminist mobilization. In J. Freeman & V. Johnson (Eds.), *Waves of protest: Social movements since the sixties* (pp. 169–194). Lanham: Rowman & Littlefield.

Thoits, P. A. (1983). Multiple identities and psychological well-being: A reformulation and test of the social isolation hypothesis. *American Sociological Review, 48*(2), 174–187.

Thurston, E. (1909). *Castes and tribes of southern India*. Madras: Madras Government Press.

Turner, J. C., Hogg, M. A., Oakes, P. J., Reicher, S. D., & Wetherell, M. S. (1987). *Rediscovering the social group: A self-categorization theory*. Oxford: Blackwell.

Turner, J. C., Oakes, P. J., Haslam, S. A., & McGarty, C. (1994). Self and collective: Cognition and social context. *Personality and Social Psychology Bulletin, 20*, 454–463.

Zagarell, A. (1997). The megalithic graves of the Nilgiri Hills and the Moyar ditch. In P. Hockings (Ed.), *Blue mountains revisited: Cultural studies on the Nilgiri Hills* (pp. 23–73). Delhi: Oxford University Press.

Chapter 9
The Concurrent Paths of Parental Identity and Child Development

Maria P. Fracasso

I can still remember the freedom of coming and going as I pleased, sleeping soundly and uninterruptedly, and buying whatever was in my budget that caught my fancy. I was a carefree, yet determined woman with a successful career, a foundation in my religious faith, and surrounded by trusted and reliable friends. Although my identity in career, faith, and friendships remained, my relaxed identity changed when I became a parent. Twenty years ago, I gave birth to an incredible baby girl, and 2 years later, her amazing brother arrived. I had accepted a new, lifelong commitment with little information about what to do, how to do it, and, most importantly, what was to become of me as an adult.

I learned very quickly that once an individual has a child, life is never the same and one's perspective on life changes in immeasurable ways. I was now a mother, and I would be a mother forever. As a mother, I assumed a new identity with unique roles and responsibilities—having children and being their mother changed who I was forever. Most importantly, I noticed my focus shifted from me to my children. I started to defer many of my own needs (for privacy and freedom) and desires (for sleep and new clothes) to the needs of my children.

What I found to be most challenging as a parent was adjusting to the fluctuations in my identity as my children moved through their life stages—from toddlers to young children, to teenagers, and to young adults. I appreciate now that my identity as a parent is quite complex in that it includes many diverse components such as caretaker, provider, teacher, and mentor, with each varying in emphasis throughout the course of my children's lives. It has been a journey for me as a parent to work hard at each stage by setting a good example—balancing the type of parent I wanted to be with the type of parent I should be—while being sensitive to their needs and making sure they became mature, strong, healthy adults. I can say without hesitation

M.P. Fracasso (✉)
Psychology Department, Towson University,
8000 York Rd., Towson, Baltimore County, MD 21252, USA
e-mail: fracasso@towson.edu

J.D. Sinnott (ed.), *Identity Flexibility During Adulthood*,
DOI 10.1007/978-3-319-55658-1_9

that becoming a parent is by far the most difficult, yet most rewarding, identity I have ever chosen in my life.

Parental Identity

Identity is central to how one perceives the world and how one is perceived. Therefore, the label of parent that is given to individuals (or is taken) has a major effect on their consciousness. Historically, identity development theory and research has focused on the period of adolescence. In this regard, Erikson (1963) suggests that the principal task for an adolescent is to resolve an identity crisis that falls on a continuum from positive (identity) to negative (role confusion). Moreover, the successful resolution of the psychosocial crisis of identity versus role confusion during adolescence is contingent upon the positive resolution of preceding crises in order to promote future positive outcomes. Marcia (1966) expands upon Erikson's adolescent identity theory by adding four identity statuses, with each indicating whether the individual had experienced an identity crisis and/or firmly committed to an identity. Identity statuses were organized hierarchically, with two indicating that adolescents who experienced an identity crisis, with or without commitment, were more mature than the two statuses where they had not experienced crises. Regardless of Erikson and Marcia's focus on adolescence as a period of identity development, current research (e.g., Arnett, 2000; Levinson, 1978; Levinson & Levinson, 1996) indicates that adolescence may be only the beginning of identity development and not the end. In fact, identity across the life span may be affected by both changing life events, such as the birth of a child, and an individual's reactions to these changes.

There is, then, no more meaningful life event nor more significant an identity crisis that an individual goes through as a human being than to become a parent. An individual who changes from being a nonparent to a parent experiences a profound shift in identity that continues throughout the course of a child's life. When a child arrives, the individual tends to give up personal freedom and replaces it with responsibility; self-love is changed to other love, and sense of self is transformed with the ongoing responsibility of child-rearing which continues to adjust as the child develops. Clearly, parents are not the same people they were before they had a child, and they will not be the same years after their child has grown. Being a parent, then, is one of the most dramatic and significant identities that an individual assumes. Interestingly, however, and unlike other identities that an individual acquires over the course of life, this is an identity that continues to transition as the child is growing and developing. That is, the parent's identity adjusts to what the child requires at specific stages of development.

Galinsky (1987) created a thought-provoking stage approach to describe parental development where she presented six stages in the life of the parent. In this model, parents are confronted with tasks they carry out over the life of their child. As their children grow, parents are faced with preparing for their arrival; becoming a nurturer, authority, interpreter, and interdependent; and, finally, preparing for their departure. Clearly parents acquire new skills and abilities, new goals, and responsibilities that are prompted by their child's stage of development. It can be argued, however, that in doing so, they embark on an incredible journey that continues to add to their identity as parents. This paper, then, makes use of this model to trace the concurrent paths of parental identity and children's growth and development with a narrative of my own experience as a parent.

Becoming a Parent

During pregnancy, parents read about what to expect as they anticipate the arrival of their baby, imagine what the birth will be like, shape how they will be as parents, envision what parenthood will bring, and prophesy how their lives will change following the birth of their child (Galinsky, 1987). Parents begin to observe relatives, friends, and even their own parents, who have made the transition from singular to plural. This commences one's identity as a parent. They visualize themselves as parents caring for their child and become "other" focused in that they start to predict what the needs of the baby will be and not necessarily what their needs will be when the baby arrives. They also envision how they are going to balance the baby's needs with other responsibilities involving partner, career, and friends. With the birth of the baby, however, parents begin to modify this image of their parent identity with reality, or at least they modify their behavior toward more realistic expectations. This is the beginning of the identity-transforming experience of parenting.

Personally, I imagined I knew what would happen when I had my first child. I would continue working conscientiously at my career; I would continue to vigorously take care of the house—paying bills, shopping, cleaning, cooking, and laundry; I would continue my relationships with family and with friends; but I would now take on the new responsibilities of child-rearing. No problem. My identity as mother would not be any different from my identity as employee, daughter, sister, and friend.

I was in for a very rude awakening once my first child arrived. I soon began to realize my focus had shifted from me and onto her—she provided the primary focus in my life, and my needs were secondary. Motherhood was a big challenge for me because it was unpredictable, filled with intense emotions that required a tremendous amount of commitment, selflessness, and patience. It was not something that I understood until I was actually in the situation with the baby. It was at this point in my life that I realized my identity as a parent was distinct from my identity as a daughter or friend. And I continued to transform in relation to the changes that occurred as my daughter developed.

Caring for My Infant

Clearly parents change when they learn how to care for their baby. It is during this first year of life that the child is dependent on its parents for survival as well as growth and development. As soon as the baby becomes a reality, parents modify the initial perception of their envisioned identity as parents during pregnancy to actual care providers for their infant. The expectations they created of what their baby would be like and how they would respond and care for their infant need adjustment with the arrival of their baby and the awareness of their actual skill in caring for the child.

I can still recall the first night my daughter came home at only 2 days old, and she cried incessantly throughout the night. She would not stop crying, and I could not soothe her. I tried everything that I read and was told would work: feeding, changing, rocking, and singing, but nothing worked. I felt that I was failing as a mother, and she had been at home for less than 24 h. I called my mother the next day, frustrated and overwhelmed, and asked how she could do this with each of her five children! She advised me about babies and assured me that I would be fine as I gained more realistic understanding of the baby.

During infancy, parents identify as care providers; they are the nurturers of their child (Galinsky, 1987). As an infant experiences a completely new world of sensory experiences, parents identify as providers of basic physiological and emotional needs—food, clothing, emotional soothing and regulation, social interaction, and comfort in affectionate, caring ways. By meeting these needs, parents enhance the emotional bonding with their child and promote physical development through ensuring proper nutrition and sleep as well as cognitive development by providing a stimulating environment and encouraging curiosity. For the infant's emotional and social development, parents engage in consistent and continuous sensitive, responsive, and affectionate interactions with their infants. Caring and warm parents establish routines and daily schedules for their individual needs that provide appropriate objects for stimulation and a safe environment for exploration. It is important, therefore, that parents understand what is happening to their infant regarding development and provide experiences that encourage that development.

As parents spend time caring for their infants, they also learn their baby's signals of when to cuddle, provide stimulation, or foster quiet time. Recognizing the baby's signs and being an accepting, emotionally available, responsive caregiver help to form a secure attachment with their infant. The infant's initial attachment impacts characteristics, such as self-esteem, identity, trust, social competence, and the ability to form attachments later in life (Erikson, 1963; Main, Kaplan, & Cassidy, 1986; Matas, Arend, & Sroufe, 1978). The quality of parent's responsiveness and initial attachment, therefore, is not only important in getting the infant off to a strong and healthy start but also in playing an important role after infancy (Thompson, 2006). Being responsive comes when parents spend lots of time engaging in daily activities and repeated interactions with the baby. There is no doubt that infants are a lot of work, and it can be challenging to care for them, but parents who enjoy caring for and being with their child and convey that joy to the child will generally have an easier time being a parent as the child grows and develops.

Although infancy is a time for the development of a secure attachment relationship with parents, it is also a time of parental questioning. Parents may start to question their priorities as well as what they should be doing with their time. Adjustments can be difficult when expectations have been unrealistic regarding being a parent or thinking they know exactly what to do all the time. I read the books about what to expect, I spoke with other parents and took care of other people's children when I was a teenager, so I "knew" what to expect from my baby. I was convinced I was prepared. I don't think anyone is truly prepared to be caretaker and nurturer of a completely dependent being, and I was no different. It took time while I watched, listened, and held my daughter, wondering what I had to do to meet her needs. It took time for me to realize how to care for her, and during this time, my identity as care provider continued to improve. I became better at reading her cues of when she was hungry or tired, and I understood what I had to do in order to be sensitive and responsive to her needs. I also began to realize that parenthood is made up of continual compromises regarding my identity as daughter, teacher, and sister and that my priorities were now on my daughter. And I was going to spend my time securing a strong attachment relationship with this completely dependent being.

Protecting and Controlling My Preschooler

As the child develops from infant to toddler and preschooler, parents begin to realize that their identity takes on a new structure. While parents started with a child that was unable to eat, dress, communicate, or get around, they now have a child that is capable of walking, talking, eating, dressing, and asserting independence daily. Children are becoming increasingly better at exploring their environment because of their physical, cognitive, and socioemotional development. Their fine and gross motor skills allow them to more effectively manipulate objects as well as travel faster and farther than before. Cognitively, they are learning about the properties of objects and about how things work while using their language to put together sentences and communicate with other people. Socioemotionally, they begin to understand emotions such as "happy" and "sad" which help them to recognize another's emotional reactions and allow them the ability to control their as well as others' emotions. As their social and emotional skills improve, they continue to develop a greater sense of self and independence (Erikson, 1963).

While children become more independent, their parents' identity as care providers is now one that needs to regulate their behavior in order to protect them from potentially dangerous situations. This can be a very difficult time for parents because they now shift their identity from nurturer to both protector and authority (Galinsky, 1987). Although physical contact and caretaking is still an important component of the parents' identity, the child is now in need of verbal lessons on appropriate behavior, exploration, and safety. Parents are more confident in their identity as sensitive and caring parents and have developed an attachment to their child but now need to develop identities that can limit and control their child. During the prenatal period, parents anticipated their disciplinary style and their ability to avoid angry outbursts and at the same time to show love for their child. However, because children are not always compliant or pleasant, and they change as they develop, parents need to develop the skills of a reasonable and responsible authority.

Consequently, parents' identity of monitoring and guiding their toddler's behavior is accomplished by introducing environments where they can engage in cooperative behavior and situations where they can encourage good behavior. During toddlerhood and preschool, parents spend time making rules and figuring out how much autonomy to give the child. Therefore, they set rules that are appropriate regarding what the child is able do. For example, the child understands what it means to "go to sleep" but may need more direction to "clean the room." As authorities, parents base rules on children's physical and cognitive development, where they initially guide their child on safety, such as not touching things that are dangerous, and then later monitor issues of behavior, such as table manners.

Since parents, especially first-time parents, often learn as they go along, they sometimes experience anxiety, frustration, and vulnerability. As their child's sensitive care provider and guide, parents promote safety in play, provide challenging experiences so the child feels confident, and communicate in an effective way to help the child develop a positive sense of self by understanding their emotions and how they feel about certain rules. They learn how to react when their child tells a lie, when it is okay for the toddler to try something new or when to step in, and when to help the child conform to guidelines both in and outside the home. Parents' identity performs a balancing act between being inflexible on some directions and adaptable on others and fostering the child's individuality while controlling behavior and enforcing rules.

When rules need to be enforced and discipline is necessary, parents should use methods that are effective and developmentally appropriate, keeping in mind the child's thoughts and feelings. Authoritative discipline at this age consists of understanding what the child is able to do as well as implementing deserved consequences for inappropriate behavior. Children can control their hands but may not be able to control their bladder, so hitting is inappropriate but wetting their pants is not. In addition, remembering that they can't play with mom's coffee cup on Monday may be completely forgotten by Tuesday. As their experienced guide, parents redirect and distract the child who is headed for something that is unsafe or unacceptable. Explaining simply and understandably why something is dangerous and why their behavior is inappropriate may seem obvious to the parent but may not be understood by the child. It is the parents' responsibility at this age to help the child understand and internalize what is considered suitable or inappropriate behavior. Parents who focus on their children's needs are sensitive and responsive as well as consistent and fair in the rules they establish. Consequently, they have more compliant children who are more frequently happy and feel better about themselves.

Moreover, preschoolers have a unique curiosity in discovery and learning. They have a sufficient understanding of language; they are affectionate, funny, and entertaining; and they believe their parents are omnipotent and omniscient. Although parents' identity during the preschool years is similar to when their child was a toddler, that is, caring, trusting, and loving, now they guide their child's transition from dependent to independent being. They monitor and supervise experiences rather than doing for the child, they answer their questions rather than disregard them, and they initiate and support opportunities that foster the development of a strong positive self-concept. Nonetheless, the parent's identity remains one that is sensitive, engaged, and adaptable, thereby creating a secure attachment in the infant, confidence in the toddler, and responsibility and cooperation in the preschooler.

When my son was born 22 months after my daughter, she wanted to help with feeding the newborn, changing diapers, as well as bathing, holding, and caressing the new baby. Unfortunately, after 3 days and a lot of infant crying, she wanted him to "leave our house" and wondered when he was "going back to the hospital." She became less interested in helping and more interested in being uncooperative, stubborn, and unpleasant, which is not that unusual for a toddler. I realized, then, that I had to be a nurturer of one child and the protector and monitor of another at the same time.

Regardless of how tired as I was with the new baby, as my daughter's protector, I reassured her that she was still very special and loved and taught her what was appropriate behavior with her new brother. I spent time doing special activities with her, like going to the park and library, playing games like hide and seek and Candy Land, reading stories at night, and including her in the daily routines to help her self-regulate her thoughts and feelings. The good news is that the same child who told me that I was "the meanest mommy ever on the planet" because I wouldn't let her play with Limoges figures earlier in the day told me after I let her help bake her favorite cookies, "If I squeezed you as hard as I love you, you would explode." The preschool period is a challenging time—lots of instruction, frustration, and emotion—for both parents and children.

Teaching My Child

During middle childhood, children develop and become more aware of their cognitive, social, and emotional abilities. They think more logically, learn to solve problems that are more complex, become interested in the properties of objects, are better able to understand the relationship between objects, and are capable of understanding another person's point of view (Piaget, 1972). Although their thinking is more logical and systematic than it was when they were younger, it is still concrete. In addition to cognitive changes during the school-age years, children begin to control their emotions and develop a more confident and realistic self-image. They gain a new sense of purpose and competence at useful skills, are eager to try meaningful new tasks and proud of their accomplishments, acquire new social skills, and enjoy activities with peers (Erikson, 1963).

During this period, parents reflect on their own self-concept, so they become aware of how they are being seen and understood by their child as well as how they encourage their child's self-concept and identity. Parents focus on what they think about themselves as parents and what they believe in and value while simultaneously figuring out what kinds of knowledge, skills, and values they want to encourage in their child. Parents become more genuine in their identity as a parent and thus start to prepare themselves for the changes they need because of their child's intellectual and social development.

Once again, parents' identity is transformed as their child moves into the next stage of development, but this time they take on the responsibility of communicating about the world and evaluating their child's responses (Galinsky, 1987). What parents think about, believe in, and value are now being transferred to their child. They are not only explaining but are listening to and making decisions for their child that are consistent with their thoughts, values, and beliefs. At this point in the child's life, parents are also maintaining while adjusting both their caring, sensitive, and regulating identity to be more in line with the child's advanced cognitive and social skills. Because of their increased cognitive ability, parents instruct the child on appropriate behavior, family obligations, and household responsibilities.

School age is also a time when children can compare themselves to others, physically, intellectually, and materially, and realize what they do and don't have in these areas. Parents also need to explain to their child what kind of life they will be providing based on what they can afford; they realize when they can acquiesce to their child's requests and when they must resist. At this age, children share with their parents' thoughtful and realistic concerns and questions—some of which are straightforward and easy, while others are more complicated. As translators for their children, parents should talk to their child about realities, like drugs and death, and experiences, like bullying and terrorism.

The relationship between parents and their child changes during middle childhood. Parents' identity shifts from one that initiates interactions and activities to one that determines how much involvement or independence should occur both at home and away. Parents begin to balance their need for connectedness with the child's need for separation and individuality in their behavior and identity. Parents realize that there are other people who have influence on their child, such as siblings, friends, and teachers who have become very important to them. It is essential for parents to acknowledge these new relationships, to determine when to become involved in them, and to decide when to let their child find their own way in order to maintain them.

Moreover, the questions that emerge at this stage of child development bring about yet further changes in parental identity. I was constantly amazed at the insightfulness, difficulty, and sheer quantity of questions my children found to ask during elementary school. Questions like, "Why can't I bounce a basketball in the house? What is gravity made of? Why do some people not live in a home? Is God real and what does he look like? Why can't I stay up as late as you? Why do people get sick and will you die? When do I learn how to breathe under water?" As the inquiries seemed unending, I was faced with the daily struggle of figuring out what to say, how to say it, and when it was appropriate. When my daughter asked me where she came from while we were sitting in church, I decided that I would tell her that she had an interesting question but that we could talk about it later when we were home. I also had to ensure that I actually understood what she was asking and discuss it at a level that she understood before attempting to educate her. Discussing where she came from might simply be a question about in what city or state she was born. When presented with the tough, insightful, and sometimes humorous questions, I had an opportunity to examine my own beliefs and address them appropriately.

Indeed, during my children's middle childhood, both were faced with trying to understand why their parents got divorced and what that meant, why their teenage cousin died in a car accident, and why their grandfather had to have open-heart surgery, all while going to school and maintaining friendships. As their parent, it was important for me to help and guide them as they experienced a wide range of intense emotions related to loss. I was sensitive to their concerns about the impact of divorce and the realities of death and provided them with support and honest open lines of communication. That said, when school-age children are assured that they are loved and cared for, they are extraordinarily resilient and remarkably adaptable.

Coregulating My Adolescent

For many parents, the teenage years produce feelings of anxiety and trepidation. Adolescents can make dangerous, risky, and even harmful decisions, while their parents can do little more than stand by and watch. Although parents think, because of the values and beliefs they have instilled in their child and their own substantial life experiences, their child will make the "right" decisions, parents know that this is the time their child might be influenced to make an unhealthy choice. Their hope is, however, that the parenting that occurred early in life provides the foundation that will deter their child's engaging in irresponsible behavior.

Of course, at this time in their life, adolescents are changing physically, cognitively, and socially which affect their parents' identity once again. Teen's bodies are changing in both shape and size. They may feel awkward, strange, or uncomfortable, which may make this a difficult time for both the adolescent and their parents. Teens become more introspective; they use reason to solve problems and begin to think more flexibly, abstractly, and hypothetically (Piaget, 1972). Along with teen's advanced cognitive ability comes increasingly more time to think about themselves, their thoughts, and the society in which they live. They become idealistic, hypocritical, and egocentric (Elkind, 1967). They develop into critical observers of the discrepancy between the possible and the actual and think about what the world might be like under ideal circumstances. There is, however, an inconsistency in what they say and what they do which leads to their occasionally pretending to be who they are not. Finally, they display egocentric thinking in their need to conform because others might be watching and judging them in their belief that they possess unique and profound insights. And they believe they are invulnerable to illness and injury. Socially, Erikson (1963) believes that the most important task for adolescents is to discover their identity by asking questions about who they are, what they like, where they fit, and what they want out of life by exploring alternatives and committing to roles. This is a time when teens want the freedom to form their own opinions, have privacy, and make decisions for themselves. However, they also want warm, loving, and attentive parents who monitor, supervise, and set rules that regulate their behavior.

Therefore, parents' relationship with their child during adolescence changes from an authority identity into one that becomes interdependent (Galinsky, 1987). Similar to the parents' identity with their toddler, they struggle with how much independence and control they should allow their teen and still remain sensitive and responsive to their needs while remaining emotionally available and accepting. As their teen's hairstyle, clothing, thinking, language, and behavior change, parents begin to revise the images of who their child was to who their child is currently. They should evaluate their identity as parents and once again examine their own values and goals. While doing so, they are able to communicate acceptable standards and expectations of behavior for their teen and continue to provide appropriate guidance and supervision. Reexamination of their own attitudes, values, and behaviors not only helps their teens formulate a value system to guide behavior but also transforms their identity as parents of a teen.

Clearly, this was my experience as a parent of an adolescent. As a teen, my son frequently listened to a range of music styles (rap, pop, hip-hop, techno), experimented with different fashion trends (hoodies, sweats), and was involved in various activities (music, athletics, chess). He also developed quite a diverse group of friends. Throughout the course of his adolescence, he explored different roles and opportunities. There have been many hours that I spent worrying and wondering about his choices but was comforted by the thought that the attitudes and values I taught him early in life would keep him on the right track. Hopefully so.

Without question, during adolescence, parents' identity shifts from one that is in control of their child's life to one that must let go and trust that the experiences they were given early in life will empower them to make good choices as adolescents. However, when teens make mistakes as they become young adults, parents still need to set limits and use appropriate supervision rather than disciplinary control. In sum, parents' identity is one that helps their adolescents to become independent, make decisions, and handle situations and at the same time provides the security that they are always available should problems occur.

In creating this new relationship, parents should acknowledge and respect that their teen will more often question their parents' decisions. At this point, open-minded and respectful communication is critical; it is essential to take the time not only to talk with their teen but, more importantly, to listen when their teen is speaking. Adolescents need their privacy that parents need to respect, but both should understand that parents not only make and enforce the rules but also allow and deny rights and privileges.

As my children became teenagers, I increasingly gave them more freedom, but we also discussed the rules and regulations that went along with this independence. One of these rules was that they had to text me if there was any change in their plans when they were away from home. My children and I discussed this directive, I explained the reason why it was required, and we came to a mutual understanding. Although neither child was outwardly happy, they both understood this necessity. They knew that if they respected our agreement, they retained their privileges; however, if they violated the rule, their freedom would be taken away. It didn't work perfectly all the time, but on the whole, conformity prevailed.

Mentoring My Young Adult

When the child advances into the next stage in life—young adulthood—parents once again evaluate their parenting experience and prepare themselves for their child's departure (Galinsky, 1987). Now, they focus on when their child will leave, how often they will be together, and what will become of their relationship. Their identity is adjusted concurrently with their child's development, and a new relationship emerges between the parent and their young adult when they leave home. They move into an adult relationship with their parents with parents acting like advisors.

Changes in the child's cognitive and social abilities prepare the young adult for their taking on new roles and responsibilities as adults. These young adults become more flexible in their thinking, more fully understanding abstract concepts, more aware that problems can have multiple causes and solutions, and less intent on finding absolute truths (Piaget, 1972). Therefore, it is a time when they develop new skills and interests, decide on personal values and beliefs, identify career and relationships, and gain independence from their parents. Young adulthood, however, is still a time of exploring different options in work, education, and social groups. They are now responsible for taking care of themselves, making independent decisions, and becoming financially independent (Arnett, 1998). In addition, these young adults are seeking out emotional and physical intimacy in relationships with friends and partners; perhaps they experience their first serious romance, develop long-term close and committed relationships, and engage in sexual experimentation (Erikson, 1963).

Experiencing their child growing up and leaving home signals a change in parents' lives and identity. Their sense of self as parents once more becomes disrupted, and their identity is once again transformed as they evaluate what their new self looks like. Parental identity never ceases to exist because the job never ends. Parents continue to be a part of their child's lives; they think and worry about, as well as help and care for them. Parents are still the nurturers and protectors, the interpreters, and the authority—their identity just changes into more of a mentorship identity based on this new parent-adult child relationship. Parents have accepted their child's separate and unique identity, respected their values and beliefs, and recognized their ability to make decisions for themselves on education, career, and relationships.

They realize that this stage of parental identity needs to provide guidance but less as an authority figure and more as a counselor and trusted advisor. Parents are now the source of confidence, support, encouragement, and unconditional love, while their adult child is embarking on a new and exciting stage of development.

I caught myself the other day thinking about the time when I would be able to at long last take a breath from my parental role and responsibilities and when would I leave behind my identity as parent. I wondered when my children finally would be finished with their education, committed to a serious relationship, established in their career, and settled in their lives. I realize that I am never going to stop caring for, worrying about, or helping them because I am their parent. It's just different now that they are physically, cognitively, and socially mature and live in separate places. I have told them on countless occasions throughout the course of their lives that I am their mother and I will always be there for them, no matter what. It may not be with a Band-Aid, hugs, and kisses as it was when they were young children, but it will be with guidance and encouragement as young adults. I was forever changed when I became a parent, and although my identity as a parent has been transformed on the concurrent paths with my children's growth and development, I am a parent for life!

References

Arnett, J. J. (1998). Learning to stand alone: The contemporary American transition to adulthood in cultural and historical context. *Human Development, 41*, 295–315.

Arnett, J. J. (2000). Emerging adulthood: A theory of development from the late teen through the twenties. *American Psychologist, 55*(5), 469–480.

Elkind, D. (1967). Egocentrism in adolescence. *Child Development, 38*(4), 1025–1034.

Erikson, E. H. (1963). *Childhood and society*. New York: Norton.

Galinsky, E. (1987). *The six stages of parenthood*. Reading, MA: Perseus Books.

Levinson, D. J. (1978). *The seasons of a man's life*. New York: Knopf.

Levinson, D. J., & Levinson, J. D. (1996). *The seasons of a woman's life*. New York: Knopf.

Main, M., Kaplan, N., & Cassidy, J. (1985). Security in infancy, childhood, and adulthood: A move to the level of representation. *Monographs of the Society for Research in Child Development, 50*, 66–104.

Marcia, J. E. (1966). Development and validation of ego-identity status. *Journal of Personality and Social Psychology, 3*, 551–558.

Matas, L., Arend, R. A., & Sroufe, L. A. (1978). Continuity of adaptation in the second year: The relationship between quality of attachment and later competence. *Child Development, 49*(3), 547–556.

Piaget, J. (1972). *The psychology of the child*. New York: Basic Books.

Thompson, R. A. (2006). The development of the person: Social understanding, relationships, self, conscience. In W. Damon & R. M. Lerner (Series Eds.) & N. Eisenberg (Ed.), *Handbook of child psychology* (Vol. 3). *Social, emotional, and personality development* (6th ed., pp. 24–98). Hoboken, NJ: Wiley.

Chapter 10
"Like a Constantly Flowing River": Gender Identity Flexibility Among Nonbinary Transgender Individuals

M. Paz Galupo, Lex Pulice-Farrow, and Johanna L. Ramirez

Gender is one of the most pervasive psychological constructs and one of the first identities we learn (Egan & Perry, 2001). Gender identity is commonly understood to represent an individual's internal sense of themselves[1] as male, female, both, or neither (Tate, 2014; Tate, Youssef, & Bettergarcia, 2014). As a multidimensional construct, it also encompasses an individual's sex assigned at birth, current gender identity, gender roles and expectations, gender social presentation, and gender evaluations (Tate et al., 2014). Cisgender and transgender are terms that can be used to describe the relationship between an individual's sex assigned at birth and current gender identity. Cisgender individuals use a current gender identity label that is the same as their sex assigned at birth; transgender individuals use a label that is different from their sex assigned at birth (Tate, Ledbetter, & Youssef, 2013).

Despite the fact that most individuals experience some flexibility in gender roles and presentation, binary distinctions based on gender (e.g., girl/boy, woman/man, cisgender/transgender) have been conceptually naturalized. However, gender identity, the private understanding of one's gender, is uniquely complicated for transgender individuals by dichotomous notions of gender/sex.[2] This is particularly true for individuals in the transgender community who experience their gender outside the binary (e.g., genderqueer, gender nonconforming, gender fluid, or agender individuals). The present research investigates the conceptualization of gender identity among nonbinary transgender individuals. As gender identity has been described as an individual's sense of self as male, female, both, or either (Tate, 2014; Tate et al., 2014), a focus on nonbinary transgender individuals may

[1] We intentionally use the singular they and them as gender inclusive pronouns.

[2] Following van Anders (2014, 2015), we use gender/sex to reference a concept that cannot be understood as only biologically or socially constructed.

M.P. Galupo (✉) • L. Pulice-Farrow • J.L. Ramirez
Psychology Department, Towson University, 8000 York Rd, Towson, MD 21252, USA
e-mail: pgalupo@towson.edu

J.D. Sinnott (ed.), *Identity Flexibility During Adulthood*,
DOI 10.1007/978-3-319-55658-1_10

provide particular insight into way people conceptualize their gender identity as "both" or "neither" and may provide a unique opportunity to explore gender identity flexibility.

Historical and Contemporary Frameworks for Understanding Transgender Experience and Gender Identity

Transgender experience has been narrowly defined and consistently pathologized in the psycho-medical literature. From this perspective, the focus on transgender experience has been on developing a typology of transsexuality (Benjamin, 1966; Blanchard, 1989a, 1989b) and diagnosing gender identity (e.g., as gender identity disorder in the DSM-III, American Psychiatric Association [APA], 1980; and gender dysphoria in the DSM-V, APA, 2013). From a medical perspective, early models of transgenderism have emphasized dichotomous conceptualizations of gender/sex where individuals were considered transsexual based upon their identification with the "opposite" of their "genetic" sex (Benjamin, 1966). Developed in relation to the experiences of transwomen (i.e., narrowly defined as individuals who were assigned male at birth and have a current gender identity of woman), medical models of transgender experience reinforce binary tropes of a "woman trapped in a man's body" and do not always resonate with the diverse experiences of transgender individuals (Serano, 2010; Veale, Clarke, & Lomax, 2012). These models have been criticized for making anatomical determinations central and de-emphasizing the role of self-identification (Bockting & Coleman, 1991; Devor, 1993).

More contemporary research emphasizes self-identification and often situates transgender experience within the larger lesbian, gay, bisexual, and transgender (LGBT) community (Fassinger & Arnseneau, 2007). From this perspective, sexual and gender minorities are conceptualized as related groups based on shared community (Fassinger & Arseneau, 2007), stigma/minority stress (e.g., Breslow et al., 2015; Meyer, 2015), and gender nonconformity/atypicality (Alexander & Yescavage, 2003; Clarke, Hayfield, & Huxley, 2012; Drescher, 2010). This approach has focused on transgender experience while privileging those accounts that best fit with a binary conceptualization of transgender experience (e.g., individuals who identify as women/transwomen and men/transmen) and, with few recent exceptions (Budge, Rossman, & Howard, 2014; Factor & Rothblum, 2008; Farmer & Byrd, 2015; Galupo, Davis, Grynkiewicz, & Mitchell, 2014; Harrison, Grant, & Herman, 2012; Saltzburg & Davis, 2010; Tate et al., 2013, 2014; Pulice-Farrow, Clements, & Galupo, 2017; Richards et al., 2016), fail to acknowledge the experiences of nonbinary conceptualizations of transgender experience. Research has begun to acknowledge nonbinary transgender identities and have found some differences between the experiences of binary and nonbinary transgender individuals (e.g., Factor & Rothblum, 2008). Despite the research that suggests that genderqueer is the most commonly endorsed gender identity among an online and nonclinical sample of transgender individuals (Kuper, Nussbaum, & Mustanski, 2012), gender identity research has not provided clarity in how nonbinary transgender individuals conceptualize their gender identity.

The Present Study

The present research investigates gender identity among nonbinary transgender individuals by analyzing the gender identity labels they choose and the descriptions they provide for gender identity. By centering on the lived experiences of nonbinary individuals, our thematic analysis focuses on identifying the aspects most salient to their gender identity. We include a diverse nonclinical sample including transgender individuals who primarily identify as gender variant or agender.

Method

Participant Demographics and Recruitment Strategy

Participants were 197 adults who self-identified as either gender variant or agender. Participants ranged in age from 18 to 70 ($M = 29.51$, $SD = 11.00$). The majority (73.6%) of participants resided in the USA and represented all 50 member states of the USA and Washington, DC. Countries that were represented outside of the USA included Canada, Australia, the UK, New Zealand, Costa Rica, and Norway, among others. Table 10.1 includes participant demographics with regard to racial/ethnic diversity, highest level of education, socioeconomic status, and sexual orientation. There was limited racial/ethnic diversity within the sample, with 70.1% identified as White/Caucasian and 19.8% of participants identified as a racial/ethnic minority and 10.1% providing no answer.

Recruitment announcements, including a link to the online survey, were posted to social media sites, online message boards, and emailed via transgender and gender variant Listservs. Some of these resources were geared toward specific sexual minority communities, while others served the transgender community more generally. Participants heard about the study primarily through online means, including Facebook (82.2%) Tumblr (2.43%), research-oriented websites/message boards (7.0%), and forwarded email from an acquaintance or Listserv (3.9%).

Table 10.1 Participant demographics

	%
Gender identity	
Gender variant	65.5
Agender	34.5
Sex assigned at birth	
Female	71.6
Male	24.9
Intersex	3.0
No answer	0.5
Sexual orientation	
Queer	26.6
Pansexual	15.9
Heterosexual	17.9
Bisexual	14.0
Lesbian	8.7
Gay	3.9
Asexual	3.9
Fluid	1.9
Other	7.2
Race/ethnic identity	
White/Caucasian	70.1
Bi-/multiracial	7.6
Hispanic/Latino	6.1
Asian/Asian American	2.5
American Indian/Alaska Native	0.5
Black/African American	0.5
Other	1.9
No answer	10.1
Education	
Did not complete high school or GED	2.5
High school	41.2
College	29.4
Graduate School	16.8
Socioeconomic status	
Working class	28.9
Lower middle class	22.3
Middle class	25.4
Upper middle class	8.6
Upper class	2.0

Measures and Procedure

The present study focused on information obtained from a demographic section of a larger online study investigating gender identity and the experiences of transgender individuals. A structured gender identity question was presented to participants where they chose their primary gender identity from discrete options: trans-masculine, trans-feminine, gender variant, and agender. The present analysis focuses exclusively on those who chose "gender variant" or "agender" as their primary identity category. We analyze the gender identity labels participants' use and their answers to an open-ended question about how they define their gender identity.

Data Analysis

Thematic analysis (Braun & Clarke, 2006) was used to characterize the way participants described their gender identity. Our research team includes a professor of psychology who self-identifies as a bi-/pansexual cisgender woman (first author), a clinical psychology graduate student who identifies as queer non-binary person (second author), and a clinical psychology graduate student who identifies as a sexually fluid cisgender woman (third author).

Analysis began with the second and third author independently coding data looking for themes related to each category of possible gender identity themes. The research team met and discussed the coding categories and agreed upon an initial set of codes. The second and third author then coded and sorted the data set using the initial set of codes and provided the first author (who served as external auditor) with a list of themes and sorted quotes based on theme. The entire research team agreed upon the coding structure and met several additional times to discuss and solidify which quotes would fit under each theme. Final quotes were chosen to simultaneously exemplify each theme and to ensure that the range of illustrative quotes best represented the diversity of gender nonconforming identities endorsed by the sample.

Two were included in our data analysis process in order to increase the credibility of our results. First, at the end of the survey, we provided participants with the opportunity to reflect upon how our questions captured (and failed to capture) their individual experiences. Participants were also asked to provide feedback to improve the present and future studies. Some of those responses obtained informed and provided a context for our analysis. Second, throughout the data analysis process, we discussed the themes and made decisions via consensus. Because of the range of our collective experiences across sexual orientation, gender identity, gender presentation, and relationship experiences, we came to these discussions with different perspectives.

Results and Discussion

Our analysis focuses on participants' answers to two questions. The first question allowed participants to write in the label or labels that they endorsed for their own gender identity. The second was an open-ended question in which participants were asked to describe their gender identity.

Gender Identity Labels

Participants self-identified with a range of gender identity labels. This data was self-generated, and participants were allowed to describe their gender identity in a way that felt authentic to themselves. A percentage of gender variant (20.9%) and agender (25.0%) participants endorsed multiple labels when providing their write in gender identity. For example, one participant responded, "I use the words genderqueer, gender fluid, trans, transgender, gender non-conforming, and occasionally transmasculine to refer to myself." (*genderqueer*)

Table 10.2 provides the frequency of labels endorsed by participants across gender identity (gender variant and agender). Labels fell into five primary categories: (1) gender labels using *binary* terms (e.g. woman, man, masculine, femme), (2) gender labels using *nonbinary* terms (e.g. androgynous, non-binary, pangender), (3) gender labels using *fluid* terms (e.g., fluid, gender variant, genderfluid), (4) gender labels using *agender* terms (e.g., genderless, agender, non-gendered), and (5) gender labels using *trans* terms (e.g., trans, transgender, transmasculine). It is important to note that although both gender variant and agender participants use labels that fall into all five of these categories, there are unique patterns of usage across gender identity. For example, 58.1% of gender variant as opposed to 33.8% of agender individuals used nonbinary labels while 3.9% gender variant and 76.5% agender individuals used agender labels. Because there are clear patterns in the way gender variant and agender individuals use gender labels, in the remaining analyses, we include direct quotes from the participants accompanied by their self-identified labels as context for understanding their varying perspectives.

Descriptions of Gender Identity

Beyond analyzing the use of gender identity labels, in an open-ended question, we asked participants to describe their gender. Six major themes emerged in participants' descriptions of their gender identity: (1) gender identity using binary terms of gender/sex, (2) gender as blended, (3) gender identity as fluid, (4) gender identity as nonbinary, (5) transgender as gender identity, and (6) agender conceptualizations. These themes are not meant to be mutually exclusive, and most participants' responses exemplified more than one of the themes.

Table 10.2 Frequency of gender identity labels by group

Self-identification	Gender variant % (*n*)	Agender % (*n*)
Binary	16.3 (21)	4.4 (3)
Butch	(1)	–
Female/woman	(10)	(1)
Femme	(2)	(1)
Feminine male	(2)	–
Male/man	(6)	(1)
Nonbinary	58.1 (75)	33.8 (23)
Androgynous	(2)	–
Androgyne	(4)	(1)
Ambigender	(1)	–
Bigender	(6)	–
Demigirl	(1)	(1)
Genderqueer	(37)	(13)
Nonbinary	(19)	(8)
Nonconforming	(3)	–
Pangender	(1)	–
Third gender	(1)	–
Fluid	27.9 (36)	4.4 (3)
Fluid	(2)	–
Genderfluid	(32)	(2)
Gender variant	(2)	(1)
Agender	3.9 (5)	76.5 (52)
Agender	(2)	(38)
Genderless	–	(4)
Neutral	(1)	(6)
Neutrois	(2)	(4)
Non-gendered		–
Trans identities	10.8 (14)	11.8 (8)
FTM	(1)	(1)
Trans	(4)	(2)
Trans boi	(1)	–
Transfemale	(1)	–
Transgender	(3)	–
Trans guy	(1)	–
Transmale/transman	(2)	(1)
Transmasculine	–	(4)
Transsexual	(1)	–
Total (*N*)[a]	(129)	(68)

[a]Column data includes the *percentage* of participants endorsing an identity based on *n;* column totals exceed 100% as many participants (20.9% of gender variant; 25.0% agender) endorsed multiple identity labels

"Some days male, some days female": Gender Identity Using Binary Terms of Gender/Sex

When describing their gender identity, our participants often described their nontraditional gender by employing traditional binary gender terms (e.g., male, female). For example, participants used the terms "male" and "female" to ultimately describe how their gender is not fully contained by either:

> *Half male and half female, without being fully one or the other.* (genderqueer/genderfluid)
>
> *Not comfortably fitting into male or female.* (agender)

Sometimes gender was discussed with the binary terms of female and male, other participants used feminine and masculine in similar ways:

> *Shifting between masculine, feminine, androgynous* (genderfluid)
>
> *I identify as a somewhat masculine individual whose (ongoing) history of being treated as a woman has become so important to my experiences and identity that I don't feel comfortable holding an identity as a man.* (nonbinary)

Although participants used binary terms in their descriptions of gender, they were often describing the ways that being confined to one of these terms does not capture their experience of gender:

> *I find it easier to identify my gender by what it is not rather than what it is. My gender is not male nor female so the traditional gender binary fails me. As such genderqueer seems like the most accurate label for me.* (genderqueer agender)

"A variable mix of both": Gender Identity as Blended

Another predominant theme was seen in the way that some participants described their gender identity as a blend or mix of maleness/femaleness or of masculinity/femininity. These descriptions resonate with the conceptualization of gender identity being "both" male and female:

> *A blend of male and female characteristics.* (androgynous, agender)
>
> *I describe myself as somewhere in between male and female, or mixing male and female ("androgyne," I also use the terms "transgender, nonbinary, and genderqueer)*
>
> *I am someone who is neither man nor woman but something else entirely I am a fabulous mix of feminine and masculine. I currently see myself as a femme boi.* (genderqueer)

Although participants used binary terms to describe their gender, those illustrating the theme of blended did so by seeing their gender as a mix, blend, or combination.

"Like a constantly flowing river": Gender Identity as Fluid

Central to some participants' descriptions of their gender was the notion of change. Many nonbinary participants' responses described their gender in fluid or flexible terms:

> *I have a gender that is 'fluid', that shifts and changes like a constantly flowing river. I am never 'just one' gender as my identity is constantly changing. (genderfluid under the nonbinary umbrella)*

> *I see myself as a fluid individual who experiences attributes that are feminine or masculine. These feelings cannot be defined by my sex. (genderqueer)*

Analogous to the way sexual fluidity has been described (Diamond, 2003, 2008; Fahs, 2009; Galupo, Mitchell, Grynkiewicz & Davis, 2014; Mock & Eibach, 2012; Zinik, 1985), participants typically described gender fluidity by referencing changes in their gender identity and expression across time and context:

> *My gender feelings/presentation change consistently (genderfluid)*

> *I flow all around the spectrum at any given point (genderfluid)*

> *My gender changes on a day to day basis. (genderfluid)*

> *I slosh about between male, female, neither, and both. (genderfluid)*

Although traditional definitions of gender identity emphasize that it is an individual's internal sense of their gender as male, female, both, or neither (Tate, 2014; Tate et al., 2014), many of our participants describe their gender in ways that do not neatly reside within just one of those options:

> *My gender changes. Sometimes I am female, sometimes I am a boy, sometimes I am both, and sometimes I am neither. (genderfluid)*

> *Sometimes I feel like I am completely a man. Sometimes I feel like I am mostly a man, with some woman/agender mixed in. (demiguy)*

> *I can switch in between a variety of genders (man, woman, androgyne, agender, third gender, polygender, etc.) day by day. (genderfluid)*

> *Gender Flexible, I feel both masculine and femmie to varying degrees. Sometimes multiple days will swing towards masculine or feminine energies. I notice my voice, mannerisms, thoughts and desires shift between the two. Although I have spent the past two years female full time, I am now rediscovering my male side with a new found respect and love. (genderqueer)*

For those participants who described their gender identity in fluid ways, it is clear that change is central to their experience of gender, as noted in their chosen identity labels and descriptions: *"flexible"* (queer femme), *"gender fluid"* (gender fluid), *"fluid"* (genderqueer). This is consistent with the high number of participants who used gender fluid or fluid as their gender identity label (Table 10.2).

"Somewhere beyond rather than between": Gender Identity as Non-binary

Another theme that was pervasive in participants' narratives was that their gender identity, in essence, was nonbinary. A rejection of binary terms and the traditional binary conceptualization of gender was central to their descriptions:

> *I don't conform to the gender binary (agender)*

> *I am beyond the binary genders and do not identify as either female or male. (genderqueer/ non binary)*

The endorsement of nonbinary gender identity was often accompanied by a need to find new and alternative descriptors for their identity because binary terms were not enough to capture their conceptualization:

> *having a different or alternative gender that does not fit into the binary (genderqueer)*

> *I identify as both nonbinary and trans because of the nature of having an identity that cannot easily be described by combining concepts related to "man" and "woman." Because I am somewhere beyond rather than between these concepts I am continually having to define myself as both trans and nonbinary in order to come close to having my gender viewed in a way that feels authentic to me. Other terms that are sometimes useful to describe my gender are queer and fluid.* (nonbinary trans person)

This need for adopting multiple gender labels parallels previous research on sexual minority individuals' sexual identity labels, where those with the most marginalized/nonnormative identities used multiple labels and provided more descriptions when referring to their sexuality (Galupo, Mitchell, & Davis, 2015).

"Being a trans guy is still a significant part of my identity"*: Transgender as Gender Identity

Some nonbinary transgender individuals described the ways they used transgender as a gender identity label that was meaningful to their experience. For example, two participants endorsed trans along with a traditional binary labels: *"I am trans and male"* and *"Female with a trans history."* Other participants expanded on their use of transgender or trans as an identity:

> *I identify as both nonbinary and trans because of the nature of having an identity that cannot easily be described by combining concepts related to "man" and "woman." Because I am somewhere beyond rather than between these concepts I am continually having to define myself as both trans and nonbinary in order to come close to having my gender viewed in a way that feels authentic to me. Other terms that are sometimes useful to describe my gender are queer and fluid. (nonbinary trans person)*

> *I don't identify within the gender binary. I mostly identify as genderqueer, which to me means I'm not a boy or a girl but some mix of the two, with other stuff thrown in. However, I identified as a trans man for a few years and took T during that time, so I feel being a trans* guy is still a significant part of my identity for now. (genderqueer trans* guy)*

"My identity is not modified by gender": Agender Conceptualizations

Many participants described their gender identity using agender terms, where they were genderless, gender neutral, non-gendered, for example. Their descriptors spoke to the way that their identity was not bound by gender:

> *In the end I feel that categorization by gender is absurd and my identity is not modified by gender. Hence non-gendered or agender. (genderqueer/non-gendered/gender non-conforming)*

> *I feel mostly genderless but occasionally I feel closer to female, and I feel like I fit in between female and agender. (bigender)*

> *neutral dress. neutral pronouns. neutral appearance. no makeup. (agender)*

> *I'm neutrois and gender-fluid. My gender identity itself doesn't "flow" but my gender presentation does. I flow between femme and androgynous but even when I present as more femme I don't identify as female/a woman. When I'm at work I use he/his pronouns and present as a guy; outside of work that varies wildly day to day. My gender identity is basically that of a shapeshifting being.*

> *I do not have an internal gender. It is not androgynous; it is not fluid; it is non-existent. (agender)*

> *I don't feel connected to femininity or masculinity respectively. I don't attach gender to things I do or understand why people do. I think of myself as a person not a "woman" or "man." (agender).*

> *If there are two axes on a graph, one for how female a person feels, and another for how male they feel, I am very close to the coordinate (0, 0). (agender)*

Conclusions

The present research focuses on understanding the conceptualization of gender identity among nonbinary transgender individuals by exploring the gender identity labels they choose and the descriptions they provide for their identity. By centering on nonbinary transgender experience, the present research allows a conceptualization of gender identity outside of the traditional research frameworks that constrain transgender experience and inherently define transgender experience (and gender identity more generally) in binary terms.

Our participants represented a convenience sample collected online. Although online sampling is useful for transgender research where privacy and access issues are unique from the general population (Riggle, Rostosky, & Reedy, 2005), online samples have been shown to disproportionately represent educated, middle-class, White individuals (Dillman, Smyth, & Christian, 2008). Because our sample demographics reflect this trend, interpretation of our findings should be done within the noted demographics. In addition, we recruited participants who identify as transgender, transsexual, gender variant, or having a transgender history, which we used as a broad terms intended to encompass many different gender identities. Because our recruitment strategy emphasized recruitment through transgender community resources, individuals who see their transgender experience as more of a history or status may be under represented within our sample. In particular, because many nonbinary transgender individuals encounter microaggressions from within the transgender community regarding whether they are *really* transgender (Galupo, Henise, & Davis, 2014), nonbinary individuals may feel distanced from the community and our recruitment efforts may not have reached these potential participants.

Despite the limitations of recruitment, we received a geographically diverse sample with representation across gender identities. The present research extends the current transgender literature by centering on individuals who identify as gender variant and agender. However, we did not specifically address comparisons or the potential overlap with individuals across the entire range of transgender identities. For example, many transwomen or transmen may also endorse nonbinary or agender labels. Future research is needed, then, to consider patterns of responses across gender identity.

The present findings do offer some suggestions for reconsidering the way we conceptualize gender identity. Participants described their gender identity in ways that both reflected and challenged research frameworks for understanding transgender experience. Recent definitions of gender identity that are transgender inclusive emphasize that it is an individual's internal sense of their gender as male, female, both, or neither (Tate, 2014; Tate et al., 2014). Although it appears that nonbinary transgender individuals would fall in the "both" or "neither" categories, our participants' responses suggest that their conceptualization of gender identity is more complicated than these two simple categories. In particular, the terms "both" and "neither" still convey binary gender options and fail to capture all the ways that nonbinary individuals conceptualize their identity.

Our participants' descriptions of gender were captured across six distinct themes (binary, blended, fluid, nonbinary, transgender, agender). Participants describing their gender identity in *blended terms* were the most aligned with the conceptualization of gender identity as being "both" male and female, while those describing their gender identity in *agender terms* were the most aligned with "neither" male nor female. Participant responses that fell into the remaining categories are not quite captured in conceptualizations of gender identity in the existing literature and may provide insight into additional conceptualizations of gender identity that cannot be neatly described as "male," "female," "both," or "neither." Although sometimes participants did use *binary terms* (male/female or masculine/feminine) to describe their gender identity, they did so to convey the ways that these terms, even combined, did not quite capture their identity. Similarly some participants explicitly used *nonbinary terminology* to convey that their identity did not reside anywhere on a continuum between male and female. Participants also described their gender in *fluid terms* where the central characterization of their gender identity rested in flexibility and change (across time and context). Additionally, because their gender identity could not be captured in binary terms, participants often used *transgender terms* as a way to describe their identity.

The findings from the present research overall suggest that our participants' gender identity could not be discretely conceptualized as "male," "female," "neither," or "both." This was demonstrated in the way many of their descriptions failed to map onto one of these four traditional options when describing gender identity and in the way that many participants endorsed multiple labels when naming their gender identity. This need for adopting multiple gender labels and multiple descriptors parallels previous research on sexual minority individuals' sexual identity labels, where those with the most marginalized/nonnormative identities used multiple labels and provided more descriptions when referring to their sexuality (Galupo et al., 2015). Nonbinary participants demonstrated flexibility both in the way that they used gender terminology and in the way that they described their own gender identity in fluid/flexible terms. These findings have important implications for transgender researchers, as they suggests a need to expand the understanding of gender identity in ways that better reflects the range of experience of transgender individuals. Ultimately, this research suggests a need for broader and more flexible definitions of gender identity.

References

Alexander, J., & Yescavage, K. (2003). Bisexuality and transgenderism. *Journal of Bisexuality, 3*(3–4), 1–23. doi:10.1300/J159v03n03_01.

American Psychiatric Association [APA]. (1980). *Diagnostic and statistical manual of mental disorders* (3rd ed.). Washington, DC: American Psychiatric Association.

American Psychiatric Association [APA]. (2013). *Diagnostic and statistical manual of mental disorders* (5th ed.). Washington, DC: American Psychiatric Association.

Benjamin, H. (1966). *The transsexual phenomenon*. New York: Julian Press.

Blanchard, R. (1989a). The concept of autogynephilia and the typology of male gender dysphoria. *Journal of Nervous and Mental Disease, 177*, 616–623. Retrieved from: http://journals.lww.com/jonmd/Abstract/1989/10000/The_Concept_of_Autogynephilia_and_the_Typology_of.4.aspx

Blanchard, R. (1989b). The classification and labeling of nonhomosexual gender dysphorias. *Archives of Sexual Behavior, 18*, 315–324. doi:10.1007/BF01541951.

Bockting, W. O., & Coleman, E. (1991). A comment on the concept of transhomosexuality, or the dissociation of the meaning. *Archives of Sexual Behavior, 20*(4), 419–421.

Braun, V., & Clarke, V. (2006). Using thematic analysis in psychology. *Qualitative Research in Psychology, 3*, 77–101. doi:10.1191/1478088706qp063oa.

Breslow, A. S., Brewster, M. E., Velez, B. L., Wong, S., Geiger, E., & Soderstrom, B. (2015). Resilience and collective action: Exploring buffers against minority stress for transgender individuals. *Psychology of Sexual Orientation and Gender Diversity, 2*(3), 253–265. http://dx.doi.org/10.1037/sgd0000117

Budge, S. L., Rossman, H. K., & Howard, K. A. S. (2014). Coping and psychological distress among genderqueer individuals: The moderating effect of social support. *Journal of LGBT Issues in Counseling, 8*(1), 95–117. doi:10.1080/15538605.2014.853641.

Clarke, V., Hayfield, N., & Huxley, C. (2012). Lesbian, gay, bisexual and trans appearance and embodiment: A critical review of the psychological literature. *Psychology of Sexualities Review, 3*(1), 51–70. ISSN 2047-1467. Available from: http://eprints.uwe.ac.uk/17812

Devor, H. (1993). Sexual orientation identities, attractions, and practices of female-to-male transsexuals. *The Journal of Sex Research, 30*(4), 303–315. http://www.jstor.org/stable/3813004

Diamond, L. M. (2003). Was it a phase? Young women's relinquishment of lesbian/bisexual identities over a 5-year period. *Developmental Psychology, 36*, 241–250.

Diamond, L. M. (2008). *Sexual fluidity: Understanding women's love and desire*. Cambridge, MA: Harvard University Press.

Dillman, D., Smyth, J., & Christian, L. M. (2008). *Internet, mail, and mixed-mode surveys: The tailored design method.* New York: Wiley.

Drescher, J. (2010). Queer diagnoses: Parallels and contrasts in the history of homosexuality, gender variance, and the *Diagnostic and Statistical Manual*. *Archives of Sexual Behavior, 39*, 427–460. doi:10.1007/s10508-009-9531-5.

Egan, S. K., & Perry, D. G. (2001). Gender identity: A multidimensional analysis with implications for psychosocial adjustment. *Developmental Psychology, 37*(4), 451–463. doi:10.1037//0012-I649.37.4.45I.

Factor, R. J., & Rothblum, E. D. (2008). Exploring gender identity and community among three groups of transgender individuals in the United States: MTFs, FTMs, and genderqueers. *Health Sociology Review, 17*, 241–159.

Fahs, B. (2009). Compulsory bisexuality?: The challenges of modern sexual fluidity. *Journal of Bisexuality, 9*, 431–449. doi:10.1080/15299710903316661.

Farmer, L. B., & Byrd, R. (2015). Genderism in the LGBTQQIA community: An interpretative phenomenological analysis. *Journal of LGBT Issues in Counseling, 9*, 288. doi:10.1080/15538605.2015.1103679.

Fassinger, R. E., & Arseneau, J. R. (2007). 'I'd rather get wet than be under the umbrella': Differentiating the experiences and identities of lesbian, gay, bisexual, and transgender people. In K. J. Biesche, R. M. Perez, & K. A. DeBord (Eds.), *Handbook of counseling and psychotherapy with lesbian, gay, bisexual, and transgender clients* (pp. 19–49). Washington, DC: American Psychological Association.

Galupo, M. P., Davis, K. S., Grynkiewicz, A. L., & Mitchell, R. C. (2014). Conceptualization of sexual orientation identity among sexual minorities: Patterns across sexual and gender identity. *Journal of Bisexuality, 14*, 433–456. doi:10.1080/15299716.2014.933466.

Galupo, M. P., Henise, S. B., & Davis, K. D. (2014). Transgender microaggressions in the context of friendship: Patterns of experience across friends' sexual orientation and gender identity. *Psychology of Sexual Orientation and Gender Diversity, 1*(4), 461–470. http://dx.doi.org/10.1037/sgd0000075

Galupo, M. P., Mitchell, R. C., & Davis, K. S. (2015). Sexual minority self-identification: Multiple identities and complexity. *Psychology of Sexual Orientation and Gender Diversity, 2*(4), 355–364. http://dx.doi.org/10.1037/sgd0000131

Galupo, M. P., Mitchell, R. C., Grynkiewicz, A. L., & Davis, K. S. (2014). Sexual minority reflections on the Kinsey scale and the Klein sexual orientation grid: Conceptualization and measurement. *Journal of Bisexuality, 14*, 404–432. doi:10.1080/15299716.2014.929553.

Harrison, J., Grant, J., & Herman, J. L. (2012). A gender not listed here: Genderqueers, gender revels, and otherwise in the national transgender discrimination survey. *LGBTQ Policy Journal at the Harvard Kennedy School*, *2*, 13–24. UCLA: The Williams Institute. Retrieved from: http://escholarship.org/uc/item/2zj46213

Kuper, L. E., Nussbaum, R., & Mustanski, B. (2012). Exploring the diversity of gender and sexual orientation identities in an online sample of transgender individuals. *Journal of Sex Research, 49*, 244–254. doi:10.1080/00224499.2011.596954.

Meyer, I. H. (2015). Resilience in the study of minority stress and health of sexual and gender minorities. *Psychology of Sexual Orientation and Gender Diversity, 2*(3), 209–213. http://dx.doi.org/10.1037/sgd0000132

Mock, S. E., & Eibach, R. P. (2012). Stability and change in sexual orientation identity over a 10-year period in adulthood. *Archives of Sexual Behavior, 41*(3), 641–648. doi:10.1007/s10508-011-9761-1.

Pulice-Farrow, L., Clements, Z. A., & Galupo, M. P. (2017). Patterns of transgender microaggressions in friendship: The role of gender identity. *Psychology & Sexuality*. doi:10.1080/19419899.2017.1343745.

Richards, C., Bouman, W. P., Seal, L., Barker, M. J., Nieder, T. O., & T'Sjoen, G. (2016). Non-binary or genderqueer genders. *International Review of Psychiatry, 28*(1), 95–102. doi:10.3109/09540261.2015.1106446.

Riggle, E. D. B., Rostosky, S. S., & Reedy, C. S. (2005). Online surveys for BGLT research. *Journal of Homosexuality, 49*, 1–21. doi:10.1300/J082v49n01-01.

Saltzburg, S., & Davis, T. S. (2010). Co-authoring gender-queer youth identities: Discursive tellings and retellings. *Journal of Ethnic and Cultural Diversity in Social Work, 19*(2), 87–108. doi:10.1080/15313200903124028.

Serano, J. M. (2010). The case against autogynephilia. *International Journal of Transgenderism, 12*(3), 176–187. doi:10.1080/15532739.2010.514223.

Tate, C. C. (2014). Gender identity as a personality process. In B. L. Miller (Ed.), *Gender identity: Disorders, developmental perspectives, and social implications* (pp. 1–22). Hauppauge, NY: Nova Science Publishers.

Tate, C. C., Ledbetter, J. N., & Youssef, C. P. (2013). The two-question method for assessing gender categories in the social and medical sciences. *Journal of Sex Research, 50*(8), 767–776. doi:10.1080/00224499.2012.690110.

Tate, C. C., Youssef, C. P., & Bettergarcia, J. N. (2014). Integrating the study of transgender spectrum and cisgender experiences of self-categorization from a personality perspective. *Review of General Psychology, 18*(4), 302–312. http://dx.doi.org/10.1037/gpr0000019

van Anders, S. M. (2014). Newborn bio/logics and US legal requirements for changing gender/sex designations on state identity documents. *Feminism & Psychology, 24*(2), 172–192. doi:10.1177/0959353514526222.

van Anders, S. M. (2015). Beyond sexual orientation: Integrating gender/sex and diverse sexualities in sexual configurations theory. *Archives of Sexual Behavior, 44*:1177. Advanced online publication. doi:10.1007/s10508-015-0490-8.

Veale, J. F., Clarke, D. E., & Lomax, T. C. (2012). Male-to-female transsexuals' impressions of Blanchard's autogynephilia theory. *International Journal of Transgenderism, 13*, 113–139. doi:10.1080/15532739.2011.669659.

Zinik, G. (1985). Identity conflict of adaptive flexibility? Bisexuality reconsidered. *Journal of Homosexuality, 11*, 7–20. doi:10.1300/J082v11n01_02.

Chapter 11
Identity Stories to Jettison

Louise Green

> *We propose to call our familiar everyday world the "world of measurement" in order to highlight the central position held by assessments, scales, standards, grades, and comparisons…*
>
> *All the manifestations of the world of measurement—the winning and losing, the gaining of acceptance and the threatened rejection, the raised hopes and the dash into despair—all are based on a single assumption that is hidden from our awareness…life is about staying alive and making it through—surviving in a world of scarcity and peril…*
>
> *Let us suppose now that a university of possibility stretches beyond the world of measurement to include all worlds: infinite, generative, and abundant…In the realm of possibility, we gain our knowledge by invention…We speak with an awareness that language creates categories of meaning that open up new worlds to explore. Life appears as variety, pattern, and shimmering movement, inviting us in every moment to engage…*
>
> *The action in a universe of possibility may be characterized as generative, or giving, in all senses of that word: producing new life, creating new ideas, consciously endowing with meaning, contributing, yielding to the power of contexts.* (Zander & Zander, 2000, pp. 17–18)

What we believe is true can shape, delineate, and limit consciousness.

At some moment, those on a boat or a plane assess that there is too much weight. The choice is made to jettison, to throw something out, possibly to improve stability in an emergency. Jetsam is a shortened version of jettison, indicating something thrown in distress. Jetsam is thrown out because the cargo has become an obstacle and must be discarded for survival.

Individually and collectively, humans all have "stories" that have become obstacles, stories that it is time to discard. We could tell an infinite number, but I chose three both universal and consistently undermining. They all live in the world of measurement, with endless variations of character, plot, dialogue, and drama. They are destructive stories, dangerous to our twenty-first-century global challenges.

L. Green (✉)
River Road UU Congregation, 6301 River Road, Bethesda, MD 20817, USA
e-mail: lgreen@rruuc.org

J.D. Sinnott (ed.), *Identity Flexibility During Adulthood*,
DOI 10.1007/978-3-319-55658-1_11

They are delusions that come from the measurement world, yet seem true unless we recognize the assumptions hidden from our awareness:

1. I am here alone (Disconnected).
2. My identities are fixed (Static).
3. There will never be enough (Starved).

We could shorthand them another way: Disconnected, Static, and Starved, DSS, a distress call. We will most likely be living in pain, blocked by obstacles, holding heavy burdens, and stuck in survival mode. All the while, we may be people with lots more resources than seem apparent. We are thinking "poor, sad me" all day and all night—helpless, out of luck, and flailing—missing any sense of "us." We all can lose our sense of creative action, because cognitive framing has us in a very small prison. Our storytelling is ensuring our pain, that's the irony. We never get assistance, because we are sure there is none. We are convinced of who we are, and so we won't allow growth. We never get enough, because we know there is little to be had. It's a story we wrote, yet it can be truly difficult to sense the construct we built.

A short humorous tale gets at this point: A shoe factory sends two marketing scouts to a remote jungle region of Latin America to study the prospects for expanding business. One scout sends back a telegram saying: "Situation hopeless. No one wears shoes. The other scout writes back triumphantly: "Glorious business opportunity. They have no shoes.""

How might we jettison these three stories? The first one: "I am here alone," I know well. It infrequently will pop up as a stress indicator, despite countless experiences of actual connectedness over decades. Something triggers the old story, I am flooded with the memory of the experience of severe disconnection, and this limbic brain story takes up a very mournful violin song. I am empathetic when it arrives now and compassionate when I see it operating in other. I know it *feels* lonely and painful. Yet, there is no doubt in my truer body/spirit alignment that the survival mind story is false, a very partial view.

So much comes in when we simply replace this "I" story with "we" consciousness: "We are interconnected beings." Then we say it until we mean it. That's what I've learned to do, to get *very* skeptical when my 11-year-old self attempts to hijack my lizard brain and hang on to this cargo. It needs to be jetsam for me to move ahead.

Second story to jettison is: "My identities are fixed." This one is big in our current cultural landscape and has consequences that are far-reaching. The more we hear the lived experience of those who have discovered fluid and changing identities (plural), the more some react and double down on their static fixedness. Whether it is gender expression, sexual orientation, the construction of race and ethnicity, and the centrality of economic class, the culture of identity formation is changing rapidly. Huge tectonic shifts threaten that very central story, "My identities are fixed." Human beings like to say: "I know my people. My tribe is homogenous and safe." The new story is *way* more open-ended: "We are fluid selves, shaped by language, culture, family, education, having identities which shift over lifetimes." This is hard on the central norms that create stasis and predictability.

One giant leap we are witnessing is in gender identity. While honest articulation of this experience is decades old, the cultural shift of 2015 was vast. Extremely high-profile transgender people have been saying loud and clear: "I am a fluid person. We are fluid selves."

We each have those moments of interior knowledge, living a story with a false front that has ended. Ultimately something needs to change. This leads us to the third story we must jettison to thrive in the twenty-first century: "There will never be enough." This one calls for another note from Zander and Zander (2000, pp. 19–20), in *The Art of Possibility*:

> *Many people's lives are in daily jeopardy, and they must and do concentrate on staying alive, as any of us would if held up on the street, or lost at sea. That is not the same as survival-thinking, which is the undiscriminating, ongoing attitude that life is dangerous and that one must put one's energy into looking out for Number One.*

This third story is playing out large, loud, and ugly on the world stage where we see zenophobia, violence, and the great escalation of tension and rage. At the same time, to be locked into polarization against this mean, spiteful, and often racist story is to be stuck in the world of measurement. We address it best by ditching the entire game, defiantly, boldly, even exuberantly inhabiting the world of possibility. To trade that life of struggle for new options, we will need to affirm with conviction as the Zanders say: "There IS a world of many possibilities." Not just say it, but make it so. We ally ourselves with people, organizations, and movements that are building that world about which we dream. Thriving only comes if we inhabit a different game. Otherwise, we risk the devolution that accompanies increasing rage.

The poet David Whyte's words encourage me to make the best, unique contribution I can muster in this story project of being "us." I close with his teaching on story (Whyte, 2012):

> *One of the most beautifully disturbing questions we can ask is whether a given story we tell about our lives is actually true, and whether the opinions we go over every day have any foundation, or are things we repeat to ourselves simply so that we will continue to play the game.*
>
> *It can be quite disorienting to find that a story we have relied on is not only not true—it actually never was. Not now not ever.*
>
> *Another form of obsolescence can fray at the cocoon we have spun about ourselves, that is, the story was true at one time, and for an extended period; that the story was even true and good to us, but now it is no longer true and no longer of any benefit. In fact, our continued retelling of it simply imprisons us.*
>
> *What if [we] acted as if it wasn't true anymore? One of the interesting mercies of this kind of questioning is that it is hard to lose by asking: if the story is still true, we will soon find out and can go back to telling it. If it is not, we have turned the key, worked the hinges, and walked out in the clean air again with a simple swing of the door.*

As we design new identity stories, we recreate the world of possibility. So much awaits our telling, and a million stories are possible. Choose the identity stories large enough to live into. Choose the ones where we can thrive.

References

Whyte, D. (2012). Many rivers newsletter. *Winter.* www.davidwhyte.com/2012/2012_brochure_letter.html

Zander, R. S., & Zander, B. (2000). *The art of possibility*. Cambridge, MA: Harvard Business School Press.

Chapter 12
Work and Identity Flexibility

Carol Hoare

Recently, the structure and availability of paid work have undergone substantial changes. Technology, particularly as it relates to automation and the widespread use of computer functions, has taken its toll by automating and eliminating many jobs. Computer functions have fostered declines in both the publishing industry and newspaper delivery, digital self-checkouts are making cashiers unnecessary, robotics are eliminating vehicle manufacturing jobs, and travel agencies are shutting down due to travel websites. Postal workers are endangered by e-mail and the potential of drone package delivery, needs for typists and word processors are replaced by voice recognition and computer-based dictation services, and librarians are increasingly made redundant due to search engines. The Bureau of Labor Statistics reports that manufacturing is the sector that is projected to decline the most by 2022, adding to declines already seen due to outsourcing. The industrial revolution, followed years later by the service era, might now be characterized as the depersonalized era. Devices now take the place of humans.

Declines in work opportunities are made more troublesome because the fastest growing industries (e.g., health-care services, computer systems design and maintenance) require employees who are highly literate, skilled, and, often, credentialed. The numbers of unskilled workers will swell unemployment rolls, with GED programs and community colleges ill-equipped to re-skill and prepare large numbers of the unemployed for replacement jobs. With the US high school dropout rate hovering around 7% (2.2 million youths) in 2013 (the latest year for which data are available), the future of work for such persons is at significant risk (National Center for Education Statistics 2015).

Most industries and organizations have adapted, slimming down their bureaucracies, offering far fewer worker benefits, and replacing full-time employees with contract and contingent workers. But heightened employer adaptability and flexibility

C. Hoare (✉)
The George Washington University, Washington, DC, USA
e-mail: choare@gwu.edu

J.D. Sinnott (ed.), *Identity Flexibility During Adulthood*,
DOI 10.1007/978-3-319-55658-1_12

in recent years seems to be inversely related to employee flexibility and retraining. This is a dilemma in that work is a source of significant meaning in most adults' lives. It rewards, in more ways than the monetary, the way adults spend at least half of their waking hours. Work is salient, its absence seen in staggering statistics of depression, substance abuse, suicide, and, more benignly, regression to a prior identity form (Kroger, 1996; Marcia, 2002; Valde, 1996). Without work, self-respect is lost along with a most important source of identity. As one employee said, "I can't quit my job; if I did I wouldn't *be* anybody" (Green, 1993, p. 10).

As I noted previously (Hoare, 2011), the literature on paid work has focused primarily on corporate needs. Organizational success has been in the spotlight, with the meaning, importance, and developmental opportunities for workers ill-considered. Workers are made "passive" by this literature, studied largely in terms of behaviors that sustain or threaten organizations (Hulin, 2014, p. 18):

> We treat workers as carbon-based elements of sociotechnical systems, uninteresting and unimportant as individuals but worthy of study because they are tardy or absent, produce something, quit their jobs, engage in organizational citizenship behavior or counterproductive work behaviors, or join a union. (Hulin, 2014, p. 17)

Industries and organizations must flexibly adapt it they are to survive. They must be agile in the midst of unpredictable and continually changing market demands and conditions. Employee flexibility is an outgrowth of organizational flexibility. Workers must now function adaptively without depending on disappearing and, often reassuring, boundaries and structures. "Traditional structures, with carefully delineated boundaries between jobs are less capable of responding to rapid change" (Tannenbaum, Salas, & Canon-Bowers, 1996, p. 118).

In this chapter, I consider employees themselves in terms of an identity that is constituted in many by the work of their lives. I look first to the meaning of identity and its attributes. I then consider contemporary work organizations and their tendency to displace permanent employees. Finally, I treat of the ways in which adults can reconstitute their identities, either by improving their skill sets or by transitioning into different kinds of work. Highlighted are the ways in which contemporary times require identity flexibility.

Identity

Erik Erikson's construct of identity is the basis of this chapter, not only because he originated the concept but also due to the connection he made between personal coherence and work engagement. Erikson held that identity is only partly conscious, with the unconscious portion primary. Identity means a "*subjective sense* of an *invigorating sameness* and *continuity*" (Erikson, 1968, p. 19, emphasis his), a quality expressed by William James in a letter to his wife:

> A man's character (identity) is discernible in the mental or moral attitude in which, when it came upon him, he felt himself most deeply and intensely active and alive. At such moments

> there is a voice inside which speaks and says: *This* is the real me!. (Erikson, 1968, p. 19, emphasis his)

"Moral attitude" means that identity is value-driven in that the person's identity development is constituted by work commitments that show fidelity of purpose, of knowing what is worth doing with one's life. Identity development is an active, ongoing, continual process of moving toward and gaining a sense of personal control and centrality. "Above all," Erikson (1974) wrote:

> the ego works at all times on the maintenance of a sense that we… are central in the flux of our experience, and not tossed around on some periphery; that we are original in our plans of actions instead of being pushed around; and finally, that we are activating (as well as being activated by) others instead of made passive or being motivated by exigencies. All this together makes the difference between feeling (and acting) whole or fragmented. (p. 92)

Erikson held that identity development is not an achievement that is accomplished once and for all. Rather, it is an ongoing, lifelong process, a "project" (Watson, 2008, p.124). "A sense of identity," Erikson (1980) held, "is never gained nor maintained once and for all. Like a 'good conscience,' it is constantly lost and regained" (p. 128). Furthermore, Erikson said that he had become aversive to the term *identity* because it was so often misconstrued. He "griped" that when his theory was cited, his thought was turned into "an Eriksonian achievement scale" (Erikson in Evans, 1967, p. 15). Empirical testing had reduced identity to an accomplishment and to that which could be measured through the use of interviews and scales. Among other reductions, this eliminated the unconscious as an important identity dimension. Despite its inherent reductionism, research has concurred that identity development continues through adult life (Cramer, 2004; Josselson, 1996; Pulkkinen & Kokko, 2000).

With respect to the unconscious in identity development, persons are influenced, in youth and later, in their choices of identity commitments. In this, a complex form of reflecting occurs in that:

> The individual judges himself in the light of what he perceives to be the way in which others judge him in comparison to themselves and to a typology significant to them; while he judges their way of judging him in the light of how he perceives himself in comparison to them and to types that have become relevant to him. (Erikson, 1968, pp. 22–23)

Thus, others are mirrors in that we see reflections of ourselves in the eyes, beliefs, and feedback of them and believe ourselves to be what we see. Individuals are thereby influenced by what others think and say about them, about their talents, traits, interests, and values. This occurs both consciously and unconsciously.

Erikson (1963) said he did now know when he had first noticed what he would later call *identity* but thought it was when he witnessed the convergence of "somatic tension, social panic, and ego anxiety" in veterans returning from World War II (p. 42). "It was as if, subjectively, their lives no longer hung together – and never would again. There was a central disturbance of what I then started to call ego identity"(p. 42). "The boundaries of their egos had lost their shock-absorbing delineation" (Erikson, 1968, p. 66). For many, the genesis of this malady appeared "in violent events, in others in the gradual grind of a million annoyances" (Erikson, 1968, pp. 66–67). For a number of the men, the military existence "provided few ideal prototypes" (Erikson, 1968, p. 67), and their egos disintegrated into "bodily, sexual, social, occupational fragments, each having to overcome again the danger of its evil prototype" (p. 68). Here, Erikson described the dissonance that foreshadowed disintegration. For example, dissonance had occurred when a medic saw "a seemingly innocent item such as a gun in his unwilling hands: a symbol of evil, which endangered the principles by which the individual had attempted to safeguard personal integrity and social status in his life at home" (Erikson, 1963, p. 42). Having learned to heal, he was now required to mutilate and kill. To such men, "isolation" occurred along with a "long preoccupation with work patterns that were not their own and could not be related to anything they had learned" (Erikson, 1968, p. 154).

Identity and Identification

It is important to note that much of the recent literature on workers uses the terms *identity* and *identification* interchangeably. This, to Erikson, was erroneous. Identifications are alignments in views and perspectives with family, friends, colleagues, and organizations. Conversely, *identity* "is a deeply ingrained commitment to purposes and values in which one stands singularly in the self and in the world" (Hoare 2006, p. 352). We might say that identity is inward, while identification extends outward, an important connection but not a human characteristic. Workers can and do identify with the social group or with the job. In circumstances in which organizational identification is poor, a powerful identification with the work team can replace a lack of connection with the organization (Saayman & Crafford, 2011).

Identification often means a sense of "cognitive connection" between the organization and the person's self-concept in which an "individual's beliefs about the organization become self-referential or self-defining" (Walsh & Gordon, 2008, p. 49). A strong identification with the organization can "anchor" workers' identities, providing a sense of agency, and of "belonging, and ownership" (Patriotta & Lanzara, 2006, p. 995).

"Identity-formation goes beyond the process "*identifying oneself* with ideal others" as on a one-way street (Erikson, 1960, p. 48). Identifications can yield strong attachments as well as models for future identity commitments. Active engagement is necessary, for identifications alone cannot forge identity. Rather, as William James claimed and Erikson (1958) concurred, such identifications constitute the self one must "murder" to move beyond (p. 166)".

In some cases, notably among those in the professions (e.g., ministers and physicians), persons show a stronger identification with their profession than with the employing organization. Here, their commitment to the work or calling of their lives substitutes for a strong employer connection. In effect, they believe that their professional work transcends organizational borders and that they can perform their work irrespective of its location or sponsorship.

Reconstituting Identity

In conceptualizing identity, Erikson worked in a time when career and job stability were the norm. An implicit social contract existed, one that promised continual employment to workers. This inspired a sense of loyalty and enhanced a strong sense of worker identification with the employing organization.

Today in the organizational literature, in descriptions of contemporary work environments, one finds terms such as "turbulent" (Chreim, Williams, & Hinings, 2007); "volatile" (Berntson, 2008), "unpredictable "(Fouad & Bynner, 2008), "precarious, insecure, uncertain, and "fragile" (Brown & Coupland, 2015); "hostile" (Molleman & van den Beukel, 2007); a "moving target" (Fouad & Bynner, 2008); and personally "dissonant" and "incoherent" (Saayman & Crafford, 2011). Work that once provided for "stable"career development (Mahler, 2008) in hierarchical, vertical organizations now exists in more horizontal, flattened, and sometimes decentralized structures. Furthermore, career is now framed as a series of jobs during the adult work span, instead of a single, stable career path established in one's 20s. The US Bureau of Labor Statistics (2015) indicates that adults now engage in an average of 12 jobs during their working lives. Such instability may lead to anxiety and disequilibrium that can "threaten" identity (Saayman & Crafford, 2011)).

Supporting data from displaced worker surveys show that 35% of long-tenured workers from 2011 to 2013 say that they lost their jobs because of plant closings or geographic changes in the organization, 33% said their job loss was due to inadequate work, and 32% cited position or shift abolition as reasons for their job displacement (US Bureau of Labor Statistics, 2014). More employees in goods-producing organizations lost jobs than workers in service-providing organizations. It is impossible to know what the future will bring with respect to the job market, but manufacturing jobs may well go the way of the lamplighter, the switchboard operator, the ice delivery worker, and the elevator operator.

Previously, well-educated and older workers had been comparatively protected from job loss. In a major change, the likelihood that a college graduate was displaced compared to a high school non-completer was 1.2 percentage points higher in 1993–1997 than during the prior decade (Rodriguez & Zavodny, 2003, p. 505). This may not seem to a significant change, but higher education was once an insurance against job loss. Furthermore, middle-aged and older workers were also more likely to be displaced in 1993–1997 than previously (Rodriguez & Zavodny, 2003). As the core workforce declined, there was an upswing in the employment of contingent (temporary) workers, contract workers, and consultants to 42.6 million in 2005 (Fox, 2014). Such workers are less costly, in part because health care and other benefits are not required. Fouad and Bynner (2008) found that, in 1990, 70% of US employees worked for a company that provided benefits. By 2005, only 60% of such employees had employer-sponsored benefits.

Portrayal of the foregoing disruptions is not meant to paint the darkest possible picture. Highly skilled workers, especially those who engage in knowledge work and those with superior technological expertise, are very much in demand. Yet, the altered work environment has brought with it the need for flexibility in the way employees frame their identities. If conventional job security is largely an attribute of the past, those who become more flexible might enjoy a new form of security, something called "flexicurity" (Berntson, 2008), that is, job security as a function of worker flexibility.

There are three principle ways in which workers can reconstitute their jobs in a way that is identity-salient. The first is to continually upgrade their knowledge and skills. The second is that of flexibly altering their skill sets so as to increase demand for their functions within the organization and increase their marketability to other employers. The third is to transition to other careers that are well aligned with their competencies, needs, and interests, that is, with their identity.

Knowledge Upgrading

With respect to the first of these, knowledge upgrading is a continuing need, with or without the turbulence of the current work environment. In the medical environment, for example, arsenic was used to treat infections in the 1920s and 1930s, mustard plasters were often prescribed for chest congestion in the 1950s, and Quaalude was popular in the 1960s for sedation and treatment of insomnia. A physician who prescribes such medications today might well be sued for malpractice. In less dramatic ways, it is a foolish employee who does not remain up-to-date with the knowledge and skills in his or her area of expertise and employment. Continual learning, sponsored by the organization or individually designed, is highlighted in the literature as a necessity of ongoing employment. Furthermore, key abilities in, for example, communicating well, able team membership, problem solving, self-direction, continual self-reflection and improvement, and continual updating of one's knowledge about the competitive environment in which the organization functions make for valued employees (Berntson, 2008). Persons with these qualities are typically more secure in their jobs than those with fewer skills and interpersonal deficits.

Self-Efficacy

Increasing one's belief in personal self-efficacy is another way a worker may be able to upgrade his or her performance. In 1977, Bandura originated the construct. He held that "an efficacy expectation is the conviction that one can successfully execute the behavior required to produce the outcomes" (p. 193). Self-efficacy has been shown to be a personal characteristic that is related to effective task and job performance. In 2007, Judge, Jackson, Shaw, Scott, and Rich reported that more than 10,000 studies of self-efficacy had been conducted during the prior 25 years, with an average of 1.67 articles appearing every day in 2004 alone.

Self-efficacy does not function in isolation. Along with, for example, general mental ability, competence in task performance, conscientiousness, openness, and experience, self-efficacy plays a role in predicting able performance at work. In the absence of these highly correlated variables, self-efficacy alone does not produce positive outcomes in attaining work-related goals. However, when competent, motivated, and experienced employees with related positive characteristics consider themselves self-efficacious, work-related performance is enhanced as is an ongoing belief in one's performance.

Employees who are comparatively low in self-efficacy may be able to raise their own levels of the attribute and demonstrate goal-directed intentions to perform well. Other than emotional arousal, which is not particularly relevant to most work contexts, employees can engage in three main modalities of self-efficacy that Bandura (1977) identified. These are "performance accomplishments," "vicarious experience," and "verbal persuasion" (p. 195). For those with low self-efficacy, reflecting on areas in which they have shown personal mastery may boost expectations for efficacy at tasks in the present work environment. In using vicarious experience, one observes others perform well at a task and then models the observed behavior.

Such role modeling can be helpful, particularly if the person doing the modeling is someone with characteristics that are similar to the person observing (e.g., gender, equal level in the organization). The third way of enhancing a sense of efficacy is through verbal persuasion. Although this is the least effective of the three modes, Bandura noted that, along with efforts to enhance or correct performance, social persuasion may contribute to positive self-efficacy results.

Thus, it can be said that workers with low or incorrect assessments of their self-efficacy may learn that they are, or can become, self-efficacious. This can be thought of as an extension of one's learning plan, a self-improvement modality. Performance improvements may well result.

Accommodating One's Identity

In the second key way of reconstituting identity, the literature reports a frequent disjunction between what individuals are taught to do so as to function well in their jobs and who they must become in order to remain employed. That is, identity must shift in order to accommodate the requirements of the job and the organization. Workers can volunteer for cross-training in which they learn to function in roles beyond their core skills and, potentially, in teams. In doing so, they become valuable across a range of needs and functions. In manufacturing, flexible, cross-trained workers "have overlapping skills and, therefore, will be able to move to a bottleneck task, to replace one another in the case of absenteeism, to assist an overloaded colleague, or to share workloads, all of which will contribute to efficiency and performance" (Molleman & van den Buekel, 2007, p. 118). Engaging in cross-functional team work in complex problem-solving tasks is also important in that such engagement shows a strong positive relationship with accountability.

Insofar as change is the only permanent work quality, involving oneself in the change process diminishes rigidity, the antagonist of flexibility. Such involvement also permits workers to influence the change process and outcomes actively, instead of resisting or remaining on the periphery of the action. Related to this are significant changes in the constitution of the workforce, one in which persons from different ethnicities, races, and cultures work side by side. Rigid workers have been known to limit their contacts with cultural others, while those who are accepting and flexible telegraph to others that they value diversity in the workforce and feel as though they and their work profit from interacting with cultural others. Ongoing identity development is far more likely in contexts where workers are exposed to divergent viewpoints and are receptive to them (e.g., Adams & Marshall, 1996; Berzonsky & Adams, 1999; Bosma & Kunnen, 2001, Erikson, 1968; Fadjukoff, Kokko, & Pulkkinen, 2010; Grotevant, 1987; Kroger, 2007; Marcia, 2001; Waterman, 1982). Not only does such this make the worker more attractive to the current organization, but it improves his or her marketability beyond organizational borders.

Openness to Experience

Openness to experience includes "ongoing learning, . . . receptivity to new and potentially conflicting information and ideas, curiosity, inventiveness, broadmindedness, and the desire to explore fresh alternatives" (Hoare, 2011, p. 413). Openness is related to employee flexibility in that open-minded workers tend to welcome divergent ways of perceiving the world and are willing to consider new and unexplored terrain and options. Clearly, values can come into play, for persons are not evenly open-minded across all views, attitudes, and perspectives. For example, not having had the benefits of maternity or paternity leave in their own prior work lives, middle-aged or older adults may resist policy changes that provide such benefits to young employees. Or, not believing that climate change is influenced by humans, employees may resist organizations' sustainability efforts.

In the work realm, studies of openness have shown that the attribute defines an ongoing way of perceiving and approaching the world (Major, Turner, & Fletcher, 2006). Persons who are high on openness characteristics tend to adapt better to changing conditions and show a willingness to consider alternatives to the traditional and familiar. Those low in openness tend to oppose change, preferring the familiar, the conventional, and the tried-and-true. They tend not to be highly creative in their approach to work problems and tasks (George, Helson, & John, 2011).

In today's work environment, openness and its expression in the employee's approach to the world and to employing creativity is a valued commodity. Uncertainty and the ongoing press for new products and ideas create the need for innovation throughout the work environment. Although openness to experience is a personality trait that can change over time (George et al., 2011), no studies were found that considered ways in which worker openness might be developed or expanded.

Context is always important, and through their managers and supervisors, organizations must be willing to support development plans for expanding worker openness. And, when workers themselves seek to expand their own openness, the positive effects on flexibility and creativity might be well work the effort.

The organizational literature is replete with claims that workers must show their willingness to be "temporally flexible as well as "spatially mobile" (Brown, 2015, p. 31). In the global economy, organizations have moved beyond US boundaries and time zones. The term "boundaryless" has been used to describe jobs and careers that "zigzag" rather than moving along a stable, hierarchical path (Walsh & Gordon, 2008). As a result, worker flexibility might mean a willingness to work in countries other than the USA and to learn a foreign language. Such openness, which is correlated with intelligence, can enhance one's current position and future employability.

Transitioning to Other Careers

The third key way in which employees can employ flexibility to alter portions of their identity is by transitioning to positions that differ significantly from their current jobs. Such a transition often occurs voluntarily when the worker concludes that the current role is no longer the most compatible with, or the best expression of, his or her identity. A manager who, in midlife, left the business environment to become a teacher, said:

> I felt like I was abandoning my values. My values had always been the working person, deep downtrodden, the less fortunate, and now I was going . . . to be management….somewhere along the line I kept being rewarded for being productive and lost that. It is kind of nice to be back to that. (Mahler, 2008, p. 263)

Recently, Danny Ludeman resigned from his position as CEO at Wells Fargo Advisors in St. Louis to attend Covenant Theological Seminary and run a nonprofit organization to help ex-convicts adjust to life after incarceration. He found his calling at midlife and now helps ex-prisoners obtain jobs and housing, thus reducing the recidivism rate substantially. He aims to close one prison every month (Finn, 2015).

Often, those transitioning had been successful in their prior work but found that such work did not meet their identity needs. This was true of both Ludeman and of George Bernard Shaw. Erikson (1956) described Shaw and his reflections on his life when he was 70 years old. Shaw experienced a crisis (to Erikson, an "identity crisis") that occurred when Shaw was 20 years old, one that occurred not because he had failed but because he had succeeded in a business occupation that he abhorred. He said he had felt like an "imposter" and feared that he might be held in the tentacles of his hated job interminably (p. 59). Thus, he left his position and began a lengthy "psychological moratorium" to discover his genuine identity:

> Thus, 'the complete outsider' gradually became his kind of complete insider. 'I was,' he said, 'outside society, outside politics, outside sport, outside the Church'—but this 'only within the limits of British Barbarism…the moment music, painting, literature, or science came into question the positions were reversed: it was I who was the insider'". (p. 64)

> Such transitions confirm the "malleability of identity construction" and typically represent "progress or growth" to the person (Dutton, Roberts, & Bednar, 2011, p. 272). "Attachment to a particular occupation or employer may come to be viewed as a confinement from which the individual longs to escape" (Kirpal & Brown, 2007, p. 219). Once an "anchor," such work has become a "chain". (Kirpal & Brown, 2007, p. 219)

Yet, dramatic transitions can be difficult to make, engendering anxiety and "a disequilibrated sense of self" (Mahler, 2008, p. 317). Although such changes are often motivated, as in Shaw's case, by antagonism between an "ideal and a current identity" (Chreim, Williams, & Hinings, 2007, p. 1530), and can eventually place the person in agentic control of his or her life (Saayman & Crafford, 2011), uncertainty can take hold. Those who are transitioning report feeling "in a vacuum," in "midair," "neither here nor there," "at loose ends" (Ibarra & Barbulescu, 2010, p. 149) and feeling as though they are "wandering in the wilderness" (Ibarra & Barbulescu, 2010, p. 143). Such feelings can precipitate a retreat from the "ideal," back to what was "real." Yet, a career transition can make a real difference in life, taking persons to a position in which they feel as though they can then "leave their footprints 'in the sands of time'" (Saayman & Crafford, 2011, p. 211).

In many respects, we are in an age of individualization. Individuals are now expected to be responsible for their own jobs, their learning, and their careers (Allvin, 2004). They must be "proactive," "seeking opportunities and initiating situations" that make them more attractive in the present and toward the future (Berntson, 2008, p. 3; see also Crant, 2000; Hall, 1996; Hall & Moss, 1998); Seibert, Kraimer, & Crant, 2001). This defines a "protean career," one in which "individuals not only set up their own career plans, goals, and ambitions, but must also find their own ways in which to realize them" (Berntson, 2008, p. 4). In the current quid pro quo psychological contract, "the employer offers competency development, interesting assignments, and various bonuses, whereas the employee, in return, offers involvement, maximum performance, and openness to change" (Berntson, 2008, p. 4; see also Conway & Briner, 2005; Kluytmans & Ott, 1999). Increasingly, employers rely on workers to "develop a proactive and 'entrepreneurial' work attitude based on multi-skilling and flexibility" (Kirpal & Brown, 2007, p. 233).

Few will claim that efforts in the direction of flexibility are easy. Yet, flexibility carries with it a promise of personal development and work engagement and, potentially, continual employment. Flexibility is the watchword in literature that describes qualities that are required of workers and organizations. Although it may be disquieting, workers must now be at the helm, nondependent on job security, and functioning in a way that makes them desirable as employees.

Conclusions

There are dramatic changes in contemporary work environments that require changes in the way workers constitute and deploy their identities. Fortunately, identity development occurs throughout adulthood and is malleable. In what is now a volatile work environment, flexible workers are in great demand. And there are ways in which workers can expand their flexibility and thus dimensions of their identities. The three ways highlighted here are knowledge upgrading, expanding skill sets, and transitioning to alternate careers that are compatible with their identity needs.

References

Adams, G. R., & Marshall, S. K. (1996). A developmental social psychology of identity: Understanding the person-in-context. *Journal of Adolescence, 19*, 429–442.

Allvin, J. (2004). The individualization of labour. In C. Garsten & K. Jacobsson (Eds.), *Learning to be employable: New agendas on work, responsibility, and learningin a globalizing world* (pp. 23–41). New York: Palgrave MacMillan.

Bandura, A. (1977). Self-efficacy: Toward a unifying theory of behavioral change. *Psychological Review, 84*, 191–215.

Berntson, E. (2008). Employability perceptiOns: Nature, determinants, and implications for Health and well-being (Unpublished doctoral thesis). Stockholm University, Stockholm, Sweden.

Berzonsky, M. D., & Adams, G. R. (1999). Re-evaluating the identity status paradigm: Still useful after 35 years. Commentary. *Developmental Review, 19*, 557–590.

Bosma, H. A., & Kunnen, E. S. (2001). Determinants and mechanisms in ego identity development: A review and synthesis. *Developmental Review, 21*, 39–66.

Brown, A. D. (2015). Identities and identity work in organizations. *International Journal of Management Reviews, 17*(1), 20–40.

Brown, A. D., & Coupland, C. (2015). Identity threats, identity work and elite professionals. *Organization Studies, 1*, 1–22.

Chreim, S., Williams, B. E., & Hinings, C. R. (2007). Interlevel influences on the reconstruction of professional role identity. *The Academy of Management Journal, 50*, 1515–1539.

Conway, N., & Briner, R. B. (2005). *Understanding psychological contracts at work: A critical evaluation of theory and research*. New York: Oxford University Press.

Cramer, P. (2004). Identity change in adulthood: The contribution of defense mechanisms and life experiences. *Journal of Research in Personality, 38*, 280–316.

Crant, J. M., & Bateman, T. S. (2000). Charismatic leadership viewed from above: The impact of proactive personality. *Journal of Organizational Behavior, 21*, 63–75.

Crant, J. M. (2000). Proactive behavior in organizations. *Journal of Management, 26*, 435–462.

Dutton, J. E., Roberts, L. M., & Bednar, J. (2011). Pathways for positive identity construction at work: Four types of positive identity and the building of social resources. *The Academy of Management Journal, 35*, 265–293.

Erikson, E. H. (1963). *Childhood and society* (2nd ed.). New York: Norton.

Erikson, E. H. (1974). *Dimensions of a new identity*. New York: Norton.

Erikson, E. H. (1980). *Identity and the life cycle*. New York: Norton.

Erikson, E. H. (1968). *Identity, youth and crisis*. New York: Norton.

Erikson, E. H. (1956). The problem of ego identity. *Journal of the American Psychoanalytic Association, 4*, 56–121.

Erikson, E. H. (1958). The syndrome of identity diffusion in adolescents and young adults and the psychosocial development of children. In J. M. Tanner & B. Inhelder (Eds.), *Discussions on child development, 1955, Proceedings of the Third Meeting of the Child Study Group*. New York: International Universities Press.

Erikson, E. H. (1960). Youth and the life cycle, an interview. In *Children*. 7 (pp. 43–49). Washington, DC.: U.S. Department of Health, Education and Welfare.

Evans, R. I. (1967). *Dialogue with Erik Erikson*. New York: Norton.

Fadjukoff, P., Kokko, K., & Pulkkinen. (2010). Changing economic conditions and identity formation in adulthood. *European Psychologist, 15*, 293–303.
Finn, E. (2015, August 3). Answering God's call. *Barron's* 21–23.
Fouad, N. A., & Bynner, J. (2008). Work transitions. *The American Psychologist, 63*, 241–251.
Fox, J. (2014). Where are all the self-employed workers? *Harvard Business Review, 5*, 1–10.
George, L. G., Helson, R., & John, O. P. (2011). The "CEO" of women's work lives: How big five consciousness, extraversion, and openness predict 50 years of work experiences in a changing sociocultural context. *Journal of Personality and Social Psychology, 101*, 812–830.
Green, A. (1993). *Wobbles, pilebuts, and other heroes*. Urbana, IL: University of Illinois Press.
Grotevant, H. D. (1987). Toward a process model of identity formation. *Journal of Adolescent Research, 2*, 203–222.
Hall, D. T. (1996). Protean careers of the 21st century. *The Academy of Management Executive, 10*, 8–16.
Hall, D. T., & Moss, J. E. (1998). The new protean career contract: Helping organizations and employees adapt. *Organizational Dynamics, 26*, 22–37.
Hoare, C. (2006). Work as the catalyst of reciprocal adult development and learning. In C. Hoare (Ed.), *Handbook of adult development and learning* (pp. 344–380). New York: Oxford University Press.
Hoare, C. (2011). Work as the catalyst of reciprocal adult development and learning. In C. Hoare (Ed.), *The Oxford Handbook of reciprocal adult development and learning* (2nd ed., pp. 396–424). New York: Oxford University Press.
Hulin, C. L. (2014). Work and being: The meanings of work in contemporary society. In F. J. Kevin, J. R. Hollenbeck, & A. M. Ryan (Eds.), *The nature of work: Advances in psychological theory, methods, and practice* (pp. 9–33). Washington, DC: American Psychological Association.
Ibarra, H., & Barbulescu, R. (2010). Identity as narrative: Prevalence, effectiveness, and consequences of narrative identity work in macro work role transitions. *The Academy of Management Review, 35*, 135–154.
Josselson, R. (1996). *Revising herself: The story of women's identity from college to midlife*. New York: Oxford University Press.
Kirpal, S., & Brown, A. (2007). The much vaunted 'flexible employee' – what does it take? In A. Brown, S. Kirpal, & F. Rauner (Eds.), *Identities at work* (pp. 211–237). Dordrecht, The Netherlands: Springer.
Kluytmans, F., & Ott, M. (1999). The management of employability in the Netherlands. *European Journal of Work and Organizational Psychology, 8*, 145–153.
Kroger, J. (2007). *Identity development. Adolescence through adulthood* (2nd ed.). Thousand Oaks, CA: Sage Publications.
Kroger, J. (1996). Identity, regression and development. *Journal of Adolescence, 19*, 203–222.
Mahler, E (2008). Defining career success in the 21st century: A narrative study of intentional work role transitions. (Unpublished doctoral dissertation). The George Washington University, Washington, DC.
Major, D. A., Turner, J. E., & Fletcher, T. D. (2006). Linking proactive personality and the big five to motivation to learn and development activity. *The Journal of Applied Psychology, 91*, 927–935.
Marcia, J. E. (2001). A commentary on Seth Schwartz's review on identity theory and research. *Identity: An International Journal of Theory and Research, 1*, 59–65.
Marcia, J. E. (2002). Identity and psychosocial development in adulthood. *Identity: An International Journal of Theory and Research, 2*, 7–28.
Molleman, E., & van den Beukel, A. (2007). Worker flexibility and its perceived contribution to performance: The moderating role of task characteristics. *Human Factors and Ergonomics in Manufacturing, 17*, 117–135.
National Center for Education Statistics (2015). Trends in high school drop and completion rates in the United States. Retrieved from nces.cd.gov/programs/coe/indicatorcoj.asp
Patriotta, G., & Lanzara, G. F. (2006). Identity, institutions, and new work roles. *The American Behavioral Scientist, 49*, 987–999.

Pulkkinen, L., & Kokko, K. (2000). Identity development in adulthood. *Journal of Research in Personality, 34*, 445–470.
Rodriguez, D., & Zavodny, M. (2003). Changes in the age and education profile of displaced workers. *Industrial & Labor Relations Review, 56*, 498–510.
Saayman, T., & Crafford, A. (2011). Negotiating work identity. *SA Journal of Insustrial Psychology/ SA Tydskrif vir Bedryfsielkunde, 37*(1), 12. http://dx.doi.org/104102/sajip.v37i1.963.
Seibert, S. E., Kraimer, M. L., & Crant, J. M. (2001). What do proactive people do? A longitudinal model linking proactive personality and career success. *Personnel Psychology, 54*, 845–874.
Tannenbaum, S. I., Salas, E., & Cannon-Bowers, J. A. (1996). Promoting team effectiveness. In M. West (Ed.), *Handbook of work group psychology* (pp. 503–529). Chichester, UK: Wiley.
U.S. Bureau of Labor Statistics (2015). *Number of jobs held, labor market activity, and Earnings growth among the youngest baby boomers: Results from a longitudinal Study*. Retrieved from nls_info@bls.gov
U.S. Bureau of Labor Statistics (2014). Worker Displacement: 2011–2013. Retrieved from cpsinfo@bls.gov
Valde, G. A. (1996). Identity closure: A fifth identity status. *The Journal of Genetic Psychology, 157*, 245–254.
Walsh, K., & Gordon, J. R. (2008). Creating an individual work identity. *Human Resource Management Review, 18*, 46–61.
Waterman, A. S. (1982). Identity development from adolescence to adulthood: An extension of theory and a review of research. *Developmental Psychology, 18*, 341–358.
Watson, T. J. (2008). Managing identity: Identity work, personal predicaments, and structural circumstances. *Organization, 55*(1), 121–143.

Chapter 13
From Student to Professional: Thoughts on Roadblocks and Keys to Success

Shaina A. Kumar

From Student to Professional: Thoughts on Roadblocks and Keys to Success

A few years back, I received my master's degree in clinical psychology and decided somewhere along the way that my ultimate career goal was to become a professor and conduct my own research in the field. I thought the best way to build my résumé for such a position would be to acquire direct experience and more formal education, but the formal education piece would have to wait until later. For now, I wanted to focus on understanding what it meant to actually be a professor. As such, I sought out an adjunct professor of psychology position at my university to increase my repertoire. I accepted the title gracefully after interviewing. Initially, I thought that holding this position would be quite easy. All I had to do was talk about topics I already understood, make activities, discuss current events, and grade papers, right? Soon after, I found this was not the case and teaching others held quite a responsibility.

I remember speaking with a number of my academic advisors regarding what it meant to be a professor before I started the position. I was given a range of responses that I will discuss later; however, I want to note that each one of them had mentioned that being a professor meant becoming a "professional" and "holding a position of authority" or something similar. That was the point where I had a minor existential crisis. I had no idea what it meant to be "professional," much less what "holding a position of authority" meant. Until now, my entire life had been spent identifying as a student. Although I previously held teaching assistant and internship positions in my field, I was still a student through and through. Whenever I introduced myself in a professional setting, I would say something along the lines of, "Nice to meet you! I am a student attending [college] and I am here to learn about [task]."

S.A. Kumar (✉)
Psychology Department, Towson University, 8000 York Rd, Towson, MD 21252, USA
e-mail: skumar@towson.edu

J.D. Sinnott (ed.), *Identity Flexibility During Adulthood*,
DOI 10.1007/978-3-319-55658-1_13

My role as a student was to listen to lectures for hours on end, write long papers every weekend, stay up into the late hours studying, miss out on much needed sleep time, excessively worry over exams, reward myself with fun times, and then repeat the cycle. That was all I knew. I was suddenly expected to leave that identity behind, an identity that I had cultivated for over 20 years. Moving from student to professional quickly became a very daunting task and I no longer felt qualified to do anything other than study. At the end of the day, I questioned myself: did I even know how to do anything other than be a student?

There have been a number of researchers that have contributed to the understanding of human psychosocial development during this life period. Perhaps the most well-known contributor, Erik Erikson (1968), paved the way for understanding existential crises experienced in what he defined as "prolonged adolescence." Erikson documented that prolonged adolescence was a period in industrialized societies where individuals explored and solidified their identities in life before taking on adult responsibilities (e.g., becoming a parent), and in modern language, this time has now been defined as "emerging adulthood" (Arnett, 2000). Expectedly, emerging adulthood is the time where Erikson's fifth stage of development, identity versus role confusion, becomes most relevant. The identity versus role confusion stage is characterized by individuals attempting to discover their own unique identity, and a successful individual coming out of this stage will gain a sense of control and independence through their late teens into their 20s (Arnett). As young adults tend to find their niche in society during this developmental period, many researchers also believe that the most important events of our lives happen within this time frame (Martin & Stayer, 1990). It helped me to understand that this crisis I was experiencing was completely normal, but honestly it did not put me at ease. Unsurprisingly, this stage of my life was just as bumpy as Erikson predicted.

I encountered a number of roadblocks through my journey. There were some roadblocks that were easily attended to while others threw me through a nonsensical loop. There are also a number of roadblocks that I am still in the process of overcoming. However, at this point, I believe I have now made a commitment to shape a new sense of identity: I am now committed to being a professional. As James Marcia (1966) would agree, I have reached what is known as "identity achievement." I have gone through a period of identity exploration and developed a new, additional self. By no means was this process easy. In this chapter, I have outlined some of the more difficult roadblocks I encountered and what I have ultimately learned from my experiences. I have also followed up with what I believe helped me achieve success. While neither of these are all-inclusive lists, I believe they have a certain degree of relatability for all those going through this transition phase.

Roadblocks

Impostor Syndrome

The biggest roadblock I encountered was what is known as "impostor syndrome" or the "impostor phenomenon." Kolligian and Sternberg (1991) define this concept quite accurately: "…buried in the hearts and minds of many high-achieving individuals is the private sense of being an impostor or fraud" (p. 309). These "impostors" fail to internalize their objective success and there is no clear-cut reason as to why, but a prevalent explanation is wrapped in distorted attribution processes (Kolligian & Sternberg, 1991). In other words, high-achieving individuals may attribute their success to an external force as opposed to their own internal hard work and effort. Many high-achieving individuals believe that they are impostors and that they are deceiving others into thinking that they are actually professionals.

I stepped into the classroom during my first semester of teaching and I was filled with this impostor-like feeling. I could not shake my student identity, and as such I felt that I was not qualified to teach other students. I felt that I somehow received this position out of luck or error. I had even thought at one point that the department chair mistook me for someone else and had looked over the wrong curriculum vitae while interviewing me. I strongly believed that I did not fit the "professional" bill or deserve this position. Looking back, my preoccupation with impostor syndrome was a disservice to both my students and myself. These feelings of ingenuity caused me to become nervous and I was not able to give my students my best self. In turn, this led me to suffer from a lack of self-esteem because I knew I could do better.

Through subsequent introspection and the aid of others, I learned to contest these feelings and I realized I did have objective success that was not due to luck or error. I also realized that many individuals experience this feeling and I should not let it weigh me down. As a matter of fact, there is a large breadth of literature behind impostor syndrome that spans decades (e.g., Bell, 1990; Clance & Imes, 1978; Cokley et al., 2015; Cusack, Hughes, & Nuhu, 2013; Gibson-Beverly & Schwartz, 2008; Kets de Vries, 1990; Li, Hughes, & Thu, 2014; Peteet, Montgomery, & Weekes, 2015; Vergauwe, Wille, Feys, De Fruyt, & Anseel, 2015). Truly understanding that I was not an impostor nor alone in this feeling was the first step I took in moving from a student to a professional self. However, once I was able to see beyond my own internal struggles, I encountered my next roadblock. The next roadblock I experienced related to the newly found responsibilities I gained. I was not quite comfortable with that shift in the beginning either. What did it really mean to be "responsible?"

Shift of Responsibilities

Furthering Erikson's early work, Arnett (2000, 2004) proposes that the time frame of roughly 18–29 years old is a unique developmental period in that individuals experience many important transitions that lead to a more solidified identity. Arnett argues that identity formation, especially in the areas of work and professionalism, occurs during this period. In particular, this is the time when individualistic character qualities come to light, notably accepting higher responsibilities for one's self and actions as well as independent decision-making. From my own personal experience, I can attest to this. I graduated with my master's degree a month after I turned 24 years old, and I shortly learned thereafter what it meant to accept higher responsibility and become more independent. Regarding the latter, I no longer had advisors and professors holding my hand, providing me with strict deadlines for assignments, and making sure I was on the right track in life. It was now time for me to take on that role for others and take care of myself as well. Of course, I still rely on them from time to time when I have to make life-changing decisions, and I am forever grateful for their help.

Regarding the former, I realized the days of late-night video gaming and Netflix marathoning had passed after teaching for a year. No longer were the days where I could sleep at 3:00 AM, wake up for class around 8:00 AM, and still somehow look alive and go to work in the late afternoon. The days of procrastinating assignments were also nowhere in sight. I now have to sleep at a decent hour, wake up at a normal time, and be alert and ready to go once class begins. If I ever have late nights, they are spent grading midterm and final exams as opposed to watching the entire collection of Studio Ghibli films in one sitting. I can no longer procrastinate on assignments because my assignments are now creating lectures, planning activities, and grading papers and tasks that involve the lives of others. I have a newly found duty to be the best person that I can be at my job and deliver high-quality content. I would again feel like I was doing a disservice to my students if I did not give my best efforts; I do not have the room to act irresponsibly. I am now a role model and a professional whose actions and decisions affect others. Each decision I make is crucial.

Despite the challenges I faced accustoming myself to my new responsibilities (read: becoming more motivated and thinking each of my decisions through), I took my job to heart and my efforts were indeed rewarded. To recount one situation at the end of my first semester, I had given positive feedback to all of my students on notecards to encourage them through the rest of their studies. I was not expecting anything in return, but a student had asked, “Can we write you feedback too?” and I hesitantly obliged. The notes I received were heartwarming. A few students had written that they wished I was their mother, and many others thanked me for my engaging lectures, activities, and discussions that I had spent hours creating. Indeed, although this job was not as easy as “just showing up to class” and studying as a student, I am satisfied with the career path I chose because it brings its own form of happiness. At the end of the day, I am thankful that I took on the responsibility to educate others regardless of the time it took to adjust. Nonetheless, becoming a professional was much more than simply accepting new responsibilities and interacting with others. Rather, it was also connecting with others on a deeper level, which was something I did not have to do as a student. Truly connecting with others was the next major roadblock I encountered, especially with those who identified differently than myself.

Diversity and Generational Differences

Although the college demographic has changed a bit in the last few years, the population remains largely the same across the United States. As reported by the National Center for Education Statistics (NCES), approximately 20,375 students had enrolled in a degree-granting postsecondary institution. Of those 20,375 students, 59.3% identified as White, while only 15.8% identified as Hispanic, 14.7% identified as African American/Black, 6.4% identified as Asian/Pacific Islander, and even smaller proportions identified as American Indian/Alaskan Native, having two or more races, or a nonresident alien (2013a). Additionally, the ages of college students were also quite homogenous across the board: 39.9% of students were in the range of 18–24 years old (NCES, 2013b). As a college student, I mostly fit the characteristics of a stereotypical profile. I had not taken too much notice regarding the diversity and generational spread in my institution. I saw every other student in equal light and did not take into account how race, age, and other factors may play different roles in the educational environment. I realize now that my outlook was the result of privilege and a lack of awareness of others (Helms, 1990, 1995), and thus I have learned to reflect on my environment in full. I later learned of a psychologist named Jean Phinney (1993) who developed a three-stage model of ethnic identity development that encompasses how we begin to explore our own ethnic identities as well as those ethnic identities around us. This model aligned with the stages of my personal journey quite clearly. While at this point I do not believe I have achieved a full understanding of ethnic identity, I do believe I have moved toward the "ethnic identity search" stage that involves exploring and seeking to understand what ethnicity means and how it interacts within the grand scheme of the world (Phinney, 1993). Truly learning how to connect with others despite major differences is quite a challenge, but I have already increased my knowledge tenfold during my time in the classroom.

The first batch of students I taught held the stereotypical demographics listed above. There was not too much spread between race and age, and neither of those factors impacted their learning experience as far as I could tell. However, one of my students did have a non-stereotypical profile that I did not mention previously: she had children. At that time, I had not yet encountered teaching a parent in the classroom. I was lucky in that she was incredibly sweet, but I did notice her learning style and contributions were unlike the rest of the class. At times, I thought that my lecture material was not resonating with her because she had a much more worldly view than I did in some respects. I took the initiative and spoke with her about this, and she assured me that the material was still relatable. However, she did suggest that I incorporate information about treating children and communicating with children in a therapeutic setting. I gathered more information relating to these topics and integrated it into my lectures. I also recounted experiences I had with children in a therapeutic context during class. She was incredibly grateful and the rest of the students enjoyed hearing the material as well. Through this experience, I learned how important it is to attempt to include everyone in the classroom (to the extent that is possible) and to connect with individuals even if they are not in the same place of life as I am.

The second batch of students I taught did not hold the stereotypical demographics mentioned above. The spread of races and ages were wide and I could see how these factors impacted their learning experience. A number of students were not fortunate enough to have regular access to a computer to check Blackboard for notifications and reading assignments, and a number of older students were not familiar with technology whatsoever. Moreover, there were a few religious individuals in my course and a handful of them were easily offended when it came to discussing controversial issues such as homosexuality, abortion, and the etiology of certain psychological disorders. There were also individuals in the course suffering from mental illness, and the content of the course was triggering for them if the material was relevant to their experiences. Although this was my most challenging group of students yet, I learned that having the ability to collaborate with others from different backgrounds, to cooperate with all the diverse personalities, to take everyone into consideration when planning and lecturing, and to genuinely empathize with individuals from all walks of life is crucial. My training as a student did not prepare me for these types of encounters in the workplace, but I learned so much from this group of students and I have carried the lessons with me ever since. Primarily, I learned the true utility of relating to others and bringing everyone's unique personality into the discussion, and I believe that has led me to become a better professional. However, at the same time, this lesson led me to the last major roadblock I encountered: what does a true professional look like anyway?

Cultivating a Professional Identity

Cultivating a professional identity was the last major roadblock I encountered. At this point, I had a better understanding of myself, my new responsibilities, and my level of knowledge and competence. I also gained a greater adaptability to the work environment and a stronger ability to connect with my students. Even so, I still felt that I was missing something that could not be gathered through literature. I spoke with a long-time colleague of mine about my dilemma and she had instantly known the answer. She told me I was too focused on the smaller details and missed the bigger picture. She then asked me what a professional looked like in my eyes, and that led me to my a-ha moment. It was difficult to describe initially, but I realized that professionals of the field carried themselves in a way that emanated a competent aura. This came through in how they addressed others, led discussions, spoke about their experiences, expressed their body language, dressed themselves, and more. I deemed this as a "professional characteristic set" and attempted to work toward what I thought a professional to look like from there.

Again, literature was not helpful here, bur rather it was personal experience as well as trial and error that assisted me in overcoming this dilemma. I realized that it was not about using bigger, incomprehensible words, wearing suits, or exuding confidence. As a friend of mine said, it was simply about "dressing and acting for the job you want to have." I began addressing others in a more professional manner, I spoke about more mature topics and educated myself about current events, I sprinkled in my own experiences when speaking with others instead of simply rattling off literature, and I reflected appropriate body language whenever around my colleagues and students. I also began dressing more businesslike, although I will still wear my favorite pair of destroyed jeans on occasion. I did not completely alter my personality, but rather I feel that I now have the ability to exhibit that professional air through daily practice. Researchers Frazier and Hooker (2006) purport that self-knowledge and character develop through interactions with others, self-reflexive thought, and our own personal strivings, so I aim to gain more experience in order to further develop my sense of self and become successful. I have not yet perfected professionalism at this point, but as I teach my students every semester, "Development is a life-long process."

On that note, I have learned what I believe to be "keys to success" during this developmental transition. While this list does not cover every possible route to success, the following points have helped me, helped others, and literature supports in some cases as well. I encourage readers to consider these four keys as solutions to the transition puzzle – other keys will be found through your own experiences.

Keys to Success

Indulging in Support Systems

I have mentioned a number of times in this narrative chapter how I sought out advice and feedback from academic advisors, colleagues, and friends. In addition, I also received advice and emotional support from my family. I write about indulging in support systems first and foremost because I believe it is the most important key to success. Defining what support systems are can be quite difficult because everyone prefers different types of support, but the overarching idea is that support systems, or social relationships, will provide you with both tangible (e.g., monetary) and intangible (e.g., emotional) assistance during times of need (Sarason et al., 1991). Literature has shown that support systems are helpful in countless ways, but the two main mechanisms by which social support is beneficial to us are (1) its ability to mitigate stress during negative situations and (2) its contribution to well-being and health through the lifespan (Lane & Fink, 2015). Moreover, social support has been tagged as an important protective factor for emerging adults experiencing stressful life transitions, in particular adjusting to professional life (Polach, 2004). So, for those of us who are experiencing this difficult life transition and struggling with adjusting to professional life, know that the literature shows indulging in social support allows us to lead happier, fulfilling, and productive lives during this time.

I realize I am very lucky in that I have a solid support system. Whenever I was overly anxious about a lecture I had to create, I knew exactly who to contact. Whenever I was feeling lost about whether I was making the correct choices during my career path, I knew exactly who to talk to. Whenever I was sad that things did not go my way, I would seek out support from those who have been there for me since the beginning. I wholeheartedly agree that my support system helped me cope through difficult events and I am not quite sure where I would be without them. My advice is to find at least one person who has the ability to act as your rock during challenging times. If you cannot find someone in real life, I recommend seeking out support on Internet communities or through hotlines. I remember one specific instance where I spoke to someone on the *7 Cups of Tea* (2016) online community and it was truly cathartic. If you are uncomfortable with that prospect, try finding comfort in pets (e.g., Johnson, 2015; Sable, 1995; Wells, 2011). I cannot tell you how many times I talked to my Pomeranian about my troubles and how much it actually helped. To be brief, I can truly say that leaning on others for support has helped ease my transition from a student to professional self. Nonetheless, my journey did not stop there. After leaning on others, I would then seek out knowledge on how to improve myself and further increase my well-being on my own.

Increasing Knowledge

British statesman Philip Stanhope once wrote in a letter to his son, "The knowledge of the world is only to be acquired in the world, and not in a closet." It is so important to move outside of your bubble and increase your knowledge whenever you can. I have learned quite well that living in ignorance equates to living in fear. If I am ever unsure about something, I read about it, I ask others about it, and I try to form my own opinions about it. Depending on what it is that I am unsure about, I will also attempt to experience it for myself. Whether you are an adolescent, emerging adult, older adult, none of the above, or somewhere in-between, you will always benefit from learning. Professional literature also supports this notion. Through learning and broadening the context of our lives, we are shown to gain higher self-esteem and feelings of self-efficacy, a deeper sense of purpose and future, an increased sense of social integration, and an ability to cope more effectively with physical and mental health complications as well as other types of adversity (Schuller et al., 2004).

When I was not sure where to start learning about a topic, I simply watched. Regarding my road to becoming a professional, I watched supervisors, professors, and colleagues in my field. As I mentioned previously, one aspect I watched was how others carried themselves. I learned what it meant to *look* like a professional. Through watching colleagues interact in my department, I also learned how to *act* like a professional. I picked out the pieces that were most relevant to who I wanted to become and experimented with different techniques. For instance, I tried combining teaching styles of my favorite professors and I ended up figuring out my own style in the process. More importantly, getting involved in the workplace and challenging myself, picking up extra experiences, and going beyond what was required contributed to a deeper sense of what it meant to be a professional. Becoming familiar with the unfamiliar is what allowed me to grow. It also allowed me to feel a greater sense of purpose and realize what I was doing was meaningful. I now also understand that my pursuit of knowledge was not only benefitting myself but others around me as well. That said, I did not eat, breathe, and sleep knowledge and experience. Self-care and making time for myself were also equally important tasks that contributed to my growth as a professional just as much. We must take care of ourselves, too.

Self-Care

Even though I am a psychology major, self-care was not as stressed in my program as I thought it should be. Looking back on all the courses I have taken and the professors I have interacted with, I had one professor who mentioned self-care in passing and another professor who dedicated a lecture to it. The lecture had noted that self-care prevented burnout, lowered levels of stress, and helped individuals refocus on tasks that originally seemed discouraging or arduous. In spite of this, I did not hear too much about self-care otherwise. Ironically enough, as I was searching for peer-reviewed literature to support my views in this section, I did not find nearly as many sources as I had for previously mentioned topics. In my opinion, this says something important about the nature of the workplace and the type of society that we live in, especially where the title of "workaholic" is revered.

My own definition of self-care is letting yourself do whatever it is that you want to do (within healthy limits). If you want to practice yoga, meditation, jogging, or writing in your self-care routine, by all means please do so. However, if you want to binge watch Netflix, play video games, or simply stare at the sky, that is fine too. Our minds become so overwhelmed with what we need to do, when we need to do it, and how to do it that we forget about ourselves in the process. As the famous French proverb states, "Rome was not built in a day." We need time to create great things. I have told myself that life is about undergoing a multitude of wonderful experiences, and we cannot create those great things if we are too focused on a singular event (e.g., work).

I remember explaining the concept of self-care to a client of mine during my graduate internship. She had experienced a great deal of adversity during her childhood that resulted in daily nightmares as an adult, and she was not taking the time she needed to heal. I explained the concept of self-care to her, as well as examples of activities that she could do, but she straightforwardly told me that she did not have time. I then asked if there were any activities she would be willing to do that she could simply dedicate 10 min to daily. She thought about it during our session and told me that she would be willing to write a small diary entry at the end of each day. Needless to say, she was surprised with the results. With the combination of therapy and her own self-care, she experienced a substantial decrease in nightmares and found herself much less stressed through the night. She was also more energized through the day. In her own words, "I finally managed to start taking care of myself as much as I take care of other people."

On a more personal note, I found myself turning toward mindfulness and meditation to ease my stress. When I found myself overly worrying about something, I brought myself back to the present and acknowledged my worries as simple thoughts. When I found myself unable to sleep due to worry, I used deep-breathing techniques to relax. By in large, these techniques decreased my level of stress and made me feel at peace. Researchers have found similar results for mindfulness and meditation practices across the board, especially for emerging adults (Greeson, Juberg, Maytan, James, & Rogers, 2014; Peer & McAuslan, 2016; Ramler, Tennison, Lynch, & Murphy, 2016; Rogers, 2013). Mindfulness was a particularly useful technique I used to overcome my impostor syndrome. It allowed me to let go of my thoughts that told me my success was due to some external force and instead acknowledge that my success was in large due to my hard work. However, I am acutely aware that it was not my hard work alone that got me where I am today. In all honesty, there are a number of other factors that contributed to my success (and some are outlined above), but a major source of credit must also be given to networking.

Networking

Networking is a bit of a strange thing. In a perfect world, every person would be judged on the same criteria and we would all be considered equal. There would be no bias whatsoever. Unfortunately, like everything else, this is not the case. A recommendation from someone who can vouch for your character, work ethic, and potential is much stronger than a résumé you have built yourself. I learned this concept fairly early on in my career and my experiences speak to its truth. I met people, who then knew other people, who in turn knew other people, and I was then able to make direct contact through that connection and reap the benefits. I have found that it is incredibly important to put yourself out there and make contacts wherever possible, whether it is in a school environment, work environment, professional conference, business meeting, or even a family gathering. No doubt, establishing relationships has helped give me the edge in getting where I want to be, and making connections has made it easier for me to make my way into the professional world. It seems that my experience is a common one: Susan Adams (2011) from the Forbes staff reported that, in data collected from 59,133 clients that were searching for jobs, an overwhelming 41% found a position through networking, while only 8% of clients were able to secure a position through direct approach. Other individuals turned to Internet job boards (25%) and agency search firms (11%), but nothing came close to the success of networking (Adams, 2011).

I have similar success stories. I was able to secure my undergraduate internship, undergraduate teaching assistantship, graduate teaching assistantship, and current adjunct position through networking. I was also able to secure all of my past and present research positions through networking. In my case, I either knew someone directly or my contacts knew of someone and provided me with recommendations to land these positions. To illustrate an obvious example, I am able to write this chapter because I made a connection with the principal author of this textbook during my undergraduate years. Earlier in my career, I thought that networking was a sneaky and underhanded way to go about achieving success, but in reality we need that edge above others to be noticed. However, do not misunderstand: whether you are able to actually secure the position you are seeking is due to hard work and effort. Networking is simply a mechanism through which the transition from student to professional is made easier, but at the end of the day, the ability to achieve real success is on you.

Conclusion

As documented through literature and personal experience, making the transition from a student to a professional is not easy. Again, the roadblocks I have outlined are not exhaustive; in truth, there are many other roadblocks that my colleagues and I have bumped into. That said, the barriers I have mentioned seem to be commonly encountered among all of us while we move along through this developmental period. My keys to success are also not exhaustive, but rather they are pieces of information that I would like to share with you, the reader, to potentially make life easier for you or for someone in your life who is going through this rough transition. I want to make it known that while my experiences have led me to no longer see myself as a "student" per se, I still believe that we are all students for as long as we continue learning. Researchers have noted that the self and identity are very dynamic and active constructs capable of change based on our experiences across the lifespan (Markus & Wurf, 1987), so I plan to continue learning in order to further refine who I am and who I want to become.

We all go through life at a different pace and cope with transition differently. Many of us become wrapped up in expectations of society and what is considered the norm during these crucial developmental periods. However, above all else that I have written here, I have learned to never lose sight of my true self and use my unique personality to my advantage. This has made my transition to a professional much smoother. In the beginning of this chapter, I wrote about advice that was given to me by my academic advisors before I took on the title of professor. I mentioned that they had stated that becoming a professor meant becoming a "professional." What I did not mention initially is that, although cliché, all of them also said, "Be yourself."

Every semester in the classroom, I begin my first lesson with talking about impression formation. I tell my students that all it takes is a tenth of a second to form an impression of a stranger on important dimensions such as attractiveness, likeability, competence, trustworthiness, and aggressiveness (Willis & Todorov, 2006). For this reason alone, I believe it is imperative to be yourself and not the stereotypical professional who is a walking scientific article with perfect prose and posture. Of course, this does not mean completely going against the norms of society, but rather it means to find a healthy balance between the two. It means staying true to who you are but also showcasing the best version of yourself. It took me quite a long time to come to this conclusion, and I am still working on finding my balance, but I know I have grown as both a person and a professional through my experiences. I am content with being a work in progress. As Ralph Emerson so brilliantly said, "Life is journey, not a destination."

References

Adams, S. (2011). *Networking is still the best way to find a job, survey says*. Retrieved from: http://www.forbes.com/sites/susanadams/2011/06/07/networking-is-still-the-best-way-to-find-a-job-survey-says

Arnett, J. J. (2000). Emerging adulthood. A theory of development from the late teens through the twenties. *American Psychologist, 55*, 469–480. doi:10.1037/0003-066X.55.5.469.

Arnett, J. J. (2004). *Emerging adulthood: The winding road from the late teens through the twenties*. New York: Oxford University Press.

Bell, L. A. (1990). The gifted woman as impostor. *Advanced Development, 2*, 55–64.

Clance, P. R., & Imes, S. A. (1978). The impostor phenomenon in high achieving women: Dynamics and therapeutic intervention. *Psychotherapy: Theory Research & Practice, 15*(3), 241–247. doi:10.1037/h0086006.

Cokley, K., Awad, G., Smith, L., Jackson, S., Awosogba, O., Hurst, A., et al (2015). The roles of gender stigma consciousness, impostor phenomenon and academic self-concept in the academic outcomes of women and men. *Sex Roles, 73*(9–10), 414–426. doi:10.1007/s11199-015-0516-7.

Cups of Tea. (2016). *Connect with caring people for online therapy & counseling*. Retrieved from: http://www.7cups.com/

Cusack, C. E., Hughes, J. L., & Nuhu, N. (2013). Connecting gender and mental health to imposter phenomenon feelings. *Psi Chi Journal of Psychological Research, 18*(2), 74–81.

Erikson, E. H. (1968). *Identity: Youth and crisis*. New York: Norton.

Frazier, L. D., & Hooker, K. (2006). Possible selves in adult development: Linking theory and research. In C. Dunkel & J. Kerpelman (Eds.), *Possible selves: Theory, research and applications* (pp. 41–59). Hauppauge, NY: Nova Science Publishers.

Gibson-Beverly, G., & Schwartz, J. P. (2008). Attachment, entitlement, and the impostor phenomenon in female graduate students. *Journal of College Counseling, 11*(2), 119–132. doi:10.1002/j.2161-1882.2008.tb00029.x.

Greeson, J. M., Juberg, M. K., Maytan, M., James, K., & Rogers, H. (2014). A randomized controlled trial of Koru: A mindfulness program for college students and other emerging adults. *Journal of American College Health, 62*(4), 222–233. doi:10.1080/07448481.2014.887571.

Helms, J. E. (1990). *Black and white racial identity: Theory, research, and practice*. Westport, CT: Greenwood Press.

Helms, J. E. (1995). An update of Helms' white and people of color racial identity models. In J. G. Ponterott, J. M. Casas, L. A. Suzuki, & C. M. Alexander (Eds.), *Handbook of multicultural counseling* (pp. 181–198). Thousand Oaks, CA: Sage.

Johnson, J. J. (2015). The experiences of pet owners' well-being gained through their relationships with their companion animals. In P. M. Gubi (Ed.), *Listening to less-heard voices: Developing counselor's awareness* (pp. 80–117). Chester, UK: University of Chester Press.

Kets de Vries, M. F. (1990). The impostor syndrome: Developmental and societal issues. *Human Relations, 43*(7), 667–686. doi:10.1177/001872679004300704.

Kolligian, J., & Sternberg, R. J. (1991). Perceived fraudulence in young adults: Is there an 'impostor syndrome'? *Journal of Personality Assessment, 56*(2), 308–326. doi:10.1207/s15327752jpa5602_10.

Lane, J. A., & Fink, R. S. (2015). Attachment, social support satisfaction, and well-being during life transition in emerging adulthood. *The Counseling Psychologist, 43*(7), 1034–1058. doi:10.1177/0011000015592184.

Li, S., Hughes, J. L., & Thu, S. M. (2014). The links between parenting styles and imposter phenomenon. *Psi Chi Journal of Psychological Research, 19*(2), 50–57.

Marcia, J. E. (1966). Development and validation of ego-identity status. *Journal of Personality and Social Psychology, 3*(5), 551–558.

Markus, H., & Wurf, E. (1987). The dynamic self-concept: A social psychological perspective. *Annual Review of Psychology, 38*(1), 299–337. doi:10.1146/annurev.ps.38.020187.001503.

Martin, P., & Stayer, M. A. (1990). The experience of micro- and macroevents: A life span analysis. *Research on Aging, 12*(3), 294–310. doi:10.1177/0164027590123002.

National Center for Education Statistics. (2013a). *Total fall enrollment in degree-granting postsecondary institutions, by level of enrollment, sex, attendance status, and race/ethnicity of student: Selected years, 1976 through 2013*. Retrieved from: http://nces.ed.gov/programs/digest/d14/tables/dt14_306.10.asp

National Center for Education Statistics. (2013b). *Percentage of 18- to 24-year-olds enrolled in degree-granting institutions, by level of institution and sex and race/ethnicity of student: 1967 through 2013*. Retrieved from: http://nces.ed.gov/programs/digest/d14/tables/dt14_302.60.asp

Peer, J. W., & McAuslan, P. (2016). Self-doubt during emerging adulthood: The conditional mediating influence of mindfulness. *Emerging Adulthood, 4*(3), 176–185. doi:10.1177/2167696815579828.

Peteet, B., Montgomery, L., & Weekes, J. C. (2015). Predictors of imposter phenomenon among talented ethnic minority undergraduate students. *The Journal of Negro Education, 84*(2), 175–186. doi:10.7709/jnegroeducation.84.2.0175.

Phinney, J. S. (1993). A three-stage model of ethnic identity development in adolescence. In M. E. Bernal & G. P. Knight (Eds.), *Ethnic identity: Formation and transmission among hispanics and other minorities* (pp. 61–79). Albany, NY: State University of New York Press.

Polach, J. L. (2004). Understanding the experience of college graduates during their first year of employment. *Human Resource Development Quarterly, 15*(1), 5–23. doi:10.1002/hrdq.1084.

Ramler, T. R., Tennison, L. R., Lynch, J., & Murphy, P. (2016). Mindfulness and the college transition: The efficacy of an adapted mindfulness-based stress reduction intervention in fostering adjustment among first-year students. *Mindfulness, 7*(1), 179–188. doi:10.1007/s12671-015-0398-3.

Rogers, H. B. (2013). Mindfulness meditation for increasing resilience in college students. *Psychiatric Annals, 43*(12), 545–548. doi:10.3928/00485713-20131206-06.

Sable, P. (1995). Pets, attachment, and well-being across the life cycle. *Social Work, 40*(3), 334–341.

Sarason, B. R., Pierce, G. R., Shearin, E. N., Sarason, I. G., Waltz, J. A., & Poppe, L. (1991). Perceived social support and working models of self and actual others. *Journal of Personality and Social Psychology, 60*(2), 273–287. doi:10.1037/0022-3514.60.2.273.

Schuller, T., Preston, J., Hammond, C., Brassett-Grundy, A., & Bynner, J. (2004). *The benefits of learning: The impact of education on health, family life, and social capital*. London: Routledge.

Vergauwe, J., Wille, B., Feys, M., De Fruyt, F., & Anseel, F. (2015). Fear of being exposed: The trait-relatedness of the impostor phenomenon and its relevance in the work context. *Journal of Business and Psychology, 30*(3), 565–581. doi:10.1007/s10869-014-9382-5.

Wells, D. (2011). The value of pets for human health. *The Psychologist, 24*(3), 172–176.

Willis, J., & Todorov, A. (2006). First impressions: Making up your mind after a 100-ms exposure to a face. *Psychological Science, 17*(7), 592–598. doi:10.1111/j.1467-9280.2006.01750.x.

Chapter 14
Play, Flow, and Tailoring Identity in Middle Adulthood

Kevin Rathunde and Russell Isabella

Identity provides a sense of meaning and direction in life by helping to clarify our role in the world and connection to others (Erikson, 1968). However, identity is not a static achievement; it evolves over time. A coherent identity may first come together in adolescence or early adulthood, but the style of individuality put together at this time is unlikely to fit well as we grow older and reach middle adulthood. As life circumstances change, therefore, so must the ensemble of goals, values, and beliefs that form the self and identity around which our lives revolve.

There are numerous circumstances and events in life that can initiate identity change in midlife. Some can be traumatic events that inject disequilibrium into life and force the self to adapt (McAdams, 1993). For instance, a chronic and debilitating illness such as cancer may force the reassessment of priorities and therefore affect how one makes sense of the self and its role in the world (Ellis, 1999). Likewise, challenges introduced through one's work or family life, accidents, or even the inevitable process of aging, as long as they are successfully engaged and do not overwhelm the person, can lead to meaningful and important changes in identity. In the absence of such events that force change upon the self, however, change depends on the willingness of the person to *voluntarily* step outside their comfort zone to engage challenges significant enough to require a reorganization of priorities and goals. It is this self-initiated aspect of identity change that we focus on in this chapter, especially in relation to the use of leisure time.

There are also numerous ways that individuals can intentionally set in motion a change of identity in middle adulthood. For example, they might choose to take on a new role at work, get involved in promoting a social change through community service, or even return to school to build new career skills. All of these paths to identity change, as long as challenges are successfully engaged, can result in new

K. Rathunde, Ph.D. (✉) • R. Isabella, Ph.D.
Department of Family and Consumer Studies, University of Utah,
225 South 1400 East, Rm. 228, AEB, Salt Lake City, UT 84112-0080, USA
e-mail: rathunde@fcs.utah.edu; russ.isabella@fcs.utah.edu

J.D. Sinnott (ed.), *Identity Flexibility During Adulthood*,
DOI 10.1007/978-3-319-55658-1_14

views of the self and its connection to others. This chapter focuses on yet another voluntary way to set change in motion: *the use of leisure time to engage challenging, intrinsically motivated leisure pursuits*. The perspective here is that such opportunities are based on the human capacity for lifelong play (Graham & Burghhardt, 2010; Montagu, 1989), a capacity that is too often left dormant in the lives of busy adults. Moreover, in relatively comfortable life circumstances without pressing external needs to change, we believe the use of voluntary leisure play is one of the best ways adults in middle adulthood can set themselves a difficult challenge that initiates positive identity growth.

After articulating a framework for thinking about play and identity development, the chapter narrows its focus to three men in middle adulthood who, despite having favorable life circumstances, elected to engage difficult leisure pursuits that had a positive effect on identity growth. By engaging this capacity for play in adulthood, these men were able to flexibly tailor their identities in ways that promoted successful aging and avoided the potential stagnation of comfort and simply letting their existing identities persist.

Play and the Possibility of Tailoring Identity: A Developmental Perspective

The analogy of *tailoring* is used in this chapter to represent the process of modifying identity in ways that enhance the quality of life by providing a better self-environment fit. The choice of this analogy was inspired by Erikson's (1950) classic definition of identity as "the style of one's individuality … that … coincides with the sameness and continuity of one's meaning for significant others in the immediate community" (p. 50). In other words, identity can be thought of as a style of individuality that we wear like a suit of clothes; the suit represents and expresses the self, and it conveys meaning about the person to others. This analogy works well for describing small or large changes that might be made to identity. Tailoring could refer to minor changes to the self such as learning a new skill that enhances a work or leisure role, or it could mean creating an entirely new outfit that fundamentally alters one's style of individuality and interaction with others. The tailoring analogy is also evocative in relation to the middle-aged men who provided the interview material in this chapter (see also Rathunde & Isabella, 2017). While not all men in middle adulthood regularly wear suits (including the authors of this chapter), tailoring implies a more discriminating process of self-development and presentation that is more likely to occur in midlife, rather than in adolescence or early adulthood, due to increased life experience and self-knowledge.

Whether one calls it flexible identity or tailoring, or whether one adopts related concepts implying a self-regulative capacity to change such as ego-resiliency (Block & Block, 2006), psychological complexity (Rathunde & Csikszentmihalyi, 2006), or psychological flexibility (Kashdan & Rottenberg, 2010), the ability to creatively adapt to new situations by differentiating and integrating information as a situation demands is a clear marker of positive functioning. The keys to understanding why some individuals manifest such flexibility are likely buried in a person's developmental history, beginning with the nurturing environments of early childhood (Biglan, Flay, & Sandler, 2012). Exploring these foundations is not the main focus here. However, in order to provide some context for understanding the emphasis on leisure play and voluntary identity change in this chapter, we offer a few, broad observations on the developmental importance of play and why rich experiences of play while growing up may be important for the possibility of tailoring identity in adulthood and beyond. For the purposes of this chapter, the terms "play" and "leisure play" will refer to the same thing, namely, a frame of mind or orientation for performing an activity, rather than a specific set of activities (see Brown, 2009; Mainemelis & Ronson, 2006). A state of play emerges, as described next, when a few key characteristics are present.

The Importance of Play for Human Development and the Role of Resources

Johan Huizinga's (1955) classic study of the role of play in the cultural achievements of Western civilization (i.e., *Homo Ludens*, or man the player) describes three of the primary characteristics of play that set it apart in human action: it is freely chosen, it is intrinsically motivated and enjoyable, and it typically occurs in a protected space that is segregated from ordinary or "real" life. Children and adults play, as do animals, because they want to; if the activity is forced or if it is done for reasons that are extrinsic to the order-creating and absorbing nature of the activity itself, then it is something other than play. This does not mean that play lacks seriousness. On the contrary, Huizinga notes that it can be every bit as intense as ordinary life, if not more so. Csikszentmihalyi's (1975) classic monograph on the flow experience, *Beyond Boredom and Anxiety*, takes a similar approach to Huizinga in highlighting the importance and intensity of play. In fact, this seminal book on flow was originally subtitled *The Experience of Play in Work and Games*, and the main elements of flow theory were first proposed in an article entitled "An Exploratory Model of Play" (Csikszentmihalyi & Bennett, 1971). Play, therefore, can be seen as the prototypical experience of flow that dissolves self-consciousness, accelerates attention, and fuses a person with their chosen activity. Flow can occur in many nonplay activities, including work, when conditions mimic those that typically characterize play settings and games (i.e., there is free choice, clear rules and feedback, intrinsic motivation, manageable novelty, and so on).

Animals, including humans, have play in common. It is only humans, however, who have a developmental trajectory that prioritizes play and maintains a robust capacity for it across the life course (Gould, 1977; Montagu, 1989). One compelling answer to why this is so is provided by Burghardt's (2005) surplus resource theory (SRT). According to the theory, animals with "a long developmental period under parental care tend to play more frequently and with greater complexity" (Graham & Burghhardt, 2010, p. 409). In other words, play more often occurs when animals are under minimal chronic stress and *have more energy than is required for growth and maintenance alone*. Because human infants and children have a neotenous pattern of growth, can often depend on their caregivers for the basic necessities of sustenance and survival, and in nurturing environments benefit from a caregiver's sensitive emotion regulation, they are more free to play. Resource advantages other than those associated with the protections provided by caregivers also make a difference. For example, better nutrition has been positively linked to the increased play of children (Espinosa, Sigman, Neumann, Bwibo, & McDonald, 1992), and the same is true of other animals (Sharpe, Clutton-Brock, Brotherton, Cameron, & Cherry, 2002).

Play does not need to be well resourced to exist in some form. In other words, the capacity to play still exists and is developmentally important for children and adults in difficult life circumstances when resources are scarce. In fact, one could make the case that play is even more important for such individuals who might benefit by the opportunities afforded by play for stress relief, mood regulation, and adaptive growth. Nevertheless, the importance of surplus resources for enhancing play cannot be denied. For example, play is depressed for children in poverty due to (1) poorer quality schools with fewer opportunities for engagement (e.g., sports, art, music, extracurricular activities), (2) fewer safe play areas outside of school (e.g., parks and playgrounds subject to violence or vandalism), and most importantly (3) economic stressors that deplete parental time, energy, and resources for providing children with enriching play opportunities inside and outside of the home (Milteer, Ginsburg, Mulligan, 2011). The same is true of adults in stressful circumstances: play does not disappear completely and remains a valuable coping tool. Veterans facing traumatic injury and mental health challenges, for example, find relief and enhanced coping skills in play-based outdoor activities that are intrinsically enjoyable (Duvall & Kaplan, 2014). Yet access to outdoor recreation, like most other leisure activities, is negatively impacted by poor health and low SES conditions (Floyd, 1999).

In addition to the experiential rewards of play that motivate its engagement, the long-term benefits of play for learning and development have been widely examined. A partial list includes the honing of mental and physical capabilities due to enjoyable practice and exercise, greater social bonding (e.g., reduced aggression, cooperation, a sense of fairness), and key for this chapter – behavioral and mental innovation and flexibility that enable better adaptation to an environment (Burghardt, 2005; Pellegrini, 1992; Spinka, Newberry, & Bekoff, 2001). If one adds to this list the many educational benefits that research has associated with the play-like states of intrinsic motivation (Deci & Ryan, 1985), flow and peak experience (Maslow, 1968; Rathunde & Csikszentmihalyi, 2006), and interest (Renninger, Krapp, & Hidi, 1992), a strong case can be made for the crucial role of play in healthy human development. Unfortunately, not all families and schools have the social and material resources to provide safe and supportive conditions for children's play.

Moreover, even when these contexts are rich in resources, play and intrinsic motivation are frequently undervalued, and children's energy is directed instead toward extrinsic tasks deemed more "important" (e.g., grade-oriented schoolwork). In these circumstances, opportunities for play are lost, and children's activities more often resemble those of adults working for rewards and social recognition.

The cost of play deprivation, whether due to poverty or an underappreciation of its role, can be enormous for child development and, by extension, adult development. Play is widely recognized as a developmentally appropriate way for infants and young children to learn about the world (Bredekamp & Copple, 1997; NAEYC, 2009). It is also seen as critical for the formation of secure attachment because it provides an enjoyable joint activity and bridge for responsive parenting (Kerns & Barth, 1995; Slade, 1987). Because of its developmental importance, the American Academy of Pediatrics (AAP) recently sounded an alarm about the social conditions that threaten to reduce play (Ginsburg, 2007). An AAP policy statement notes that "play is so important to optimal child development that it has been recognized by the United Nations High Commission for Human Rights as a right of every child."

Consistent with a resource theory of play, in a follow-up report, the American Academy of Pediatrics suggested that the amount and quality of play are especially threatened for children from low SES families (Milteer et al., 2011). Ironically, in addition to the problem of play deprivation in underresourced neighborhoods, the AAP also warned that children with an abundance of resources were also at risk for play deprivation due to a too-early focus on academics (Ginsburg, 2007). In other words, beginning in kindergarten or even preschool, many educational programs are reducing free play, recess, creative arts, and outdoor activities in order to emphasize reading and mathematics (Dillon, 2006). Parents who are unaware of the research literature on the benefits of play fall prey to social pressures that encourage them to hurry their kids into adult roles and get them on the fast track to a coveted spot at a good university, and this misguided pressure can actually undermine their child's ability to reach their full potential in adulthood.

Whether as the result of poverty and reduced opportunities for play or misconceptions about play that lead parents and teachers to undervalue it through the formative years of child and adolescent development, one of the long-term costs of play deprivation is likely to be a reduced adult capacity for learning and creativity and the identity development that depends on such processes (Rathunde & Csikszentmihalyi, 2006). Although play is appropriately seen as a biological and evolution-based process primarily associated with youth and early development, it is wrongly dismissed from adult development because of a failure to understand the evolutionary strategy at work. What appears to be unique about the human strategy for survival and flourishing is the importance of lifelong cognitive complexity and flexibility. For this reason, play – arguably one of the progenitors of such flexibility in human development – is just as important to adult growth as it is to children's physical, cognitive, and social development. If it is true that Western civilization has benefited greatly from the play orientation of humans (Huizinga, 1955), that flow is associated with great creative achievement (Csikszentmihalyi, 1996), and that the promise of human neoteny is to remain playful and flexible through the entire life span (Montagu, 1989; Gould, 1977), then continuing to play in adulthood remains vitally important.

The Advantages of Leisure Play for Identity Development in Middle Adulthood

If play is sometimes undervalued in childhood, even when families and schools have abundant resources to support it, this undervaluing is even more prevalent in adulthood. Much of this bias comes from associating play with entertainment or wasting time and not appreciating its potential intensity and relationship to learning and creativity. However, if adult identity development is conceptualized as an outcome resulting from these processes (i.e., *as information about the self and its role in the world that is learned and creatively constructed)*, then it is easy to see why play might enhance identity development. As mentioned above, many unanticipated life events and challenges, including negative or traumatic ones, can trigger identity growth and change (McAdams, 1993). However, play may be one of the best ways to initiate changes to the self in relatively positive life circumstances. In other words, when individuals have some protected space, are not under chronic stress, and have more energy than is necessary just for growth and maintenance, the advantages of play can emerge. Middle adulthood can sometimes offer such positive conditions. Unfortunately, many fail to take advantage of the opportunities it may afford because they do not recognize the value of play.

The intention here is not to idealize middle adulthood. This period of life (approximately ages 45–64, according to the US Census) can be a difficult one for those whose lives are burdened with declining health, competing time demands, or financial pressures (for a review, see Lachman, 2004). Still, for many in affluent Western countries and for an emerging middle class in some Asian countries with expanding economies, midlife can open up more space for identity exploration and change. One primary reason is that children require less parental attention as they become older and more self-sufficient and eventually leave home to start a job or go to college. In addition, despite the economic and relationship uncertainty that will affect a sizeable number of individuals at this time of life, many others find themselves in well-established careers and marriages. In these fortunate circumstances, less attention needs to be spent worrying about job and relationship security, and these resources can be invested in growth-oriented activities. Classic developmental perspectives add that the self-knowledge and maturity/wisdom gained by middle adulthood are helpful for setting new priorities, enhancing individuation by reintegrating neglected aspects of the self, and strengthening social and community engagements (Erikson, 1950; Jung, 1955; Levinson, 1978; Neugarten, 1968).

With favorable circumstances, therefore, midlife can free more resources and energy (cognitive, financial, and time) than are needed simply for the maintenance of life, and these resources can be invested in play for the benefit of health and continued cognitive growth. Whereas adolescents are able to forge an identity with the help of a *moratorium* granted by parental and societal protection that provides a sheltered space to play, explore, and learn about themselves and the world (Erikson 1968), some middle-aged adults may gain a second moratorium to explore identity if they are fortunate enough to have the "protection" of a stable life structure. As a result, they are in a better position to carve out what Joseph Campbell (2011, p.115) referred to as *sacred space* where one could tailor a sense of self while experiencing deep engagement:

> This [having a sacred space] is an absolute necessity for anybody today. You must have a room, or a certain hour or so a day, where you don't know what was in the newspapers that morning, you don't know who your friends are, you don't know what you owe anybody, you don't know what anybody owes to you. This is a place where you can simply experience and bring forth what you are and what you might be. This is the place of creative incubation. At first you may find that nothing happens there. But if you have a sacred place and use it, something eventually will happen.

Play is beneficial for everyone, regardless of whether they have an abundance of resources or not. The many physical and cognitive benefits associated with active, play-oriented lifestyles in midlife could result in an improved quality of life and sizeable health care savings for an aging population (Brown, McGuire, & Voelkl, 2008; Stebbins, 1982; Valliant, 2002). Unfortunately, because of the misunderstandings and negative perceptions of frivolity that surround the idea of adult play, even good health, free time, financial resources, relationship security, cognitive maturity, and a protected space may not be enough to guarantee its occurrence. These same advantages, in fact, can result in sedentary, comfortable lifestyles devoid of novel physical and cognitive challenges. That is where, we believe, an absorbing leisure play activity can enter the picture. Such an activity sets in motion an intense learning and creative process that involves enjoyable exploration and great effort, individual differentiation, and social connection. While some are fortunate to find such play in their work lives, many others find leisure activities offer their best opportunity to explore new facets of the self. Leisure provides the freedom of choice that is so fundamental to play and often missing from the work environment. Therefore, a person can select activities that they feel best represent their path to self-actualization and an identity that fits their skills and interests. Kleiber (1999, p. xvi) suggests the same: "To the extent that we are in an age where structural determinants of behavior and personality such as religion, occupation, nationality, and regional identification have lost much of their determining hold, leisure becomes especially relevant to development as it is individually constructed; if people are in a position to invent themselves, it will occur most readily within the freedom that is available."

One of the advantages of leisure play for identity development is that the intrinsic person-environment connection established generates a seemingly inexhaustible source of energy and attention that can be invested in a chosen activity. For example, if a person encounters an extrinsically motivated challenge at their job, the energy that adheres to the problem can melt away in the evening when the workday is over. In contrast, a person encountering a challenge while engaging in a passionate interest may sometimes be unable to engage the challenge because of other pressing time demands, but their willingness to do so is ever present. In any free moment, they would happily devote themselves completely to exploring the challenge and finding a resolution. This is so because intrinsic motivation propels the person-environment transaction, and a person engages in an activity because the engagement itself is rewarding (i.e., the rewards emerge from the interaction; see Dewey, 1913). Such engagements do not require less effort and concentration than work; in fact, they can be equally "serious" and often surpass the most intense forms of work engagement (Stebbins, 1982).

Another great advantage of leisure play for identity development is that intrinsic motivation and freedom of choice are conducive to having occasional flow experiences. When one has a chance to temporarily escape some of the constraints of everyday life and become fully engrossed in some activity, flow is triggered. These intense states provide a tremendous momentary boost of energy that accelerates the path of learning and creativity through its various phases (Csikszentmihalyi, 1996; Csikszentmihalyi, Rathunde, & Whalen, 1993). If identity is thought of as a specific type of learning or creativity involving insights about the self and its place in the world, then it is easy to see why play provides an optimal way to tailor one's identity. Alan Waterman's (1990, 1993) extensive empirical and theoretical work on identity development supports this assertion. He found that an intrinsic motivational orientation led to more *personal expressiveness* and meaningful identity exploration and commitment. Drawing on Aristotle's philosophy of living a good life, Waterman referred to such an orientation as resulting from pursuing one's highest potentials or daimon (true self): "Experiences of personal expressiveness, from feelings accompanying intrinsic motivation, through flow, to peak experiences, constitute a sign that one is acting in a manner consistent with one's daimon" (1990, p. 56).

Self-Differentiation, Social Integration, and Flow in Identity Development: An Interpretive Framework

The conceptual framework used in the second part of the chapter to interpret the interviews on play and identity borrows from (1) theories of identity development emphasizing exploration/commitment dynamics and self-other connections and (2) insights gained from examining models of design, learning, and creativity. The resulting framework is referred to here as the *tailoring model of identity development*. While it shares similarities to other perspectives on identity, it differs from them by placing a stronger emphasis on passionate leisure engagements and flow experiences as central to the dynamics of exploration and commitment, both in terms of having identity-relevant personal insights (i.e., self-differentiation) and connecting those insights in meaningful ways to others who uphold and support one's sense of self (i.e., social integration).

Marcia (1980) extended Erikson's ideas about identity using the notions of *exploration* and *commitment*. The former involves a search for new information relevant to forming an identity; commitment is the sorting through of this information and the selection among alternatives to arrive at a coherent set of goals and values. Marcia suggested that the ideal identity status (i.e., identity achievement) occurred when a commitment was made after first exploring a variety of options. Other identity theorists have focused less on stable outcomes and more on the *style* one uses to form an identity. Nevertheless, the same dynamic of exploring alternatives before selectively making a commitment is considered optimal (Berzonsky, 1990; Schwartz 2001). It is worth noting here that these divergent/convergent dynamics are consistent with experimental evidence on optimal arousal and flow theory; that is, arousal and the quality of experience are optimal when novelty and order (or challenges and skills in flow theory) are kept in balance and not skewed too much toward one extreme or the other. In other words, identity development works best, as is the case with any form of learning, when divergent and convergent processes work in combination to sustain deep engagement and avoid the extremes of anxiety (overarousal) or boredom (under-arousal) (Berlyne, 1971; Rathunde and Csikszentmihalyi, 2006).

In addition to the interplay between exploration and commitment, the interrelationship between self-differentiation and social integrations plays a fundamental role in classic theories of identity. Erikson integrated psychological and sociocultural considerations in his definition and thought of identity as providing a sense of meaning both internally for the self *and* externally for others. Schwartz (2001, p. 9) notes that most post-Eriksonian theories carry forward this link between the personal and the social: "Ego identity…represents a coherent picture that one shows both to oneself and to the outside world." Conceptions of identity informed by symbolic interaction theory also emphasize the role of the self in collaboration with social feedback. Part of one's identity is first shaped through personal experience and self-reflection. However, that private sense of meaning is not the endpoint of the process; a person's identity is also validated and further shaped through social interaction as suggested by the concepts of a *looking-glass self* and *taking the role of the other* (Cooley 1902; Mead 1934; Turner 2013).

The interrelationship between self-differentiation and social integration is not unlike the movement between an *idea* and its *application* in models of design, learning, and creativity. For example, when designing a suit or some other item, designers first map out ideas and then develop prototypes to test them in the real world (Norman 2013; Onarheim and Friis-Olivarius 2013). Likewise, in Kolb's model of experiential learning (see Kolb, 1984; Kolb, Boyatzis, & Mainemelis, 2001) and Wallas' (1926) classic depiction of the stages of creativity (see also Csikszentmihalyi, 1996; Hansen, Lumpkin, and Hills, 2011), there is a common movement from an idea phase of a learning/creative process to one of application in the world and then back again in a dialectical cycle. In all of these models, divergent and convergent dynamics play a prominent role in the birth of an idea and its successful application (Rathunde & Isabella, 2017).

We think of tailoring identity as following a similar pattern (see Fig. 14.1): identity development often is initiated through exploration and commitment in relation to self-differentiation. Through engaging in new challenges and imaginatively combining what is learned, a person can broaden a sense of self in ways that set the stage for new ways of interacting in the world. However, these self-differentiating steps

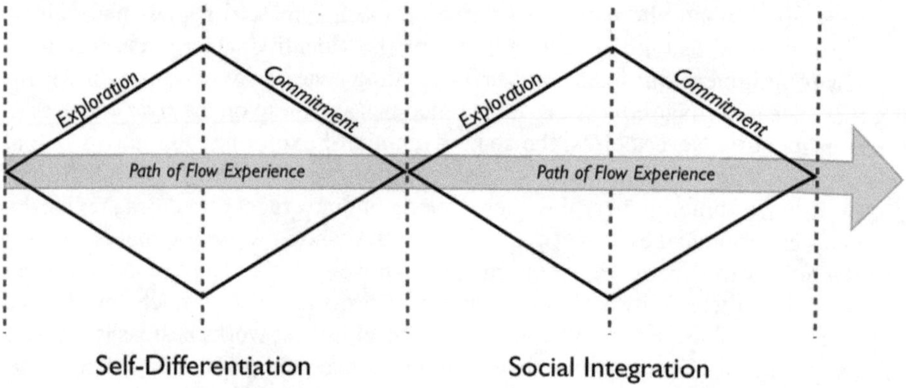

Fig. 14.1 The process of tailoring identity

are *incomplete* until they are actualized in social contexts. Social integration connects one to others and gives a sense of belonging to a larger group and being recognized by it (McCall & Simmons, 1978). It requires a new divergent-convergent cycle of exploration and commitment but this time in an outward, other-directed process as an "individual constructs an identity out of socially possible faces and voices" (Adams and Marshall 1996, 431).[1]

In summary, the flexible tailoring of identity in middle adulthood is presumably enhanced by engaging intrinsically motivated, freely chosen leisure play activities. Such activities set in motion a divergent-convergent process of exploration and commitment that reveals new facets of the self (self-differentiation) and new ways to connect with others (social integration). From a developmental perspective, such a capacity in midlife is likely enhanced by positive early environments that nurture play and thereby set the stage for adult learning and flexibility. While play is a universal human phenomenon that can occur regardless of available resources, just as is the case in childhood, play is more likely to emerge in midlife when conditions are such that stress is at a minimum and surplus energy exists for investing in growth-oriented activities that are not, strictly speaking, necessary for the maintenance of life. For those in midlife with the good fortune to have safe and supportive environments, passionate leisure activities provide an optimal context for self-directed, intrinsically motivated challenges that can unleash great energy, trigger

[1] The tailoring identity model is proposed here as a heuristic guide to understanding the multifaceted process of identity development. In other words, the sequential nature of the model (i.e., self-differentiation and *then* social integration) generally captures the way identity growth unfolds; however, we recognize that the process is less linear in the lives of real people. For example, social integration typically follows after a process of self-differentiation; however, social integration sometimes requires additional phases of self-differentiation before it is successful. In addition, dialectical models such as this are greatly influenced by the timeframe one adopts (i.e., the insights gained from examining identity change over the period of a few months would be very different than those resulting from looking at change over the period of several years).

flow experiences, and tailor identity in ways that enhance personal expressiveness and social connection.

Examples of Tailoring Identity Through Leisure Play

As part of an ongoing study of identity development in middle-aged men, a series of interviews were conducted and examined using interpretive phenomenological analysis (IPA), an idiographic/qualitative approach that is useful for generating in-depth, experiential accounts with a small number of study participants (Biggerstaff, &Thompson, 2008; Reid, Flowers, & Larkin, 2005). In order to add detail and flesh out the conceptual ideas presented in the first half of the chapter, we focus next on excerpts from three interviews that fostered key insights on how leisure play can be used to generate significant challenges that instigate identity growth. The interviewees ranged in ages from 49 to 55 years old. Jerry was passionate about photography, Finn loved paragliding, and Tim was deeply engaged with writing. These names and other potentially revealing details from the interviews have been anonymized to protect the privacy of the interviewees.

If leisure play activities are to affect identity or result in flow experience, opportunities to engage them must be recognized and readily available. Such opportunities are presumably enhanced by favorable resource conditions that sometimes arise in midlife due to supportive marriages and lessened parental/family responsibilities, stable financial and career circumstances, and cognitive maturity and self-knowledge. These conditions do not guarantee play and may contribute instead to feeling comfortable and satisfied with one's existing identity. This was not the case with our interviewees who, instead of choosing the predictability of the status quo, mentioned these factors as relevant for finding the time to use their passionate interests as a means for challenge and growth. Excerpts from these interviews are presented next, followed by accounts of the interviewees' identity-relevant experiences and flow.

Finding Opportunities for Leisure Play

Support from a spouse and the relaxation from some family and parental responsibilities can be key factors in finding time for leisure play. After admitting that photography can be an expensive pursuit, Jerry laughed nervously as he recalled the reaction from his wife when boxes show up from B&H Photo: "She doesn't say don't go and do it, but it's more like what have you been spending our money on now?" Her predictable question, however, did not signal a problem in their relationship; instead, it conveyed her deep understanding of Jerry. This understanding, as well as the lessening of other family-related responsibilities, made it easier for both of them to find time for their leisure interests: "We don't have the domestic demands that we may have had five years ago. We live in an old house … which took quite a lot of renovations … we had a lot of projects going on … we sort of finished that and freed up more time for us compared to what we had a few years ago."

Finn added more detail about how supportive family dynamics can help provide time and space. After pointing out that "paragliding is really difficult to schedule" because it is "totally weather dependent," and this unpredictability "makes it challenging for the balance between work and family life," he asserted that you have to be "ruthless" in clearing time when the weather conditions are right and "everything is on." He continued, "What that means is you have to be willing on those days to drop everything … you have to be able to tell your family I'm off, forget about me. I will not talk to you for the next ten hours." The family situation works, however, for several reasons. Like Jerry, Finn has a spouse who is supportive and understands how important the activity is to his sense of self. In addition, Finn prepares for those last-minute disappearances by being helpful the rest of the year and accumulating good will: "You do more dishes, you do more laundry, you take the kids, everything … You do this in all the contexts where you can, just to be ruthless on this one day, or these couple days." It also helps tremendously that his two children are getting more independent. When they were young, "it really cut down on the hours I could fly … I mean, if I would look at my log book … I didn't get more than 20 hours a year of flight time back then, if at all actually." Now that his oldest child has entered adolescence and his younger one is about to, it "gives us much, much, more [time because] they are much more independent." When Finn is off flying, his wife, who has a demanding professional career, is less burdened because their children can do things on their own, and "that gives me more time … because they're more independent."

Just as positive marital and family routines can be established by middle adulthood, work and career dynamics can likewise gain in stability and free up attention for engaging leisure play activities. One of the best examples of this was provided by Jerry.

> I always had career aspirations to go to a certain level and that had gone on for probably 20 years. I had reached a plateau, a plateau that I was very comfortable with … and I … mentally freed up a bit more time instead of [being] career focused … I'd still work the same number of hours but maybe I had a slightly different mindset once I … made that decision.

Part of this mindset involved making subtle time-use decisions when traveling for work, such as not scheduling many business dinners: "I don't always accept all these dinners … I will accept these three invitations and decline the other two … and then the two nights … [I] am not sitting in the hotel room just watching the T.V., I'm probably out enjoying my photography." Even when not traveling, he became strategic with his time. If it were possible, he scheduled conference calls or meetings around opportunities for photography.

None of these changes in mindset or scheduling negatively affected Jerry's work; in fact, it was just the opposite. He accepted "that I have to work X hours a week" and "his work got done." He thought his involvement with photography actually *contributed* to his ability to manage the intensity of his work and sustain it without experiencing burnout.

> In a funny sort of way, and this might seem illogical, I actually think it's helped my career because … it's given me an escape … which has allowed me to sustain this role and keep traveling for all these years … So it may have changed me as a person and allowed me to sustain what I've been doing where I might not have been able to do it otherwise.

Such insight is consistent with developmental perspectives that highlight increasing maturity in middle adulthood and insight that is beneficial for setting new priorities (Jung, 1955; Levinson, 1978; Neugarten, 1968).

Tim likewise came to see his interest in writing as a "supplemental tool" that helped him in his work life. After being laid off from his job a few years earlier, he had time to accept a 30-hour-a-week internship with a successful writer during which he "learned a tremendous amount." Then, after beginning to work full time again, he found that his renewed interest in writing actually helped him in his new work role.

> [I] do corporate training now and I tend to love that … I think if you're not as happy with … what you're doing at work then maybe I'd focus more on the writing to say, hey, this [work] is a distraction or diversion. But since I like what I do as well, it's kind of a supplemental tool … Seems like when I'm training, I bring up … things about me and say, hey, I'm an aspiring writer and I do this. So there's usually one or two people who come up afterward and say, well hey, I've been writing … [or there is] some connection with them about something.

Finn's involvement with paragliding also led to insights that informed his understanding of work. Rather than seeing it as directly helpful as did Jerry and Tim, however, he perceived his work-leisure relationship as complementary and useful for maintaining an optimal balance in life.

> I'm a competitive person. … I'm devastated if I don't, based on my assessment, don't do well. … I think the activity of flying, of paragliding … really resonates strongly with me because it has these qualities. … So, the question is really — what am I searching for? What I'm looking for here … is this kind of intensity of experience, what I said earlier, you know, it's hell and heaven. So this really, very intense experience of doing something. … I don't get it in my job anymore. … It doesn't give me this intensity. … So that's something that I learned that I need to maintain because it's a really important part of myself.

Self-Differentiation and Social Integration Through Leisure Play

If positive conditions in midlife and increasing self-knowledge are able to facilitate more opportunities for leisure play, such activities can be a powerful impetus to self-differentiation and social integration. On a personal level, they can instigate exploration of new information and skill development; on an interpersonal level, they can connect emerging aspects of the self to others who provide support, a sense of connection, and a social mirror of recognition and feedback. Our study participants spoke often about the importance of these aspects of their leisure pursuits.

As Jerry told us of devoting a great deal of time, thought, and money to photography, he emphasized that there was "huge potential for learning." He explained, "With just the techniques, the technology evolves, [so] you start to maybe experiment more, do different things. … I try to [get better] … just taking a lot of photos. So yes, practice. One hopes one improves just by doing more of it." These processes of exploration and skill development, in fact, provided Jerry with the primary reason for his continued passion for photography:

> [What keeps me coming back to photography is] the desire to do it better and get better shots. Better shots or different shots. … If you have been to a certain place and have taken a certain photograph and feel … you've maximized the potential of doing that, maybe you wouldn't go back. But say at a sporting event you always know there's going to be new opportunities because … every game is different. What motivates you is to get better shots and new images, different images.

Apparent as well from Jerry's interview was the uniqueness of his relationship with photography with regard to these self-differentiation components. He explained this by comparing photography to golf: "With photography I can aspire to sort of get better and better. Where with golf, I think I've reached the ceiling of my physical limits or whatever it may be, my coordination, and I'm satisfied to just sort of hack around and have good company with friends." Jerry goes further, distinguishing between the two outlets in terms of friendly socialization, which lightens the challenges of golf:

> So for golf, as opposed to photography, golf provides a very good social outlet, you know. I have friends, we talk while we're out on the course, we're not very good but we're all about the same and there's a social side to that. I wouldn't really describe there being too much of a social life to my photography. You go out there, even if you're out there on an outing with the camera club, and you're somewhat in the zone. Maybe there's a social element in the car getting to and from the venue, but beyond that you're focused on doing it.

Finn also spoke extensively about challenges that were inherent to paragliding and how learning was literally necessary to his survival. "There are many days … when you fly to prepare for those days when you enhance your skills. … I'm very systematic about how to approach this because … I know how to advance performance. I can … focus on training to get really good and … I'm really ambitious about this." Speaking at length about more specific challenges he faced, Finn introduced the notion of risk and the important role it played in his preparation.

> Now I'm flying cross-country which means I'm flying new routes. So I'm flying stuff people have flown but I have never flown before. And one of the biggest challenges in this is to get this really right balance between how much risk are you taking [and] how much are you pushing. … Risks associated with this are unknown terrain — you land in a spot where retrieval is really difficult. … When do you take the risky route? When do you take the slower route? That's a continuous challenge for me. … I want to go far which means I have to … be willing to take higher risks but … I want to take reasonable risks.

Identity theory makes clear that insights about self and identity never occur in a social vacuum. Identity is both a personal and social phenomenon. Parts of the self that are formed through personal experiences are also public, and feedback from others is part of the identity-development process. For Finn, some of the feedback from others is not identity relevant and simply reflects the dangers of paragliding: "It is a really lunatic activity for many people." There are significant others, however, who recognize the essential parts of him connected to this activity. For example, even though Finn's father-in-law worries about paragliding being an unnecessary risk, Finn sees a tension in his perceptions: "My father in law … there is a little bit of fascination in him. … He's proud when he sees me fly. … He's also retrieving me so I can give him a call and he says ok I'll pick you up. So he's facilitating some of it." Most importantly, Finn knows that his wife understands the part of him that is intimately connected to paragliding: "[She's] supportive. I mean, she knows it's critical, and she understands that it's critical for my balance. If I haven't flown in a while I'm in a really bad mood."

Like Finn, Jerry also recalled how some of his acquaintances did not fully understand how photography was connected to his sense of self and identity:

> Say … I want to take a certain shot, and I want people to move out of the shot so I stand in a certain space. And I'm waiting and there's still other people. They'll say: 'Haven't you yet taken the photograph?' And the answer is no, I've been waiting for this opportune moment and it hasn't yet arisen. And people are frustrated, 'Well just take it and move it,' you know that sort of mind set. … I think others can see my sort of commitment to it as excessive.

However, also like Finn, there were significant others who recognized his commitment and what it meant to him, especially his wife: "She's understanding you know … after all this … she knew I was an active photographer … She's known this from day one … So it's part of the package … It didn't sneak up on anyone." In addition, although it did not radically alter his self-image, there were occasions when the positive reactions of friends bolstered Jerry's sense of self: "You know it gives you a bit more self-confidence because you take images that people want copies of or people truly recognize. … It changes the way I think about myself."

Making connections with a wider group of people played an important role in how Tim viewed himself as an aspiring writer. He recalled how he was part of a writing group, a member of the society of children's book writers, and how for the last number of years he had been attending a lot of conferences and "visiting with a lot of people."

> I think I'm more willing to be open to things now … There's a value that comes from feedback and being aware of things that you can't see. And before I don't think that with [writing] critique groups [I] participated with some of them in the past … the fear was always … is this person going to know any more than my neighbor, my spouse, to give feedback … And maybe something with the age and where I'm at has helped as well to say there's great feedback from everybody.

One time he received feedback from an agent on a couple pages he had written that was an affirmation of his growing skills: "If they [agents] like it, they may request more. Then they may request a whole manuscript … I have had an agent request the full novel which I thought was a good sign." Even more important than this affirming recognition, Tim appreciated the intimate connections with others he was able to make through his stories:

> Something about just that creative process, about just taking something that's not there and that's only in your head that you've seen, or your slant on that, and being able to put it down on that paper so you can get somebody else who isn't inside your head to … see what you've seen and share in that experience or that kind of moment.

Tailoring Identity and Flow

In addition to the similarities across the interviews with respect to finding time for their interests and instigating personal growth and social connection, all three interviewees described states of deep engagement that occurred while doing their chosen activities. Although none of them used the specific concept of "flow," there was little doubt that the in-the-moment states they depicted fit this descriptor of optimal experience. According to Waterman (1990), peak and flow experiences can be seen as confirmations that a person's activities are personally expressive of identity and reflect parts of themselves that are meaningful. This was clearly the case for our interviewees. Whereas some individuals choose their leisure primarily for relaxation, distraction, or perhaps simply to connect with friends, our interviewees talked about their activities as deeply absorbing and moving them closer to their unique potentials. In this sense, flow signaled that they were actively tailoring their identities and not just accepting an "off-the-rack" style of individuality.

Flow involves the dynamic negotiation of an optimal state of arousal (Rathunde, 2013; Rathunde & Csikszentmihalyi, 2006). In terms of the tailoring model presented earlier in Fig. 14.1, flow associated with identity development would indicate being proactive in relation to under- or overstimulating settings. In other words, sometimes the path to flow requires exploring new challenges, and sometimes it calls for committing to mastering them. The interviews we conducted provided evidence of these divergent-convergent dynamics (see also the autoethnographic account of leisure music making in Rathunde & Isabella, 2017). As demonstrated by the following quotes, Tim was keenly aware of the ups and downs of the writing process and its occasional fulfillment in moments of flow:

> Some days it can be you're in the zone and you know it's just coming fast and furious, you're getting ideas, there's a lot of excitement, a lot of energy about the possibilities and about the future. … And maybe on the worst days it's the frustration of this is all a bunch of crap. … You experience a wide range of emotions and then when you can make it work again [you experience] that euphoric feeling of I've conquered this or I've figured out how to take this jumbled messed up thing and actually make it work. … Sometimes it happens in the same day. You start out good and then you hit a bump and you're … trying to think through something.

> Sometimes you're just laying in bed at night and you get ideas for new stories or something comes into your mind … so ideas are coming up … and then it's a matter of jotting that down cause some inspiration hangs around longer than others. … You're always thinking about it … and I usually try to have something with me at all times so I can be jotting something down or if I hear something, keep tabs on that. … Depending what you're writing on, you're always going back to try to make it accurate or authentic so that it's more historic or

> you're trying to research something to see if that's how it really is done. … Everything from mechanics all the way through to just new ideas and information, and then sometimes you have an epiphany.

Flow-like moments of illumination also occurred for Tim when he was interacting with others. Tim thought of himself as an observer of the world: "If you're a dentist you look at people's teeth, if you're a shoe salesmen you look at people's shoes … and so you [a writer] tend to look at people and just be an observer of life and what's going on around you." He found it enjoyable to share his observations with others in his writing group. One example involved a passage he had written about a teenage girl. A group member commented, "a teenage girl wouldn't really do that." Tim thought for a second and responded, "Ok then I'll trust you. You probably know that better than I would." He continued:

> You think you're pretty good [at writing] then … people start pointing things out you sometimes just can't see or you don't know what you don't know. … Being able to have someone else point that out is very illuminating.

These experiences of euphoria, epiphany, and illumination were important reasons why Tim proclaimed, "I love exploring and that creating process." The writing process furthers Tim's identity development not only because it expresses a passion for writing that can be traced back to his love of reading, comic books, and art when he was an adolescent, but also in terms of things he values in life.

> Things that matter to you at the time come out in that writing and so it may be … as you're looking back on things, things that mattered to you, or things that you were thinking about, tend to make its way into that writing consciously or subconsciously. So if you really focus on it, you can really say, ahh yes, this is when I was dealing with this, or … I was thinking a lot about this topic of time or family.

Finn was likewise articulate about the complex dynamics of spontaneous discovery and careful planning that resulted in occasional "wow" moments of flow and being focused in the moment.

> I was maybe 11 and 1⁄2 or 12 thousand feet high … and I thought, this is the day. I need to commit. And I flew over [the mountain]. … It was the right day, it was the right conditions, I had the right equipment, and I was prepared because I really had planned on it. … This is the thing that is so exciting, for me, about paragliding. When you fly cross-country you are an explorer. You turn from someone who is doing very conventional things, you know, sitting in your office … into someone who is discovering something totally new. And that really drives me … this kind of wow. … And of course there's an incredible beauty to it … and you see things you never would see otherwise. … If you fly slow you can go down to 10 – 15 miles per hour. And so you see stuff that you never see on a bicycle, not in a car, or in an airplane, or a helicopter. That makes it really intriguing. … I mean this is a very emotional thing about it. … One of the things I find very intriguing is I look at [other paragliders] and I see a lot of individual differences. I'm super intense when I fly. I can't listen to music. It would totally distract me. And I need everything, I need every sensory input I can get. And then there are people who when I fly with them, I look at them, and you know, I look at signs, grass bending, leaves rustling, they have no idea that this stuff is happening. So they don't get the feel for the thermal that's coming up the hill this moment, which means you launch into it and you immediately climb out. They launch any time [because they miss the sensory input] and they sink out. … And I think you need this intensity to do these things.

As was the case with Tim's description of the process of writing, Finn's account of paragliding involved moments of exploration and discovery counterbalanced by ones of reflection and planning. Each of these aspects of the process played an essential part in the negotiation of optimal arousal and triggering the intense moments of absorption in flow. While Jerry did not describe these divergent-convergent adjustments in the process of taking photos, he provided one of the clearest descriptions of the phenomenology of flow, one that came extremely close to its widely documented characteristics (Csikszentmihalyi, 1996).

> I enjoy doing it. I still get satisfaction, pleasure, from getting … an image that is really good. I still get the thrill. I don't know whatever term you want to use. … It's still not mundane to me. It still energizes me and it gets me sort of excited. … In the field I try to be focused on taking images … and not get distracted. People will say that I'm focused, focused on doing something and there's a huge cry for help 50 yards away, I might not even notice cause I'm focused on the task in hand. People will say I'm kind of cut off from the rest of the world.

Conclusion

There are numerous circumstances in midlife that can initiate identity change. Becoming a grandparent, winning a lottery, or simply the natural process of aging might lead to a reformation of beliefs about one's role in life. In addition, traumatic events and unexpected health challenges might force adaptations that affect identity (Ellis, 1999; McAdams, 1993). In the absence of such events that force change upon the self, however, identity development often depends upon the willingness of a person to *intentionally* engage in challenges significant enough to require a reorganization of priorities and goals. In these self-directed circumstances, there are also numerous ways to set the process in motion. One might volunteer at a local school, get involved in promoting a candidate for state office, or start a new business out of one's home. All of these paths to identity change can introduce challenges that might alter the self and its connection to others. The present chapter focused on another voluntary and important way to instigate identity development: investing time in challenging and intrinsically motivated leisure play pursuits. The perspective here is that middle-aged adults too often miss such growth-oriented opportunities, even when they have favorable life circumstances and resources to support them. These missed opportunities, in turn, inhibit successful aging and represent a significant loss for the quality of mental and physical health (Brown et al., 2008; Stebbins, 1982; Valliant, 2002).

Part of the explanation for these missed opportunities, we believe, lies in misunderstandings about the continued role of play in adulthood and its capacity to motivate engaging new challenges. Passionate leisure interests in middle adulthood reflect the human capacity for lifelong play, a capacity that is likely enhanced by age-appropriate play experiences during childhood and adolescence (Rathunde & Csikszentmihalyi, 2006). The long list of benefits research has associated with play

(Burghardt, 2005; Pellegrini, 1992; Spinka et al., 2001) and similar intrinsically motivating states (Csikszentmihalyi, 1996; Deci & Ryan, 1985; Maslow, 1968; Renninger et al., 1992) make a strong case for its consequential role in human development. Although play is an evolution-based process that is primarily associated with childhood, it remains vitally important in adulthood because the human strategy for survival and flourishing is the capacity for mental flexibility and lifelong learning (Kashdan & Rottenberg, 2010; Montagu, 1989).

The interview protocol used in our identity study was not designed to probe the play histories of the interviewees or to address the developmental hypothesis that childhood play positively affects the capacity to tailor identity in mid-adulthood. Nevertheless, it is worth noting that all three interviewees perceived a connection between the intense experiences they associated with their current leisure interests and their deep engagement with athletics when younger. Tim described his involvement with track and basketball from junior high through high school as "pretty all encompassing for quite a number of years." Finn enjoyed playing handball in his youth, eventually competed on a national team, and said it was "a very formative experience during adolescence." When Jerry was younger, he enjoyed playing rugby and went to a high school where sports were "actively encouraged" and "part of the school culture." He specifically perceived an "intersection of two interests" with sports and photography that was carried forward in his adult interests. None of these anecdotal connections provide unequivocal support for a developmental link between youthful play and the adult capacity for play and identity growth. They also do not shed any light on our interviewees' play in early childhood, a developmental period that is arguably even more important than adolescence (Biglan et al., 2012). However, when these anecdotes are seen in the context of the literature on play, it is reasonable to assume that deep engagement experiences earlier in life were part of the developmental histories of our interviewees (see also Brown, 2009).

Whatever its origin, the capacity for play demonstrated by Jerry, Finn, and Tim benefited from surplus resource conditions (Burghardt, 2005). Such conditions, unfortunately, are not a given in midlife, and some individuals find themselves dealing with financial or other difficulties that compress time for play and leisure (Lachman, 2004). Others may find themselves in favorable conditions and still elect to maintain the status quo without attempting to explore ways to differentiate the self or establish new social connections. Our interviewees, in contrast, leveraged their positive conditions to challenge themselves through leisure play. Although they represent a small and very select group of men and it is impossible to generalize widely from their idiosyncratic stories, we believe these stories are instructive for illustrating the potential benefits of embracing intrinsically motivating and difficult challenges. Instead of opting for comfort, their examples illustrated that good marital relationships and communication, lessening parental and family responsibilities, stable career and financial circumstances, and growing self-knowledge can free resources in middle adulthood that then can be invested in leisure play. These investments facilitated the identity development of our interviewees through self-differentiation and personal growth, as well as social integration that helped reaffirm and support changes to the self. Their vivid descriptions of the phenomenology of play were consistent with the literature describing such experiences (Csikszentmihalyi, 1996), their divergent-convergent dynamics that mirror the exploration-commitment dynamics of identity development (Berzonsky, 1990; Marcia, 1980; Schwartz, 2001), and the way such optimal experiences can reveal meaningful aspects of identity (Waterman, 1990).

Whether attempting to understand adult identity development or some other outcome requiring exploration and flexibility, leisure play is a valuable route to lifelong learning that is often overlooked. While there is little doubt that favorable resource conditions can help trigger a state of mind characterized by intrinsic motivation, freedom of choice, and feeling outside the constraints of ordinary life (Huizinga, 1955), play is a path to growth for all adults regardless of the circumstances they face. Studies like the present one serve to highlight this potential of play by suggesting how it can provide tremendous energy and motivation for engaging significant challenges.

References

Adams, G. R., & Marshall, S. K. (1996). A developmental social psychology of identity: Understanding the person-in-context. *Journal of Adolescence, 19*, 429–442.

Berlyne, D. E. (1971). *Aesthetics and psychobiology*. New York: Appleton-Century-Crofts.

Berzonsky, M. D. (1990). Self-construction over the lifespan: A process perspective on identity formation. In G. J. Neimeyer & R. A. Neimeyer (Eds.), *Advances in personal construct theory* (Vol. 1, pp. 155–186). Greenwich, CT: JAI.

Biggerstaff, D., & Thompson, A. R. (2008). Interpretative phenomenological analysis (IPA): A qualitative methodology of choice in healthcare research. *Qualitative Research in Psychology, 5*(3), 214–224.

Biglan, A., Flay, B. R., Embry, D. D., & Sandler, I. N. (2012). The critical role of nurturing environments for promoting human wellbeing. *American Psychologist, 67*(4), 257–271.

Block, J., & Block, J. H. (2006). Venturing a 30-year longitudinal study. *American Psychologist, 61*, 315–327.

Bredekamp, S., & Copple, C. (1997). *Developmentally appropriate practice in early childhood programs*. Washington, DC: NAEYC.

Brown, C. A., McGuire, F. A., & Voelkl, J. (2008). The link between successful aging and serious leisure. *International Journal of Aging and Human Development, 66*(1), 73–95.

Brown, S. (2009). *Play*. New York: Avery.

Burghardt, G. M. (2005). *The genesis of animal play: Testing the limits*. Cambridge: MIT Press.

Campbell, J. (2011). *The power of myth* (with Bill Moyers). New York: Knopf Doubleday.

Cooley, C. H. (1902). *Human nature and the social order*. New York: Scribners.

Csikszentmihalyi, M. (1975). *Beyond boredom and anxiety: The experience of play in work and games*. San Francisco: Jossey-Bass.

Csikszentmihalyi, M. (1996). *Creativity*. New York: HarperCollins.

Csikszentmihalyi, M., & Bennett, S. (1971). An exploratory model of play. *American Anthropologist, 73*(1), 45–58.

Csikszentmihalyi, M., Rathunde, K., & Whalen, S. (1993). *Talented teenagers: The roots of success and failure*. New York: Cambridge University Press.

Deci, E. L., & Ryan, R. M. (1985). *Intrinsic motivation and self-determination in human behavior*. New York: Plenum Press.
Dewey, J. (1913). *Interest and effort in education*. Cambridge, MA: Riverside.
Dillon, S. (2006, March 26). Schools cut back subjects to push reading and math. *New York Times*. Retrieved from http://www.nytimes.com
Duvall, J., & Kaplan, R. (2014). Enhancing the well-being of veterans using extended group-based nature recreation experiences. *Journal of Rehabilitation Research and Development, 51*(5), 685–696.
Ellis, C. (1999). Heartful autoethnography. *Qualitative Health Research, 9*(5), 669–683.
Erikson, E. H. (1950). *Childhood and society*. New York: Norton.
Erikson, E. H. (1968). *Identity: Youth and crisis*. New York: Norton.
Espinosa, M. P., Sigman, M. D., Neumann, C. G., Bwibo, N. O., & McDonald, M. A. (1992). Playground behaviors of school-age children in relation to nutrition, schooling and family characteristics. *Developmental Psychology, 28*(6), 1188–1195.
Floyd, M. (1999). Ethnic and racial diversity of National Park System visitors and non-visitors. Technical Report. *NPS Social Science Research Review, 1*(2), 1–23.
Ginsburg, K. R., The Council on Communications and Media, & The Committee on Psychosocial Aspects of Child and Family Health. (2007). The importance of play in promoting healthy child development and maintaining strong parent-child bonds. *Pediatrics*. Retrieved from http://pediatrics.aappublications.org/content/119/1/182.full.html
Gould, S. (1977). *Ontogeny and phylogeny*. Cambridge, MA: Harvard University Press.
Graham, K. L., & Burghhardt, G. M. (2010). Current perspectives on the biological study of play: Signs of progress. *The Quarterly Review of Biology, 85*(4), 393–418.
Hansen, D. J., Lumpkin, G. T., & Hills, G. E. (2011). A multidimensional examination of a creativity-based opportunity recognition model. *International Journal of Entrepreneurial Behaviour & Research, 17*(5), 515–533.
Huizinga, J. (1955). *Homo ludens*. Boston: Beacon Press.
Jung, C. G. (1955). *Modern man in search of a soul*. New York: Harcourt.
Kashdan, T. B., & Rottenberg, J. (2010). Psychological flexibility as a fundamental aspect of health. *Clinical Psychology Review, 30*, 865–878.
Kerns, K. A., & Barth, J. M. (1995). Attachment and play: Convergence across components of parent-child relationships and their relations to peer competence. *Journal of Social and Personal Relationships, 12*, 243–260.
Kleiber, D. (1999). *Leisure experience and human development*. Boulder, CO: Westview Press (Basic Books).
Kolb, D. A. (1984). *Experiential learning*. Englewood Cliffs, NJ: Prentice Hall.
Kolb, D. A., Boyatzis, R. E., & Mainemelis, C. (2001). Experiential learning theory: Previous research and new directions. In R. J. Sternberg & L. F. Zhang (Eds.), *Perspectives on cognitive, learning, and thinking styles*. Mahwah, NJ: Lawrence Erlbaum.
Lachman, M. E. (2004). Development in midlife. *Annual Review of Psychology, 55*, 305–331.
Levinson, D. J. (1978). *The season's of a man's life*. New York: Knopf.
Mainemelis, C., & Ronson, S. (2006). Ideas are born in fields of play: Towards a theory of play and creativity in organizational settings. *Research in Organizational Behavior, 27*, 81–131.
Marcia, J. E. (1980). Identity in adolescence. In J. Adelson (Ed.), *Handbook of adolescent psychology* (pp. 159–187). New York: Wiley.
Maslow, A. H. (1968). *Toward a psychology of being*. New York: D. Van Nostrand.
McAdams, D. P. (1993). *The stories we live by: Personal myth and the making of the self*. New York: Morrow.
McCall, G. J., & Simmons, J. L. (1978). *Identities and interactions*. New York: Free Press.
Mead, G. H. (1934). *Mind, self, and society*. Chicago: University of Chicago Press.
Milteer, R. M., Ginsburg, K. R., Mulligan, D. A., The Council on Communications and Media, & The Committee on Psychosocial Aspects of Child and Family Health. (2011). The importance of play in promoting healthy child development and maintaining strong parent-child bonds:

Focus on children in poverty. *Pediatrics*. Retrieved from http://pediatrics.aappublications.org/content/129/1/e204.full.html

Montagu, A. (1989). *Growing young*. Boston: Bergin & Garvey.

National Association for the Education of Young Children (Position statement) (2009). *Developmentally appropriate practice in early childhood programs serving children from birth through age 8*. Retrieved from http://www.naeyc.org/files/naeyc/file/positions/position statement Web.pdf

Neugarten, B. L. (1968). Adult personality: Toward a psychology of the life cycle. In B. L. Neugarten (Ed.), *Middle age and aging: A reader in social psychology*. Chicago: University of Chicago Press.

Norman, D. A. (2013). *Design of everyday things: Revised and expanded*. New York: Basic Books.

Onarheim, B., & Friis-Olivarius, M. (2013, Ocotober). Applying the neuroscience of creativity to creativity training. *Frontiers in Human Neuroscience, 7*, 656. 10.3389/fnhum.2013.00656

Pellegrini A. D. (1992). Rough-and-tumble play and social problem solving flexibility. *Creativity Research Journal, 5*(1), 13–26.

Rathunde, K. (2013). Experiential wisdom and lifelong learning. In J. Sinnott (Ed.), *Positive psychology and adult motivation* (pp. 269–290). New York: Springer.

Rathunde, K., & Csikszentmihalyi, M. (2006). The developing person: An experiential perspective. In R. M. Lerner (Ed.), W. Damon (Series Ed.), *Handbook of child psychology: Vol. 1. Theoretical models of human development* (6th ed.) (pp. 465–515). New York: Wiley.

Rathunde, K., & Isabella, R. (2017). Playing music and identity development in middle adulthood: A theoretical and autoethnographic account. In R. Mantie & G. D. Smith (Eds.), *Oxford handbook of music making and leisure* (pp. 131–149). Oxford: Oxford University Press.

Reid, K., Flowers, P., & Larkin, M. (2005). Exploring lived experience. *The Psychologist, 18*(1), 20–23.

Renninger, K. A., Hidi, S., & Krapp, A. (Eds.). (1992). *The role of interest in learning and development*. Hillsdale, NJ: Erlbaum.

Schwartz, S. J. (2001). The evolution of Eriksonian and neo-Eriksonian identity theory and research: A review and integration. *Identity: An International Journal of Theory and Research, 1*(1), 7–58.

Sharpe, L. L., Clutton-Brock, T. H., Brotherton, P. N. M., Cameron, E. Z., & Cherry, M. I. (2002). Experimental provisioning increases play in free-ranging meerkats. *Animal Behaviour, 64*(1), 113–121.

Slade, A. (1987). Quality of attachment and early symbolic play. *Developmental Psychology, 23*(1), 78–85.

Spinka, M., Newberry, R. C., & Bekoff, M. (2001). Mammalian play: Training for the unexpected. *Quarterly Review of Biology, 76*(2), 141–168.

Stebbins, R. A. (1982). Serious leisure: A conceptual statement. *The Sociological Review, 25*(2), 251–272.

Turner, J. H. (2013). *Contemporary sociological theory*. Newburry Park, CA: Sage.

Vaillant, G. E. (2002). *Aging well*. Boston: Little Brown and Company.

Wallas, G. (1926). *The art of thought*. New York: Harcourt Brace.

Waterman, A. S. (1990). Personal expressiveness: Philosophical and psychological foundations. *Journal of Mind and Behavior, 11*, 47–74.

Waterman, A. S. (1993). Two conceptions of happiness: Contrasts of personal expressiveness (Eudaimonia) and hedonic enjoyment. *Journal of Personality and Social Psychology, 64*(4), 678–691.

Chapter 15
Optimizing Challenges: Eminent Elders Meet Adversity with Identity Flexibility

Grant J. Rich

This chapter examines optimal development in older adults through two case studies of eminent elders who achieved great success and international reputations in their professions. Analysis of these cases is utilized as a basis for theoretical exploration of the theme of this volume, that adult identity is not as fixed, concrete, and permanent as previously thought. This chapter examines these "evolving selves" (Csikszentmihalyi, 1993) through the lens of flow, a core positive psychology concept (Rich, 2014), and a focus on how sustained engagement with an activity when challenges and perceived skills are high, yet nearly balanced, can facilitate optimal experience, achievement, and well-being. In particular, the description of case studies in this chapter will note how these eminent creators utilized identity flexibility in pursuit of their goals, despite tremendous life challenges. Interviews and other case materials support an argument, that for these high-achieving individuals, setbacks were converted to opportunities, and life challenges ultimately were viewed as having a silver lining. The two interviewees that form the focus of this chapter are Fred Hersch, the eminent jazz pianist, and Saths Cooper, the well-known South African psychologist and head of the International Union of Psychological Sciences (IUPsyS).

Since the launch of the positive psychology movement about 15 years ago, one of the most influential leaders has been Mihaly Csikszentmihalyi, who, along with Martin Seligman, was a cofounder of this new branch of psychology, which aims to offer a corrective to the business as usual psychology focusing on psychological disorders, by instead focusing on human strengths and virtues (e.g., Seligman & Csikszentmihalyi, 2000). One of the positive psychology concepts that has been most extensively and carefully researched has been flow, Csikszentmihalyi's term for a psychological state of optimal experience that has much in common with what others have termed peak experiences (Maslow, 1971) or intrinsic motivation

G.J. Rich (✉)
Consulting Psychologist, Juneau, Alaska, India
e-mail: optimalex@aol.com

J.D. Sinnott (ed.), *Identity Flexibility During Adulthood*,
DOI 10.1007/978-3-319-55658-1_15

(Deci & Ryan, 1985). In fact, Csikszentmihalyi's work on flow predates the positive psychology movement, as, for example, in his work published in the 1970s concerning flow in populations including dancers and rock climbers (Csikszentmihalyi, 1975) and later work examining flow in adolescents (Csikszentmihalyi & Larson, 1984) and a broad range of other populations across the life span and around the globe (Csikszentmihalyi, 1990).

Though it does have similarities to related constructs, such as humanistic accounts of peak experiences, flow is distinct from them, as has been demonstrated by ample quantitative and qualitative data (Rich, 2014). In particular, Csikszentmihalyi has detailed nine elements to the flow experience that are worth noting here. First, there are clear goals at each step of the process. Next, the person receives immediate feedback on their performance. There is a balance between the perceived challenges of the activity at hand and the perceived skills one brings to the activity. This flow element is especially relevant to the present chapter, as will be discussed later. Fourth, the action of the activity and conscious awareness become merged. Fifth, distractions from the main activity are kept out of conscious awareness. Six, in flow, the person is not worried about or thinking about failure. Next, self-consciousness disappears. Eighth, the person's sense of "clock" time disappears, expanding or contracting, as attention is focused on the main activity. The final ninth element occurs if the previous eight elements are in large part met. In this case, the main flow activity becomes an end in itself, or, in Csikszentmihalyi's terms, autotelic. Such an activity is pursued for its own sake, not solely for pursuit of extrinsic rewards, such as praise from others, or financial gain.

Flow has been applied both to short-term and long-term motivation, change, and development. For instance, Csikszentmihalyi has detailed what he calls microflow experiences, which may last just moments or minutes, and are enjoyable and engaging, though the experience is much less intense than Maslow's peak experiences or full-blown flow experiences. For example, a person who is bored at a meeting may absorb the rest of idle consciousness by doodling, or a person in a hospital waiting room may fill the gap in attention by playing mental counting games. Twiddling one's hair while reading a less than gripping novel may be another instance of microflow (Csikszentmihalyi, 1975, 1990). Most flow research has focused on flow experiences that last many minutes or perhaps hours, such as may occur during a deeply engaging conversation, an athletic activity, or a scholarly work session, such as conducting an experiment in a lab or writing a section of an academic publication. Least studied have been long-term, ongoing flow experiences. In fact the relationship between short-term flow experiences and long-term flow experiences merits further discussion and analysis by researchers in the next generation. Though persons who experience brief microflow and typical length flow experiences may indeed experience flow at many times in life, this is not true for all persons, and no one yet discovered is in full flow every hour of every day of every year of a life span. That said, attempts have been made to connect the flow moment to flow lives, by analyzing flow in youth as well as adults. For instance, in a large 5-year longitudinal national student study of 33 high schools, students who spent more time in flow were compared with students who spent significantly less time in flow

(Csikszentmihalyi & Schneider, 2000). Those students in flow while conducting "work- or academic"-related activities tended to show greater well-being and optimal development with respect to activities that related to positive career and educational development. Though this was only a 5-year study of adolescents, the implications for longer-term development are clear. If one enjoys and derives flow from activities related to school or work, one is likely to want to repeat these activities in the future, even if there are no extrinsic rewards such as teacher or parental praise or monetary compensation. Practice perhaps makes perfect, and young people in flow while doing work or academic activities are thus likely to develop stronger, more advanced skills in these activities than young people who do not experience flow in work or academic activities. Those not experiencing flow in such activities are likely to stop such activities as soon as possible (for instance, after graduation or even by leaving school).

Extending the flow experience further across the life span, scholars have demonstrated how the flow experience can be linked to high levels of achievement in many disciplines. For example, using interviews with nearly 100 well-known persons aged 60 and above who had made significant contributions to their respective domains, Csikszentmihalyi (1996) examined the creativity process and motivations in later life for continued work and success. The sample included Nobel, Pulitzer, and Grammy award winners, in disciplines including science, art, music, and literature. Many, if not all, of these eminent elders are in places where they have already accomplished much professionally, and thus one could argue that the persons could retire, having already achieved many extrinsic rewards in terms of money and praise. Yet, as a group, the interviewees demonstrated strong desires to continue in their careers, reflecting the intrinsic nature of flow activities. That said, and perhaps offering further confirmation of the flow experience, as a group these creators tended note as they aged that they enjoyed the ability to pick and choose which projects to work on and so could better select projects as older adults that appealed to them, rather than needing to take on assigned projects as when younger and less well-known, for instance, to ensure financial stability or career advancement. The interviews revealed that enjoyment in the main activity domain was a major motivator for these creators over their careers and lives. Such enjoyment helped the creators persist in their professions even before achieving eminence and carried many of the participants through hard times, times when those who did not receive as much flow from their domain may have left the profession for other pursuits (e.g., musicians who leave music for less competitive careers or academics who leave academe after finding it difficult to maintain funding or secure a tenured position).

In his book *The evolving self,* Csikszentmihalyi (1993) has offered an extended discussion of how flow may be viewed as an explanatory framework for optimal growth and development across the life span. Persons seek experiences that offer them flow and then seek to repeat such experiences, developing increasing sophistication and complexity in their flow activity domain, as their skills increase with such practice. That such peak experience and focus is linked with overall well-being is recognized by Martin Seligman, who names engagement as the second of the five pillars of his PERMA well-being theory of positive psychology (2011). Engagement, writes Seligman, positive psychology's cofounder, "is about flow" (the other four pillars are positive emotion, relationships, meaning, and accomplishment) (p. 11).

The aspect of the flow experience that is the focus of this chapter is the issue of balancing perceived challenges and perceived skills. According to Csikszentmihalyi (1990), if challenges significantly exceed skills during an activity, the person will experience anxiety and likely will not experience flow or enjoyment. In contrast, if one's skills during an activity significantly exceed the challenge, one will likely experience boredom, and this not likely experience flow or enjoyment. In addition, if the skills and challenges of activity are balanced but low, the person may experience apathy. For example, many personal hygiene and maintenance activities require few skills and present few challenges; brushing one's teeth, for instance, takes little effort, and most people find such activities rather mundane and certainly not a peak experience. However, when the challenges presented by an activity require one to use one's skills to at or near their fullest, flow often occurs. In keeping with the theme of this volume on identity flexibility in adulthood, it is important to note how the self must continue to change, evolve, and adapt over the life course in order to continue to experience flow and the enjoyment it brings. For example, as an athlete ages, physical muscle strength may decline despite conditioning. Thus challenges in an activity increase as at least some skills may decrease, changing the nature and dynamic of activities that previously offered flow. To maintain flow then, such an athlete may (1) choose athletic events that better fit her or his changing strengths, (2) increase conditioning so as to meet the new challenges, or (3) find a different activity that produces flow, perhaps in a different or related professional domain, such as moving to a position as a coach or trainer, becoming involved as a sportscaster or sports journalist, or perhaps returning to school to pursue a degree in a new field, such as physical therapy or medicine. In the remainder of this chapter, two case studies of eminent elders in their professions will be examined to see how being open to flexibility in the challenge-skill balance has helped these individuals, both in the short term and in the long term, to maximize well-being and success, despite encounters with serious adversity, including a life-threatening personal health crisis, incarceration, and racial/ethnic prejudice.

Fred Hersch is an eminent American jazz pianist. Born in 1955, he was raised in Cincinnati, Ohio, until relocating to the East Coast as a young adult. At present, he has been nominated for eight Grammy Awards (most recently in 2015), has served as faculty at several respected music conservatories (his former students include well-respected jazz pianists Ethan Iverson and Brad Mehldau), and has earned awards or grants such as a Rockefeller Fellowship and funding from the National Endowment for the Arts. He has collaborated with many famous names in jazz and classical music, including Gary Burton, Kurt Elling, Charlie Haden, Marc Johnson, Julian Lage, Bill Frisell, Kevin Eubanks, Art Farmer, Lee Konitz, Stan Getz, Toots Thielmans, Joe Henderson, Joey Baron, Joshua Bell, Roomful of Teeth, Dawn Upshaw, and Renée Fleming. He ranked third in the 2015 critics' poll on jazz pianists in the famous industry publication, *Downbeat*, and will be a cover story in an issue later in 2015.

In terms of flow, in individual musical performances in the short term, an interview with Hersch indicates the experience rings true for him. When asked what his primary motivation to make music is, Hersch notes "there is a certain feeling, especially with other musicians when you are all in the zone and creating something together, that's kind of indescribable, and you're speaking this very intimate language with other people, and as much as I love to compose and do all kinds of other stuff, ultimately that's what makes me want to keep playing- that potential that every time you sit down something can happen!" He notes that when he is playing something he enjoys: "I disappear and it's just music. I'm not really conscious of the technical impediments; I'm just pretty much able to do what I hear, within reason… and there's no way to describe that feeling- people try to write about it and it's a very hard thing to put into words- but it's one of those things, that once you've done it, you want to keep doing it, because it is so much fun. It is very special when it occurs, and you can't will yourself to do it, you have to allow it to happen, so I try to put myself in the frame of mind of allowing things, rather than presenting something" (Rich, 2015).

When asked if there is anything he does that makes it more likely that he will have a peak performance, Hersch notes that he tries to be rested and not "overplay in a rehearsal or sound check or warmup," just ensuring that his "fingers are working." Such comments fit the flow model in terms of balance of challenges and skills. With over-practice right before a performance, the material may perhaps seem less challenging, and skills could dominate over them, perhaps leading to performer boredom. However, being rested and simply ensuring sufficient finger facility, the performer is ready to delve deeply into the performance with his full focus and attention, increasing chances that flow may occur. Hersch also notes that he does not like to have a full set list of material pre-planned before a performance; this flexibility allows responsiveness to the balance of challenges and skills that will evolve over the evening and is another way that the performer ensures an optimal match between his inner life and skills that evening and the outer reality of the reception by the audience and the match to the difficulty of the program. As Hersch comments: "I'm always better off if I play what's in front of me or what occurs to me at that very moment… it's the question of the right thing at the right time in terms of the programming that really helps me stay connected" (Rich, 2015).

In another interview (Regen, 2013), Hersch had commented that his *Alive with the Vanguard* trio set was his best to date and that the musicians had brought a "sense of danger and respect to the bandstand." When asked to clarify what he meant, the pianist noted that the musicians "pick things up really quickly and that allows for spontaneity and the interaction, and jazz is kind of unique in that respect"; the danger is "when all of a sudden you're in unchartered territory- you're playing something that you never played it before and that's when all your experience and the experience of the people you are playing with comes into play and you can really create something fresh together- and that's exhilarating and a little dangerous because you don't know what's going to happen- it can crash or burn or it can be really cool, but you have to be willing to take chances, and your experience helps you pull them off" (Rich, 2015). This sense of playing at or near the edge of a balance between challenges and skills is again evidence that is consonant with flow theory and may indeed suggest why Hersch has constantly improved, both in his own eyes and that of the critics.

Fred Hersch is an openly gay man. He moved out of Cincinnati, Ohio, in the 1970s, beginning life as a gay man in Boston in 1975 and recalls the first time he marched in a gay pride march was about 1979 or 1980, which "felt like a big step" (Rich, 2015). In the 1980s, he discovered he was HIV positive and has been living with AIDS for a number of years. Hersch reports that his period of coming out, such as to fellow jazz musician Stan Getz was "the beginning of my gaining confidence as a composer. I had to get out there while I still had time" (Hajdu, 2011, p. 144). In 2008, he faced a number of severe health challenges. First, he developed an AIDS-related dementia that led to intense paranoia and delusions of persecution. Hersch says this included "a three-month psychotic break when the AIDS virus went into my brain [and] I was completely, really nuts" (Rich, 2015). Next, he entered a 2-month long coma after developing "a really shitty, pneumonia… it was just a bad pneumonia that was not diagnosed in time – it was not an AIDS-related coma," and during that period, he had regular dialysis and had a tracheotomy. For 8 months, he could not eat food or liquids and lost nearly all motor function. Months of physical therapy helped him relearn to walk, and he could "not hold a pencil, let alone play the piano" (Hajdu, 2011; Rich, 2015). Hersch attributes his resilience and recovery to several factors, including medications including Zyprexa and two new HIV medications that came out and reduced his viral load, as well as support from his partner Scott, who negotiated with the healthcare team, massaged Fred's hands, and offered his love with daily visits. Hersch also notes several personal qualities. He reports "I wanted to live and get back to playing. I did not want to fade out. When I was psychotic I wanted to end it all. After the coma, I was really determined to not let this define my life" (Rich, 2015).

His post-coma recovery is evident in the many accolades, including multiple Grammy nominations, received since 2008. His longtime engineer, who has worked with Hersch on over 40 albums, has commented that "since his illness, he's matured musically and also emotionally, saying 'everything I do has to have meaning and has to be my best game, because I do not have a lot of time.' I have seen a huge change in him with the illnesses- just stop the fooling around, stop wasting time" (Hajdu, 2011, p. 147). Hersch agrees, noting that "in my playing five years, six years, out of my coma maybe I am even playing better than I was before or than I ever have" (Rich, 2015).

Being a gay man and identifying himself publicly in this way has impacted his career, but Hersch cautions strongly against facile interpretations. For instance, he recoils at critics or audiences who think he plays "pretty" because he is gay. He notes that "I don't play the way I do because I am gay. I play the way I do because I'm Fred" (Hajdu, 2011, p. 146). Though he has selected musical projects that focus on gay musicians or poets, such as albums devoted to the music of Billy Strayhorn or musical settings of Walt Whitman's poetry, Hersch comments "when I did *Leaves of Grass* some people though 'Whitman was gay, Fred is gay, makes sense,' but I didn't give a shit, his words were inspiring and I was able to use his words, and music would help them come alive, so that's why I did it… [the fact that Whitman was gay] is not what attracted me, what attracted me was what he had to say" (Rich, 2015). These caveats in mind, Hersch does acknowledge the impact that HIV/AIDS and being a gay man has had on his career. He notes: "when I was diagnosed, it was a death sentence; you were just waiting for the shoe to drop. I spent many, many years thinking this is the last record I will ever make or this is the last fill in the blank and feeling defective and somehow 'less than' or feeling guilty and blaming myself for not having been more careful – all those kinds of things… so my whole career as a musician under my own name has had that cloud over it…. [but now] it's pills, and something I watch and manage. I will be 58 in the fall and sixty is looking like a no brainer, but I never thought I'd be forty, so it does change you." He adds: "I am determined… to make records and do projects so if I died, I'd leave at least something behind; I would want people to at least know who I was. I think that was a motivator and I am pretty driven in some respects" (Rich, 2015).

Hersch describes his experience after he first came out the coma as follows: "I had to learn to work with a more limited palette, technically, as a pianist… [yet] at the same time I felt stronger than ever creatively. I found I had more things to say musically, I had more to express, and what I had to say didn't require pyrotechnics" (Hajdu, 2011, p. 144). In flow theory, one would say he modified the challenges to fit his new skill set, at least until his recovery was completed and physical abilities restored. Such techniques have been employed by other musicians to great success. For example, the Grammy award winning Canadian jazz pianist Oscar Peterson suffered a severe stroke in the early 1990s in which he "practically lost the use of [his] left hand" (Csikszentmihalyi & Rich, 1997; Peterson, 2002; Rich, 1994, 2012a). To cope, Peterson reports he "had to learn how to possibly stretch that restriction as [he] played and to stretch it to the point where [his] playing would increase" (Rich, 1994). One way that he altered his professional identity was to focus more for a time on recording projects than on live performance, as in a recording studio there is no large audience, and a performer could attempt multiple takes until the desired level or performance was achieved. He also became more involved with composition and synthesizers and with ensembles that used a guitar that could over most of the chords that he would have previously played with his left hand (Marin, 2008). In addition, Peterson selected a project with the well-known classical violinist Itzhak Perlman that would again reflect a flexible response to the changing balance of skills and challenges resulting from his stroke and due to the ensemble composition would highlight his strengths, rather than the relative weakness of his left hand, before returning step by step to a small series of live concerts.

One project that resulted from Hersch's 2008 health challenges is the ambitious jazz theater piece *My Coma Dreams* (Hersch, 2013), which Hersch notes was a large, risky project and his first time using technology and video in this way, and also utilized a larger ensemble than he had typically written for in the past. The piece is the story of Fred and his partner Scott and their experience from right before his coma until right after the end of his coma, and the title refers to the series of often jazz-inspired dreams Hersch remembered having while in the coma. In one of the extra features on the DVD of *My Coma Dreams*, Hersch reports: "Six years after the coma I think I'm playing much, much better than before" and notes a shift in self-concept, commenting "if you play a wonky chord, no one will die" and indicating "I'm lucky to be here. I'm lucky I get to do what I do. I don't have anything to prove; I'm much more relaxed. *My Coma Dreams* was cathartic and therapeutic… *My Coma Dreams* is a souvenir and allowed me to be myself. It is the job of the artist – when something comes to you, you can't ignore it." When asked what challenge was hardest to overcome, Hersch replies "In a way, myself, to learn how to get out of my own way- and just be, instead of trying to impress people or worrying about what I think I should be- just to be myself- and that be OK- except when I am being a jerk- but that has been the hardest thing- regulating self-esteem, not getting too grandiose, or not getting too, on the other hand, down on myself, or feel underserving or like a sack of shit- just finding that balance, knowing who I am, what I can do, what I want to do, keeping that balance" (Rich, 2015). His advice to himself seems to fit the advice he would give jazz musicians, which is, he says, "what I tell any young musician – be yourself!" On this point, Hersch seems to have come full circle. His mother tells a story that when 3-year-old Fred was in the grocery store, a stranger came up to him and asked "and who do you belong to?" Fred replied, "I don't belong to anybody I belong to myself" (Hajdu, 2011, p. 149). Hersch's resilience and celebration of life is present in his many successful projects today, including not only his own music but in his teaching, activism, and personal life. *My Coma Dreams*, the jazz theater project, exemplifies many ways in which life challenges can be successfully met with identity flexibility and careful balancing of challenges and skills. As *My Coma Dreams* writer and director Herschel Garfein comments: "the happy ending is right there on the stage" (Hersch, 2013).

Like jazz pianist Fred Hersch, South African psychologist Saths Cooper has contributed significantly not only in his discipline but to the broader world as well. In Cooper's case, his contributions are not only in psychology but also in the anti-apartheid struggle and fight for human rights in South Africa (Rich & Kuriansky, 2015). Born in 1950, in a rural area outside Durban, South Africa, Cooper self-identifies as Black, though he is from an Indian heritage. In the 1970s, Cooper encouraged Indian activists to endorse the Black Consciousness Movement (BCM), an anti-apartheid movement led by his colleague Black student Steve Biko. Due to his activism, Biko was beaten to death by police, and ultimately Cooper was arrested and incarcerated for 9 years, mostly at the infamous Robben Island prison, with much of that time in the same cell block as Nelson Mandela, where he interacted with Mandela daily. Later Cooper completed his education, including his doctorate, and helped create the Psychological Society of South Africa (PsySSA) in 1994, shortly before Nelson Mandela became South Africa's President. The PsySSA was South Africa's first psychology organization that accepted members regardless of race or gender. Cooper was its president for a number of years.

In 2012, Cooper was elected president of the International Union of Psychological Sciences (IUPsyS), the first African to hold the position of this organization which includes over 82 national psychology associations internationally. In 2013, he was named Extraordinary Professor at the University of Pretoria, and the following year, the American Psychological Association awarded him its prestigious Distinguished

Contributions to the Advancement of International Psychology award. Well-respected psychologist Rainer Silbereisen has said, "Dr. Cooper is recognized as one of the key psychology leaders to have restored credibility to South African psychology" (*Cape Times,* 2012). To understand the significance of this comment, one must remember the history of South African psychology (Rich & Gielen, 2012). South African Hendrik Frensch Verwoerd, who was one of the major architects of the apartheid regime, was a psychologist and was appointed in 1928 as chair of Applied Psychology and Psycho Technique at the major Afrikaner University near Cape Town. Verwoerd later became South Africa's prime minister from 1958 until his assassination in 1966. As historian Leonard Thompson comments, "During Verwoerd's premiership, apartheid became the most notorious form of racial domination that the postwar world has known" (2000, p. 189). Given such struggles, one better understands how truly extraordinary are Cooper's life and accomplishments.

At first, one may wonder how flow could play a role through such challenging life circumstances, which include prejudice and discrimination, denial of education, incarceration, and torture. It is important to remember first, that flow is a morally neutral experience; it can be associated with morally or ethically positive experiences or with morally or ethically questionable or negative experiences. For examples of the latter, one can cite the research on combat flow (e.g., Harari, 2008) or the work on Japanese motorcycle gang members (e.g., Csikszentmihalyi & Csikszentmihalyi, 1988); both groups may engage in activities that bring flow, but that cause damage, destruction, and perhaps death to others. Additional examples may include the experience of flow in exotic dancers in a strip bar (Barton & Hardesty, 2010), in speeding motorists (Chen & Chen, 2011), and in problematic internet use (Thatcher, Wretschko, & Fridjhon, 2008). Some early research on flow specifically focused on flow in solitary ordeals, in examining successful coping with adversity. In particular, Logan (1988) cites ample evidence for such experiences, by examining narratives from individuals who have experienced solitary ideals, including a prisoner of the Nazis in World War II, one of writer Aleksandr Solzhenitsyn's fellow prisoners in the Soviet Union, Henri "Papillon" Charrière's time in the infamous penal colony in French Guiana, psychiatrist Victor Frankl's experience in a Nazi concentration camp, and Charles Lindbergh's famous solo trans-Atlantic flight on *The Spirit of St. Louis* in the 1920s. Also worth recalling is that the flow experience is typically only enjoyable after it is over. During the experience, the person is so focused on the task at hand; little or no attention is left over to contemplate the nuances of one's own mental and emotional state. Only after the experience concludes does the person typically reflect that the experience was enjoyable and a peak experience one would like to repeat in the future (Csikszentmihalyi, 1990; Rich, 2014).

An examination of Cooper's life reveals many examples of the type of adult identity flexibility associated with managing and adapting the balance of skills and challenges to maximize the possibility of optimal experience. For instance, in negotiating the challenging terrain of Apartheid South Africa as a student, though technically of Indian heritage, Cooper made a decision in terms of racial/ethnic identification to self-identify as Black. As he comments (Rich & Kuriansky, 2015),

> We identified intellectually as part of the oppressed. So all those who would have previously been called non-White, we said, we are not really non-White, because if you left out "White" out of that term, you were left as "non," and we are not "non." We are not "nons," we are people. We have an identity and we identify as Black, with Black meaning anybody who had a different way. So it was a politically loaded student organization. Remember this was in the late 1960s, when there was a lot of political organization and opposition, so they secretly had spies everywhere. Everyone was listening, phones were tapped. It was a very oppressive system; it was a police state …, I was banned. You could be tortured. You could not have a fixed gathering. I could not meet with more than one other person. If I met with two people, it could be seen as a gathering. I was under house arrest ... Being in my twenties, it was severe restriction ... All this happened, and so my identity was a Black consciousness ideology in South Africa. Ethnically, I am the fourth generation of indentured stock, but I identified as part of the oppressed majority, and I played that role. I identify myself now as a South African, and I regard myself as Black, especially when an oppressive system is in place. I am a fellow human being; whether Jewish from Brooklyn or Black from South Africa, your ethnicity is given to you, and your religious identity is between you and your maker. We are imprisoned by those labels. We shouldn't be. We should be recognized by the richness we bring to our human interaction.

Aligned with soon-to-be-martyred activist Steve Biko, this group led protests such as the 1973 Durban Strike. At around this time, Cooper became Publicity Secretary at the Black People's Convention and was arrested the next year for assaulting a policeman. At this stage of his young adult life, a balance of skills and challenges meant activism that could be dangerous and indeed violent. However, as he entered a period of his life where he was alternatively banned or jailed, or released, to thrive, he needed to adapt flexibly to changing conditions in terms of skills and challenges. For example, he was incarcerated for about 9 years in total, mostly at the notorious Robben Island prison (1974–1982). There, most of the time, he shared a cell block with Nelson Mandela, interacting with him daily. While some activists who excel at protests, clandestine activities, and organizing demonstrations may have collapsed under the prison environment, Cooper adapted and made extraordinary use of the time. For instance, he had many political discussions with Mandela on the anti-apartheid struggle and on learning to better understand their differing perspectives. In addition, Cooper studied for a BA in psychology degree via correspondence while incarcerated. This pursuit of a psychology degree is especially powerful, given the history of psychology in South Africa, and the reality that the top three administrators at the prison were psychologists, as well as a number of his other captors. Despite the apartheid regime's abuse of psychology, Cooper had the skills to confront these challenges by seeing how psychology as a discipline could potentially offer insight into people and ultimately empower them. In addition to the conversations with Mandela, and degree pursuits, another important aspect of Cooper's successful coping during this time, involved mental flexibility in terms of his consciousness and how he decided to view himself, despite the physical confinement. He reports in his life that he never accepted the indentured servant mentality (Rich & Kuriansky 2015) and comments:

> This is personal liberation. You can be liberated in an oppressive system. In my worst moments, when I had been tortured and been at the mercy of my interrogators, I recognized that even though they may have been huge burly guys, they were more afraid, despite their

> size, of what you stood for. So you played on that. That developed my psychological repertoire, a certain understanding of why people do such things, why people do the worst unremitting forms of racism the world has ever known. We would never do to them what they do to us. So I became a master of surprise. When you are persecuted, you don't want to do that to other people. Once you experience it, you understand why people commit it, and you don't want to use the methods of the oppressor.

While prior to his incarceration, Cooper met the challenges of the apartheid through direct protesting and activism that *worked against establishment practices*; after earning his psychology PhD at Boston University and returning to South Africa, he worked to change the establishment regime and, as apartheid officially came to a close in the 1990s, *worked to create new establishment practices* and systems that would best serve post-apartheid South Africa. Thus, in some respects, he has become part of the new establishment. Confronting these new challenges required utilizing some of the organizational skills from his young adulthood student protest days, but now these skills were adapted to the new conditions. Here Cooper's approach includes working to create new psychology organizations in South Africa, such as the Psychological Society of South Africa (PsySSA), which accepted members without regard to race or gender. Cooper served as its president from 1996 to 1999 and from 2006 to 2007 (Rich & Kuriansky, 2015). Having experienced firsthand the abuses psychologists in apartheid South Africa had inflicted upon so many, Cooper has worked tirelessly to ensure the new psychology is one that embraces the humanity of all and includes all South Africans, not just those of a certain social or economic status or race or ethnicity. As he comments, South Africa has a "burgeoning community psychology movement that is making psychology available to severely impoverished people, especially in remote and outlying areas. Some people think psychology is a luxury—they say, you can't eat it, you can't feed people with psychology, so what's the point? However, when we bring psychology to rural areas, we quickly get overbooked… South Africa's compulsory year of public service for newly licensed clinical psychologists has created a culture in which psychologists interact with very disadvantaged communities, helping empower them to deal with the pressures of life. Without these programs, psychology would remain an elite domain" (Dingfelder, 2013).

Since his organizational leadership is so impressive and his experience in this regard is so extensive, one may wonder how the young adult Cooper from his student protest days under apartheid relates to the Cooper today, who has led officially recognized, major national and international psychology organizations in a post-apartheid world. He is clear that he is still an activist, not an armchair philosopher, or the type of academic who writes only for other academics on arcane topics of little practical value. As he remarks, in the context of a discussion concerning the high level of violence in the world, psychologists:

> … don't need to continue to research and write about it; what we need now is to start doing, by looking at our research findings and putting them into policy that can start changing the view that society tolerates violence …. we can take all the research that we have and begin to formulate policies, proposals, and help policymakers understand those proposals and the necessary preventions and interventions that need to happen to (1) prevent violence, and (2)

> intervene when violence breaks out. We need to go back to basics and create a culture of peaceful coexistence and better understanding amongst human beings, and this can only happen if we go back to teaching kids about this in Kindergarten and school levels. It can also happen by having positive messages come out in the multimedia.

In sum, Cooper's life demonstrates how being responsive to changing challenge and skill balances can be associated with successful coping in adversity. Skills that may be appropriate and useful outside prison may be useless or detrimental inside prison; likewise, skills useful inside prison may be less useful outside prison. For example, before he went to prison, in efforts to change the apartheid system, Cooper was expelled from university and thus could not utilize those academic skills at that time and instead was effective then in staging group protests to work to end that system. However, while in prison, leading active group protests of prisoners would likely result in severe repercussions, while devoting oneself to study and conversations with other incarcerated leaders served Cooper's long-term goals of positive social change quite well. Meeting extremely challenging circumstances with identity flexibility not only helped Cooper survive, but ultimately he thrived, optimizing use of extremely difficult conditions while not losing sight of his long-term goals. While clearly the topics and situations Cooper found himself in are quite different than the flow situations often discussed in sports or music success stories (e.g., Jackson & Csikszentmihalyi, 1999; Parente, 2015; Rich, 2012a, 2012b), such flow experiences in difficult experiences have been documented by previous researchers in a range of challenging political and social conditions including incarceration (Logan, 1988). Indeed, some flow researchers argue that at least in some situations for some people, the sense of enjoyment one experiences after a flow experience may better be described as satisfaction coming from deep engagement with a meaningful task (Csikszentmihalyi, 1990; Rich, 2014). Clearly Cooper is a truly extraordinary psychologist whose life and career reflect deep engagement and an abiding interest in advocating for change through social action. Examination of his life and career demonstrates a number of ways in which identity flexibility is associated with successful coping and optimal development, despite great challenges.

In sum, examination of these case studies offers an illustration of how Csikszentmihalyi's flow theory may be applied to adult development. More specifically, one aspect of the flow experience in particular, the balance of challenges and skills, has been related to identity flexibility in adulthood, to successful coping with intense life challenges, and to optimizing both professional success and personal well-being. The two cases in this chapter are different in many ways, in terms of career choice, nationality, race/ethnicity, sexual orientation, and health status, among other dimensions, though the two men do share several similarities, including experience with prejudice and discrimination and experience as well-respected leaders in their respective professional domains, and they are about the same age (Hersch was born in 1955, and Cooper was born in 1950). Though as cautious psychologists, one would not draw firm conclusions from only two cases, the experiences of the two men do offer examples of how identity may be managed and may evolve flexibly to meet changing life circumstances, such as a life-threatening health crisis or prolonged periods of incarceration under an unethical and immoral government. Coupled with a long tradition of flow theory and research that supports the findings of these two cases, including prior research on flow as a mechanism for life-long growth and change and as a phenomenon that has been demonstrated to occur even under adverse conditions, one begins to understand how the case studies in this chapter may point the direction for further research, with larger samples and with both qualitative and quantitative data, to better understand how the balance of skills and challenges may influence flow, well-being, and optimal development over the life course. So that psychologists better understand how such findings may generalize beyond these case studies, such research should employ a broader, more diverse sample, in terms of age, race/ethnicity, nationality, profession, gender/sex, educational level, and so on. Such work seems well worth pursuing, as the potential implications for ultimately developing and assessing new types of interventions, including therapies and recommendations for clients and other persons facing life adversity, may be significant indeed.

References

Barton, B., & Hardesty, C. L. (2010). Spirituality and stripping. *Symbolic Interaction, 33*(2), 280–296.
Chen, C., & Chen, C. (2011). Speeding for fun. *Accident Analysis and Prevention, 43*(3), 983–990.
Cooper receives top psychology award. (2012). *Cape Times*, p. 5.
Csikszentmihalyi, M. (1975). *Beyond boredom and anxiety*. San Francisco: Jossey-Bass.
Csikszentmihalyi, M. (1990). *Flow*. New York: Harper Collins.
Csikszentmihalyi, M. (1993). *The evolving self*. New York: Harper Collins.
Csikszentmihalyi, M. (1996). *Creativity*. New York: Harper Collins.
Csikszentmihalyi, M., & Csikszentmihalyi, I. (Eds.). (1988). *Optimal experience*. Cambridge, UK: Cambridge University Press.
Csikszentmihalyi, M., & Larson, R. (1984). *Being adolescent*. New York: Basic Books.
Csikszentmihalyi, M., & Rich, G. (1997). Musical improvisation: A systems view. In K. Sawyer (Ed.), *Creativity in performance* (pp. 43–66). Greenwich, CT: Ablex.
Csikszentmihalyi, M., & Schneider, B. (Eds.). (2000). *Becoming adult: How teenagers prepare for the world of work*. New York: Basic Books.
Deci, E. L., & Ryan, M. (1985). *Intrinsic motivation and self-determination in human behavior*. New York: Plenum.
Dingfelder, S. (2013). South Africa's shameful past and hopeful future. *Monitor on Psychology, 44*, 32.
Hajdu, D. (2011). Giant steps: The survival of a great jazz pianist. In A. Ross (Ed.), *Best music writing 2011* (pp. 137–149). Cambridge, MA: Da Capo.
Harari, Y. N. (2008). Combat flow: Military, political, and ethical dimensions of subjective well-being in war. *Review of General Psychology, 12*(3), 253–264.
Hersch, F. (2013). *My coma dreams* [DVD]. Palmetto Records. Jackson, S., & Csikszentmihalyi, M. (1999). Flow in sports. Champaign, IL: Human Kinetics.
Jackson, S., & Csikszentmihalyi, M. (1999). *Flow in sports*. Champaign, IL: Human Kinetics.
Logan, R. (1988). Flow in solitary ideas. In M. Csikszentmihalyi & I. Csikszentmihalyi (Eds.), *Optimal experience* (pp. 172–180). Cambridge, UK: Cambridge University Press.
Marin, R. (2008). *Oscar*. Toronto, Canada: Groundwood Books.
Maslow, A. (1971). *The farther reaches of human nature*. New York: Viking.

Parente, T. J. (2015). *The positive pianist: How flow can bring passion to practice and performance*. New York: Oxford University Press.
Peterson, O. (2002). *A jazz odyssey: The life of Oscar Peterson*. New York: Continuum.
Regen, J. (2013). Fred Hersch: On success, survival, and the search for a singular sound. *Keyboard Magazine.*
Rich, G. (1994). *Interview with Oscar Peterson.*
Rich, G. (2012a). The flow experience in jazz pianists: Positive psychological motivation and cognition. *Indian Journal of Positive Psychology, 3*(4), 340–344.
Rich, G. (2012b). A cinematic lens on healthy talent development in piano prodigies: Considerations for positive psychology. [Special issue: Positive Psychology]. *Psychology, 3*(12A). doi: 10.4236/psych.2012.312A171
Rich, G. (2014). Finding flow: The history and future of a positive psychology concept. In J. Sinnott (Ed.), *Positive psychology: Advances in understanding adult motivation* (pp. 43–60). New York: Springer.
Rich, G. (2015). *Interview with Fred Hersch.*
Rich, G., & Gielen, U. (2012). Reflections on the 2012 International Congress of Psychology in Cape Town, South Africa. *International Psychology Bulletin, 16*, 44–48.
Rich, G., & Kuriansky, J. (2015). Saths Cooper: Post-Apartheid psychology and leadership in South Africa and beyond. In G. Rich & U. Gielen (Eds.), *Pathfinders in international psychology*. Charlotte, NC: IAP- Information Age Publishing.
Seligman, M. E. P. (2011). *Flourish*. New York: Free Press.
Seligman, M. E. P., & Csikszentmihalyi, M. (2000). Positive psychology: An introduction. *American Psychologist, 55*(1), 5–14.
Thatcher, A., Wretschko, G., & Fridjhon, P. (2008). Online flow experiences, problematic internet use, and internet procrastination. *Computers in Human Behavior, 24*(5), 2236–2254.

Chapter 16
Identity Flexibility and Buddhism

Jeff Rosenberg

"Thus Did I Experience"[1]: Seeing Identity Arise for Oneself

The Buddha emphasized that each of us needs to be a "radical empiricist." This was true for his own awakening and in his instructions to others that each individual needs to "come to know for themselves" (Benedict 2009). The term "insight" is central to one's spiritual growth and can be defined as an "understood experience" (Khema, 1997). This subjective awareness, tempered with such qualities as acceptance and compassion, is used to attend especially to the workings of the mind. The mind is paramount as underscored by the opening of the Dhammapada: The Sayings of the Buddha (Byrom, 1993):

> We are what we think.
> All that we are arises with our thoughts.
> With our thoughts we make the world.
> Speak or act with an impure mind
> And trouble will follow you
>
> As the wheel follows the ox that draws the cart.
> We are what we think.
> All that we are arises with our thoughts.
> With our thoughts we make the world.

[1] Given that the Buddha was fond of puns and word plays, my intention is to honor his spirit by using "Thus Did I Experience," a reflection of the standard beginning of Suttas (Discourses of the Buddha): "Thus Have I Heard"

J. Rosenberg, Ph.D., M.B.A., M.A. (✉)
Clinical Psychologist and Executive Coach, 4501 Connecticut Avenue,
NW Suite 223, Washington, DC 20008, USA
e-mail: docjeffrosebud@me.com

J.D. Sinnott (ed.), *Identity Flexibility During Adulthood*,
DOI 10.1007/978-3-319-55658-1_16

Speak or act with a pure mind
And happiness will follow you
As your shadow, unshakable.[2]

And so, in the spirit and instruction of the Buddha, I begin with this personal accounting.

Smug and Separate, Acceptance and Connection

I was at a workshop on death and dying. There was an exercise, and my partner was a friend – an elderly, retired scientist. As the exercise unfolded, I became aware of feeling smug, what one might call a perverted sense of contentment. In a setting of beauty and quiet with people I trusted, I tuned into this smugness with curiosity. "I don't usually feel smug; this is odd. This feeling arose once I started this exercise with John." I observed his kind face and leathery skin. This smugness sustained itself as we entered a new phase. One of us was to lightly touch the other; John would touch me first. His touch seemed incongruous, for it was like a child's touch with its own sense of curiosity, wonder, and playfulness. Insight! The smugness shattered; it had been created, I realized, at the expense of separateness. I could afford to be smug because John was *different*; he was the old one, the one who was going to die. He had the leathery skin, the hearing aids, and the cloudy eyes. My "immortality project" (Brasington, 2015a, 2015b) rested on the shaky foundation of an identity of being "younger" and "healthier." And it was purchased at the price of forming an identity that separated me from John. Bemusement, humility, sadness, even a little fear at what I had created (I could see how this could lead to prejudice and persecution of others not belonging to my group.) all arose. Yet, I was happy to give up my assumed identity – to acknowledge and accept my inevitable aging and decay and ultimate death – to truly connect in an intimate way with my fellow being. We are one; we are the same; we all live with aging, illness, and death.[3]

---

[2] There are many translations of this well-known opening. In one translation (Maitreya, 1995), "Mind is the forerunner of all actions. All deeds are led by mind, created by mind…" In another that I use in the opening (Byrom, 1993), "We are what we think. All that we are arises with our thoughts. With our thoughts we make the world…" And (Thera, 2003), "1. Mind precedes all mental states. Mind is their chief; they are all mind-wrought…" So is it "actions," "thoughts," "mental states"? – Maria Heim (2014) solves it with this translation: "Mind is the forerunner of all things [my bold]. Mind is chief, and they are mind-made. If one speaks or acts with a wicked mind, suffering follows even as the cartwheel follows the hoof of an ox. Mind is the forerunner of all things. Mind is chief, and they are mind-made. If one speaks or acts with a pure mind, happiness follows even as one's shadow stays near." Within Buddhist psychology, these different terms are noteworthy. Nonetheless, each translation underscores both the centrality of mind and its initiating role (e.g., as in "forerunner," "led by mind," "arises with," "precedes").

[3] His Holiness the Dalai Lama (http://www.lionsroar.com/watch-the-dalai-lama-break-down-the-illusion-behind-prejudice/) said that on a fundamental level, we are all the same. At a second level, we find/even search for differences. It may be race, country, etc., and if these gross differences aren't there, then we search for others. Is this a matter of tribalism or belonging? This would imply

Buddhist psychology refers to the "three fires" – greed, aversion (sometimes called ill will or hatred), and delusion. These fires name different ways that we can react to unfolding experiences. A small child may have a yummy treat and, as a result, stuff more in his or her mouth before finishing what's already there lest their sibling gets it. This is an example of greed and, unfortunately, is not limited to young children.[4] Let's now apply this, along with other Buddhist constructs, to my experience with John.

Being the animals that we are, the Buddha stated that one of the basic building blocks of an experience is vedana[5] – often translated as "feeling" (SN 36.15) but perhaps "valence" (Brasington, 2015a) might be better as we value or appraise the experience (really, a mind moment) as pleasant, unpleasant, or neutral. This is automatic, and there is no control over this initial valuing. At the workshop, I valued (without my awareness) this experience reflecting my mortality as unpleasant. And I reacted by desiring to distance myself (aversion) from the unpleasant. This is resistance; I wished things to be other than they are. Fortunately, mindfulness came to the fore in that I observed a mental state/emotion[6] of smugness. This was my reality, and I accepted with awareness the arising of "smug Jeff," not how I like to see myself. I went into an investigative frame. The insight rushed in, helped along significantly by the incongruity of John's childlike touch, as I appreciated what this organism labeled "Jeff" had done.[7] It had created an identity. I belonged to the "younger," "healthier," "death is not my problem" group. I was able to do this as I created and sustained a duality that used John (with smug satisfaction) as NOT being in the group.

---

both safety and security. Is it just that we're wired to see differences? And could those differences be used to feel superior or good about ourselves (at the cost of others) or to fuel any number of interpretations or stories about "how it is"? He says this difference seeking is the primary cause of our "man-made" problems.

[4] Delusion contributes in this example by thinking we are better off by being greedy. See Goldstein (2013), pages 218–219, for discussion on "Taking What Is Unsatisfactory to Be Happiness." He says on page 219: "It's said that after the Buddha's enlightenment, he was moved to teach by compassion, because he saw all beings seeking happiness, wanting happiness, yet doing the very things that caused suffering."

[5] Vedana is one of five aggregates or bundles (form, feeling (vedana), consciousness, perception, and "habits of mind" (sankhara which has many other translations such as fabrication)) which are assembled (much like a "chariot" is assembled) to form a mind moment. Goldstein (2013) within his section called "Mindfulness of Dhammas" says: "In this light, what we call the birth and death of a person, of a being, of self, are seen as just the arising and passing of different aggregates. The power of the teachings lies in their directions for us to experience this for ourselves." (page 172) This has important implications for identity, both in terms of its dynamic nature and flexibility, as will be discussed over the course of this chapter.

[6] Please note that I did not label this being "smug" as a "feeling" as I'm reserving that for the initial reaction – vedana – which is often translated as "feeling."

[7] You may have noticed the inquiry as a contemplation based on R.A.I.N. (e.g., Brach, 2012; Chap. 5). They stand for: (1) recognize reality as it is, (2) allow or accept that reality, (3) investigate or inquire, and (4) non-identification, or, in the words of Ajahn Sumedho's book title *Don't Take Your Life Personally*.

One might respond that while there is aversion, there's also delusion. "Hello, Jeff, you're going to die." Good observation; that's correct. In Buddhist psychology, there's always some element of delusion in creating this separateness and thereby these identities. And once the insight arose, the separateness and created identity were shattered.

Buddhism Is Much More Than Meditation

A central practice in Buddhism is called "the five contemplations." Here is one version of them:

I am of the nature to age; I cannot avoid aging.
I am of the nature to be ill; I cannot avoid illness.
I am of the nature to die: I cannot avoid death.
Everything that is mine, dear and delightful, will change and vanish.
I am the owner of my karma[8]*; I am born of my karma; I live supported by my karma; I will inherit my karma; whatever I do, whether good or evil, that I will inherit.* (AN V.57)

There can be a tendency to think in the West that Buddhism equals meditation. Over the years, I have come to learn and appreciate the value of the tremendous breadth and scope of Buddhism both in terms of its teachings and practices. Meditation, much like a microscope, is a tool that gives us access to "see" things we otherwise would not. For example, when first starting to meditate, one may be aghast at the avalanche of thoughts, emotions, etc. in our minds. In light of this discovery, people might conclude that "meditation is not for them." The irony is that *because* of their meditation, they were able to see this avalanche – a virtually universal phenomena shared by most everyone. Others may be equally stunned by the level of judgment, both of others and perhaps especially of themselves, as they apply this powerful tool of self-examination.[9]

[8] "Karma" is one of those overused and misconstrued words (e.g., "Karma is a bitch.") now in our lexicon. In the Buddha's time, the idea of cause and effect, that one's actions have consequences for oneself, was radical in the sense that it infringed on the notion that desired outcomes could be influenced through the purchase, in essence, of various Brahmin rituals. As reflected in the Dhammapada quotations at the outset, the mind is key. Thus, even moreso than behavior, one's volition behind the behavior is central to karma. This brings to mind a favorite Tibetan proverb: "Everything rests on the tip of one's motivation." This clearly points to the importance of ethical conduct and that cultivation of wholesome mind states is key. For a more in-depth discussion, see, for example, Goldstein (2013), pages 329–335. Karma is also discussed later in the chapter.

[9] Matthew Lieberman (2013), in his book *Social: Why Our Brains Are Wired to Connect* provides an evolutionary perspective on all this activity. This includes when we "think we are not thinking," and in fact, our default mode network (sometimes thought of as a "self-referential network") is quite active trying to figure out and wrestle with social interactions. It's interesting to note that the brain is the biggest consumer of calories of all the organs in the body. An article by Mehrmann & Karmacharya (2013) provides another perspective on the default mode network which reflects more on its possible role in the "disease process" (page 10) in depression, anxiety, and other disorders. Perhaps this is partly why individuals may be a bit "freaked out" when they observe so much of such activities in the mind.

To return to the five contemplations, these are but one example of the contemplative dimension in Buddhist psychology. The first three items to contemplate – aging or decay, illness, and death – confront directly the "rules of life" (Brasington, 2015a) which we are so wanting to deny, minimize, rationalize away, avoid. Stephen Batchelor (2004), in his book *Living with the Devil*, refers to these forms of coping as dealing with "the radical contingency of experience." These coping mechanisms are ways of avoiding, of not acknowledging and confronting directly, these "rules of life." The price we pay is suffering, for we are resisting life as it is.

Confrontation and the Choice to Investigate and Change: Or Not

Confrontation is central to my work as a therapist and in my own self-examination as described above. I view it as a two-step process: (1) observation and (2) invitation to explore. To be effective, one must observe and communicate that observation with "right speech." The Buddha emphasized the importance of right speech, in part, by listing a whole variety of ways we often do not practice it. He underscored that confrontation, as I'm using the word, must be communicated with the intention of non-harming, to be timely, and to be truthful (Bodhi (1994). My self-observation of "smugness" was done in this spirit aided significantly by my being in the setting of the workshop and having trust in the teacher, the group as a whole, and my partner John.

I accepted the invitation to explore my smugness. A key to my insight was to experience and see clearly the resistance to acknowledging death. I craved,[10] so to speak, immortality or the denial of death. And so a duality was created in which my self was identified as being in the "Forever Young" group (Dylan, 1973), and of course, this required John to NOT be in that group. We create identities oftentimes to avoid the "rules of life" which also includes the fourth item in the five contemplations: "Everything that is mine, dear and delightful, will change and vanish."

Based on our particulars in terms of temperament and environment (often referred to and under the rubric of "causes and conditions" by Buddhist practitioners), the following can develop and lead to identity *in*flexibility:

[10] Craving is a key concept to Buddhist psychology, and the critical insight of the Buddha is turning it off to end suffering. Leigh Brasington (2015a) explains craving as analogous to a light switch. There are many components to turning on the light – a functioning bulb and wire, power source, etc. The key is that this switch is all that's needed to turn off or keep off the light. We don't need to eliminate the power source, remove the bulb…we just need to keep the switch off or to turn it off. And craving, in relation to suffering, is that switch. (Sometimes, this is represented by the equation, pain x resistance = suffering. If there is zero resistance, then there is no suffering. Pain is inevitable; suffering is optional. When there is no resistance to experience unfolding (and thereby no craving), there may well be pain (e.g., the elderly Buddha's back pain discussed later in this chapter) but no suffering. I believe this equation is attributed to Shinzen Young (http://www.shinzen.org/Articles/artPain.htm), and many meditation teachers refer to it.)

The thought manifests as the word,
The word manifests as the deed,
The deed develops into habit,
And the habit hardens into character.
So watch the thought and its way with care,
And let it spring from love
Born out of concern for all beings. (Dhammananda, 1989)

This quote underscores the pernicious tendency to automatically fall into our habits – of thought, speech, and action – when we are not being mindful. I think of this as similar to "default" settings on a computer. And we can further confuse the issue by making attributions about this being our "character," as if these tendencies are equivalent to us. Ricard (2015) puts it this way:

> True, our character traits change little, so long as we do nothing to improve them.[11] But they are not frozen in place. Our basic traits, which result from the combined contributions of our genetic heritage and the environment in which we grew up, make up only the foundation of our identity. Scientific research in the field of neuroplasticity shows that any form of training leads to a reconfiguring in the brain, on both the functional and structural levels. "(page 239)

I think "foundation of our identity" is just right as this reflects a seeming solidity but one which can be changed (though not so easily and at the risk of collapsing the imagined structure of a seemingly permanent self).[12] Also, implicit in "the environment in which we grew up" are the adaptations/choices we, as organisms, made to navigate that environment. In some respects, this is the key (maybe the glue, the mortar) for our foundation. These adaptations and choices may have helped us to survive back then but now, having hardened, may lock us into limited and inflexible behaviors, perceptions, and identities.

---

[11] Not only do they not change, they are likely to become that much more solidified by confirming our view of the world, influencing what we pay attention to, and how we perceive (label) that which we attend to.

[12] And here's a good example of just how attached we can get, just how seemingly solid that foundation can be (Richardson, 2015 titled "Ballad of the Sad Climatologists"):

> Scientists are problem solvers by nature, trained to cherish detachment as a moral ideal. Jeffrey Kiehl was a senior scientist with the National Center for Atmospheric Research when he became so concerned about the way the brain resists climate science, he took a break and got a psychology degree. Ten years of research later, he's concluded that consumption and growth have become so central to our sense of personal identity and the fear of economic loss creates such numbing anxiety, we literally cannot imagine making the necessary changes. Worse, accepting the facts threatens us with a loss of faith in the fundamental order of the universe. Climate scientists are different only because they have a professional excuse for detachment, and usually it's not until they get older that they admit how much it's affecting them—which is also when they tend to get more outspoken, Kiehl says. "You reach a point where you feel—and that's the word, not think, feel—'I have to do something.'

Within my field, the concept of "neuroplasticity" faced substantial resistance. Sharon Begley in her book *Train Your Mind, Change Your Brain* recounts this resistance. This is but one example of our tendencies to resist paradigm shifts.

In sum, potential for change is virtually limitless, but this magnitude of change comes with a high "price tag." Not only do we confront and experience the five contemplations like a head-on collision, we also come to realize that our very being, our identities, our sense of belonging, and our self are without substance. This literally "rocks our (constructed) world." Smith (2010) describes this world: "Character is reinforced through our narrative, the ongoing story of 'me'." We confirm our current reality through the recollection of how we have always been." And "this assumed reality might not be any more reliable then reading last year's newspaper for today's news" (page 19). Imagine this story dissolving; really, it means "me" is dissolving!

Working on the Foundation of One's Self/Identity in Day-to-Day Life

My experience was at a workshop. And, in a later section of this chapter, Dr. Nikki Mirghafori's comments on the Foundation of One's Self/Identity in Day-to-Day Life are based on her experiences at extended multi-month meditation retreats. What about experiences in day-to-day life?[13] Let's take a look at a psychotherapy client's report entitled: "The Hurt Phenomena Arising and the Organism's Reaction/Response." VC is a high-achieving, middle-aged professional. With a childhood of poverty, abuse in the form of primarily violence from his mother and abandonment by the father, VC coped by "walking on eggshells, complying which included working very hard in school, and if attacked by 'going into a shell'" in contrast to fighting back. In a recent session, VC reports feeling "anger" at being accused by his partner of selfish motives for wanting to change his travel plans. This especially stings as, while he acknowledges a part of him may be selfish, his primary motivation is to be present to support his partner at a time of particular career stress and as he recognizes this is a "tender time" for their relationship. He realizes he's angry; he doesn't want to react in his habitual style of absorbing the attack/accusation. He becomes aware of a bodily sensation in the upper abdomen – an area/sensation he's come to associate with "guilt" (as in "I'm wrong" and taking on the responsibility as in "It's his fault"). This area/sensation seems to now be activated by anger!

He reports that he was able to "stay with it," to say "no" to some coworker requests, and to give himself some space to be with his experience. We discuss how perhaps guilt and anger are both responses to a common denominator of feeling "hurt," that having his partner criticize is the hurt, with guilt and anger being two

[13] There is a tension or trade-off between being a monastic and being what is called a "householder," someone living in the real(?) world of jobs, kids, commuting, shopping, etc. While a monk or nun has the luxury of sustained and regular periods for formal meditation, there are not the same kinds of opportunities to confront the challenges of the householder life, especially the dynamics of interpersonal relationships as illustrated in this short case study.

responses. His reaction, his habitual response,[14] is to "absorb" – to literally curl up as if his mother assaulted him and/or to feel bad or responsible on a psychological level.

He asks about taking a martial arts class as a way to "practice" this new response. He asks: "What do you think?" I'm generally supportive and encourage him to be very careful in screening the teacher.

I return to his capacity to give himself space, to be with his experience. I talk to him about Rumi's poem the "Guest House" and the importance of welcoming such experiences and learning from them, as painful as they may be. We tie together his current-day partner's response (criticism) to a primarily empathic act on his part with, historically, his mother's pattern of "blowing up" when he would come home with "only" 9/10 correct on school work. It's like the mother could only see the "-1" and not the "+9," while his partner could only see the selfishness and not the empathy. A strong resonance, a powerful connection, was made in that he could appreciate the parallel with the current-day experience including both the pattern of the other person's response (to whom in each instance he has a strong emotional attachment) and the intensity of his response.

I label these kinds of experiences (wherein one appreciates the connection, the affective resonance, of current and past experiences) as "emotional time." It's as if all of these experiences are activated and contribute to the intensity of one's somatic/affective response in the present moment. These are central to reworking our mind, the foundation of our identity, in the sense that we can both reinterpret what has/is happening and, importantly, see the habitual responses involved and the opportunity to rebuild them. Perhaps, VC is evolving from mild-mannered professional to Superman: both capacities are there and which manifests will depend on what is cultivated, along with causes and conditions, at any given point in time.

This is consistent with Paul Gilbert's work (e.g., Gilbert, 2013, 2014) which he calls compassion-focused therapy. Let's assume VC is able to get to the place where he can respond with either guilt or anger. There's certainly flexibility in response and how both he and others might view him as a result. However, these responses are still coming from a place of hurt. I suspect, if VC continues this work, he might get to a place where he doesn't take the criticism so personally. Increasing confidence in his own intentions and conduct (this is referred to as "sila" or ethical conduct in Buddhism Bodhi, 1994) could be cultivated so that he interprets the criticism targeted at him as really about his partner, that is, the criticism is a reflection; it's like a mirror that's been held up, and the criticism is a reflection of the partner's own insecurity, way of coping with uncertainty, etc. In this context, VC, rather than interpreting the criticism as a threat, is able to respond with compassion. In other words, he is able to stay in touch with his own love and good will both for himself and his partner. Different brain modules would then be activated in contrast to responding

[14] It can be useful to label habitual responses as "reactions" in contrast to "responses" which come out of mindfulness – the capacity to pause and reflect on what is unfolding and then opening to perhaps a range of responses. In my clinical work, I call this "being a PRO" (pause, reflect/relax, and open) which comes from Gregory Kramer's work with Insight Dialogue (Kramer, 2007).

to a threat. VC's capacity to respond has, under this scenario, qualitatively expanded. We might even say that his identity isn't easily defined – he responds as called for by the situation following the values of good will (loving-kindness and compassion), empathetic joy, and equanimity (see Burton 2003 for a discussion of these qualities referred to in Buddhism as "Brahma Viharas").

In a subsequent session, VC comes into the session with a joyful smile. He reports that his partner is wrestling with "forgiveness." There is recognition by the partner of the sincerity of VC's efforts, and there is no doubt of VC's love for his partner. Yet, for his partner, it's hard to let go and, yet again, his partner recognizes that the resentment and criticism are really being carried not by VC but by himself/herself (the partner). He reports that the change in the energy and ease between them is palpable.

Further, VC reports that for the first time, probably in years, he was able to talk with his mother without "irritation." He comes to see the parallel and recognizes that he, as well, is wrestling with forgiveness. He reports appreciating his mother's very real limitations and is beginning to see how this would manifest itself in her behavior toward him. Talking with her, at least in this instance, did not activate irritation and the quality of the call changed markedly.

But will it continue? He wants this so very badly – both with his partner and with his mother. We discuss the way in which this could easily turn into craving. I suggest that any number of causes and conditions may affect these interactions in the future. They could contribute to continued ease or perhaps a reverting back to old patterns. We talk about "right effort" (Bodhi, 1994) and how this might serve as an alternative way of relating to these interactions. In other words, can he continue in a mindful, investigative mode and recognize that whatever happens, he can hopefully learn more about what contributes to how any given interaction unfolds? His intention is therefore steady regardless of the outcome. This is a mode of *responding* that is NOT *reactive* to vedana – clinging to the pleasant, aversive to the unpleasant, and indifferent or "zoned out" to the neutral. This is going beyond the worldly, animal response. This reflects the intention of switching off the craving and, from a stance of equanimity, observing the unfolding of experience; however, it may arise and pass away.

This stance is nicely reflected by a quote attributed to none other than Thomas Paine: "I love those who can smile in trouble, who can gather strength from distress, and grow brave by reflection. 'Tis the business of little minds to shrink, but they whose heart is firm, and whose conscience approves their conduct, will pursue their principles unto death'."

In this session, VC reports having experiences that take him out of the realm of "hurt." This is a more fundamental shift in identity flexibility than the movement from "guilty VC" to "angry VC." This leaves the realm of hurt, which is really about threat and can activate VC's fight/flight/freeze module, to one that enters the realm of affiliation and compassion.

Practice: Mindfulness of What Is Wholesome/Unwholesome, Cultivating Unworldly Pleasures

Is there anything we can do to cultivate our identity flexibility? We could argue that both VC and I happen to be introspective, psychologically minded while others are not. While the Buddha did indicate that some may be more readily inclined to have such insights than others, his main message was "Practice!" Practice, in short, enables us to clearly see the consequences of our actions. Seeing clearly, we increasingly choose wholesome responses, ones that are more fulfilling even at the cost of short-term gratification. Practice cultivates an attitude toward our lives that promotes curiosity and equanimity – the "desire" to have insight into our actions even when the momentary experience is unpleasant while also literally "changing our brain" (Begley, 2007). With these practices, we are not so locked into habitual responses and thus our identity, so to speak, can be more fluid.

The fundamental rationale for practice is reflected in the fifth of the five contemplations regarding karma. Here, again, is the contemplation: "I am the owner of my karma; I am born of my karma; I live supported by my karma; I will inherit my karma; whatever I do, whether good or evil, that I will inherit." Goldstein (2013) says: "According to the law of karma, the results of our actions follow us like a shadow. When we integrate this realization into our lives, we pay more attention to our choices and actions, and to where they are leading" (page 329).

In the Buddha's time, this notion of karma was revolutionary. My actions (and especially the volitions fueling the actions) have consequences for me. Therefore, if I practice and promote good or wholesome actions, this will have positive consequences. The emphasis on volition and intention (Heim, 2014) is intriguing as this is emphasizing motivation, intention, and introspection (see also Olendzki, 2014).

In *The Middle Length Discourses of the Buddha: A Translation of the Majjhima Nikaya* (MN) in Suttas 18, 19, and 20, the Buddha lays out instructions for how to cultivate good or wholesome karma. For example, "Bhikkhus [Buddhist monks] whatever a bhikkhu frequently thinks and ponders upon, that will become the inclination of his mind" (Sutta MN.19, Verse 6, page 208). Much of the Sutta provides instruction on how to work with various thoughts, be they wholesome or unwholesome. And he urges his monks at the end of the Sutta: "Meditate, bhikkus, do not delay or else you will regret it later. This is our instruction to you" (Sutta MN.19, Verse 27, page 210).

Ricard's (2015) words closely echo those of the Buddha: "But by training one's mind, the meditator carries out a maximum inner enrichment. Research in neuroscience carried out over a dozen years in which I myself have taken part shows that attention, emotional balance, altruistic love, compassion, and other human qualities can be cultivated, and that their development is accompanied by profound functional and structural transformations of the brain" (page 243).

Khema (1997) underscores the importance of gaining insight into the pleasure that can be realized without responding to our animal nature of simply satisfying our sense desires.[15] To highlight this further, we can contrast this from Freud who claimed that really all of our actions were in response (be it direct or a derivative) of two fundamental drives, libidinal and aggressive (Heffner, 2014). In a way, it is remarkable that the Buddha, who apparently lived in a time seemingly dominated by such drives, was able to have the key insight that pleasure does not have to be borne of sensual desire.

It took the Buddha 6+ years to reach this critical insight leading to his awakening. He had mastered the concentration practices of two teachers, survived extreme ascetic practices, and yet was still flummoxed. His insight, as it is told, emerged as he remembered a time as a boy when he sat under a tree absorbed by the light on the tree's leaves during the harvest season. He had fallen into a meditative absorption (the first jhana). His insight was that there was pleasure in this state even though there was no striving for sensual desire. "I thought, "'Why am I afraid of that pleasure that has nothing to do with sensual pleasures and unwholesome states?' I thought: 'I am not afraid of that pleasure since it has nothing to do with sensual pleasures and unwholesome states'" (Goldstein, 2013; citing MN, Sutta 36, page 340).

Ayya Khema, in her discussion of jhanas or meditative absorptions, beautifully describes the insights that come from experiencing these states. While cultivating these states is useful for facilitating vipassana or insight practice, they are also very important in terms of the insights they themselves derive:

> To recapitulate briefly: the first brings the insight that what we are looking for in the world is already within us; the second, that our sense-contacts can never provide us with the joy we experience in the jhana itself; the third, that contentment and peacefulness can only arise where there is wishlessness. (page 93)

In other words, these experiences trump the gratification of sensual desire. They provide experiences that inform us that there is so much more than just pursuing the "pleasure principle." Without these experiences and insights, we can continue to mistake our pursuit of pleasure as a means to happiness or fulfillment. Here is how she puts it:

> We realize that there can only be contentment and peace, if there is no wish for anything. This makes such an impact that we will undoubtedly try to carry it over into our everyday life. Not that we will always be successful. The mind has every kind of desire, some quite refined, others absurd. But we now know that with every desire we have, we are only hurting ourselves, and that the contentment and peace we experience in the third jhana is far superior to the fulfillment of any desire. Realizing this, we can very often drop the desire, and by so doing, drop the dukkha[16] – the wanting, the restlessness, the attempts to get and achieve. (pages 59–60)

---

[15] To be complete in addition to sensual desire, there are also the desire for becoming and the desire for non-becoming. See Bhikku (2010) and for a concise summary http://www.buddhanet.net/4noble12.htm).

[16] Dukkha is a keyword in Buddhist psychology. It is often thought of or translated as "suffering," but this can be misleading. Another translation is "unsatisfactoriness" nicely illustrated by Goldstein's (2013) discussion of mindfulness of the four postures on pages 57–58. In essence, if we pay attention, we're often making adjustments to relieve pain, discomfort, or tension. Brasington

Joseph Goldstein (2013) in his book *Mindfulness* has a chapter on "worldly and unworldly feelings." He lists several types of experiences conducive to unworldly feelings including generosity, love and compassion, renunciation, and clear seeing along with concentration as Ayya Khema has described. The pleasant unworldly feeling of "clear seeing" is hopefully evident in the rendition of both my and VC's experiences. It is hard to describe the excitement, joy, and contentment that I feel in experiencing a significant insight. There may well be pain and grief that accompany such insight, but it is meaningful pain and grief. As a therapist, there can be pleasure in the profound connection with another as they share their suffering. It feels like an honor to me when this quality of genuine connection takes place. Generosity can be fun with pleasure in anticipation, in the giving, and in recollection.

Who Is My Self?: Penetrating the Impermanence of Everything, Including Self

Who Is My Self? is the title of the book already cited by Ayya Khema, a Buddhist nun. She taught and wrote with a clarity that reflects her wisdom and compassion. She explains:

> We must remember that the Buddha taught on two levels: that of relative truth and that of absolute truth. When we first come into contact with the teachings, we have no idea what absolute truth is, and when we encounter some part of it, our minds boggle at it. (Khema, 1997, page 2)

The examples from my workshop experience and that of VC are on the level of relative truth. This, by no means, diminishes their significance. We both had "transcendent" experiences. We had insights that showed us and led us to truly appreciate what are unworldly experiences. That is, we were able to take pleasure in experiences that were NOT driven by our "animal instincts" (Goldstein, 2013).

I like to think of these two truths, relative and absolute, as similar to Newtonian physics and quantum physics. Both are functional in the sense that they enable us to understand phenomena, to make predictions. If I'm in my fancy, worldly car and a trucker truck (my son's term) is on a collision course, I'm grateful to Newton's laws that inform me, given impending mass and velocity, to get out of the way. And yet, when it comes to the behavior at the subatomic level, Newtonian physics needs to step aside.

Here's how Ayya Khema summarized it:

> Today's science supports this experience, but it is better put the other way around – the words of the Buddha support today's science. Most of our scientists are not enlightened beings, although they know the truth that the universe consists of nothing but particles that

(2015a) defines it as "not a lasting source of satisfaction." If we're not aware, these adjustments, strivings, restlessness… are endless and ultimately do not and cannot provide a "lasting source of satisfaction."

come together and fall apart. Yet they have not realized that the one who knows, is exactly the same. (page 3)

Here's a brief taste of this absolute truth. Nikki Mirghafori, in an interview with Gil Fronsdal entitled "Into the Abyss," (2015) describes it as follows:

> Pa Auk Sayadaw carefully led and directly pointed to a series of specific insights in succession, many of which shook me to the core. All of those accumulated into a shift. Once, for example, when my mind was deeply concentrated, I saw all the experience of every moment disintegrating. Everything was disassembling as quickly as it arose. Then, there was the knowledge that everything that was ever going to arise – every experience, every moment – was also going to die, perish, pass. *Everything*. There was absolutely nothing to hang onto.

At first, this insight brought up a sense of existential despair, which then coalesced into a deep acceptance of the way things are in this human life. I felt a sense of "okayness" and equanimity with respect to everything that has happened, happens, and will ever happen… The state of ease that I talk about holds the suffering, the craziness, and everything that this world is – and knows that it's all okay. It's a sense of transcendence, not outside of but within the fullness of life" (*Inquiring Mind,* pg. 16–17).

Identity Flexibility: A Contradiction in Terms?

This is a good juncture to consider how we might define and what we've learned about "identity flexibility." My experience of being "smug" could be viewed as an illustration of the "birth of an identity." The craving to deny my mortality led to a solution involving the creation of an identity. This identity requires duality. For me to be identified as belonging to the "Forever Young" group, the need arose for others to not belong and John, my partner in the exercise, was the perfect foil. If this adaptation were ongoing, I could imagine sustaining the smugness that has a certain kind of contentment or satisfaction to it. Increasing scorn, ridicule, and even disgust could be heaped onto John and others of his kind. They could be scapegoated. They could carry the burdens of aging, mortality, and the like with which my kind cannot be bothered.

Now, I'm a bit trapped in that I really have to value my "Forever Young" group. One idea of identification is that we "identify with," we value that to which we belong.[17] This may make it challenging to find value in the other. How do I reconcile

---

[17] Lieberman (2013) in his book *Social: Why Our Brains Are Wired to Connect* discusses from an evolutionary perspective about how our "belonging" is more than just a psychological maneuver or defense. Belonging to the tribe, if you will, is fundamental to our sense of security. Oxytocin, the "love" hormone, while promoting affiliation, also promotes belonging within the group or tribe. It can thereby enhance a group member's suspicion of outsiders, of those from other groups. Identity, to the extent it enables a sense of belonging, can be fundamental to our well-being and thus difficult to release.

the wisdom that the elders may contribute when they're supposed to be "old farts," obsolete, living in the past, and unable to cope with today's pace?

Presumably, another by-product of my solution to this pesky problem of mortality could become the "hardened" character trait of "smugness." Self-deception or delusion could help me to not see this. Or I might rationalize it, maybe even see it as a sign of my superiority, my being my own person. "Yes, I may grate people, but whose problem is that, really?"

Let's move to the example with VC. His "guilt" and tendency to be compliant can be viewed as long-standing adaptations or habits. Might friends say: "VC, he's always guilty, he doesn't speak up, that's just the way he is." Like Clark Kent, would we identify him as "mild-mannered?" Is that who VC is; is that his assumed identity? When clients say: "That's just me." I typically edit them: "What you're describing is just an overlearned, longstanding, habitual pattern of response." So, VC and those who know him may identify him as "mild-mannered" though the vignette suggests that that may be changing or becoming more complex. Critically, he "sees" the parallel between his partner's criticism and his mother's criticisms/assaults. He appreciates that part of his present-day response is due to the resonance with his past. His partner is not his mother.

In the postscript, we certainly see how his partner has capacities apparently not available to VC's mother. I would suggest that this helps VC to develop acceptance and equanimity with his mother such that he's not irritated on the phone call. He is more able to see his mother for whom she is and to accept her in that light. He, at least for the call, is no longer threatened by her, to me, a reflection of the irritation historically. This opens up opportunities for him to be responsive in new ways – perhaps being more curious, patient, able to ask questions, etc. He can be in an affiliative mode rather than in one of threat (Gilbert, 2013, 2014). He can meet her with good will (compassion) and equanimity.

So far, we see how craving, attachment to a particular outcome and/or way of viewing the world, leads to the creation of identity and can increasingly trap and limit one's flexibility not only in action but also perception and outlook. Acceptance, letting go of craving, releases one from particular identities, be it in the sense of characteristics or belonging to certain groups. The capacity to respond flexibly, one's "response-ability," is enhanced by "letting go" of craving and realizing pleasure through unworldly practices such as generosity and compassion.

Lastly, there is the interview of Nikki Mirghafori. Is she really talking about identity flexibility? On one level, we could say "Yes." She is stating that her sense of "ease" and profound acceptance of the okayness of whatever unfolds (by the way, she partly got into Buddhism in reaction to contracting Lyme's disease) enables her to meet experience without being threatened. There's the sense that she can bring equanimity to whatever arises including her own illness. But is it "her own illness?"[18] To repeat from above, she says:

[18] Laurie Hope (2010) has compiled a range of quotes from interviewees (including herself) and quotes from authors and others regarding how we relate to and learn from illness in her book *The Unchosen Path*. Her third chapter, entitled "Who Am I?" considers how illness compels us to look at the ways we've defined or identified ourselves and questions who are we really.

> Everything was disassembling as quickly as it arose. Then, there was the knowledge that everything that was ever going to arise – every experience, every moment – was also going to die, perish, pass. *Everything.* There was absolutely nothing to hang onto.

This is a deep penetration into impermanence (anicca) – one of the three factors of existence. The other two – unsatisfactoriness (dukkha, or more precisely, "not a lasting source of satisfaction" Brasington, 2015a) and no-self (anatta, or more precisely, "no permanently abiding self or soul" Smith, 2010, page xii) – are also expressions of impermanence. She is saying there is no permanent Nikki. "*This total disappearance of the feeling of 'self' is the culmination of the path*" (my italics – Khema, 1997; page 168). This does not mean that there isn't a body. For example, the Buddha as he aged had back pains such that he would start but not finish talks. But imagine if we operated with the insight (again, understood experience, not just the concept) that there was no permanent self. There was the unfolding of experience of which this organism, labeled "I" for convenience, was just part of that unfolding. I suppose we could say that that would be the height of "identity flexibility" or that the term loses its meaning on this level.

The Buddha taught for roughly 45 years. The mark of a "master teacher," he apparently was able to meet students where they were at. At times, this has caused confusion, as we might see inconsistencies in his teaching when, alternatively, they could reflect his exquisite ability to say what was needed in the situation as it arose. I would say that the "Tathagata" – a name for the Buddha – reflects one who has penetrated the truth. If we think of this as nonduality, then how can there be identity on this level? The discussion of identity, for sure, assumes an other – another group, another characteristic, something which implies the separation or division of what is whole. Perhaps on this level, "identity flexibility" becomes a bit of a contradiction or paradox. As one realizes greater and greater capacities to be flexible, there is less and less need for an identity.

Thanissaro Bhikkhu (2010), in *The Paradox of Becoming*, describes the need, or lack thereof, for an identity (really identities) in this way:

> …Each and every desire, in fact, has its own separate world; and within those worlds, we take on different identities. The Buddha had a word for this experience of an identity inhabiting a world defined around a specific desire. He called it *bhava*, which is related to the verb *bhavati*, to "be," or to "become." He was especially interested in bhava as process – how it comes about, and how it can be ended. (page 3)
>
> And later: …The Buddha's Awakening also taught him that the craving and clinging leading to stress are identical to the craving and clinging that lead to becoming. So becoming is inevitably stressful…Regardless of what identity you assume, or however you experience the mountain of the world, it's going to entail some degree of stress. (page 4)
>
> And finally: …Freed from both suffering and becoming, the mind would be totally released from the limitations of any identity or location – a freedom that beggars the imagination, but captures it as well. (page 5)

The insight, the penetration of seeing things or one's self as separate being "true" only on the level of relative truth, is liberating. Nothing has changed. There is a famous Zen expression: "Before enlightenment, I chopped the wood and carried the water. After enlightenment, I chopped the wood and carried the water." And yet everything has changed in that there is no need for identity, no need for becoming, as both Ayya Khema and Thannisaro Bikkhu describe. There is simply the organism, as dependently arising phenomena, unfolding in process, with other dependently arising phenomena. Perhaps we get a momentary taste of this – be it musical, artistic, athletic, etc. – when we "get out of the way" and the magic happens.

And, in this sense, Clark Kent and Superman are both "real" but not "true."[19] We take on all kinds of assumed identities and, in the moment on the relative truth level, they are real. We can be mild-mannered; we can be extraordinary, far beyond the [usual] powers; it appears that the potential may be limitless (consider, e.g., the extraordinary capacities of those diagnosed with dissociative identity disorder or what used to be called multiple personality disorder – while perhaps disorders and certainly reflective of much suffering – their capacities to carry multiple identities is remarkable). (e.g., Hughes, Kuhlman, Fichtner, and Gruenfeld (1990) and Reinders et al. (2014)) And yet, at the level of absolute truth, both Clark Kent and Superman are not true but stream of dependently arising phenomena interacting with no distinguishing identities.

References

AN V.57 Anguttara Nikaya, *The book of the fives, 57 themes. Discourses of the Buddha.* http://suttacentral.net/an5.57/en

Batchelor, S. (2004). *Living with the devil: A meditation on good and evil.* New York: Riverhead Books.

Begley, S. (2007). *Train your mind, change your brain: How a new science reveals our extraordinary potential to transform ourselves.* New York: Ballantine Books.

Benedict, G. (2009). *Buddhist wisdom: The path to enlightenment.* London: Watkins Publishing.

Bhikku, Thanissaro (2010). *The paradox of becoming.* Barre, MA: Dhamma Dana Publications, Barre Center for Buddhist Studies (Here's a free version available on-line: http://www.accesstoinsight.org/lib/authors/thanissaro/paradoxofbecoming.pdf

Bodhi, B. (1994). *The noble eightfold path: Way to the end of suffering.* Onalaska, WA: BPS Pariyatti Editions.

Brach, T. (2012). *True refuge: Finding peace and freedom in your own awakened heart.* New York: Bantam Books.

Brasington, L. (2015a). From his talks and responses to questions on retreat, August 6–16, 2015. See also his web site (www.leighb.com) which references much of this material.

Brasington, L. (2015b). *Right concentration: A practical guide to the Jhānas.* Boston: Shambhala Publications.

Buddhanet. (n.d.) http://www.buddhanet.net/4noble12.htm (A concise summary of the Three Kinds of Desire. No specific author identified. See also Bhikku (2010)).

---

[19] Rinpoche.T, a meditation teacher, in the first chapter of his book *Fearless Simplicity* tells a story in which he freezes at the prospect of crossing a bridge. From this experience, he used the phrase: "Real but not true." It is "real" on the relative level in that his body and mind reacted as they did based on his past conditioning but "not true" in the context of the present circumstances. My use of "real" and "true" in the main body of the text is different than how they are used in *Fearless Simplicity*. In case you read this book, my intention here is to clarify that difference.

Burton, L. (2003). *Jhanas and the Brahma Viharas*. An essay found at: http://www.leighb.com/jhnbrmvhr.htm
Byrom, T. (translator) (1993). *Dhammapada: Sayings of the Buddha*. Boston: Shambhala Publications.
Dhammananda, K. Sri (1989). *How to live without fear and worry*. Somerville, MA: Wisdom Publications. (For an interesting review of this and similar quotes see: http://quoteinvestigator.com/2013/01/10/watch-your-thoughts/).
Dylan, B. (1973). *Lyrics to forever young*. http://www.azlyrics.com/lyrics/bobdylan/foreveryoung.html
Gilbert, P. (2013). Compassion-focused therapy. Presentation at a Meng Wu Lecture on 28 February 2013 at the Center for Compassion and Altruism Research and Education at Stanford University. Find this talk and others at http://www.compassionatemind.co.uk/resources/video.htm
Gilbert, P. (2014). The origin and nature of compassion focused therapy. *British Journal of Clinical Psychology, 53*(1), 6–41. Go to http://self-compassion.org/the-research/ for access to a PDF of this article.
Goldstein, J. (2013). *Mindfulness: A practical guide to awakening*. Boulder, CO: Sounds True.
Heffner, C. (2014). For a summary of Freud's drive theory. http://allpsych.com/personalitysynopsis/drives/#.Ves6RM78GfT
Heim, M. (2014). *The forerunner of all things: Buddhaghosa on mind, intention, and agency*. New York: Oxford University Press.
His holiness the Dalai Lama in an interview with Melvin McLeod of Shambhala Sun, April, 2015. http://www.lionsroar.com/watch-the-dalai-lama-break-down-the-illusion-behind-prejudice/
Hope, L. (2010). *The unchosen path: Reflections from the inner journey of illness*. Ojai, CA: Copper Press.
Hughes, J. R., Kuhlman, D. T., Fichtner, C. G., & Gruenfeld, M. J. (1990). Brain mapping in a case of multiple personality. *Clinical Electroencephalography, 21*(4), 200–209.
Khema, A. (1997). *Who is my self?: A guide to Buddhist meditation*. Somerville, MA: Wisdom Publications.
Kramer, G. (2007). *Insight dialogue: The interpersonal path to freedom*. Boston: Shambhala Publications.
Lieberman, M. (2013). *Social: Why our brains are wired to connect*. New York: Crown Publishing.
Maitreya, A. (1995). *The Dhammapada: The path of truth*. Berkeley, CA: Parallax Press.
Majjhima Nikaya (MN) Suttas 18,19, 20, 36. *Discourses of the Buddha*.
Mehrmann, Craig, Karmacharya, Rakesh (2013, July/August) Principles and neurobiological correlates of concentrative, diffuse, and insight meditation. *Harvard Review of Psychiatry*, *21*(4), 1–16. http://www.academia.edu/10300722/Principles_and_Neurobiological_Correlates_of_Concentration_Diffuse_and_Insight_Meditation
Mirghafori, N., Fronsdal, G. (2015). Inquiring mind. *31*(2), 16–17. Interview titled "Into the Abyss".
Olendzki, A. (2014). A master lecture – a Buddhist contribution to neurophenomenology. https://www.youtube.com/watch?v=jDCmFum-Jbg
Paine, T. Quote: http://www.goodreads.com/author/quotes/57639.Thomas_Paine
Reinders, A. A. T. S., Antoon, T. M., Willemsen, den Boer, J. A., Herry, P. J., Dick, J., et al. (2014). Opposite brain emotion-regulation patterns in identity states of dissociative identity disorder: A PET study and neurobiological model. *Psychiatry Research: Neuroimaging, 223*, 236–243. http://dx.doi.org/10.1016/j.pscychresns.2014.05.005.
Ricard, M. (2015). *Altruism: The power of compassion to change yourself and the world*. New York: Little, Brown and Company.
Richardson, J. H. (August, 2015 issue of *Esquire*). http://www.esquire.com/news-politics/a36228/ballad-of-the-sad-climatologists-0815/
Rinpoche, T. with Eric Swanson (2012). *Fearless simplicity: Awakening the power of essence love*. New York: Harmony Books.

Rumi, M. J. (Born 9/30/1207 in Balkh (Afghanistan)). *Guest House* http://christophertitmuss.org/blog/the-guest-house-by-rumi-and-the-buddha (Titmuss also discusses the use of the "guest house" as a simile by the Buddha).

Smith, R. (2010). *Stepping out of self-deception: The Buddha's liberating teaching of no-self.* Boston: Shambhala Publications.

SN 36.15. Samyutta Nikaya 36 connected discourses on feeling, 15 Ananda (1); Discourses of the Buddha. https://suttacentral.net/en/sn36.15

Sumedho, A. (2010). *Don't take your life personally.* Totnes, UK: Buddhist Publishing Group (BPS).

Thera, B. (2003). *The Dhammapada: The Buddha's path of wisdom.* Kandy, Sri Lanka: Buddhist Publication Society.

Young, S. (specific date unknown – copyright for content 1998–2010). Break through pain: Practical steps for transforming physical pain into spiritual growth. http://www.shinzen.org/Articles/artPain.htm

Chapter 17
Identity Revised: A Clinician's Perspective on What an Identity-Based Model of Mind Looks Like

Vedat Şar

It is not the strongest or the most intelligent who will survive but those who can best manage change. (L. C. Megginson (1963) (a quote usually misattributed to Darwin))

Identity is usually conceived in its social aspects such as cultural, ethnic, and religious components rather than as an individual integrative mental capacity which plays a role in health and disease. Hence, identity has been a relatively underreferenced concept in psychiatry and clinical psychopathology. In DSM-5, the official classification system of the American Psychiatric Association (2013), the only diagnostic category to explicitly address a disturbance of identity is dissociative identity disorder (aka multiple personality disorder) and its subthreshold forms as described among other specified dissociative disorders (OSDD). An identity disturbance due to prolonged and intensive coercive persuasion is also mentioned as a diagnostic category in the latter group. Last but not least, some type of disturbance of identity is listed among diagnostic criteria of borderline personality disorder.

It is of particular interest that dissociative identity disorder, other specified dissociative disorders, and borderline personality disorder are categories related to chronic traumatization (e.g., abuse and/or neglect) in childhood (Sar, Akyuz, Kugu, Ozturk, & Ertem-Vehid, 2006). Although not yet represented as such in official classification systems of psychiatry, "complex" post-traumatic stress disorder (PTSD) is a further living diagnostic entity related to developmental traumatization as well as to a disturbance of self-perception among other symptoms (Sar, 2011). Whereas identity may be affected in several other psychiatric conditions such as schizophrenic disorder (Ebisch and Gallese, 2015), those with a relation to environmental stress, during the early years of life in particular, seem to be in closer connection with identity formation (Wilson, 2006). Namely, identity is formed not only by

V. Şar, M.D. (✉)
Koc University School of Medicine (KUSOM), Rumelifeneri Yolu, 34450 Istanbul, Turkey
e-mail: vsar@ku.edu.tr

J.D. Sinnott (ed.), *Identity Flexibility During Adulthood*,
DOI 10.1007/978-3-319-55658-1_17

identificatory-fusionary processes (e.g., seeking behavior) but also by frustrations which shape personal boundaries. Under certain conditions, frustrations may assume the scope of a *traumatic experience* leading to maladaptive development and to an eventual fragmentation of identity.

This paper is concerned with the interplay between clinics and everyday life, individual and society, and components of the "internal world" of the individual in the context of identity. One aim of this paper is to inquire into the limits and nature of the flexibility of identity in the contemporary world. An inquiry on "flexibility" of identity necessarily has to be associated with the concept of psychological "trauma" (Sar, 2015b). Traumatic experiences of any life period may affect identity, although in a different way, because they may constitute turning points in one's life or trigger trauma-related mental constellations of earlier periods. It is not known whether an eventual "flexibility" of identity, vice versa, may serve as a potential "buffer" against traumatic experiences (or, alternatively, may even develop as a consequence of the latter). Hence, the current paper is intended to address the dialectic which, paradoxically, allows change and continuity in a simultaneous fashion, while psychosocial mutuality is necessarily maintained during this dynamic interplay.

Autonomy and Boundaries

The concept of identity covers both *continuity* and (*psychosocial) mutuality* as its core features. In his opus magnum "Childhood and Society," Erik Erikson (1950/1963) defined identity as "… accrued confidence that the sameness and continuity prepared in the past are matched by the sameness and continuity of one's meaning for others" or "what (one) appear(s) to be in the eyes of others as compared with what (one) feel(s) (he/she is)." He also made a link to clinical phenomena: "the bizarrness and withdrawal in the behavior of many very sick individuals hides an attempt to recover social mutuality by a testing of the borderlines between senses and physical reality and between words and social meanings." Even associating this with bodily sensations (operative as early as the infancy period), he stated that "such consistency, continuity, and sameness of experience provide a rudimentary sense of ego identity which depends… on the recognition that there is an inner population of remembered and anticipated sensations and images which are firmly correlated with the outer population familiar and predictable things and people." Pursuing his thesis on psychosocial mutuality, he added: "ultimately, the children become neurotic not from frustrations, but from the lack or loss of the societal meaning in these frustrations." Hence, "the amount of trust derived from earliest infantile experience does not seem to depend on absolute quantitites of food or demonstrations of love, but rather on the *quality* of the maternal relationship."

Identity as an individual mental construct carrying uniqueness and continuity necessarily implies a certain delineation of personal boundaries. Any formulation about boundaries must also consider the factors which guarantee the autonomy of the person not only against the external world but in the context of one's *internal world*. This is related to the mental integration level of the individual, which is necessary to maintain a sense of self and a sense of agency. It is also a prerequisite to maintain self-regulation and self-control against retreat to a rather restricted "safe mode" (Ford, 2009) in a "fear and defense cascade" (Kozlowska, Walker, McLean, & Carrive, 2015) due to perceived or real threat.

Autonomy of the individual has been an issue for many theorists. In a well-known phrase, postulating an innate tendency of instinctual drives in constant need of satisfaction, Sigmund Freud stated: "where id is there shall ego be" (1923/1975). The subsequent movement of psychoanalytic "ego psychology" challenged this notion by assuming the newborn adjusted to the "average expectable environment" from the beginning rather than solely from exposure to conflicts between instinctual drives and the requirements of external reality (Hartmann, 1937/1958). Hence, ego psychologists underlined the existence of primary and secondary mental apparatuses which guarantee the autonomy of the "ego" not only from the environment but also from the "id" (Rapaport, 1958). One of the leading figures of this movement, it was Erikson who introduced the concepts of *identity*, *identity crisis*, and *identity confusion* to psychiatry and clinical psychology. While trying to expand psychoanalytical theory to include psychosocial components of healthy individual development as well, he formulated the issue of identity; i.e., the core individual capacity representing the human subject as a unique entity.

On the other hand, the obvious dependency of the individual, and of the newborn in particular, on the external world, has been considered a crucial component of development by both scientific research and psychoanalytical thinking. Several British psychoanalysts, in particular, devoted their work on so-called object relations theory to describe the process of development of a "psyche" in relation to others. The influential work of John Bowlby (1973) focused attention on interpersonal attachment as a lifelong need. The prominent figure of North American psychoanalysis and self-psychology Heinz Kohut (1971) introduced the concept of self-object; i.e., individuals' mental extensions to the external world. In this way, he tried to address boundary problems evoked by a rather "weak" self in conditions of pathological narcissism. The latter concept has been attributed to developmental trauma by some authors (Battegay, 1992; Howell, 2003). On the other hand, social psychology, as the scientific discipline devoted to the domain between individual and society, influenced clinical work with small groups (Sherif, 1954).

Notwithstanding these many and diverse efforts, the *interface between* society and individual has remained an understudied area. This was particularly for those working in clinical settings. In fact, this domain began to gain priority in the past century in a process which remains ongoing. Compared to most of the contemporaneous societies, the nineteenth-century individual was rather *tradition-directed* (i.e., directed by personally assimilated sociocultural traditions) or *inner-directed* (i.e., directed by individual desires and wishes). In contrast, throughout the twentieth century, the development of urbanization, industrialization, mass media, public relations, and marketing created a new type of individual prone to be controlled from outside (Battegay, 1987).

More recently, emergence of digital computers, electronic communication devices, the Internet, and, last but not least, "social" media have accelerated this trend. Finally, the shift toward "other-directedness" (Riesman, 1950) took a new dimension in the recent wave of "globalism" of an unprecedented scope when communities were forced to undergo rapid changes without being prepared in terms of lifestyle, law, ethics, traditions, and social rituals. Such developments inspired questions about whether and how the contemporary individual's identity is challenged by external demands and influences. Last but not least, not only social and cultural changes but also increased geographic mobility in the era of globalism created challenges for immigrant youth in particular. While their potential flexibility may be constrained by socioeconomic, ethnic, and racial stratification systems in "host" societies (Fuligni &Tsai, 2015) and psychiatric complications are not rare (Staniloiu, Borsutzky, & Markowitsch, 2010), there are impressions about creativity-boosting aspect of "dual identities" (Gocłowska & Crisp, 2014), i.e., carrying the qualities of the "host" and "original" cultures concurrently.

An Identity-Based Model of Mind

Danish existentialist philosopher Sören Kierkegaard (1813–1855) gave hints about how to proceed. In his famous study published in 1849 (*Sickness Unto Death*), he described the dual aspect of the human self: "A human being is a spirit. But what is spirit? Spirit is the self. But what is self? The self is a relation that relates itself to itself or is the relation relating itself to itself in the relation." What he did not underline is that the human spirit is rather *the relation between the two aspects of self.*

To address the theoretical gap not only in healthy but also clinical aspects of the interface between society and the individual, Sar and Ozturk (2007) introduced a duality model of mind based on *sociological* and *psychological* selves which correspond to Kierkegaard's two aspects. Although the "sociological self" serves as an interface between society and the individual, unlike a collective self, it is proposed to be an individual mental faculty as is the psychological self. The latter is meant to deliver observations and estimations about subjective experiences. It maintains the capacity of "pure love," an intention toward "maturity," and a sense of individual "uniqueness" and "self-orientedness." Both selves are proposed to represent patterns of thinking, experiencing, and behavior which can utilize and interact with other mental capacities in their own ways. However, healthy interpersonal relationships are proposed to be based on a harmonious development and coupling of the "sociological" and "psychological" selves.

According to this model, developmental traumatization leads to detachment of the two selves from one another. Once detached, and in contrast to the more unitary psychological self, the sociological self becomes fragmented if overloaded, leading to an instability of identity. Enlargement and fragmentation of the sociological self subsequent to traumatization restrict the further development of the psychological

Table 17.1 Properties of sociological and psychological selves

Sociological self	Psychological self
Modeling, imitation, copying	Creativity
Eclecticism	Authenticity
Dogmatism	Possibilities
Polarization	Synthesis
Negotiation	Choice
Reversibility	Constancy
Competition	Self-expression
Single-focus awareness	Multi-focus awareness
Cruelty	Compassion
Affiliation	Contact
Fusionary relationships	Boundaries
Metaphors, metonymies, symbols	Signs
Fantasy, fiction, distortion	Facts
Heroes and heroines	Icons
Religion	Spirituality

Adapted from Sar and Ozturk (2007, 2013)

self and keep it "frozen." The universal properties of the sociological and psychological selves become more prominent after detaching (Table 17.1).

Developmental detachment of the two selves may also be exacerbated by disintegrating experiences in adult life such as cumulative traumatization, a single disruptive traumatic experience, and/or deep disappointment. In order to nurture the capacity of endurance – or, alternatively, to induce over-adjustment in the new generation – societies and families may enhance the development of the sociological self among their offsprings (Ozturk & Sar, 2005). Once detached, and in contrast to the sociological self, the psychological self has limited authority over the actions of the individual. Yet expansion of the sociological self does not facilitate better relationships with the external world either. Rather, it becomes an obstacle to achievement of maturity due to the avoided and consequently frozen psychological self.

At the clinical level, this model addresses trauma-related psychiatric conditions in particular. This is because the specific task of the "sociological" self is to save the "psychological" self from the destructive influences of others and to buffer psychological trauma. However, application to the clinical sphere requires an enrichment of this duality model to cover the experienced phenomenology as well as the dynamics of change in clinical symptomatology. Sar and Ozturk (2007) propose a "tripartite" solution for this problem while introducing a third concept of self: the "trauma-self" (aka the "symptomatic" self) which operates as the intermediary between the "sociological" and "psychological" selves. The contention of the authors is that the trauma-self is a special portion of the "psychological" self which emerges as a fragment after traumatization, detaches from its origin, and is subsequently co-opted by the "sociological" self.

While striving to solve the traumatic impasse, the trauma-self orients to and remains in a perpetual state of help seeking, thus becoming symptomatic clinically. Because so close to immediate lived experience, various features of the trauma-self can be observed in everyday life as well as in clinical conditions. Typical features of the trauma-self in everyday life include increased fragility and vulnerability to outside influences, self-pity, a complaining attitude, hostility, un-cooperativeness, experiencing oneself as a "victim," impaired self-regulation, polarization of responses (overreaction versus numbness), and distance and temperance problems in relationships (such as detachment and withdrawal or fusionary attachment). Phenomena observed in clinical settings are "secondary" dissociative symptoms (self-mutilation, somatosensory symptoms, amnesia, suicidality), "resistances" in psychotherapy (depression, trauma-related obsessions, lack of therapeutic mutuality), and fluctuations between stability and crisis (Sar & Ozturk, 2005).

Separate from the tripartite self-system, the "moderator" is another entity responsible for regulation of emotions, coordination of thought and behavior, and maintenance of coherence. It also maintains interpersonal distances as an "orbital" interpersonal system (rather than a "common pool"), time perception, and sense of order.

When the moderator is overwhelmed (is out of order temporarily), loss of self-regulation, affect dysregulation, states of altered consciousness (trance), and even brief psychotic attacks of dissociative type may be observed (Sar & Ozturk, 2005). Emotions can be co-opted by distinct mental states (fragments of the sociological self) and/or by the trauma-self. As the final figure, the "natural" self is only a rudimentary organ oriented in "life energy" and motivation (Fig. 17.1).

Trauma, Memory, and Dissociation

Traumatic stress is in a special relationship with formation as well as transformations and disturbances of identity (Wilson, 2006). Firstly, trauma may affect memory which influences perception of one's life (Brewin, 2011). Mental intrusions (e.g., vivid memories) and omissions (e.g., amnesias) may undermine one's sense of self and agency. Post-traumatic fear, anger, guilt, and shame constitute not only external but also "internal" (trauma-related) phobias one has to avoid (Steele, Van der Hart, & Nijenhuis, 2001). Hence, PTSD is only one of the clinical possibilities subsequent to the traumatic situation. Various types of complex clinical constellations may emerge. *Dissociation* is the common component among the diverse clinical post-traumatic conditions (Sar, 2011).

It is obvious that "trauma" is not identical with the stressor event itself. Trauma is a configuration which has both objective and subjective aspects. It is a *situation* characterized by the vital discrepancy between objective threat and the subject's ability to cope (Fischer & Riedesser, 1999). Trauma also describes a *reaction*: the response of the subject to the stressor event (if possible at all). An adequate response may not have been possible in the traumatic situation and the process may

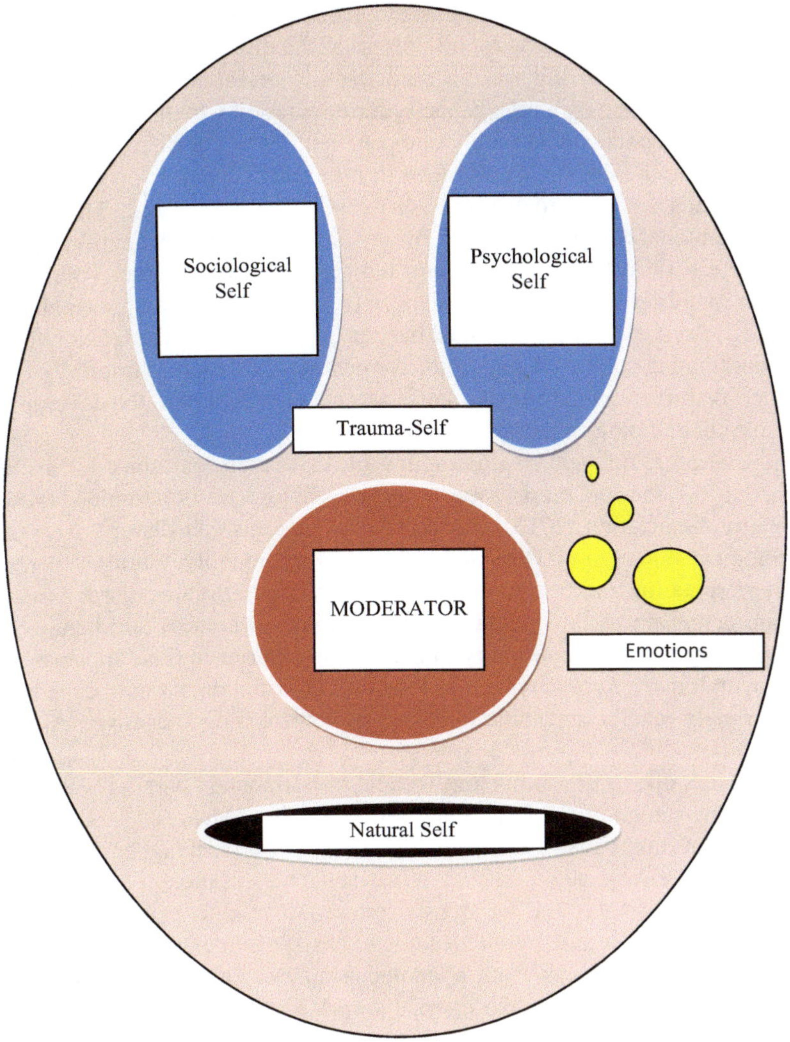

Fig. 17.1 An identity-based model of mind

not have been possible to complete (Fischer & Riedesser, 1999). Last but not least, trauma is an interrupted sociopsychological *process* which needs to be completed (Horowitz, 1976/1986). The impossibility of a completed response and/or interruption of the process may lead to generalization of the traumatic dilemma of the crisis to one's entire life (Sar & Ozturk, 2005). This means that the inner world continues to traumatize the patient after the traumatic event, creating an "inner enemy" (Kalsched, 1996). "The enemy who started on the outside is transformed into an inner torment" (Van der Kolk, 2011). Hence, trauma is not only about the past but also about the future (Sword, Sword, Brunskill, & Zimbardo, 2014). What typifies a traumatic reaction is that the traumatic event cannot be entirely grasped from within the interpretative background present at the moment of its occurrence.

According to pioneering trauma clinician and researcher Pierre Janet, mental health is characterized by a high capacity for integration which unites a broad range of psychological phenomena within one personality (Van der Kolk & Van der Hart, 1989). To achieve this, and in addition to a general capacity for synthesis in the central nervous system, "realization" of experiences is required. This is possible only by "personalization" (claiming ownership) and "presentification" (ability to differentiate between past, present, and future) of the experience. Trauma jeopardizes these abilities leading to dissociation. In both normal and abnormal functioning, reflexive self-awareness is crucial but can be disturbed by the tension that arises from coordinating subjective and objective perspectives about oneself.

Hence, disturbances in reflexive self-awareness are central to the development of severe psychopathology (Auerbach & Blatt, 1996).

Dissociation is defined as a disruption of, and/or discontinuity in, the normal integration of one or more aspects of psychological functioning (American Psychiatric Association, 2013). Dissociative symptoms can disrupt every area of psychological functioning: consciousness, memory, identity, emotion, perception, body representation, motor control, and behavior. Experientially, dissociative symptoms are perceived as (a) unbidden intrusions into awareness and behavior, with accompanying losses of continuity in subjective experience (i.e., "positive" dissociative symptoms) and/or (b) inability to access information or control mental functions normally readily amenable to access or control (i.e., "negative" dissociative symptoms).

This occurs due to the competing vertical or horizontal "parallel" mental structures resisting integration. In horizontal disintegration (Meares, 1999), exhaustion or other reasons may cause a liberation of lower systems from higher control (escape from mental hierarchy, automatisms). In vertical disintegration, loops covering elements from every level of the hierarchy (from primitive reflexes to complex cortical activities) may operate side by side leading to passive influence or interference phenomena from time to time. Both phenomena may occur due to threats from the external world or conflicts in the internal world. The economy of this endeavor is the overcoming of the threat by evolutionary given abilities which are relatively rapid and automatic in response. Due to competition between complexes which are no longer integrated, Bob and Faber (2006) propose the description of "parallel distributed processing" (PDP).

As demonstrated in a recent anecdotal case study on "vampirism" (both an ancient and contemporary symbol which is surprisingly little studied by psychiatry and psychology), the dissociated, hence autonomous, mental cycle established by disillusioning experiences in early life may lead to self-perpetuating individual violence and periodic disruptive behavior (Sakarya, Gunes, Ozturk, & Sar, 2012). Lloyd deMause (2002) regards even war and institutional violence as a societal reenactment of widespread traumatizing child-rearing practices. He underlines the unspoken conflict and competition between different childrearing practices ("psycho-classes") as one of the underlying factors prominent in civil wars

(Betancourt, 2015; Nandi, Crombach, Bambonye, Elbert, & Weierstall, 2015). Dissociation plays a role in intergenerational and transgenerational transmission of trauma, i.e., trauma passed down directly from one generation to the next or transmitted across a number of generations (Atkinson, 2002). As a function of the "sociological" self, the transmission of intergenerational and transgenerational trauma causes disruption in identity formation.

Attachment, Dissociation, and Identity

The key to avoidance of confusion is recognition that *dissociation is not a static but a dynamic condition.* A particular issue to be considered is that individuals suffering from dissociation do not experience only discontinuities and/or disruption of their mental functions. Simultaneously, they are in an intense striving to achieve the normal integration toward wholeness (Tagliavini, 2014). Many patients with dissociative identity disorder unsuccessfully struggle with their condition for several years by themselves to achieve an improvement (self-reparation or self-treatment) before the appropriate diagnosis is made by a clinician. On the other hand, dissociation is not only an intrapsychic but also *an interpersonal phenomenon* (Liotti, 2006). The latter factor contributes to the dynamism of dissociation in terms of the contextual factors affecting the condition of the individual.

Significantly, rather than as an intrapsychic defense against mental pain, Liotti (2006) proposes that pathological dissociation should be viewed as a "primarily intersubjective reality hindering the integrative processes of consciousness." Additionally, early defenses against attachment-related dissociation may lead to interpersonal controlling strategies that further inhibit the attachment system. Dissociative symptoms emerge as a consequence of the breakdown of these defensive strategies on exposure to events that activate the attachment system.

Bowlby (1973) proposed that inadequate care-seeking interactions with primary caregivers could lead the infant to develop multiple internal representations of self and attachment figures which he called internal working models (IWM). One IWM becomes dominant in regulating interpersonal relationships in a context, while the other IWMs remain separated. The latter become active in stressful situations to regulate emotions and cognitions in a way that may to some degree be alien to the person's usual sense of self (Liotti, 2006). This model accords with others which rely on "distinct mental states" (Putnam, 1997) or "ego states" (Watkins & Watkins, 1997).

According to Sar and Ozturk (2013), the "alternate personality states" of people with dissociative identity disorder modulate the insecure attachment with the abusive "caretaker" via "triangulation"; (i.e., they are involved as a third element). According to the perspective of game theory, the "triangle" is the smallest stable relationship system which tolerates more tension than a dyad (Bowen, 1978). If the tension is too high for one triangle to contain, it spreads to a series of "interlocking" triangles (i.e., emergence of additional alter personalities). Following the properties of the fragmented sociological self (Table 17.1), alter personality states are prone to take “role(s)” in the classic “drama triangle” (Karpman, 1968), that is, not only as rescuer(s), but also as abuser(s) and victims “inside.” Liotti (2006) also suggests that shifts among the multiple IWMs fits the drama triangle; i.e., the interactions between the main characters oscillate between the roles of the benevolent rescuer, the malevolent persecutor, and the helpless victim (Karpman). The link between attachment theory and the drama triangle is represented in the models of “attachment to the perpetrator” (Ross, 1997) or “identification with the aggressor” (Papiasvili, 2014) which allow the victim a subjective sense of control in the abusive condition. Such appearances have become a focus of interest in diverse perspectives such as the Stockholm Syndrome (Cantor & Price, 2007).

Identities Hijacked in the Society

Such dynamics may influence identity formation in normative conditions as well. To compensate for the painful experience of impaired sociopsychological mutuality, one may enter into fusionary relationships with potential “rescuers” in the form of “heroes” or “heroines” (Sar & Ozturk, 2013). These are individuals, organizations, or ideas perceived as “dominant others” (Arieti & Bemporad, 1980). These heroes may be substituted by any dominant other, such as religion, ideology, passionate love, or even fashionable brands and trademarks. They may also be partially or totally interchangeable. In postmodern conditions beset by simulacra (Baudrilliard, 1994), “imaginary” heroes and heroines may emerge. In “preserved” communities where real relationships and tangible “heroes” or “heroines” prevail (such as the popular girl of the neighborhood or the old wise man of the village), there is no need for imaginary versions of them.

Heroes, including those that are “negative,” may transiently become overt or covert leaders in the community who are “followed” and to whom one submits. To restore impaired self-esteem, fusionary relationships with heroes may have a positive orientation and elicit feelings of love and admiration (Sar & Ozturk, 2013). The relationship has a self-protective function. Alternatively, the subject may enter into the control of the hero which leads to blurred personal boundaries. In this case, the heroes with whom one is fused contribute to denial of low self-esteem rather than restoration of it.

Heroes and heroines differ from “icons” of “true quality” in the subjective values attributed to them. Unlike the icons with their universal and timeless positive qualities (which are usually adopted by relatively integrated individuals), heroes and heroines may be either positive or negative and bound with the spirit of the era. Both heroes and icons circulate among individuals, groups, and society and assist transformation of identities in every age group. Icons nurture the “psychological” self, while heroes and heroines serve the enlargement of the “sociological” self. Tragically, a detached and enlarged sociological self may turn out to be a malevolent and non-empathic force not only for the individual but for the family and society. Moreover, an enlarged sociological self may be misused by others and by the overall society because people with an enlarged sociological self may skillfully deploy it to their own gain and to the detriment of others. As such, the sociological self provides the basis of social alters which can collude with others in group relationships (deMause, 2002). Extreme dominance by the sociological self enables a socially dangerous and destructive style.

DSM-5 listed identity disturbance due to prolonged and intensive coercive persuasion (e.g., brainwashing, thought reform, indoctrination while captive, torture, long-term political imprisonment, recruitment by sects or by terror organizations) among other specified dissociative disorders (OSDD). Individual and organized violence (e.g., terrorism, wars, and other acts of assault) prevail globally leading to victimization of individuals and whole communities. Incidents of individual violence against civilians and children occur from time to time in prosperous Western Europe and North America and also leave unanswered questions (Thoresen, Aakvaag, Wentzel-Larsen, Dyb, & Hjemdal, 2012). Adoption of such "negative identities" (Erikson, 1950/1963) seems to attract young individuals with an ultramalignantly hypertrophied, detached, and degenerated "sociological self" (Sar and Ozturk, 2007, 2013). However, paradoxical it sounds, overadjustment to the environment at the cost of individual autonomy may have devastating consequences both individually and socially (Rapaport, 1958). Prone to enter fusionary relationships with a person, group, idea, or institution (Battegay, 1992; Kohut, 1971), such individuals suffer from an internal detachment between their sociological and psychological selves. This is dissociation without dissociative symptoms, that is, losing the "relation which relates oneself to oneself" (Kierkegaard, 1849/1983) or an "escape from oneself" (Kogan, 2007).

"Sociological self" has implications for possession experiences among dissociative individuals as well as in nonclinical populations which occur in the "transitional" area (sociological self) between individual and society (Winkelman, 2011). They are perceived as external entities controlling the person; i.e., unlike the individual alter personalities, they can affect, control, and even intrude on others as well (hence, they are "shared" entities in the community). A study conducted among women in the general population of an Anatolian town in Turkey found that possessing entities had human (living or dead person) or nonhuman (e.g., jinns, ghosts) qualities (Sar, Alioğlu, & Akyüz, 2014). Given its relationship with traumatic stress and dissociation, the experience of possession seems to be evoked by the need for assistance (rescue) in the face of helplessness.

As a further option, Sar and Ozturk (2007, 2013) proposed the "reversible personality." Rather than constituting an adaptive "dialogical self" (Blackman, 2005), "reversibility" is an ultra-formalist obsessive position of the sociological self associated with an increased tendency to be directed by others. While the "reversible" person on the surface may appear to be a strong opponent of dominant societal structures, he or she may become a covert (or overt) "ally" of the "power" (Sar & Ozturk). This "in between" status may serve as a tool to avoid the experience of estrangement or disruption when dealing with conflictual demands.

Core Disturbances of Identity

Core clinical phenomena related to identity differ from symptoms secondary to those of identity disturbance. Various types of core disturbances of identity are listed and described below.

Identity Distress

Identity distress (Berman & Montgomery, 2014) involves intense or prolonged upset or worry about personal identity issues including long-term goals, career choice, friendships, sexual orientation and behavior, religion, values and beliefs, and group loyalties. Research suggests that trauma exposure and subsequent PTSD symptoms may negatively affect identity development and psychological adjustment. After a major natural disaster, identity distress was positively associated with age, hurricane exposure, PTSD symptoms, and internalization of problems. Linear regression analyses showed that identity distress was uniquely associated with internalizing symptoms and that there was an indirect effect of hurricane exposure on identity distress via PTSD symptoms. PTSD symptoms moderated the link between identity distress and internalizing symptoms, with a significant positive slope found for youth who had more PTSD symptoms (Scott et al., 2014).

Identity Crisis

With his concept of identity crisis, Erikson (1950/1963) described a normative occurrence of adolescence. In fact, Erikson's chart of psychosocial development is based on the assumption of normative crises in each of the eight developmental periods of life. These crises around the core conflict of the period need to be solved with a positive balance to be delivered as a strength to the next period, in fact, to be put at risk for further enrichment as it occurs when trying to experience intimacy by meeting identities.

Identity Diffusion

The opposite of establishment of a firm identity is identity diffusion. While frequently normative in the period of adolescence, an extension of this phenomenon to early adulthood points to a disturbance. For instance, in a screening study on a college sample in Turkey, one in ten students fitted the diagnostic criteria for DSM-IV borderline personality disorder (Sar et al., 2006). Higher than expected for a nonclinical and high-functioning population, this rate possibly reflected the effects of identity diffusion rather than a personality disorder.

Identity Confusion

Identity confusion is characterized by an internal struggle between one's diverse internal tendencies (Steinberg, 1994). Experiences of passive influence originating from within, or even dissociative hallucinations associated with parts representing distinct identities, may affect decision-making processes.

Identity Alteration

This exceeds the limits of identity confusion when aspects of fragmented identity can take executive control of mind and behavior episodically. One may have dissociative amnesia for some of these episodes or rather experience depersonalization due to lack of the feeling at ownership when in executive control of another personality state (Steinberg, 1994).

Negative Identity

Originally proposed by Erikson, this represents direct attainment of identity features in contrast to what was wished for by parents, caregivers, authorities, etc.

Transition Between Identities

Some types of psychopathology mark a transitional period between two identity states resembling a "rite de passage" (Van Gennep, 1909). The latter is known to be composed of three phases: separation, liminality, and incorporation. Depression may be a final common pathway for such conditions clinically. Various types of the resistance of the trauma-self may have a role in development of persisting clinical syndroms. Such psychopathological conditions correspond to the "liminality" phase of the transition.

Transformation of Identity

This seems to be a defense which usually occurs when individuals are exposed to individual or societal oppression (Sandole and Auerbach, 2013; Sar & Ozturk, 2013).

Disintegration of Identity

This leads to a severe crisis at a clinical level, i.e. usually with psychotic features of depressive or dissociative type unless it is a consequence of a more severe mental disorder such as schizophrenia. Unless being delusional to compensate such as experience of "nonexistence," this condition cannot be maintained for a long time. The subject may become highly suicidal or the condition may recover itself by reinstating the control of the "host" personality state on the fragmented mental contents (Sar, 2014; Tutkun, Yargic, & Sar, 1996). According to the proposed model, the functions of the "moderator" are in a breakdown either temporarely (e.g., during a transient dissociative psychosis) or permanently (schizophrenia).

Resiliency or "Antifragility"

Only 15 % of adults who experience an overwhelming, single traumatic event will go on to develop PTSD (Yehuda, 2003). This is why psychotraumatology should inquire into the factors expected to prevent maladaptation in the face of unusual stress. Concepts such as resiliency and post-traumatic growth have become areas of research interest for this purpose. While the former has been utilized to assess the varying levels of coping of subjects exposed to traumatic stress, it is still controversial. For instance, even some individuals with PTSD have been proposed to be resilient in a certain way (Southwick, Bonanno, Masten, Panter-Brick, & Yehuda, 2014). Cultural critic Nassim Nicholas Taleb (2012) has recently added a new concept to this notion, that of "antifragility," while challenging "robustness" as an innate feature of resiliency. With antifragility, he considers the possibilities for managing unpredictability when solid and enduring structures may be limited in their repertoir of response types in such conditions.

Typically, psychosocial factors associated with depression and/or stress resilience include positive emotions and optimism, humor, cognitive flexibility, cognitive explanatory style and reappraisal, acceptance, religion/spirituality, altruism, social support, role models, coping style, exercise, capacity to recover from negative events, and stress inoculation (Southwick, Vythilingam, & Charney, 2005). In one study, *positive affect* was significantly negatively related to several symptoms of psychopathology, including depression, dissociation, self-destructive behavior, PTSD, and global psychopathology (Etter, Gauthier, McDade-Montez, Cloitre, & Carlson, 2013). Lower positive affect was predicted by lower childhood social support and greater severity of childhood adversity (i.e., sexual abuse).

Can dissociation contribute to one's antifragility? Psychotraumatology is a dialectical field and such questions may raise contradictory responses concurrently. Many diseases are based on the immune reaction due to the presence of an external agent intruding on the body. However, while it is a defense, an immune reaction may be destructive itself. A mental "disorder" can never be considered as a strength.

One has to consider, however, that mental defenses are meant to facilitate survival. Peritraumatic dissociation is a predictor of PTSD (Van der Hart, Van Ochten, Van Son, Steele, & Lensvelt-Mulders, 2008); hence, it apparently leads to maintenance of the clinical symptoms. On the other hand, dissociation is known to be an adaptive response to overwhelming stress as well. There are even hypotheses addressing dissociation as a potential neuroprotective factor after traumatic experience (Ross, Goode, & Schroeder, 2015).

Post-traumatic psychopathologies may, indeed, be strategies of survival rather than "degenerative" processes themselves. Dissociation seems to be protective only if stress exceeds the clinical threshold and becomes intolerable while there is no evidence showing that it contributes to flexibility and healthy adaptation under "normative" conditions. Such division may be a preference of the organism to survive by using its limited resources for a particular function, while others (the less vital ones) need to become dormant at least for a period. This is how the body functions when in shock due to loss of a significant proportion of total blood volume: The biggest portion of the blood volume is directed to the brain (as it is the least solid against spooling) by constriction of the vessels leading blood to other organs. However, unless timely assistance from outside is available, this becomes an unfortunate strategy: The non-preferred organs are thereby degenerated irreversibly by necrosis. Akin to that, in a less fatal way though, dissociation may have also costs in the long run.

Nevertheless, dissociation is treatable. Unlike schizophrenia, it is based on a mechanism available to everyone rather than being pathological or degenerative per se. Typically, among patients with dissociative identity disorder, one encounters child personality states which possibly represent one's mental state before traumatic disillusion. Such states may be laden with anger and turn to so-called persecutory personality states which threaten the "host" personality who is no more popular in their eyes due to its overadjustment, and even "attachment, to the perpetrator" (Ross, 2007) in a hostile environment. Functional somatic disturbances (usually of neurological nature) are common among patients with dissociative and other post-traumatic conditions. Recently, some types of these symptoms have been labeled "shutdown dissociation" (Schalinski, Schauer, & Elbert, 2015). This highlights their way of preventing the mental system from overwhelming.

Dissociation may assist an individual or a community to survive in a world of conflicting messages (Krüger, Sokudela, Motlana, Mataboge, & Dikobe, 2007). In such conditions, it may thus be an appropriate tool for maintaining a balanced, coherent self in society (i.e., an individual connected to other people). However, this is only possible via an intervening personal psychological process which filters information. In addition to the first filter consisting of brain resources dealing with externally originated sensory information, a second "dissociative filter" screens sensory, emotional, and thought-related information so that only a manageable selection of information occupies the person's consciousness. With its capacity to deal with diverse facets of reality, the "sociological self" functions as such a filter.

A recent study on adolescents with dissociative identity disorder and its subthreshold forms in Turkey found no significant differences on childhood trauma histories and family dysfunctionality as assessed by self-report measures (Sar,

Önder, Kilinçaslan, Zoroglu, & Alyanak, 2014). However, the group with dissociative identity disorder or its subthreshold forms had greater separation anxiety disorder concurrently compared to controls with other psychiatric disorders. This finding underlined the possibility of attachment disturbances in the dissociative sample possibly originating from an overprotecting-overcontrolling child-rearing style (Brothers, 2014) which is relatively common in Turkey as a culturally accepted, normative child-rearing style. The latter is usually a self-compensatory behavior of traumatized parents which leads to intergenerational transition of subtle trauma. This attitude threatens interpersonal boundaries (as well as private individual spheres) and may be insidiously overwhelming for the rising generation (Kogan, 2007) and increase "fragility." Not rarely, such "apparently normal" families (Öztürk & Sar, 2005) are characterized by affect dysregulation (Briere & Runtz, 2015) among their members leading to transient outboursts of anger during crisis periods only. Nevertheless, the combination of "overprotection" and "affect dysregulation" is not expected to build any strength.

Implications for "Healing"

One definition of identity is the "accrued experience of the ego's ability to *integrate*" (Erikson 1950/1963). Both directly and indirectly, identity is one of the potentially significant dimensions of psychotherapy in post-traumatic clinical conditions in particular (Sollberger et al., 2015). For example, life-review interventions are systematically implemented and investigated not only in elderly patients with depression or cognitive decline in oncology units and hospices but also in adolescents with various mental problems (Maercker & Bachem, 2013). They are focused on life balance (balanced accounting of negative and positive memories), finding meaning, and elaboration of memory (greater detail of what is remembered actively).

By articulation of trauma, identity can be successfully reinvented. This requires a renewed evaluation of traumatic experience in the context of the "psychological" self rather than the "sociological" self. Winkelman (2011) proposes the "integrated mode of consciousness" necessary for such episodes. As early as the seventeenth century (1689), John Locke stated in "An Essay Concerning Human Understanding" that "consciousness is…the repeated self-identification of oneself." This phrase is inspirational for an identity-based understanding of psychotherapy: *Integration takes place by letting the individual perceive oneself as oneself in the face of each diverse reality while developing sociopsychological connections between these realities and kernels of self.* Technically, to change the schemata which have been learned previously, reconsolidation researchers underline the necessity of the phenomenon they term a "mismatch," "prediction error," or "juxtaposition" experience. Reactivation without concurrent discrepancy fails to induce deconsolidation, and the memory remains stable (Ecker, 2015).

Aware of the challenges in maintaining an authentic self, Polish psychiatrist Kazimierz Dąbrowski (1996) proposed the theory of *positive disintegration* in the

1960s. He believed that the initial personality integration, based upon socialization, does not reflect true personality. Rather the latter must be based upon a system of values that are consciously and volitionally chosen by the person to reflect their own "personality ideal." In order for challenge to the initial integration to occur, crises and disintegrations are needed and are usually provided by life experiences. This model is not a developmental theory of stages leading to maturity which is applicable to everyone. According to Dabrowski, only those who can manage the difficult transitions can reach the higher levels. On the other hand, Dabrowski's "positive disintegration" does not represent "clinical dissociation." Rather, clinical dissociation seems to be a consequence of failure to achieve "positive disintegration" in a suboptimal environment.

In the realm of mental health, effective management of "chaos" is only possible if the individual can maintain the role of survivor rather than victim while undergoing psychosocial reorganization. Using the terminology of the model inquired in this paper, it depends on the presence of a harmonious relationship between "psychological" and "sociological" selves and a mental processing in the context of the former rather than the latter and the trauma-selves.

Basically, a shift from "sociological" to the "psychological" self is indicated for the majority of individuals who seek psychotherapy which is expected to address the issue of identity (Fig. 17.2). Consistent with the model proposed here, it is the "trauma-self" (symptomatic self) to which the clinician is exposed, while "sociological" and "psychological" selves operate as contexts in the background.

While addressing the whole system is crucial for solving the problem in general and for rearticulating the identity, this process cannot work unless the resistances of the trauma-self are resolved. Additionally, in post-traumatic conditions, the dysfunctionality in the tripartite self-system may overwhelm the "moderator," leading to its temporary and reversible disturbances. Both resistances of the "trauma-self" and the secondary disturbances of the "moderator" lead to clinical phenomena which resemble several psychiatric syndromes (depressive phenomena, functional neurological- somatic symptoms, and even a brief psychotic attack) which cannot be treated successfully by algorithms shaped for their primary forms. This is the main cause of "treatment resistance" among some of the (usually traumatized) patients encountered in daily clinical work. Positive outcomes can be assessed both by the disappearance of core symptoms of identity disturbance and of secondary symptoms (psychiatric "comorbidities").

There is a general critique which targets the tendency in the disciplines of clinical psychology and psychiatry to identify the individual as the locus for therapeutic intervention rather than the social conditions associated with various forms of distress. Social changes cannot "heal" the individual (i.e., the subjective repercussions of traumatic experience). Yet, social change not only occurs in the context of groups but is predicated upon the power of changes in the *internal world of the individual*, i.e., the subject. Namely, in the absence of healing, the traumatized individual lacks the strength to defend himself/herself and remains at risk of maintaining the role of victim rather than that of survivor. Thus, a dysfunctional individual may undermine any potential healthy environmental change by disrupting of his/her relationships

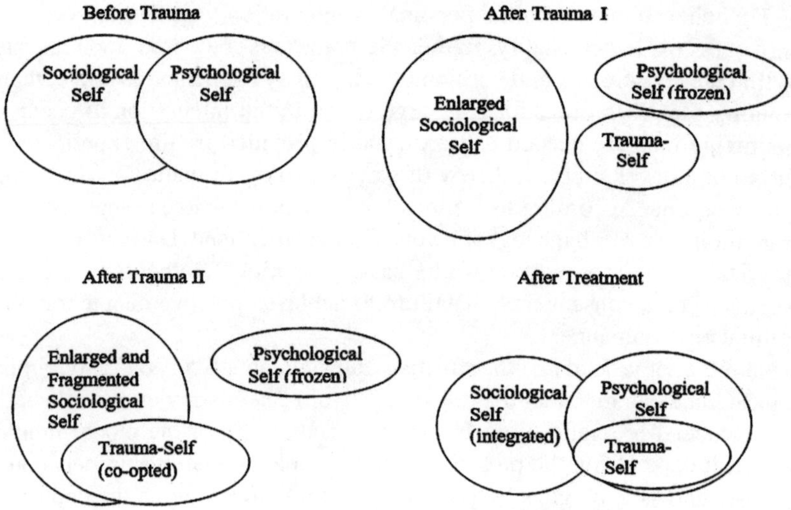

Fig. 17.2 Functional dissociation of the self before and after traumatic experience

with potential allies. Effective treatment requires a fulcrum of leverage "inside"; by using "internal resources" (Bernet, 2000). Such treatment always has an "ego states" (Barabasz, 2014) aspect aimed at "integration" inside of the "internal world" of the subject (Barlow & Chu, 2014).

At the same time, trauma is unlikely to be resolved without the assistance of others, i.e. help from the external world. The self-perpetuating internal "ghetto" is resistant to change until effective therapeutic intervention is available (Frankel & O'Hearn, 1996). Trauma is not only an absence and departure but also a call to survival through new forms of contact with others (Caruth, 1995). This evokes Kierkegaard's statement about the human spirit (self) which is relational in the broadest sense of the word (i.e., both in the internal world of the individual and interpersonally). Here one can speculate that a *healthy flexibility* of identity is correlated with *relational fertility* of the subject in both directions.

A common belief is that "western" cultures underline individuality, whereas "eastern" cultures emphasize relatedness. The problem of personal autonomy is not a linear one; however, and cannot be solved by focusing on a single component. Interestingly, Turkish social psychologist Cigdem Kagitcibasi (1996, 2011) stated that autonomy and relatedness are not end points of a continuum, as is often assumed. As distinct dimensions, either pole of the agency dimension can coexist with either pole of the interpersonal distance dimension. According to her model, this renders four different types of self possible: the *autonomous-separate self*, the *heteronomous-separate self*, the *heteronomous-related self*, and the *autonomous-related self*.

Another aspect of trauma treatment is "creativity" which may be required in approaching the unknown in order to make it meaningful (Daniels, 2010). In Jacques Lacan's understanding, trauma is an intrusion of the "real" into the "symbolic"

(Zizek, 2007). The "traumatic truth" cannot be pinned down by the symbolic/imaginary framework (i.e., the mental schemata) that preceded it. Hence, there is a striking resemblance between "trauma" and French philosopher Alain Badiou's (2005) notion of the "event": both are characterized by a relation of "incommensurability" with regard to the preexisting context in which they emerge (Bistoen, Vanheule, & Craps, 2014). An "event" is the sudden appearance, with maximal intensity, of a previously nonexistent element of a world. It reveals the radical contingency of any way of ordering the multiple, with the potential to change all other appearances and degrees of existence. In short, the distinction between an "event" and a fact can be made via reference to the consequences (i.e., the degree of change) that it has for the world in which it takes place. Badiou's "event" can only be comprehended retroactively, because understanding of it can only take place on the basis of a new horizon of possibilities generated by the event, hence, with a message about the future (Sword et al., 2014). In other words, the event announces the possibility for a "new world" to arise (Bistoen et al., 2014).

Conclusions

Identity is challenged by traumatic stress which usually represents a change in internal (psychological) and external (sociological) realities, thereby temporarily threatening the mutuality between "sociological" and "psychological" selves of the individual. The opposite is also true: a challenge to identity may be "traumatic." Such challenges may lead to a crisis characterized by a disruption in psychological functions and even by emergence of clinical symptoms. Dilemmas inherent to a particular crisis may be generalized to the entire life if a resolution has not been achieved. Timely resolution of such impasse seems to be associated with the availability of internal and external psychological resources, a capacity to be open to implement newly learned principles while keeping a basic level of continuity. Critical in this context is a well-integrated identity to allow the internal and external communication which facilitates healthy decision-making. Such "integrative synthesis" would benefit from nurturance of "cognitive-social competence" on the basis of an "autonomous-related self" (Kagitcibasi, 2011) and as shown in the 22-year longitudinal study of Turkish Early Enrichment Project (TEEP) designed to promote overall human development in the context of rural-to-urban migration in Istanbul, Turkey (Kagitcibasi, Sunar, & Bekman, 2001; Kagitcibasi, Sunar, Bekman, Baydar, & Cemalcilar, 2009).

In his seminar on *identification* (1961–1962), and from the perspective of logic, Jacques Lacan indicated that identity can be defined as an entity that is equal to (i.e., A = A) itself (Vanheule & Verhaeghe, 2009). In his theater-piece "Biography: A Play," which he regarded as a comedy, Swiss novelist Max Frisch (1969) explored the possibility and impossibility of "correcting" or "reinstating" identity. Thus the unique phenomenon of identity remains not only a topic of inquiry for scholarly debate but an endless resource of artistic inspirations.

Acknowledgments The author thanks Pam Stavropoulos, PhD, for her help in editing this manuscript.

References

American Psychiatric Association. (2013). *Diagnostic and statistical manual of mental disorders* (5th ed.). Washington DC: American Psychiatric Association.

Arieti, S., & Bemporad, J. R. (1980). The psychological organization of depression. *American Journal of Psychiatry, 137*, 1360–1365.

Atkinson, J. (2002). *Trauma trails: The transgenerational effects of trauma*. Melbourne: Spinifex.

Auerbach, J. S., & Blatt, S. J. (1996). Self-representation in severe psychopathology: The role of reflexive self-awareness. *Psychoanalytic Psychology, 73*(3), 297–341.

Badiou, A. (2005). *Being and event* (O. Feltham, Trans.). New York: Continuum.

Barabasz, A. (2014). Evidence based abreactive ego state therapy for PTSD. *American Journal of Clinical Hypnosis, 56*(1), 54–65.

Barlow, M., Chu, J. (2014). Measuring fragmentation in dissociative identity disorder: The integration measure and relationship to switching and time in therapy. European Journal of Psychotraumatology, 5. doi: http://dx.doi.org/10.3402/ejpt.v5.22250

Battegay, R. (1987). Narzisstische Störungen im Lichte der modernen psychoanalyse (narcissistic disorders in the light of modern psychoanalysis). *Schweizer Archiv für Neurologie und Psychiatrie, 138*, 45–59.

Battegay, R. (1992). *Narzissmus und Objektbeziehungen*. Bern: Hans Huber Verlag.

Baudrillard, J. (1994). *Simulacra and simulation*. Michigan: University of Michigan Press.

Berman, S. L., & Montgomery, M. J. (2014). Problematic identity processes: The role of identity distress. *Identity: An International Journal of Theory and Research, 14*(4), 13–245.

Bernet, R. (2000). The traumatized subject. *Research in Phenomenology, 30*, 160–179.

Betancourt, T. S. (2015). The intergenerational effect of war. *Journal of American Medical Association (JAMA) Psychiatry, 72*(3), 199–200.

Bistoen, G., Vanheule, S., & Craps, S. (2014). Badiou's theory of the event and the politics of trauma recovery. *Theory & Psychology, 24*(6), 830–851.

Blackman, L. (2005). The dialogical self, flexibility and the cultural production of psychopathology. *Theory & Psychology, 15*(2), 183–206.

Bob, P., & Faber, J. (2006). Dissociation in brain and mind as a consequence of competitive interactions. *Prague Medical Report, 107*(3), 297–304.

Bowen, M. (1978). *Family therapy in clinical practice*. Northvale, NJ: Jason Aronson Inc.

Bowlby, J. (1973). *Attachment and loss, Vol. 2: Separation: Anxiety and anger*. London: Hogarth Press.

Brewin, C. R. (2011). The nature and significance of memory disturbance in post-traumatic stress disorder. *Annual Review of Clinical Psycholology, 7*, 203–227.

Briere, J., & Runtz, M. (2015). Dissociation in individuals denying trauma exposure findings from two samples. *Journal of Nervous and Mental Disease, 203*, 439–442.

Brothers, D. (2014). Traumatic attachments: Intergenerational trauma, dissociation, and the analytic relationship. *International Journal of Psychoanalytic Self Psychology, 9*(1), 3–15.

Burakova, Z. (2010). Finding identity through trauma. In S. Kolar, Z. Burakova, & K. Sandorova (Eds.), *Reflections of trauma in selected works of postwar American and British literature* (p. 129). Kosice: Pavol Josef Safarik University, Faculty of Arts.

Cantor, C., & Price, J. (2007). Traumatic entrapment, appeasement and complex post-traumatic stress disorder: Evolutionary perspectives of hostage reactions, domestic abuse and the Stockholm syndrome. *Australian and New Zealand Journal of Psychiatry, 41*, 377–384.

Caruth, C. (1995). Trauma and experience: Introduction. In C. Caruth (Ed.), *Trauma: Explorations in memory* (pp. 3–12). Baltimore: The Johns Hopkins University Press.

Dąbrowski, K. (1996). *Multilevelness of emotional and instinctive functions. Part 1: Theory and description of levels of behavior*. Lublin: Towarzystwo Naukowe Katolickiego Uniwersytetu Lubelskiego.

Dąbrowski, K. (1966). The theory of positive disintegration. *International Journal of Psychiatry, 2*, 229–244.

Daniels, S. (2010). A kaleidoscopic view: Reflections on the creative self. *Roeper Review, 20*(3), 154–158.

deMause, L. (2002). *The emotional life of nations*. New York: Institute of Psychohistory.

Ebisch, S. J. H., & Gallese, V. (2015). A neuroscientific perspective on the nature of altered self–other relationships in schizophrenia. *Journal of Consciousness Studies, 22*(1–2), 220–240.

Ecker, B. (2015). Minding the findings: Let's not miss the message of memory reconsolidation research for psychotherapy. *Behavioral and Brain Sciences, 38*, e7. doi: http://dx.doi.org/10.1017/S0140525X14000168.

Erikson, E.H. (1950/1963). *Childhood and society*. New York: Norton.

Etter, D. W., Gauthier, J. R., McDade-Montez, E., Cloitre, M., & Carlson, E. B. (2013). Positive affect, childhood adversity, and psychopathology in psychiatric inpatients. *European Journal of Psychotraumatology, 4*, 20771. http://dx.doi.org/10.3402/ejpt.v4i0.20771.

Fischer, G., & Riedesser, P. (1999). *Lehrbuch der Psychotraumatologie*. München: Ernst Reinhardt Verlag.

Ford, J. (2009). Dissociation in complex posttraumatic stress disorder or disorders of extreme stress not otherwise specified. In P. F. Dell & J. A. O'Neil (Eds.), *Dissociation and dissociative disorders. DSM-V and beyond* (pp. 471–483). New York: Routledge Publs.

Frankel, A. S., & O'Hearn, T. C. (1996). Similarities in responses to extreme and unremitting stress: Cultures of communities under siege. *Psychotherapy: Theory, Research, Practice, Training, 33*, 485–502.

Freud, S. (1923/1975). Das Ich und das Es. In *Psychologie des Unbewussten*. Freud- Studienausgabe, Bd.III, A.Mitscherlich, A.Richards, J.Strachey (pp. 273–327). Frankfurt: S. Fisher.

Frisch, M. (1969). *Biografie: Ein Spiel*. Suhrkamp: Frankfurt am Main.

Fuligni, A. J., & Tsai, K. M. (2015). Developmental flexibility in the age of globalization: Autonomy and identity development among immigrant adolescents. *Annual Review of Psychology, 66*, 411–431.

Gocłowska, M. A., & Crisp, R. J. (2014). How dual-identity processes foster creativity. *Review of General Psychology, 18*(3), 216–236.

Hartmann, H. (1937/1958). Ego psychology and the problem of adaptation. In H. Hartmann & D. Rapaport (Trans.), *Journal of the American Psychoanalytic Association,* Monograph series (Vol 1, pp. 121). Madison, CT: International Universities Press.

Horowitz, M.J. (1976/1986). *Stress response syndromes*. Northwale, NJ: Jason Aronson Inc.

Howell, E. F. (2003). Narcissism, a relational aspect of dissociation. *Journal of Trauma & Dissociation, 4*(3), 51–71.

Kagitcibasi, C. (1996). The autonomous-relational self: A new synthesis. *European Psychologist, 1*, 180–186.

Kagitcibasi, C. (2011). Sociocultural change and integrative syntheses in human development: Autonomous-related self and social-cultural competence. *Child Development Perspectives, 6*(1), 5–11.

Kagitcibasi, C., Sunar, D., & Bekman, S. (2001). Long-term effects of early intervention: Turkish low-income mothers and children. *Journal of Applied Developmental Psychology, 22*, 333–361.

Kagitcibasi, C., Sunar, D., Bekman, S., Baydar, N., & Cemalcilar, Z. (2009). Continuing effects of early intervention in adult life: The Turkish early enrichment project 22 years later. *Journal of Applied Developmental Psychology, 30*, 764–779.

Kalsched, D. (1996). *The inner world of trauma. Archetypel defenses of the personal spirit.* London: Routledge.

Karpman, S. B. (1968). Fairy tales and script drama analysis. *Transactional Analysis Bulletin, 7*(26), 39–43.

Kierkegaard, S. (1849/1983). *Sickness unto death.* Princeton, NJ: Princeton University Press.

Kogan, I. (2007). *Escape from selfhood. Breaking boundaries and craving for oneness.* London: IPA (International Psychoanalitical Association) Limited.

Kohut, H. (1971). *The analysis of the self: A systematic approach to the psychoanalytic treatment of narcissistic personality disorders.* New York: International Universities Press.

Kozlowska, K., Walker, P., McLean, L., & Carrive, P. (2015). Fear and the defense cascade: Clinical implications and management. *Harvard Review of Psychiatry, 23*(4), 263–287.

Krüger, C., Sokudela, B. F., Motlana, L. M., Mataboge, C. K., & Dikobe, A. M. (2007). Dissociation: A preliminary contextual model. *South African Journal of Psychiatry, 13*(1), 13–21.

Lacan, J. (1966). La Seminaire XIII, L'objet de la psychoanalyse, (1965–1966), unpublished seminar of 19 January 1966. (cited by B. Fink: The master signifier and the four discourses. In D. Nobus (Ed.), *Key concepts of Lacanian psychoanalysis* (pp. 29–47). London: Rebuss Press.

Levine, P. A. (1997). *Waking the Tiger: Healing trauma.* Berkeley, CA: North Atlantic Books.

Levine, P. A. (2008). *Healing trauma.* Boulder, CO: Sounds True.

Liotti, G. (2006). A model of dissociation based on attachment theory and research. *Journal of Trauma & Dissociation, 7*(4), 55–73.

Maercker, A., & Bachem, R. (2013). Life-review interventions as psychotherapeutic techniques in psychotraumatology. *European Journal of Psychotraumatology, 4*, 1. doi:http://dx.doi.org/10.3402/ejpt.v4i0.19720.

Meares, R. (1999). The contribution of Hughlings Jackson to an understanding of dissociation. *American Journal of Psychiatry, 156*(12), 1850–1855.

Megginson, L. C. (1963). Lessons from Europe for American business. *Southwestern Social Science Quarterly, 44*(1), 3–13.

Nandi, C., Crombach, A., Bambonye, M., Elbert, T., Weierstall, R. (2015). Predictors of posttraumatic stress and appetitive aggression in active soldiers and former combatants. *European Journal of Psychotraumatology, 6*. doi: http://dx.doi.org/10.3402/ejpt.v5.22250

Ozturk, E., & Sar, V. (2005). 'Apparently normal' family: A contemporary agent of transgenerational trauma and dissociation. *Journal of Trauma Practice, 4*(3–4), 287–303.

Papiasvili, E. D. (2014). The contemporary relevance of Sándor Ferenczi's concept of identification with the aggressor to the diagnosis and analytic treatment of chronic PTSD. *Psychoanalytic Inquiry, 34*(2), 122–134.

Putnam, F. W. (1997). *Dissociation in children and adolescents. A developmental perspective.* New York: Guilford Press.

Rapaport, D. (1958). The theory of ego autonomy: A generalization. *Bulletin of the Menninger Clinic, 22*, 13–35.

Riesman, D. (1950). *The lonely crowd.* New Haven, CT: Yale University Press.

Ross, C. A. (1997). *Dissociative identity disorder. Diagnosis, clinical features, and treatment of multiple personality.* New York: Wiley Press.

Ross, C. A., Goode, C., & Schroeder, E. (2015). Hippocampal volumes in a sample of trauma patients: A possible neuro-protective effect of dissociation. *The Open Psychiatry Journal, 9*, 7–10.

Sakarya, D., Güneş, C., Öztürk, E., & Şar, V. (2012). "Vampirism" in a case of dissociative identity disorder and PTSD. *Psychotherapy and Psychosomatics, 81*(5), 322–323.

Sandole, D. H., & Auerbach, C. F. (2013). Dissociation and identity transformation in female survivors of the genocide against the Tutsi in Rwanda: A qualitative research study. *Journal of Trauma & Dissociation, 14*(2), 127–137.

Sar, V. (2011). Developmental trauma, complex PTSD and the current proposal of DSM-5. *European Journal of Psychotraumatology, 2*, 5662. doi:10.3402/ejpt.v2i0.5622.
Sar, V. (2014). The many faces of dissociation: Opportunities for innovative research in psychiatry. *Clinical Psychopharmacology and Neuroscience, 12*(3), 171–179.
Sar, V. (2015a). Establishing the common ground in European psychotraumatology. *European Journal of Psychotraumatology, 6*, 28213. doi:http://dx.doi.org/10.3402/ejpt.v6.28213.
Sar, V. (2015b). The psychiatric comorbidity of dissociative identity disorder: An integrated look. In A. P. van der Merwe & V. Sinason (Eds.), *Shattered selves: Voices of triumph and testimony*. London: Karnac Press.
Sar, V., Akyuz, G., Kugu, N., Ozturk, E., & Ertem-Vehid, H. (2006). Axis I dissociative disorder comorbidity in borderline personality disorder and reports of childhood trauma. *Journal of Clinical Psychiatry, 67*(10), 1583–1590.
Sar, V., Alioğlu, F., & Akyüz, G. (2014). Experiences of possession and paranormal phenomena among women in the general population: Are they related to traumatic stress and dissociation? *Journal of Trauma & Dissociation, 15*(3), 303–318.
Sar, V., Krüger, C., Martinez-Taboas, A., Middleton, W., & Dorahy, M. (2013). Sociocognitive and posttraumatic models of dissociation are not opposed. *Journal of Nervous and Mental Disease, 201*(5), 439–440.
Sar, V., Önder, C., Kilinçaslan, A., Zoroglu, S. S., & Alyanak, B. (2014). Dissociative identity disorder among adolescents: Prevalence in a university psychiatric outpatient unit. *Journal of Trauma & Dissociation, 15*(4), 402–419.
Sar, V., & Ozturk, E. (2005). What is trauma and dissociation? *Journal of Trauma Practice, 4*(1–2), 7–20.
Sar, V., & Ozturk, E. (2007). Functional dissociation of the self: A sociocognitive approach to trauma and dissociation. *Journal of Trauma & Dissociation, 8*(4), 69–89.
Sar, V., & Ozturk, E. (2013). Stimulus deprivation and overstimulation as dissociogenic agents in postmodern oppressive societies. *Journal of Trauma & Dissociation, 14*(2), 198–212.
Schalinski, I., Schauer, M., Elbert, T. (2015). The shutdown dissociation scale (Shut-D). European Journal of Psychotraumatology, 6. doi:http://dx.doi.org/10.3402/ejpt.v6.25652.
Scott, B. G., Sanders, A. F. P., Graham, R. A., Banks, D. M., Russell, J. D., Berman, S. L., et al. (2014). Identity distress among youth exposed to natural disasters: Associations with level of exposure, posttraumatic stress, and internalizing problems. *Identity: An International Journal of Theory and Research, 14*(4), 255–267.
Sherif, M. (1954). Sociocultural influences in small group research. *Sociology and Social Research, 39*, 1–10.
Sollberger, D., Gremaud-Heitz, D., Riemenschneider, A., Agarwalla, P., Benecke, C., Schwald, O., et al. (2015). Change in identity diffusion and psychopathology in a specialized inpatient treatment for borderline personality disorder. *Clinical Psychology & Psychotherapy, 6*, 559–569.
Southwick, S., Bonanno, G., Masten, A., Panter-Brick, C., Yehuda, R. (2014). Resilience definitions, theory, and challenges: Interdisciplinary perspectives. European Journal of Psychotraumatology, 5. doi:http://dx.doi.org/10.3402/ejpt.v5.25338
Southwick, S. M., Vythilingam, M., & Charney, D. S. (2005). The psychobiology of depression and resilience to stress: Implications for prevention and treatment. *Annual Review of Clinical Psychology, 1*, 255–291.
Staniloiu, A., Borsutzky, S., & Markowitsch, H. (2010). Dissociative memory disorders and immigration. In W. Christensen, E. Schier, & J. Sutton (Eds.), *ASCSO: Proceedings of the 9th Conference of the Australasian Society for Cognitive Science* (pp. 316–324). Sydney, Australia: Macquarie Centre for Cognitive Science.
Steele, K., Van der Hart, O., & Nijenhuis, E. R. S. (2001). Dependency in the treatment of complex posttraumatic stress disorder and dissociative disorders. *Journal of Trauma & Dissociation, 2*(4), 79–116.
Steinberg, M. (1994). *Structured clinical interview for DSM-IV dissociative disorders-revised (SCID-D-R)*. Washington, DC: American Psychiatric Press.

Sword, R. M., Sword, R. K. M., Brunskill, S. R., & Zimbardo, P. G. (2014). Time perspective therapy: A new time-based metaphor therapy for PTSD. *Journal of Loss and Trauma, 19*(3), 197–201.

Tagliavini, G. (2014). Dissociation and traumatization from Pierre Janet to Gianni Liotti and beyond: Connecting some dots in European psychotraumatology. Paper presented in the symposium on European Perspectives on Trauma: Finding the Common Ground. Hamburg, Germany: Annual Conference of the German-Speaking Society of Psychotraumatology (DeGPT).

Taleb, N. N. (2012). *Antifragile: Things that gain from disorder*. New York: Random House.

Thoresen, S., Aakvaag, H., Wentzel-Larsen, T., Dyb, G., & Hjemdal, O. (2012). The day Norway cried: Proximity and distress in Norwegian citizens following the 22nd July 2011 terrorist attacks in Oslo and on Utøya Island. *European Journal of Psychotraumatology, 3*. doi:http://dx.doi.org/10.3402/ejpt.v3i0.19709

Tutkun, H., Yargic, L. I., & Sar, V. (1996). Dissociative identity disorder presenting as hysterical psychosis. *Dissociation, 9*, 241–249.

van der Hart, O., van Ochten, J. M., van Son, M. J. M., Steele, K., & Lensvelt-Mulders, G. (2008). Relations among peritraumatic dissociation and posttraumatic stress: A critical review. *Journal of Trauma & Dissociation, 9*(4), 481–505.

van der Kolk, B. A. (1996). The complexity of adaptation to trauma: Self-regulation, stimulus discrimination, and characterological development. In B. A. Van der Kolk, McFarlane, & L. Weisaeth (Eds.), *Traumatic stress* (pp. 182–213). New York: Guilford Press.

van der Kolk, B. A. (2011). Introduction. In D. Emerson & E. Hopper (Eds.), *Overcoming trauma through yoga*. Berkeley, CA: North Atlantic Books.

van der Kolk, B. A., & Van der Hart, O. (1989). Pierre Janet and the breakdown of adaptation in psychological trauma. *American Journal of Psychiatry, 146*(12), 1530–1540.

Van Gennep, A. (1909). *Les rites de passage*. Paris: Émile Nourry.

Vanheule, S., & Verhaeghe, P. (2009). Identity through psychoanalytic looking glass. *Theory & Psychology, 19*(3), 391–411.

Watkins, J. G., & Watkins, H. H. (1997). *Ego states. Theory and therapy*. New York: Norton.

Wilson, J. P. (2006). Trauma and the epigenesis of identity. In J. P. Wilson (Ed.), *The posttraumatic self. Restoring meaning and wholeness to personality*. New York: Routledge Publ.

Winkelman, M. (2011). A paradigm for understanding altered consciousness: The integrative mode of consciousness. In E. Cardeña & M. Winkelman (Eds.), *Altering consciousness: Multidisciplinary perspectives* (Vol. 1, pp. 23–41). Santa Barbara, CA: Praeger.

Yehuda, R. (2003). Clinical relevance of biologic findings in PTSD. *Psychiatric Quarterly, 73*(2), 123–133.

Zizek, S. (2007). From objet a to subtraction. *Lacanian Ink, 30*, 131–141.

Chapter 18
Caregiving Identity and Flexibility

Kim Shifren

This chapter focuses on caregiver identity development and the importance of flexibility in their identity. The chapter begins with a discussion of identity development followed by work on caregiver identity development. Next, the assessment tools available for the study of caregiver identity development are presented. Finally, the chapter concludes with directions for future research.

Identity Development

Erikson (1968, 1980) is credited with paving the way toward our understanding of identity development, with work by Marcia (1966, 1993) on identity statuses further helping to broaden our understanding of identity development. Erikson discussed identity development as something in which the individual develops a sense of who he/she is and how he/she fits into the world. Erikson believed that we form our identity from contemplating a range of choices within our cultural group for personal relationships, occupation, sexual orientation, and beliefs and values. Erikson discussed identity development in terms of a "crisis" as part of the process in which someone constructs his/her identity. However, Marcia used the term "exploration" instead, because exploration is viewed as a more positive approach to study possible identities. Marcia distinguished four types of identity status or states of ego development: identity achievement, identity foreclosure, identity moratorium, and identity diffusion (1966, 1993, 1994). Identity achievement involves the period of exploration followed by a commitment to a particular goal, action, or decision (e.g., deciding to go to college). Identity foreclosure involves having a commitment without any exploration of alternative goals, actions, or decisions (e.g., going along with

K. Shifren, Ph.D. (✉)
Psychology Department, Towson University, 8000 York Road, Towson 21252, MD, USA
e-mail: kshifren@towson.edu

J.D. Sinnott (ed.), *Identity Flexibility During Adulthood*,
DOI 10.1007/978-3-319-55658-1_18

parents' view of religion). Identity moratorium involves exploration of alternative goals, actions, or decisions, but not making a commitment (e.g., individual is contemplating which job to accept). Identity diffusion involves no exploration and no commitment.

Over time other researchers have presented their own definitions of identity development (e.g., Berzonsky, 1990). For example, Waterman's (1984) definition of identity refers to the sense of personal identity, and this is a self-definition including the goals, values, and beliefs to which a person is passionately committed. In his early work, Waterman (1982) discussed the importance of parents, and parenting styles in relation to the development of one's identity, along with the amount of experiences that are available for individuals to have healthy role models and the importance of social expectations in identity development. Some researchers have compared theoretical and methodological differences in identity constructs and found similarity in results for instruments used in research, despite different theoretical approaches to identity development (Schwartz, Mullis, Waterman & Dunham, 2000). In the 1990s, Deaux (1993) argued that identity can be broken into two parts: personal identity and social identity. Deaux suggested that personal identity includes traits and behaviors that are self-descriptive and are associated with at least one of the identity categories. Deaux suggested that social identity includes our roles such as a daughter or teacher or membership in a group such as African. Others concur that social identity includes race, gender, religion, sexual orientation, etc. (Jones & McEwen, 2000). As we continue to refine our ability to measure identity development, the definition of identity development has been expanded and clarified, and it is likely to continue to do so. Over time many studies have been done on identity development (e.g., Sneed, Whitbourne & Culang, 2006; Waterman, 2015) including studies on women's identity development (Josselson, 1996), sexual identity (Parker & Yau, 2012), dual age identity in later adulthood (Weiss & Lang, 2009), spirituality and identity (Kiesling, Sorell, Montgomery & Colwell, 2008; Sinnott, 2002), and cultural, racial, and ethnic identity (Cross & Cross, 2008; Helms, 1990; Phinney, 1992; Smith & Silva, 2010; Willis, 2012).

Identity Flexibility

Some researchers argue that identity can change throughout the life-span (i.e., identity flexibility), with modifications of earlier identifications into a new identity, based, in part, on new experiences and changes in one's life (Erikson, 1968, 1980; Marcia, 1993). Our ability to adapt to change, to be able to modify the performance of our abilities such as our memory or physical strength, can be improved with practice or training. This ability to adapt to change or "plasticity" has been described as a key principle of life-span development (Baltes, 1987; Baltes, Lindenberger & Staudinger, 1998). Plasticity or flexibility in one's abilities is important contribution for healthy identity development.

Not all researchers agree with the idea of flexibility in identity development over the life-span. Some researchers argue that we all begin life with more flexibility, and we become more rigid as we age. Researchers using a neuroscience framework have suggested that individuals with healthy brains will show a cognitive shift in how they self-regulate their identity. Individuals will show changes in their identity, but then identity will become more continuous as they age because of a reduced capacity for their brain to allow change in their identity as they age (Tucker & Desmond, 1997). Tucker and Desmond do not suggest that there is no plasticity in the adult brain. Instead, they argue that there is a reduced level of plasticity. Brains may be less able to accommodate new data into existing brain networks as we age; consequently, we become more rigid in our identity.

Earlier research on identity development and plasticity did not include the newer technologies available today to assess the human brain. In some ways these two conflicting views are like comparing apples and oranges. One view is based on years of research involving interviews, surveys, and much paper and pencil assessments of identity development (e.g., Erikson, 1968, 1980) that still continues to this day (Lloyd, Bond & Flaxman, 2013; Sneed et al., 2006; Waterman, 2015). However, the other view, of less plasticity as we age, stems from the use of newer technology to better understand the human brain, the networks involved, and monitor such changes over time (Lockhart et al., 2015). Regardless of which view one might take, researchers do agree that some level of plasticity in the human brain is essential for our survival and healthy development. Individuals with more flexibility can deal better with situations, and better flexibility is associated with better mental health (Lloyd et al., 2013).

Identity flexibility has been defined in similar, though not identical ways, over the years. For instance, Grotevant, Thorbecke, and Meyer (1982) defined identity flexibility as a type of process that was deliberately done to compare an individual's current identity with other possible identities. Whitbourne (1986) defined identity flexibility as "the consideration of alternative identity involvements in the areas of family and work, or both simultaneously" (p. 166). Whitbourne found that individuals with more identity flexibility were more likely to make changes in their lives than those who showed less flexibility in their identity.

Whitbourne (1986) found that age predicted identity flexibility, with older adults (in this study individuals were 24–61 years old) being less flexible. In this early research on identity flexibility, Whitbourne argued that the older participants (i.e., middle-aged adults) in the study went through a process of adapting to their current situations, and they were able to accept the constraints of their age. However, education and employment played an important role too. Better educated individuals were more likely to attempt to alter their lives than those who have less education. Whitbourne also found that working women were more likely to make changes in their lives compared to women who did not work outside of the home.

There can be no doubt that the need to adapt to an ever-changing environment is most apparent when individuals find themselves in caregiver roles, and caregiving is an experience that can occur at any point in the life-span from childhood through older adulthood (Shifren, 2009). Depending on the kind of care recipient needs (acute versus chronic, mental, and/or physical health problems), caregivers may provide care for both basic (bathing, feeding, dressing) and instrumental (finances, shopping, housework) activities of daily living for care recipients, often with little or no warning. Caregiver roles can change quickly or slowly over time. Regardless of the pace of changes that occur, flexibility in one's identity is important in order to adapt to the caregiver role in a healthy manner (Montgomery & Kosloski, 2009; Savundranayagam & Montgomery, 2010).

Research from 2014 and earlier shows that approximately 66 million caregivers (i.e., 29 % of the US adult population) provide or have provided care to a relative, friend, or associate (The National Alliance for Caregiving and AARP, 2009). The most recent study on caregivers provides an estimated prevalence of caregiving for an adult at 16.6 %, or 39.8 million Americans, with females as the majority of caregivers (60 %), and the average age of caregivers at 49 years old (The National Alliance for Caregiving and AARP, 2015). There is also an estimate of 1.3–1.4 million young caregivers in the USA who experience the role of caregiver in childhood and/or adolescence (Hunt, Levine & Naiditch, 2005), and 3.6–5.5 million individuals between 18 and 29 years old were reported as caregivers in a national survey on young adult caregivers (Levine et al., 2005).

Because of this large percentage of individuals providing care for others, many researchers have conducted studies examining the relationship between a wide variety of variables including personality, social support, and coping techniques and the mental and physical health of caregivers for a variety of diseases and disorders. In fact, such an abundance of studies have been conducted that many literature reviews (e.g., Gardiner, Brereton, Frey, Wilkinson-Meyers & Gott, 2014; Nicholls, Hulbert-Williams & Bramwell, 2014) and meta-analyses (e.g., Jensen, Agbata, Canavan & McCarthy, 2015; Wang, Huang, Chou & Yu, 2015) have been performed to determine the strength and consistency of findings. Despite the plethora of research on caregivers, caregiver identity development research appears to be the focus of only a few studies within the USA (e.g., Montgomery & Kosloski, 2009, 2013) and abroad (e.g., Alpass et al., 2013; del Río-Lozano et al., 2013; Olson, 2015; Ranjbar, 2014). Below is a discussion of caregiver identity development and the limited research on this topic.

Caregiver Identity Development

When one takes on the role of caregiver, this includes changes in the caregiver's identity (Miller, Shoemaker, Willyard & Addison, 2008; Savundranayagam & Montgomery, 2010). The caregiver role may start as just an extension of a daughter's role or spouse's role in a family; however, this role may change to become more of a caregiver role over time, depending on the care recipient's needs. Not all caregiver experiences are the same, and some caregivers will not have much time to adjust to changes in their identity.

Researchers have eloquently described the process of caregiver identity in their ongoing research on this topic. Montgomery and colleagues (Montgomery, Rowe & Koslowski, 2007; Montgomery & Kosloski, 2009) developed caregiver identity theory, and they describe it in terms of five phases:

1. Begin to take on a task that was not part of your family role before this time.
2. Begin to view the tasks you are doing as part of a caregiver role rather than your original family role, and now view yourself as a caregiver.
3. When tasks become too difficult, and make both caregiver and care recipient uncomfortable, the caregiver may need to leave the caregiver role. If you don't leave the role, then over half of relationship is as a caregiver.
4. More demands as intensity of caregiving increases will make the person feel that the caregiver role is the main role in the relationship with care recipient.
5. Once care recipient is moved to a setting where others take over the role of caregiver, this will allow the caregiver to reduce the caregiver role (Montgomery & Kosloski, 2009, pp. 49–50).

Montgomery and colleagues (2007) and Montgomery and Kosloski (2009) have suggested that the caregiver role generally develops from the relationships that already exist within a family such as a spouse, a daughter, or a daughter-in-law. This is because family members tend to develop perceptions over time for which of the family members may be best suited for the caregiver role, and the norms of society and social role expectations affect these perceptions.

As many researchers have indicated, both gender and ethnicity, the amount that individuals perceive themselves as part of a specific ethnic group affects who is perceived as the person most capable of being the caregiver (del Río-Lozano, del Mar García-Calvente, Marcos-Marcos, Entrena-Durán & Maroto-Navarro, 2013; Josselson, 1996; Kramer, 2005; Lawrence, Murray, Samsi & Banerjee, 2008; Smith & Silva, 2010; Willis, 2012). Many societies view the role of caregiver as a woman's role, and researchers argue that being a caregiver is viewed as an extension of the responsibilities of a woman in the first place (Cala Santi & King, 2007; del Río-Lozano et al., 2013; Friedemann & Buckwalter, 2014). This perception of a caregiver as a "woman's role" includes very young girls (as young as 4 or 5 years of age) as caregivers for siblings and adult relatives (Shifren, 2009). There is also much evidence that one's ethnic identity plays a role in assumptions about caregivers (Alpass et al., 2013), with minority groups showing a perception of females as natural caregivers (Smith & Silva, 2010).

Montgomery and Kosloski (2013) believe that caregivers will evaluate their role to help them decide if this role is concurring with their own beliefs about the role of caregivers. If caregivers perceive their role is including more duties or responsibilities than caregivers thought was appropriate for their role, then this can lead to poor mental and physical health outcomes for caregivers. This may be true for ethnic minority caregivers as well (Phinney & Ong, 2007; Smith & Silva, 2010).

In addition to the work by Montgomery and colleagues, Coeling, Biordi, and Theis (2003) discuss a theory of caregiver and care receiver dyadic identity development as "A mutually agreed upon informal care dyadic identity is developed when both parties have negotiated or are continuing to negotiate, a set of rules about their conduct together in the caregiving and care receiving relationship" (p. 22). Unfortunately, not all of these relationships are mutually agreed upon between caregivers and care recipients. When they don't agree, or if it isn't even discussed, the relationship does become more stressful for both individuals (Coeling et al., 2003).

As stated previously in this chapter, there are few studies on caregiver identity development, despite the importance of this topic for caregiver research. Below is a discussion of research on caregiver identity development and flexibility in caregivers' identity.

Research on Caregiver Identity and Flexibility

One's ability to focus on a current situation, but then take actions when needed to achieve goals, may be crucial parts of psychological flexibility (Lloyd et al., 2013). It can be inferred that such flexibility in one's caregiver identity development may be a valuable contribution to maintaining positive aspects of mental and physical health, as can be seen by the research discussed next. Savundranayagam and Montgomery (2010) conducted a study with 358 spouse caregivers, with 68 % female and 32 % male caregivers, and the majority of the caregivers were Caucasian. In their cross-sectional study conducted with telephone interviews, Savundranayagam and Montgomery (2010) found that discrepancies between the caregiver's perceptions of his/her caregiver role mediated the relation between stressors and different types of burden assessed in their study. Though helping with activities of daily living may appear a burden to those not in the caregiver role, it only seems to relate to burden when viewed by the caregiver as going beyond his/her expectations about the role. Savundranayagam and Montgomery (2010) found that certain problem behaviors such as aggression and wandering were more stressful for the caregivers than helping with activities of daily living, and aggression and wandering exceeded the expectations about the caregiver role for the caregivers.

Friedemann and Buckwalter (2014) assessed 533 caregivers for older adults, and these caregivers included spouses and adult children and both men and women. Their sample included a diverse ethnic background including 12 % Black from Caribbean Islands, 30 % Cuban, and 18 % from other Hispanic countries. From the in-home interviews that were conducted, Friedmann and Buckwalter (2014) found that women provide more care than men, are more stressed than men, and have more depressive symptoms than men. Women appear to have a stronger emotional attachment to the care recipient, and women appear to be less flexible in their ability to adjust to the caregiver role compared to men. In fact, as the role demands increase, female caregivers provided care to the point of being emotionally and physically exhausted. Women, it seems, have less social support from others, in part, because they don't ask for the help. Also, less help is offered to women too (Brank & Wylie, 2014). It appears that women are at a disadvantage when it comes to the caregiver role.

Male caregivers appear able to avoid at least some of the emotional aspects of the situation, and they can focus on the tasks without the kind of problems that appear to occur with the female caregivers. Researchers argue that male caregivers maintain their "masculinity" by turning the caregiver role into a challenging role, and this challenging role allows them to feel proud of their accomplishments in this role (Friedemann & Buckwalter, 2014; Phinney, Dahlke & Purves, 2013). The findings of Friedemann and Buckwalter appear to support the idea of a "gendered" approach to caregiver identity (Montgomery & Kosloski, 2013).

This "gendered" approach to caregiver identity has been found in other studies too. del Río-Lozano et al. (2013) conducted semi-structured interviews with a Spanish sample of 16 men and 16 women in caregiver roles. They found that once women take on the caregiver role, they do not perceive themselves as able to pursue or have the opportunity for other roles. Female caregivers have less rest time than male caregivers, and they appear unable to protect their rest time. Women reported that as caregivers, they felt they stopped being their own person, and they stated they were "body parts for another person" (p. 1516). As suggested from findings in prior research (Friedemann & Buckwalter, 2014; Montgomery & Kosloski, 2013), del Río-Lozano et al. found that female caregivers won't ask for help and it leads to their own health issues. Male caregivers appear to be more flexible with how they are able to provide care, more willing to ask for help and/or delegate responsibilities for care than female caregivers. Male caregivers revealed that they try to avoid having the caregiver responsibilities affect their own health, something female caregivers seem unable to do. In a longitudinal study of both spouse caregivers ($n = 254$) and adult children caregivers ($n = 208$), caregivers reported a more positive view of the caregiver role when they were satisfied with the support offered to them in this role (Savundranayagam, 2014). If female caregivers won't ask for help and/or are not offered as much help as male caregivers, then it is not surprising that female caregivers may have poorer health outcomes than male caregivers. Unfortunately, whether caregiving demands are hidden intentionally or just not noticed by others, the lack of help from others can affect caregiver identity development in a negative way (Moore & Gillespie, 2014).

In addition to the importance of gender differences in caregivers, researchers have studied the role of cultural beliefs among caregivers too. Friedemann, Newman, Buckwalter, and Montgomery (2014) conducted a cross-sectional study with structured interviews on 613 caregivers, majority female (79 %), including White, Black, and Hispanic caregivers who were spouse, adult children, or other caregivers. Though they found that cultural beliefs helped predict how much tasks the caregivers performed for the care recipients, the care recipient needs were a better predictor of how much care was provided by the caregivers than their cultural beliefs.

Though there are few studies on caregiver identity development and flexibility in this identity, these studies have provided our first important understanding of how changes in identity or lack thereof can affect the caregiver's ability to provide care and maintain his/her own health. Perhaps one reason for so few studies on caregiver identity development has to do with the limited options for assessing this important construct. Below is a discussion of the assessment tools available for research on identity development and, more specifically, caregiver identity development.

Assessment of Caregiver Identity Development and Flexibility

Marcia developed a way to assess "identity statuses" with the identity status interview (Marcia, 1966, 1994, 2002). This was a semi-structured interview on personal identity and the process involved in the development of this identity, with the four identity statuses measured. Hauser (1971) used both interview questions and the Q-sort technique to study identity development. The development of interviews and the Q-sort technique has been helpful, but these techniques are also time consuming.

Over time other researchers have developed questionnaires for use in identity research. There are instruments available on identity development in general, identity development for women, racial identity, ethnic identity, sexual identity (see Moran, 2003 for assessment of a group of identity instruments), and vocational identity (Holland, Daiger & Power, 1980). Costos (1990) discussed gender role identity development and assessment (1990), in part, by adapting Waterman's sex role identity interview. Whitbourne (1986) measured identity flexibility with the adult identity interview which includes descriptions of one's identity with regard to work and family relations and questions on flexibility focus on consideration of any kind of change happening at the present time or in the future. Racial identity clusters have been created in research (Scottham & Smalls, 2009) using the multidimensional model of Black identity (Sellers, Smith, Shelton, Rowley & Chavous, 1998). There is also a well-known measure of multigroup ethnic identity (Phinney, 1992). Any of these measures may be useful for adaptation in caregiver identity development research.

However, most research on caregiver identity development is conducted with semi-structured or structured interviews including open-ended questions and some psychometrically sound measures of concepts related to identity development, roles, and discrepancy of roles. Sometimes researchers will test models including multiple components of caregiver identity theory. For example, Friedemann et al. (2014) created and tested a model that included beliefs about the caregiving role with the Caregiving Roles Instrument (Friedemann, 2009), measures of care recipient functioning assessed with measures of ADLs/IADLs and scores on a mental status exam, assessments of caregiver stress, caregiver workload, perceived need for resources, and resource use. Friedemann et al. then used structural equation modeling to assess their model. While this method may provide important theoretical contributions on caregiver identity development, it may also deter some researchers from conducting research on this important topic.

Thus, much like the early work on identity development which was time consuming, there may be a need to continue to develop assessments of caregiver identity development that are easy to use and provide an accurate and thorough assessment of this important construct. The development and validation of assessment techniques for caregiver identity development research is not an easy task. Researchers have critiqued many instruments intended to assess identity development (Evans, Forney & Guido-DiBrito, 1998), and they have found instruments lacking in psychometric properties. As others have argued, the study of identity development is not a simple task because it is multidimensional (Moran, 2003). Though it is a challenging endeavor, it is one worth the effort in helping us better understand factors that may benefit caregivers.

Directions for Future Research

It is very important when conducting research on caregiver identity flexibility to realize that not all individuals in a caregiver role identify as male or female (Washington et al., 2015; Wiseman & Davidson, 2011), and/or they may have an alternative sexual orientation (gay, lesbian, or bisexual). Those with alternative gender identity or sexual orientation may not have the same kind of support as caregivers with traditional gender identities and/or sexual orientation where both biological support and legal support are more likely to be available (Croghan, Moone, & Olson, 2014). Those with alternative gender identities or alternative sexual orientations may rely instead on friends for support when in a caregiver situation. It will be important for future studies to include caregivers of alternative gender identity and/or sexual identities in studies on caregiver identity development to determine the issues that affect their caregiver identity development.

Also, one's ethnic identity (Phinney, 1989, 1990; Phinney & Ong, 2007) should continue to be examined in future research, because ethnic identity may contribute at least some of the explanation for mental and physical health outcomes of caregivers (Alpass et al., 2013). Smith and Silva (2010) due caution that other variables such as age and acculturation may also play an important role in the relation between ethnic identity and well-being, so these variables should also be included when conducting future studies on caregiver identity development.

Conclusion

With the exception of work by a small group of researchers (e.g., Friedemann & Buckwalter, 2014; Montgomery & Kosloski, 2013; Savundranayagam, 2014), there appears to be a paucity of research on caregiver identity development, and the importance of flexibility in one's caregiver identity remains a topic worthy of further exploration. Ultimately, we need research that includes a life-span approach to the study of caregiver identity flexibility. The development of longitudinal studies including gender and ethnicity with other aspects of caregiver identity would be a timely contribution to caregiver research.

References

Alpass, F., Pond, R., Stephens, C., Stevenson, B., Keeling, S., & Towers, A. (2013). The influence of ethnicity and gender on caregiver health in older New Zealanders. *The Journals of Gerontology: Series B: Psychological Sciences and Social Sciences, 68B*, 683–693.

Baltes, P. B., Lindenberger, U., & Staudinger, U. M. (1998). Life-span theory in developmental psychology. In R. M. Lerner (Ed.), *Handbook of child psychology: Vol. 1. Theoretical models of human development* (5th ed., pp. 1029–1143). New York: Wiley.

Baltes, P. B. (1987). Theoretical propositions of life-span development psychology: On the dynamics between growth and decline. *Developmental Psychology, 23*, 611–626.

Berzonsky, M. D. (1990). Self-construction over the lifespan: A process perspective on identity formation. In G. J. Neimeyer & R. A. Neimeyer (Eds.), *Advances in personal construct theory* (Vol. 1, pp. 155–186). Greenwich, CT: JAI.

Brank, E. M. & Wylie, L.E. (2014). Differing perspectives on older adult caregiving, *Journal of Applied Gerontology, NLM ID*: 8606502.

Calasanti, T., & King, N. (2007). Taking 'women's work' 'like a man': Husband's experiences of care work. *The Gerontologist, 47*, 516–527. doi:10.1093/geront/47.4.516

Coeling, H. V., Biordi, D. L., & Theis, S. L. (2003). Negotiating dyadic identity between caregivers and care receivers. *Journal of Nursing Scholarship, 35*, 21–25.

Costos, D. (1990). Gender role identity from an ego developmental perspective. *Sex Roles, 22*, 723–741.

Croghan, C. F., Moone, R. P., & Olson, A. M. (2014). Friends, family, and caregiving among midlife and older lesbian, gay, bisexual, and transgender adults. *Journal of Homosexuality, 61*, 79–102. doi:10.1080/00918369.2013.835238.

Cross, W. E., Jr., & Cross, T. B. (2008). Theory, research, and models. In S. Quintana & C. McKown (Eds.), *Handbook of race, racism, and child development* (pp. 154–181). Hoboken, NJ: Wiley.

Deaux, K. (1993). Reconstructing social identity. *Personality and Social Psychology Bulletin, 19*, 4–12.

Del Río-Lozano, M., del Mar García-Calvente, M., Marcos-Marces, J., Entrena-Durán, F., & Maroto-Navarro, G. (2013). Gender identity in informal care: Impact on health in Spanish caregivers. *Qualitative Health Research, 23*, 1506–1520.

DeMars, C. E., & Erwin, T. D. (2004). Scoring "neutral or unsure" on an identity development instrument for higher education. *Research in Higher Education, 45*, 83–95.

Erikson, E. (1968). *Identity: Youth and crisis*. New York: Norton.

Erikson, E. H. (1980). *Identity and the life cycle*. New York: Norton.

Evans, N. J., Forney, D. S., & Guido-DiBrito, F. (1998). *Student development in college: Theory, research, and practice*. San Francisco: Jossey-Bass.

Friedemann, M. L. (2009). Culture, family patterns and caregiver resource use. (Final Study Report, Project SO6GM08205). In *National Institute of General Medical Sciences*. Washington, DC.

Friedemann, M.-L., Newman, F. L., Buckwalter, K. C., & Montgomery, R. J. V. (2014). Resource need and use of multiethnic caregivers of elders in their homes. *Journal of Advanced Nursing, 70*, 662–673. doi:10.1111/jan.12230.

Friedemann, M.-L., & Buckwalter, K. C. (2014). Family caregiver role and burden related to gender and family relationships. *Journal of Family Nursing, 20*, 313–336.

Gardiner, C., Brereton, L., Frey, R., Wilkinson-Meyers, L., & Gott, M. (2014). Exploring the financial impact of caring for family members receiving palliative and end-of-life care: A systematic review of the literature. *Palliative Medicine, 28*, 375–390. doi:10.1177/0269216313510588.

Grotevant, H. D., Thorbecke, W., & Meyer, M. L. (1982). An extension of Marcia's identity status interview into the interpersonal domain. *Journal of Youth and Adolescence, 11*, 33–47.

Hauser, S. T. (1971). *Black and white identity formation*. New York: Wiley-Interscience.

Helms, J. E. (1990). *Black and white racial identity: Theory, research, and practice*. Westport, CT: Praeger.
Holland, J. L., Daiger, D. C., & Power, P. G. (1980). *My vocational situation*. Palo Alto, CA: Consulting Psychologists Press.
Hunt, G., Levine, C., & Naiditch, L. (2005). *Young caregivers in the U.S.: Findings from a national survey*. Bethesda, MD: National Alliance for Caregiving, in collaboration with the United Hospital Fund. Available online at 222.uhfnyc.org.
Jensen, M., Agbata, I. N., Canavan, M., & McCarthy, G. (2015). Effectiveness of educational interventions for informal caregivers of individuals with dementia residing in the community: Systematic review and meta-analysis of randomized controlled trials. *International Journal of Geriatric Psychiatry, 30*, 130–153.
Jones, S. R., & McEwen, M. K. (2000). A conceptual model of multiple dimensions of identity. *Journal of College Student Development, 41*, 405–414.
Josselson, R. (1987). *Finding herself: Pathways to identity development in women*. San Francisco: Jossey-Bass.
Josselson, R. (1996). *Revising herself: The story of women's identity from college to midlife*. London: Oxford University Press.
Kiesling, S., Motgomery, & Colwell. (2008). Identity and spirituality: A psychosocial exploration of the sense of spiritual self. *Psychology of Religion and Spirituality, 5*, 50–62. doi:10.1037/1941-1022.S.1.50.
Kramer, M. K. (2005). Self-characterizations of adult female informal caregivers: Gender identity and the bearing of burden. *Research and Theory for Nursing Practice, 19*(2), 137–161.
Levine, C., Hunt, G. G., Halper, D., Hart, A. Y., Lautz, J., & Gould, D. A. (2005). Young adult caregivers: A first look at an unstudied population. *American Journal of Public Health, 95*, 2071–2075.
Lawrence, V., Murray, J., Samsi, K., & Banerjee, S. (2008). Attitudes and support needs of black Caribbean, South Asian and white British carers of people with dementia in the UK. *British Journal of Psychiatry, 193*, 240–246.
Lloyd, J., Bond, F. W., & Flaxman, P. E. (2013). The value of psychological flexibility: Examining psychological mechanisms underpinning a cognitive behavioral therapy intervention for burnout. *Work and Stress, 27*, 181–199.
Lockhart, S. N., Luck, S. J., Geng, J., Beckett, L., Disbrow, E. A., Carmichael, O., & DeCarli, C. (2015). White matter hyperintensities among older adults are associated with futile increase in frontal activation and functional connectivity during spatial search. *PLoS ONE, 10*, doi:10.1371/journal.pone.0122445
Marcia, J. E. (1966). Development and validation of ego-identity status. *Journal of Personality and Social Psychology, 3*, 551–558.
Marcia, J. E. (1993). The ego identity status approach to ego identity. In J. E. Marcia, A. S. Waterman, D. R. Matteson, S. L. Archer, & J. L. Orlofsky (Eds.), *Ego identity: A handbook for psychosocial research* (pp. 3–41). New York: Springer-Verlag.
Marcia, J. E. (1994). Ego identity and object relations. In J. Masling & R. Bornstein (Eds.), *Empirical approaches to object relation theory* (pp. 59–103). Washington, DC: American Psychological Association.
Marcia, J. E. (2002). Identity and psychosocial development in adulthood. *Identity: An International Journal of Theory and Research, 2*, 7–29.
Miller, K. I., Shoemaker, M. M., Willyard, J., & Addison, P. (2008). Providing care for elderly parents: A structurational approach to family caregiver identity. *Journal of Family Communication, 8*, 19–43.
Montgomery, R., Rowe, J., & Kosloski, K. (2007). Family caregiving. In J. Blackborn & K. Dulmus (Eds.), *Handbook of gerontology: Evidence-based approaches to theory, practice, and policy* (pp. 426–454). New York: Wiley.

Montgomery, R. J. V., & Kosloski, K. (2009). Caregiving as a process of changing identity: Implications for caregiver support. *Generations: Journal of the American Society on Aging, 33*, 47–52.
Montgomery, R. J., & Kosloski, K. D. (2013). Pathways to a caregiver identity and implications for support services. In R. D. Talley & R. J. Montgomery (Eds.), *Caregiving across the life span: Research practice and policy* (pp. 131–156). New York: Springer.
Moore, H., & Gillespie, A. (2014). The caregiving bind: Concealing the demands of informal care can undermine the caregiving identity. *Social Science and Medicine, 116*, 102–109.
Moradi, B., & Subich, L. M. (2002). Feminist identity development measures: Comparing the psychometrics of three instruments. *The Counseling Psychologist, 30*, 66–86.
Moran, C. D. (2003). Conceptualizing identity development: Unmasking the assumptions within inventories measuring identity development. *NASPA Journal, 40*, 43–55.
Nicholls, W., Hulbert-Williams, N., & Bramwell, R. (2014). The role of relationship attachment in psychological adjustment to cancer in patients and caregivers: A systematic review of the literature. *Psycho-Oncology, 23*, 1083–1095.
Olson, R. E. (2015). Exploring identity in the "figured worlds" of cancer care-giving and marriage in Australia. *Health and Social Care in the Community, 23*, 171–179.
Parker, M. G., & Yau, M. K. (2012). Sexuality, identity and women with spinal cord injury. *Sex Disability, 30*, 15–27.
Phinney, J. S. (1989). Stages of ethnic identity development in minority group adolescents. *Journal of Early Adolescence, 9*, 34–49. doi:10.1177/0272431689091004.
Phinney, J. S. (1990). Ethnic identity in adolescents and adults: A review of research. *Psychological Bulletin, 108*, 499–514.
Phinney, J. S. (1992). The Multigroup ethnic identity measure: A new scale for use with diverse groups. *Journal of Adolescent Research, 7*, 156–176.
Phinney, A., Dahlke, S., & Purves, B. (2013). Shifting patterns of everyday activity in early dementia: Experiences of men and their families. *Journal of Family Nursing, 19*, 348–374. doi:10.1177/1074840713486727
Phinney, J. S., & Ong, A. (2007). Conceptualization and measurement of ethnic identity: Current status and future directions. *Journal of Counseling Psychology, 54*, 271–281. doi:10.1037/0022-0167.54.3.271.
Ranjbar, V. (2014). The HIV/AIDS caregiver identity ad a double-edged sword: A discourse analysis on HIV/AIDS caregiving in South Africa. *African Journal of AIDS Research, 13*, 261–269.
Savundranayagam, M. Y. (2014). Receiving while giving: The differential roles of receiving help and satisfaction with help on caregiver rewards among spouses and adult-children. *International Journal of Geriatric Psychiatry, 29*, 41–48.
Savundranayagam, M. Y., & Montgomery, R. J. V. (2010). Impact of role discrepancies on caregiver burden among spouses. *Research on Aging, 32*, 175–199.
Schwartz, S. J., Mullis, R. L., Waterman, A. S., & Dunham, R. M. (2000). Ego identity status, identity style, and personal expressiveness: An empirical investigation of three convergent constructs. *Journal of Adolescent Research, 15*, 504–521.
Scottham, K. M., & Smalls, C. P. (2009). Unpacking racial socialization: Considering female African American primary caregivers' racial identity. *Journal of Marriage and Family, 71*, 807–818.
Sellers, R. M., Smith, M. A., Shelton, J. N., Rowley, S. J., & Chavous, T. M. (1998). Multidimensional model of racial identity: A reconceptualization of African American racial identity. *Personality and Social Psychology Review, 2*, 18–36.
Shifren, K. (Ed.). (2009). *How caregiving affects development: Psychological implications for child, adolescent, and adult caregivers*. Washington, DC: American Psychological Association.
Sinnott, J. D. (2002). Introduction. *Journal of Adult Development, 9*, 199–200.
Smith, T. B., & Lynda Silva, L. (2010). Ethnic identity and personal well-being of people of color: A meta-analysis. *Journal of Counseling Psychology, 58*, 42–60.
Sneed, J. R., Whitbourne, S. K., & Culang, M. E. (2006). Trust, identity, and ego integrity: Modeling Erikson's core stages over 34 years. *Journal of Adult Development, 13*, 148–157. doi:10.1007/s10804-007-9026-3.

The National Alliance for Caregiving and AARP. (2009). Caregiving in the U.S. National Alliance for Caregiving. Washington, DC.
The National Alliance for Caregiving and the AARP Public Policy Institute. (2015). Caregiving in the U.S. 2015. http://www.caregiving.org/caregiving2015/
Tucker, D. M., & Desmond, R. E., Jr. (1997). Aging and the plasticity of the self. In K. W. Schaie's & M. P. Lawton's (Eds.), *Annual Review of Gerontology and Geriatrics, vol. 17* (pp. 266–281). New York: Springer Publishing Company.
Wang, T.-F., Huang, C.-M., Chou, C., & Yu, S. (2015). Effect of oral health education programs for caregivers on oral hygiene of the elderly: A systemic review and meta-analysis. *International Journal of Nursing Studies, 52*, 1090–1096.
Washington, K. T., McElroy, J., Albright, D., Oliver, D. P., Lewis, A., Meadows, S., et al. (2015). Experiences of sexual and gender minorities caring for adults with non-AIDS-related chronic illnesses. *Social Work Research, 39*, 71–81.
Waterman, A. S. (1982). Identity development from adolescence to adulthood: An extension of theory and a review of research. *Developmental Psychology, 18*, 341–358.
Waterman, A. S. (1984). Identity formation: Discovery or creation? Journal of Early Adolescence, 4, 329–341.
Waterman, A. S. (2015). In K. C. McClean & M. Syed (Ed.), *The Oxford handbook of identity development* (pp. 195–209). Oxford: Oxford University Press.
Weiss, D., & Lang, F. R. (2009). Thinking about my generation: Adaptive effects of a dual age identity in later adulthood. *Psychology and Aging, 24*, 729–734.
Whitbourne, S. K. (1986). *The me I know: A study of adult identity*. New York: Springer.
Willis, R. (2012). Individualism, collectivism, and ethnic identity: Cultural assumptions in accounting for caregiving behavior in Britain. *Journal of Cross Cultural Gerontology, 27*, 201–216.
Wiseman, M., & Davidson, S. (2011). Problems with binary gender discourse: Using context to promote flexibility and connection in gender identity. *Clinical Child Psychology and Psychiatry, 17*, 528–537. doi:10.1177/1359104511424991.

Chapter 19
Dual Identities and the Artist: A Personal Reflection

Valerie A. Smith

The following is a synopsis to illustrate how my personal experiences helped me to develop my artistic style and ability to integrate within specific groups.

Over the years of trying to "fit in" with my peers, my creative abilities suffered. I wanted to be like everybody else; however, my solutions to problems and the way I thought were very different. As I matured, I accepted the fact that I am different from others.

I am an illustrator and a painter who creates colorful surrealist artwork. I am the storyteller who entertains with witty and funny stories of what I've done, seen, or heard. I am the woman who tried so hard to belong.

I began my creative activities very early in life. Since I was a child, I dreamed of becoming a world-renowned artist. I grew up in the poorer section of New York where there were people of all races and religions living as neighbors. Communicating with other children my age was difficult because either I did not speak their languages or I was just too shy to make friends.

When I was a teenager, my family moved to Baltimore, and, being in a new environment, it took some time for me to adjust to the stark differences between the South Bronx and Northwest Baltimore. For me, everything was different: the weather, the people, the sights, and smells. I became a loner in my new environment; I felt lost and out of place. The change presented a challenge for me: to relate with, and to be accepted by, other teenagers in my neighborhood. As time passed, I began to acclimate myself to the differences. Still very shy and self-contained, I had problems connecting with others my age.

At 15, I began dating and at 16, I became a single parent. I was transferred from my high school to the school for unwed mothers. My family and four younger siblings were not very supportive. I felt so alone with my pregnancy. All I thought about was the shame and pain of being singled out and taunted. The change of

V.A. Smith (✉)
Utopian Dreamer, Artist's Closet, Baltimore, MD, USA
e-mail: utopiandreamer1954@gmail.com

J.D. Sinnott (ed.), *Identity Flexibility During Adulthood*,
DOI 10.1007/978-3-319-55658-1_19

schools with its change of atmosphere was devastating to me. I became reclusive and my anger grew into silence. I talked to no one for a solid year. I graduated high school to begin my life as a young single parent, a new learning experience for me.

Being a young mother and working greatly stifled my creative thought. I worked many places, mainly in sub-shops and stores and basically stayed to myself. At 18, I moved out away from my family leaving my daughter with my mother to care for while I continued to work and learn how to take care of myself.

As I worked and learned, my horizons stretched to other aspects of work. I discovered that my inborn talent was having a strong sense for intricate details and a love for colors. I was given opportunities to study in the fields of Architectural Design, Secretarial School, the Maryland Institute of Art and Basic Electronics. However, the catch was that the state paid for only 1 year in each course. I excelled in each of the classes that I studied. But because I still felt intimidated and afraid to express myself, I was faced with a special communications challenge within each of the four social groups that I joined.

Immediately after getting a certificate in basic electronics, I was hired with a company that repaired Xeroxes, dictating machines and small electronic equipment. I was faced with the challenge of comfortably talking to the older white men I worked with. Frequently, I was chosen to do repair calls at outside companies, which kept me out of the office. When the novelty of having a young black woman repairing electronic equipment wore off, given my lack of cultural knowledge and discipline, my job ended.

Being equipped with basic technical knowledge and a quick learner, I applied for temporary technical jobs. I quickly learned to become versatile and to meet each trial with enthusiasm. I felt that I had no concrete direction, and no stability, but my creativity grew in spite of the cultural and communications barriers I faced. My paintings took on a new surreal look with a distinct flair for architectural-mechanical design. But I was no Frank Lloyd Wright and few thought I had any real talent in that direction.

Within the next few years, I fell in love and had another daughter shortly. Now I was a single parent with two girls by my side. Without very much money, we lived in the poorer sections of Baltimore where people did not go to plays, listen to jazz sets, or read poetry. Learning to survive with two children left no time for creativity. Still I tried to hold on to what I learned and dabbled a bit.

In spite of the obstacles that I faced daily, I began to have concrete ideas of which direction I wanted to take my creative work. However, my limited communications skills and discipline made it harder for me. I found myself indifferent to working in standard jobs and work became only a means of support for myself and my two girls. I had many different types of jobs, just to make ends meet.

As my girls grew, I found the time to attend a commercial art school, which greatly honed my talent for detailed pencil work and the ability to see objects and situations others take for granted. I studied in the commercial arts school for 3 years and graduated with honors. Shortly afterwards, I was hired in a temporary position to do blue-lined pencil work to be photographed for manuals for the armed services. There, I learned different types of skills, and I polished the skills that I learned at the

Professional School of Commercial Art. I belonged to a group of drafting engineers, a very prestigious group.

At 35 years old, I accepted employment at an insurance company. I traded my dreams of becoming an artist for studying to become an insurance agent. I joined the "Toastmasters Club," because I wanted to be able to effectively communicate with others outside of the area where I lived.

While working at the insurance company, I was asked to create the "data deputy" character to help raise the morale of the data entry employees. A stuffed motif and posters of my rendering of a kangaroo with boxing gloves was created and passed around the company. I received recognition and an award for my efforts.

After the insurance company sold out to a larger insurance company, I lost my interest in being an insurance agent and I was laid off. While unemployed, I began pulling from my previous training with computers and secretarial abilities. I started a home business of resume writing to supplement my income. Even though my resume writing business was short-lived, I did well.

I was hired at Towson University as an in-house temporary employee, beginning in the math department and moving to a permanent position in the registrar's office. Shortly afterwards, I applied for the secretary position at the chemistry department and have been there since.

Initially, it was a difficult task to become a member of such an elite group of scientists and chemists. I worked very hard to understand and to be understood not as a black woman but as an individual with special skills and creative ideas. The task was arduous and my communications skills suffered greatly. In spite of so many failures in my previous employments, I refused to let anything get in the way of having a career with Towson University.

Slowly, I began to discipline myself, and I learned to pronounce my words completely and correctly. Most importantly, I learned to express myself and change my attitude toward people from other cultures. Gradually, I peeled away my cloak of ignorance about the world around me; I began to blossom and became more sure of myself.

While employed at Towson University Department of Chemistry, I began working on the weekends at the Marriott Inn as a server/waitress. This was a new adventure for me to work with this diverse group of people in the food service industry. There I rose to the rank of carver-server and sometimes bartender. I took extra pride in my work and I began to notice the small changes in myself. I was becoming self-assured and confident. I worked there for 3 years until my back began to bother me.

After being employed at Towson University for 13 years, my breakthrough arrived. That's when I presented my art work as a "one-woman" show. Everyone inside and outside of the department enjoyed viewing my paintings and listening to my poetry. I had one hour of fame, it was all I needed to begin breaking down the communications barriers with my colleagues. As an administrative assistant and receptionist, I needed to communicate on different levels with many different people from many cultures. I became more at ease while conversing.

I met a special person who appreciated my art and showed a deep understanding of my personal struggles. We became great friends. He introduced me to the other side of culture. Through him I met people who enjoy the arts and understood me and my art. He enlightened and urged me to exhibit my work; he taught me how to communicate and understand others that are involved in music, art, and the entertainment fields. He inspired me, even when I felt that I was too shy to communicate about my artistic ability. He encouraged me to believe in myself and to overcome obstacles that prevented me from progressing in my work. Sadly, he passed away a couple of years ago and I miss him greatly. I made a promise to him and myself that I would keep going and not drop the ball, so to speak.

Presently, I am active in volunteering to usher at different playhouses around the city. I am an active member of three different galleries and have a number of showings around the city on a monthly basis. I belong to a creative writer's club, where I once read a story that I wrote to a group in the Poe Room of the main library and I got a standing ovation. I learned to create opportunities for myself to show my work. I learned to be prepared to take advantage of each opportunity offered.

Dual Identities and the Artist

Sometimes I feel like I am leading a double life, one part in the office and the other in my studio and in the galleries. I arrive at work every day as the problem solver, innovator, and communicator. Everyday there is a different chore that I am called upon to perform.

In the evenings when I am creating and dreaming, I become the dreamer, and the creator, making my surreal dreams come to life. Other times, at the galleries, I am the cool collective artist showing my work and discussing the problems of the world as I see them. My life is never humdrum or boring as I weave my way from one identity to another.

Through my struggle to understand and be understood, I have become the versatile woman, the conversationalist, the artist, and the employee. I am nothing at all like I was a few years ago, afraid to speak to an audience of any size.

Today, I will gladly tell my story on stage if asked. I am also identified as an African-American female, daughter, mother, and grandmother who gives advice, hugs, and kisses without thinking about it.

To change like a chameleon from one social group to another takes time and courage. One must discover the common thread between herself and each group. I tend to focus on the common interests that are shared in each group and share that interest with other groups that I am involved in. I meet each person with a willingness to listen and to offer advice. This allows me to form a mutual relationship and respect with each group. I learned to speak with anyone at any level of conversation and anyone can speak with me.

Most importantly, I believe in myself as an artist. My creativity and work ethics has blossomed and continues to grow. The discipline necessary for producing art begins early in life with regular daily practice, the learning of techniques, the development of insight, and the accumulation of experience, which gradually builds up.

The furtherance of a career in art then depends as much on the artist's personal qualities and planning as it does on serendipity. Unconventional artists, with aging, may blossom into creativity by mellowing, with a serenity that assists in integrating their concepts and interpretations. They may maintain a wave of optimism and freshness, which may result in a renaissance of their careers. Alternatively, while the artist may be creative at 40 or 50 years of age, this may be followed by a decline in productivity for a variety of causes: depression, divorce, death of a spouse, economic reverses, family strife, political refuge, to name a few, with a subsequent latter peak of creativeness and productivity at age 75–85 (Simonton, 1989a, 1989b). This may happen to me too.

References

Simonton, D. K. (1989a). Age and creative productivity: Nonlinear estimation of an information-processing model. *International Journal of Aging and Human Development, 29*, 23–37.

Simonton, D. K. (1989b). Creativity and individual development. In T. Husen & T. N. Postlethwaite (Eds.), *International encyclopedia of education: Supplementary volume one* (pp. 181–184). New York: Pergamon Books.

Chapter 20
The Sick Self: A Personal Reflection

Elizabeth Stellhorn

On an icy day in February 2015, my orthopedist called me about an MRI done hours before for some troubling back pain I'd experienced for months. In one sentence, he plunged me into the ultimate alien territory: "Your MRI shows evidence of cancer in the [back] bones."

I had always taken a smug and slightly superior attitude toward the disease. "Nobody in my family has gotten it." It was true; there had been no cancer among my parents, sibling, grandparents, aunts, uncles, cousins. The only thing that ran in my family was longevity. I called a friend who was a nurse practitioner (NP). She came over shortly, stayed a long time, and listened patiently to me talk and cry noisily as she tried to be reassuring.

Less than 2 weeks later, my diagnosis of multiple myeloma (MM), a blood cancer that attacks the bones, was confirmed. MM is a highly treatable, but ultimately incurable, cancer with widely varying prognoses from a few years to 15- or 20-year survival rates. Over the coming weeks and months, I vacillated from calm to angry denial and everything in between. It was months before I stopped thinking I'd wake up from a bad dream. What kind of pain from symptoms or treatment awaited me? There was anger and grief at possible future missed travel and relationship opportunities. Would I not see my grandchildren grow up, not know where they'd go to college; would I die before they would have clear memories of me? What records of memories could I leave them? What did I still want to tell my children? What did I want to do, write, and see, before it was too late?

Our society has long had a set of unspoken expectations for a "sick" person. One is usually treated with a kind forbearance by people who are aware of one's condition. One is not expected to be as productive to society as a "well" person. On the positive side, I found with surprise that a world of privileges was accorded to me, from a handicapped parking pass to ease of getting new prescriptions filled to

E. Stellhorn (✉)
LCSW-C, private praactice, 15107 Interlachen Drive #506, Silver Spring, MD 20906, USA
e-mail: elizabeth.stellhorn@gmail.com

J.D. Sinnott (ed.), *Identity Flexibility During Adulthood*,
DOI 10.1007/978-3-319-55658-1_20

friends in social groups easily letting me off the hook when it was my turn to host an event. When I found a local organization that was dedicated exclusively to free services for cancer patients, my reaction was twofold. Some of the support groups were extremely helpful. Other times, on the negative side, I hated that the elegant old mansion that housed the organization contained a world of activities unto itself, as though I was now sequestered into Cancer World. After a yoga class one morning, I went into the restroom and shed tears. Does having cancer mean I have to have exercise classes only in Cancer World? I couldn't stand one more (what seemed to be) sappy smile from the staff. I left the building, feeling compelled to go and be in the "real" world of Starbucks, Barnes, and Nobel and everyday tasks. I was to remain highly conflicted for a long time about accepting the strange perks of illness which were both helpful and stigmatizing and humiliating at the same time.

Soon after the initial diagnosis, I was reading an x-ray report of my whole skeletal system. I had always had strong bones, even postmenopause. Reading the report describes the "lytic lesions" in my back and in one place in the skull, and "diffuse osteopenia (thinning of bone tissue) throughout" was oddly helpful and grounding. For some reason, my wise mind was calmly beginning to accept impermanence, to accept the new state. This damaged skeleton was now "me," damaged literally down to my bones. As we discuss important feelings, we often say, "I feel it deep down in my bones," or "I've got a sense in my bones about …." If something was indeed in my bones, my basic frame of being, it was indeed real. I had been a meditator and this was my first experience of a Buddhist perspective on my illness; "this too," meaning, yes, this can happen even to me, as it could to anyone in this constantly changing life. The core concept of impermanence, basic to Buddhist philosophy, resonated in a new way. Oh, so it's like this now.

I began what was to be a 6-month long regimen of weekly chemotherapy. For the most part, I felt well, with the exception of Friday, the day immediately following chemo, when nausea was my constant buddy. Usually then, I awoke Saturdays feeling just fine. Despite being aware of what was to come and planning for it, I was struck by the intense emotional neediness and general pessimism that occurred on Fridays and my sense of victimhood. Every 4 weeks, a blood draw would reveal my progress in treatment and I began to focus my self-esteem around what number my kappa light chains were to be that month. Despite having been told by the oncologist's P.A. that it wasn't uncommon for the number to occasionally plateau or even to increase slightly, I was crushed the first time it occurred and endured a long period of misery before the next draw, which happily showed another drop. When others in my support group reported progress that was significantly greater than mine, I would outwardly express happiness for them and inwardly feel like a middle schooler wondering why her acne was worse than the next girl's.

Choosing to disclose one's illness, or not, has had a profound impact on my sense of self. Many cancer patients I've talked with have told me they were highly selective as to whom they told about their diagnosis. I was the opposite. As difficult as it was to tell friends and some emotionally fragile relatives, I felt myself on a dogged path to tell almost everyone I knew. I think this was a way to make the diagnosis real to me. The idea of having cancer was so alien that it wouldn't be real unless everyone

I knew also knew about it as well. My fragile self/ego couldn't contain the knowledge alone. It was as though I wanted to be in a hall of mirrors and needed the fact of my illness reflected back to me constantly. But one can divulge excessively. At first, I talked at length to my NP friend. Then I realized I had confided too much in her and treated her like a spouse or therapist. A few months later, she angrily accused me of "using" my illness for "secondary gain." She actually criticized me for not looking nice one evening while at a restaurant. My hair was thinning, I had no makeup (I'd had to throw all the old stuff out due to risk of contamination), and I wore my glasses because I'd lost a contact lens. She claimed I was doing it to get attention, to be "melodramatic." I decided to cease discussing the topic of my illness with her altogether. While this choice was self-protective, it intensified the sense of isolation of my sick self. For the first time in a very long time, I missed not having a spouse or partner.

Periods of peace and awareness alternated with inner conflict. I couldn't shake the notion that my body had betrayed me. There was preoccupation with my inability to do simple tasks, pleasures that formed parts of my identity. This illness had made me so "NOT me." I couldn't go for long hikes anymore and couldn't swim without back pain, and I was worried about possible discomfort during active travel. Reduced work hours due to fatigue left me with less money; thus, there were even more things I could no longer do because of financial constraints. I would look at strangers around me, my nose metaphorically pressed against the glass, with a curious envy at their (apparent) good health. My "self" was becoming a small, secretive, pinched-off version of who I used to be. I carried a hidden, awful fact when out in public that made me different from all the healthy strangers around me.

Buddhist teachings again became useful here. The Buddha spoke of the three marks of existence: *dukkha*, or chronic unsatisfactoriness; *anicca*, or impermanence; and *anatta*, meaning insubstantiality or non-self. I began to realize that "my" cancer was really "the" cancer, a condition that, after all, will manifest itself in one out of every three or four people over a lifetime. A useful thought has been to remind myself, when out in public, that there are undoubtedly people in the same store/restaurant/parking lot with me, who have cancer as well. Compassion and awareness, also Buddhist concepts, began to gently flower. From that perspective, the small, pinched-off self gradually began to dissolve into a wider, almost welcoming, environment. It was the sense of relief one feels when kicking off a too-tight shoe or when, after some hesitation, one dives into a body of water and immediately feels the delicious sense of cool weightlessness and calm.

Several years before I was in quiet misery over a recently broken romantic relationship. I began a session with a therapy client inwardly wondering how I could possibly help her when preoccupied with my own grief. Our session had barely begun when she burst into heavy sobbing over a multiplicity of troubles. As I looked at her, I experienced a type of profound relief. It was as though a great warm ocean of sadness had poured into the room and surrounded us, she at one end of the body of water and I at the other, yet both in it together. It was no longer "my" grief or "her" grief. It was grief, sad, warm, universal, and reassuring. I was no longer my pinched-off self in quiet misery but warmly bathed in a common ocean.

Sometimes the sheer normality of my life, despite the changes, surprised me. Planning for a stem cell transplant in late October, I took a hiatus from work in September to prepare for the myriad screenings and other preparations necessary before hospitalization. Ultimately I was off work for nearly 4 months, by far my longest absence in over 25 years. Despite some unpleasant side effects of treatment, I grew attached to the idea of not working and began to dread returning. However, within a few weeks of resuming, it was as though I'd never left. I had had to take 4 months off to realize how bored I had become at home. During my absence, only two clients decided to stay with their interim therapists, and poignantly, one, a woman younger than myself, died unexpectedly of diabetic complications. But I remained.

We all wonder and fantasize at times about when our end will come and how. Due to the genes of my ancestors, I always assumed I'd someday develop coronary artery disease and congestive heart failure or have a series of strokes that would gradually usher me out of the world. Having worked in nursing homes, I worried about the possibility of someday being a resident of one. I had dreaded the possibility of dementia. There is now a strange sense of relief that I probably won't live to see that happen. Probably, no diapers or wheelchairs for me, no Alzheimer's disease, and no lonely waiting in the nursing home for family to dutifully pay a visit. No having to live to see all my friends die off one by one, leaving me behind. Instead, says fate, you get this: Hmm. Oh, so this is what I get. This is how my body will ultimately, gently, remind me that I'm mortal. A calm peace says: oh, OK, I have this. Everyone will have something, and I got this one. A whole raft of diseases lurks benevolently, and we all will get one, or a few, of them.

A year out, there are times I don't recognize the non-sick self I once was. Gone is the sense of entitlement, of outrage, of how dare fate throw me this curve ball? All around us, curve balls are flying, whether to a Syrian refugee, to a homeless person, to an accident victim, or to a patient with diabetes, Parkinson's, cancer, or ALS. I like to think there are things we as a society can do to help the refugees and the homeless whose fates are driven by policy rather than disease. We can also hopefully work for research policies of drug development and distribution that are not based on greed.

And I still think wistfully sometimes of the healthy, active, gray-haired grandmother in her early 80s. I once thought I'd be, interacting with teenage grandchildren and getting to see their high school or college graduations and perhaps even their weddings. There's a statistical possibility I could be that grandma, but I no longer take it for granted. I remain immersed in this process and will be for a long time to come.

Chapter 21
"Just When I Knew All of Life's Answers, They Changed the Questions": A Eudaimonist Perspective on Identity Flexibility During the Adult Years

Alan S. Waterman

Among the creators of "grand theories" of personality, Erik Erikson (1963, 1968) advanced the theory most attuned to understanding development changes across the life span. His epigenetic, eight-stage theory of psychosocial development contained a recognition that while each personality component had its "time of special ascendency," each was manifested in different ways at every stage of development. Thus, change and flexibility with respect to personality is inherent with respect to virtually all aspects of how we function throughout our lives. No matter how much we might wish it to be otherwise, we cannot be the same person at age 50 that were at 30 (or whatever other pair of ages could be placed within this sentence). The greater the distance in time between the ages that could be placed in the preceding sentence, the greater the likely difference between how we live. Consistent with the theme of this volume, in this chapter I will focus on the nature of identity changes during adulthood, the challenges changes pose for psychological well-being, and role of identity flexibility in adapting to inevitable changes in identity over time.

Two theoretical perspectives will guide the analysis of identity flexibility I advance here. The first is Erikson's theory of psychosocial development, both as a broad theory for understanding change across the life span and specifically with respect to his conceptualization of identity functioning during Stage V (identity vs. role confusion) and Stage VI (generativity vs. stagnation) (Erikson, 1963; 1982). The second is eudaimonic identity theory (Waterman, 2011; Waterman & Schwartz, 2013), a theory of well-being integrating aspects of Erikson's theorizing with philosophical eudaimonism as represented in the work of both classical and contemporary eudaimonist philosophers.

A.S. Waterman (✉)
Department of Psychology, The College of New Jersey, Ewing Township, NJ, USA
e-mail: archerwater@tds.net

J.D. Sinnott (ed.), *Identity Flexibility During Adulthood*,
DOI 10.1007/978-3-319-55658-1_21

Identity and Identity Flexibility

Since the time when Erikson brought the concept of identity to fore as a central aspect for understanding personality functioning, the term has morphed in many ways to cover aspects of psychological functioning that I suspect Erikson would not recognize as being part of the construct that was the focus of his attention. For this reason, it is important that the term be explicitly defined here so that readers will be aware of how it is being used in this chapter.

Identity refers to a person's self-definition, in terms of goals, values, and beliefs, whether developed through a process of conscious choice, identification with significant others, or ascription, that provide direction, purpose, and meaning in life. This definition covers three aspects of identity functioning: (a) the content of identity (i.e., goals, values, and beliefs), (b) the processes of identity formation (i.e., choice, identification, and ascription), and (c) the motivational functions of identity (i.e., providing direction, purpose, and meaning). This definition is not intended to exclude other possible definitions of identity; rather it is a reflection of my particular concerns as a psychological theorist and researcher.

The developmental task of establishing identity-defining goals, values, and beliefs occurs in a variety of life domains including, but not limited to, vocation, gender role expression and sexuality, family life, religion and philosophical values, political orientation, ethnicity/race, and avocational interests. For each domain, societies pose an array of possible options as to how to live and in most instances require that individuals choose among those options. As the definition of identity indicates, the process of "choice" may occur through processes of conscious decision-making, identification, or ascription, and the appearance of choice may be expressed by merely being responsive to the expectations of others without personal investment in any particular course of action. Not all domains of identity concern will be of equal salience for any given individual, and there will be extensive difference from person to person regarding which domains of perceived as being of greatest importance. Further, there may well be differences in the salience of domains based on age, gender, socioeconomic variables, and ethnicity, among other potential moderating variables.

Identity flexibility in this context refers to the capacity for change over time in the goals, values, and beliefs a person holds and pursues. Such changes in identity may be occasioned by altered circumstances in a person's life, whether a product of personal choice or imposed upon the person by external events over which there was no control. In general, the more stable and consistent the life context in which the person is functioning, the less likelihood there is for changes in identity. But one element in life is always "in motion" and that is age. As will be discussed below, age serves as a catalyst for a host of other changes in life circumstances not only for the expectations that others have for us but also for the expectations we have for ourselves. It should be recognized that changes in identity over time may be in the direction of increased or decreased well-being. Indeed, what constitutes well-being for us may change as we grow older.

Eudaimonic Well-Being

Well-being is itself another term that should be defined at the outset of this chapter. As indicated in the title, my particular focus here is on eudaimonic well-being. The origins of philosophical eudaimonism can be traced back to the Classical Hellenic period where it had its most notable treatment in Aristotle's *Nichmachean Ethics* (Aristotle, 1985). It is a philosophy concerned with the understanding of what makes for a good life or, as the theme is currently considered, what is the nature of well-being. Eudaimonia has traditionally been translated as "happiness" (Cooper, 1975; Kraut, 1979; Tatarkiewicz, 1976), though contemporary philosophers often prefer the translation as "flourishing" (Keyes & Annas, 2009; Rasmussen, 1999). Happiness is posed as the ultimate end-in-itself, that is, something sought for its own sake rather than for its instrumental value in promoting the likelihood of some other end. For example, money is valued not for itself but for what it can buy; what is bought is valued not for itself but for how it can improve one's life; but happiness is valued because it is, in itself, integral to a good life, that is, well-being. The philosophical question of central importance here concerns the nature of happiness/flourishing as an end in itself (Haybron, 2008, Norton, 1976).

Eudaimonist philosophers, from Aristotle on, reject the hedonic view that equates happiness as a subjective state equivalent to pleasure. A well-known line from Aristotle is "The many, the most vulgar, seeming conceive the good and happiness as pleasure, and hence they also like the life of gratification. Here they appear completely slavish, since the life they decide on is a life for grazing animals" (Aristotle, 1985, p. 7). Against this view of hedonic happiness, Aristotle offered the proposition that eudaimonia (happiness) is "activity expressing virtue" (p. 284), where virtue may be variously considered to be the best thing, the best within us, or excellence (Ackrill, 1973; McDowell, 1980).

I derive the definition of eudaimonic well-being used here in part from an etymological analysis of the term eudaimonia itself. The word is composed of three parts:

(a) *eu* – Meaning good or desirable, as in (e)utopia, an ideally desirable society.
(b) *-daimon* – Originally this meant a guiding spirit or tutelary god provided at birth to help set a person on the right path. The idea of the daimon was later internalized, as reflected in the view of Heraclitus that "man's character is his daimon." The daimon can thus be thought of as a "true self" representing the person's best potentials, latent talents, resonating values, and ways of living that he or she is capable of expressing.
(c) *-ia* – This syllable typically refers to ways of feeling, as in euphoria (feeling happy), melancholia (feeling sad), or anhedonia (the inability to feel happy). The implication here is that there are particular feelings associated with experiences of acting of the basis of one's true self.

The definition of eudaimonic well-being used within the context of eudaimonic identity theory is: The identification of a person's best potentials in any of a variety of domains of identity concern, the development of skills and talents necessary for the realization of those potentials, and the use of those skills and talents in pursuit of personally meaningful goals. Activities consistent with the development and expression of our best potentials are accompanied by a distinctive set of subjective experiences that I have termed "feelings of personal expressiveness" (Waterman, 1990, 1993b), of which "flow" has been the most widely studied (Csikszentmihalyi, 1990).

With these definitions of identity and eudaimonic well-being established, their relevance for psychological development from adolescence and emerging adulthood through adulthood will be discussed with particular relevance to understanding the nature of identity flexibility.

Identity Development During Adolescence and Emerging Adulthood

Whereas the focus of this volume is on identity flexibility during adulthood, it is, nevertheless, important to understand how a sense of identity is formed during the stages of adolescence and emerging adulthood. It is the personal identity established during these years that is carried forward into adulthood. Consistent with Erikson's concept of epigenesis, the tenet that prior stages of development form the foundation for later stages, the extent and quality of identity flexibility exhibited during adulthood will in large measure be a function of identity, was formed during earlier stages.

The developmental stage of adolescence and emerging adulthood, covering a span from puberty to the mid-twenties (and perhaps somewhat later), is the time frame when Erikson's Stage 5 component of identity vs. role confusion reaches its time of special ascendency, that is, the period when this is the focus of developmental concern. For this reason, the most empirical research on identity has been focused on these stages. Two of the most productive research approaches for the study of identity have been Marcia's identity status paradigm (Marcia, 1966; Marcia et al., 1993) and Berzonsky's identity styles paradigm (Berzonsky, 1989, 2011).

Marcia (1966, 1980) conceptualized identity formation in terms of two process dimensions: (a) exploration and (b) commitment. Exploration entails active consideration of alternative possible goals, values, and/or beliefs in various domains of identity concern. Commitment involves the forming unwavering investment in particular goals, value, and/or beliefs, with these serving as the basis for how one lives. Based on these dimensions, Marcia identified four identity statuses. Identity achievement is characterized by a period of active exploration leading the establishment of firm, personally meaningful commitments in any variety of domains of identity concern. Moratorium refers to the period of active exploration of alternatives, and while such exploration is ongoing, identity commitments are not present. The foreclosure status entails establishing identity commitments, but without having gone through a period of exploration. Such commitments are typically established through a process of identification with the goals, values, and beliefs or significant others in the person's life, but may also develop through forming a commitment to the first possibility actively considered. Identity diffusion is characterized both by the absence of meaningful commitments and the lack of serious efforts to form them. There may or may not have been a period of exploration of alternatives in the past, but none currently. Progressive developmental changes in identity formation during adolescence and emerging adulthood involve movement from the diffusion status into foreclosure or moratorium, from foreclosure into moratorium, and from moratorium into the identity achievement status (Waterman, 1982). Regressive movement among the statuses is also possible.

There is a large body of research indicating that adolescents and emerging adults in the identity achievement and foreclosure statuses are faring best on measures of subjective well-being, self-esteem, and other indices of psychological health (Kroger & Marcia, 2011; Marcia, 1993). Those in the identity diffusion and moratorium statuses show more poorly on such measures, with the moratorium status associated most strongly with anxiety. Identity exploration is clearly a stressful process, albeit an integral part of subsequent identity achievement.

Berzonsky, using a socio-cognitive model, conceptualized identity functioning in terms of the processes individuals employ when making identity-related decisions (Berzonsky, 1989, 2011). He identified three identity-processing orientations of styles. Individuals using an informational processing orientation deliberately seek out information relevant for making decisions, are open to new ideas, and seek to make rational, informed decision in domains of identity concern. Those with a normative-processing orientation are seen as internalizing and adhering to the goals, values, and prescriptions drawn from significant others and do so in a largely nonreflective manner. They do not tolerate ambiguity well and tend to be dogmatic with respect the expression of their goals, values, and beliefs. The third style, a diffuse-avoidant processing orientation, is associated with a confused, fragmented sense of self, reluctance to deal with identity concerns and responsiveness to situational demands. Those employing this style appear more concerned with impression management than with forming personally meaningful goals, values, and beliefs. Similar to findings with respect to the identity statuses, the identity styles differ with respect to measures of the quality of psychological functioning. Individuals employing a diffuse-avoidant processing orientation generally appear to function more poorly than those characterized as using either an informational- or normative-processing style (Berzonsky, 2011). Further, as would be expected, there empirical research indicates the convergence of these paradigms in that informational processing orientation is associated with the identity achievement and moratorium identity statuses, the normative-processing orientation is associated with functioning in the foreclosure statuses, and the diffuse-avoidant processing orientation is associated with identity diffusion (Berzonsky, 2011).

The identity status and identity style paradigms both focus on understanding the processes by which identity is formed during adolescence and emerging adulthood, that is, "how" self-defining goals, values, and belief commitments become established and how those processes relate to psychological well-being. The research literature clearly demonstrates that the presence of such commitments is associated with significantly greater well-being than their absence. Not considered within these paradigms, however, is the quality of the commitments that are made during these stages. It seems self-evident that some potential goals, values, and beliefs a developing person might commit to are "better" than other alternatives equally available. Thus, the benefits associated with commitments may not be a function of commitment, per se, but rather to the presence of better quality commitments. Commitment to poorer alternatives will not likely confer the same benefits. It was a concern for understanding what might constitute better quality commitments that led to the development of eudaimonic identity theory.

It is beyond the scope of this chapter to delve into diverse aspects of eudaimonic identity theory. (See Waterman 1990, 1992, 1993a, 2011, and Waterman and Schwartz 2013 for more extensive treatment of the theory.) My focus here will be on how better quality identity options can be recognized by adolescents and emerging adults. Recall that the concept of eudaimonia, as defined above, has two components. The first is represented by the actual, best potentials of each person, the nature of those potentials varying from person to person. Better identity choices would be the ones consistent with those potentials. The second component of eudaimonia is the distinctive subjective experiences (feelings of personal expressiveness) present when engaged in activities consistent with one's best potentials. Such eudaimonic experiences may take the form of feelings of a personal connection with some activities and spontaneous self-discovery. For example, when engaged in an activity, perhaps for the very first time, there is the reaction "Where has this been all my life? Why didn't I know about this sooner? This is fun!" It should be recognized, however, that it is not the activity itself that generates this feeling. An activity that some people feel intrinsically connected to will be experienced by others with indifference and still others with aversion. The experience of connection and self-discovery is a product of a meshing of aspects of the activity with aspects of the person, specifically the person's latent potentials.

Within the context of eudaimonic identity theory, identification of a person's best potentials is just the first step in the process of identity formation. Those latent potentials within any domain of identity concern, once identified, must be developed into actual skills and talents through dedicated effort. As these skills are being developed, there is also a need to determine the goals or purposes toward which they are to be directed. Further, it is necessary to identify opportunities within one's cultural, social, and economic context through which such goals and purposes can actually be pursued. A central proposition within the theory is that the benefits that have been identified with the identity achievement and foreclosure statuses and the information and normative-processing orientations are functions of the success the person is experiencing with regard to these four steps. The compromised well-being shown by individuals in the identity diffusion status and those expressing a diffuse-avoidant processing style is the consequence of their failure to any substantial progress with respect to any of these steps.

Since adolescence and emerging adulthood is the time frame within which identity is being formed, identity flexibility is the hallmark of development in this regard.

The greater the extent of exploration of identity alternatives that is occurring, the greater the identity flexibility involved. For individuals successfully forming identity commitments, identity is transitioning from an inchoate state to one with firmly established goals, values, and beliefs to guide one's actions. The key difference between identity functioning during full adulthood and the prior stages is that adulthood is a time of implementing identity commitments made earlier. The nature of implementation of commitments is predicated on a relatively stability of those commitment now in place. It is certain to be expected that while the capacity for identity flexibility is present, it will be called upon with far less frequency and will be less extensive than was the case during adolescence and emerging adulthood.

An Epigenetic Perspective on Identity Flexibility During Adulthood: Identity and Generativity

Throughout this section, I will focus my attention on adults in the 30–55 age range who are presumed to have achieved relative success in establishing a personally meaningful sense of identity, an identity consistent with their true potentials and natural inclinations. In other words, these adults will have answered effectively the developmental questions encountered during adolescence and emerging adulthood and who should be experiencing eudaimonic well-being to a considerable extent. They know who they are and where they seek to go in their lives. As title of this chapter proposes, now in their adult years, such individuals will encounter a quite different set of developmental questions than they had previously. They learned the answers to the questions of pervious stages, but now must find answers to different questions if they are to continue experiencing eudaimonic well-being.

Erikson (1963) saw the personality component of generativity vs. stagnation as reaching its time of special ascendancy during the adult years. Generativity involves productivity in terms of attaining a reasonable degree of success in the pursuit of one's own goals and projects and taking responsibility for the welfare of others in one's family, community, workplace, and more broadly the society in which one lives. Stagnation, its polar counterpart, reflects relative failure with respect to implementing one's chosen identity commitments and an almost exclusive self-focused orientation with respect to how one lives and related to others, both in one's immediate social context and the broader community. Adolescence and emerging adulthood are periods for planning how one would wish to live; full adulthood is a period of making those plans a reality. From an epigenetic perspective, it is evident how success at the earlier stages provides the foundation for possible success in adulthood. Without knowing who one is, and where one seeks to go in life, in other words, if one is identity diffuse, then aimlessness in adulthood is an inevitable result.

But having established personally meaningful goals, values, and beliefs in various domains of identity concern does not provide any assurance that the person will be able to implement them effectively. Just as during adolescence and emerging adulthood when feelings of personal expressiveness, including flow experiences, helped the individual to identify personal potentials and to reinforce activities consistent with those potentials, so too during full adulthood feelings of personal expressiveness serve to distinguish occasions when progress is being made toward personally meaningful goals and when activities engaged in are unrelated to generative goals. It is quite possible that activities unrelated to such goals may be thoroughly enjoyed in terms of subjective, hedonic experiences, but those activities do not contribute to, nor help to sustain, eudaimonic well-being.

Even if the person has initial success in making progress toward implementing one's previously chosen identity commitments, there can be no assurance that such progress can be sustained in the face of the various challenges that adulthood poses. Sustained eudaimonic well-being during the adult years hinges upon identity flexibility in responding to those challenges. Below, I will first identify those challenges, describing how they are related both to the expression of one's talents and skills and the pursuit of personally meaningful goals and then discuss the ways in which identity flexibility offers the promise to successfully meet those challenges.

Challenges to Sustaining Eudaimonic Well-Being in Adulthood

Domain-Specific Challenges

There is a broad array of challenges to sustaining eudaimonic well-being in adulthood that may be encountered that vary by domains of identity concern. In the paragraphs that follow, I will sketch out some of the more frequently encountered challenges in domains of identity concern that have received the most attention in theoretical and research literature on identity. No attempt is being made here to generate a comprehensive account of all of the challenges that might arise within any given domain or to cover all of the domains in which individuals define themselves.

Vocational Identity After completing one's education and seeking to find employment in one's chosen field, there is no assurance that an entry-level position will actually be found. If there is success in finding employment, it is possible that the position may be lost for reasons having nothing to do the quality of one's job performance, for example, corporate downsizing due to recession or other economic conditions, mergers, or technological change. Once unemployed, there is no assurance that one can obtain another position in the same field, particularly if there have been notable advances in that field since leaving school. If one continues in the same field, and for the same employer for a significant length of time, there is the risk of job burnout, due to boredom from repetitive routines and/or the lack of interesting new challenges. Also, with increasing age, changes in physical performance, appearance, or reaction time that make it impossible to continue to do what one had been doing, for example, in the fields of athletics, acting, and firefighting. If burnout does occur, it may be difficult to change jobs, particularly if this would entail significant new schooling and a loss in economic stability achieved in one's current position.

Identity Associated with Marriage and Family Life Although one may know what one seeks in a romantic partner, there is no assurance that a person with those qualities, and interested in a relationship, will be found. If a successful marriage (or other relational arrangement) is achieved, it may not be sustainable as the partners in the relationship change over time, as evidenced by the high rate of divorce. Not all couples seeking to become parents will be able to do so, and adoption may or may not be perceived as an option. Inevitably, becoming parents changes the interpersonal dynamic within a relationship, in part because the time demands of parenting means there is less time for a couple to be a couple. Still later, when the children are of an age to leave the parental home, there is a sharp reduction in opportunities to engage in identity-related parenting activities.

Religious/Spiritual/Philosophical Identity While the establishment and maintenance of religious beliefs is under greater personal control than many other aspects of personal identity, it can be subject to a variety of "tests of faith." Deep personal loss may shake the foundations of religious beliefs as can scandals involving religious institutions and religious leaders. Historical changes in cultural values and more within one's community may challenge religiously based standards for what is considered morally appropriate, for example, the "sexual revolution" of the 1960s and the more recent changes in the understanding of the nature of marriage. Inconsistencies in religious or philosophically based value systems may be exposed over time, or such values may come into conflict with what is required for success in other identity-related domains.

Political Identity Defining oneself through the adoption of a political ideology, whether liberal, or conservative, or something else, entails a relatively high degree of idealism. Idealism in this context refers to the belief that the world would be a better place if some set of political, social, or economic standards were more widely practiced. It may be hard to sustain such idealism in the face of experiences that not only is it difficult to convince others of the wisdom of the perspective advocated but also that even when governments attempt to enact policies consistent with the preferred ideology, the outcomes are not always what was anticipated. Disillusionment and cynicism are possible consequences of repeated failures in one's attempt to make a difference in the political sphere.

Ethnic/Racial Identity Particularly for individuals emigrating to a new culture and for the children of recent immigrants, ethnic values and practices may constitute an important part of their identity. However, acculturation pressures from the host nation may work to undermine ties to their ethnic origins in the interest of assimilation into the society in which they now live. While such pressures may be resisted, there is inevitably ambivalence and ambiguities as to how one should act when there are conflicts between one's culture of origin and the community in which one now lives. Generational differences within families, particularly marriage outside of one's ethnicity or race, may represent a particular challenge to older individuals who have centered their identity within this domain. In addition, discrimination, whether institutionalized, structural, and overt, or more individualized, symbolic, or subtly expressed, constitutes a challenge to how one sees oneself and wishes to live.

Categories of Challenges to Sustaining Eudaimonic Well-Being

The panoply of challenges catalogued in the preceding section can be divided into five categories: (a) problems of affordance (opportunity); (b) life disruptions that interfere with ongoing activities toward identity-related goals; (c) age-related changes in role opportunities and the deterioration of some skills; (d) burnout, whether from boredom or disillusionment; and (e) the experience of time as a limited resource. Some challenges impact the use of talents and skills, some interfere with the pursuit of personally meaningful goals, some risk undermining personal values and beliefs, and some affect multiple aspects of one's self-definition.

Problems of Affordance Being able to make use of one's talents and skills in the active pursuit of personally meaningful goals requires the availability of options and opportunities within one's cultural, social, and economic context through which such activities may occur. If those contexts do not afford a reasonable array of opportunities for the pursuit of one's goals, then frustration is a virtually inevitable result. In the absence of opportunities, choosing unrealistic goals could be viewed as poor decision-making during adolescence and emerging adulthood. However, an emerging adult may consider particular goals of such importance to their personal identity that they resolve to take on the challenge of creating opportunities where none currently exist or to emigrate to an environment where those opportunities are being afforded.

More commonly, the personally meaningful goals one chooses are determined in part by the recognition that one's society affords opportunities for their pursuit and attainment. However, the affordances available do not necessarily exist in sufficient numbers to allow all those choosing to pursue a particular goal to have the opportunity to do so. In this respect, affordances can be viewed as a limited resource with some portion of the population denied the opportunities to enact chosen identity elements. More individuals may wish to enter a particular career field than there are entry-level positions available in that field. Those valuing a particular marriage lifestyle may find themselves outnumbering potential partners with similar values. Even with respect to aspects of identity related to recreational activities may be subject to limited affordances due to a lack of available partners for participation in a chosen pursuit, economic considerations, or other contextual constraints.

Life Disruptions That Interfere with Ongoing Activities Toward Identity-Related Goals The array of events that may serve as life disruptions is extensive and varied. Some are specific to particular identity domains such as being laid off in the vocational domain and the loss of a romantic partner through divorce or death in the domain of family life. Others are likely to affect opportunities for engaging in personally expressive activities across multiple domains simultaneously, for example, serious illness or injury to a person directly or to a loved one, weather-related disasters such as tornados or floods, or involvement in some traumatic event. Such life disruptions can have the effect of focusing one's attention on day-to-day survival, rather than on personally expressive activities promoting eudaimonic well-being. Maslow (1970) termed this the prepotency of basic needs over needs associated with self-actualization.

Age-Related Changes in Role Opportunities and the Deterioration of Some Skills As individuals transition from emerging adulthood into full adulthood and progress through the adult years, there are not only increases in some opportunities and progressive increases in some skills but also the loss of other role opportunities and the progressive deterioration of some skills. For example, in sports, the age of peak performance varies by the demands of the sport and the gender of the sport participant (Ericsson, 1990; Schulz & Curnow, 1988). For actors and actresses, the types of parts they are likely to be offered change with age. As opportunities change or skills diminish in a domain that has been central to a person's identity, the prospects for eudaimonic well-being can be expected to be adversely affected.

Burnout Burnout involves the loss of motivation within a domain that earlier had been a source of personal expressiveness and well-being. There are two primary reasons for burnout: boredom and/or disillusionment. Boredom occurs when individuals perform the same set of activities over a prolonged period of time. Subjective experiences of flow for any activity result from the presence of a balance of challenges encountered and skills brought to it. As Csikszentmihalyi (1990) has observed, the nature of flow is such that it is naturally progressive. With repeated performance of an activity, skills are very likely to improve, and thus the challenge posed of the activity at the level performed will decrease. This imbalance of challenges and skills results in the subjective experiences associated with the activity changing from flow to boredom (the subjective state associated with a high level of skill and a low level of challenges). The only way in which to restore experiences of flow is to take on a higher level of challenge with respect the particular undertaking, one that is commensurate with the level skill now attained. This higher level of challenge will, in turn, motivate the individual to strive for still better levels of skill, an inherently progressive cycle of performance. While there are many benefits to be derived from this progressive cycle, in adulthood identifying and taking on new challenges may be particularly difficult as an increasing number of daily activities become routine.

Disillusionment involves a change in values over time such that what once was valued very highly is no longer viewed in the same way. Such a change may occur due to learning that one's efforts do not provide the types of outcomes one had anticipated. For example, in the helping professions, observations that for many clients improvements in functioning appear to be only temporary may lead to questioning whether transient benefits are worth the effort. Similarly, repeated exposure to reports of ethical failures among government officials, religious leaders, educators, and other holders of public trust as well as by prominent individuals from varied fields promotes cynicism and undermines the belief that there are values worth upholding.

Time as a Limited Resource In adulthood there is a broad increase in the extent of responsibilities a person is likely to have as a spouse, parent, worker, member of civic organizations, among others. The more roles taken on, the less time is available to devote to each one. "Multitasking" is sometimes viewed as a strategy to deal with time as a limited resource, but the consequence of trying to do multiple things at one time is that none receive a person's full attention or is performed up to the best of one's potentials. With serious time pressures to accomplish the tasks one has agreed to take on, there is a risk that conscious compromises will be made with respect to quality of performance. Such compromises will have repercussions for eudaimonic well-being. It is hard to feel good about what one is doing when there is a recognition that a better outcome was possible. "Good enough" may be what time permits but that is not an identity expressing who one truly wishes to be. And with all the time spent doing things for the benefit of others, whether employers, employees, customers, clients, students, spouse, children, friends, neighbors, the community, etc., where is the time to come from to do something for oneself?

Resolutions to the Challenges to Eudaimonic Well-Being in Adulthood

The central element to resolving the challenges to eudaimonic well-being in adulthood just described is the perceptive use of identity flexibility. Just as was true during adolescence and emerging adulthood, the requirements for experiencing eudaimonic well-being continue to be the identification of personal potentials, their development over time, the choice of goals toward which developed talents can be directed, along with identification of opportunities afforded within one's social context for the pursuit of those goals. As during the earlier developmental periods, the experiences of feelings of personal expressiveness, including flow, serve as indicators of productive efforts to achieving new, personally expressive outcomes. Since the identity-related questions have changed, so too must different answers emerge. However, it can be anticipated that the processes involved in successfully dealing with the developmental questions of the earlier stages will continue to be relevant to addressing the questions of adulthood.

With respect to changes in identity over time reflecting identity flexibility, Stephen, Fraser, and Marcia (1992) described recursive patterns of movement into and out of the moratorium status, that is, *moratorium-achievement-moratorium-achievement*, that they termed MAMA-cycles. Neither Erikson (1968) nor Marcia (1980) viewed the outcomes of the identity exploration process of adolescence and emerging adulthood as fixed guideposts for future endeavors. Inevitably, with age, changes in social contexts, and unpredictable historical events, identity commitments previously made can be expected to wax or wane in personal salience.

Just as going through the moratorium period during earlier stages was associated with elevated levels of anxiety, so too, reentry into moratorium during adulthood will be unsettling. It may be anticipated that such renewed exploration will be more psychologically distressing than it was earlier. Exploration during adolescence and emerging adulthood occurred when there were no long-term patterns of established patterns of action; during adulthood renewed exploration may well be an unwanted occurrence after years of successful personal expression.

Eudaimonic identity theory covers four broad categories of resolution efforts: (a) finding new outlets for current skills and values along established lines, (b) finding new outlets for current skills and values along new lines of endeavor, (c) identifying and developing new talents and means for their expression, and (d) resetting priorities and improving time management to promote goal attainment.

Finding New Outlets for Current Skills and Values Along Established Lines After encountering blocks to continuation of personally expressive activities with respect to a domain of identity concern, least disruptive to one's sense of identity is to find new contexts in which well-established skills can be employed in the pursuit of ongoing goals. Within the domain of vocation, for example, after a layoff can one find similar or related employment in another company, whether in the same or a different field, which will allow for the ongoing utilization of one's talents? Is going out on one's own an option? Are there other fields of endeavor that require the same sets of skills that one has productively employed up to this point in time (and which are also consistent with what is personally valued)?

The stresses associated with need to make changes with respect to personally rewarding ways of living, even those entailing utilizing essentially the same talents and values, should not be underestimated. One's willingness to be persistent when seeking to resolve a new moratorium is likely to be an important factor toward achieving such an outcome. Indeed, the level of persistence is an important indicator of the strength of the values associated with those talents and goals. The less confidence one has in one's skills or in the value of the goals being pursued, the less will be the willingness to continue striving to an uncertain outcome. In addition to the strength of belief in one's talents and goals, having (or finding) a social community supporting one's continuing efforts is likely to increase the willingness to be persistent. However, there can be a fine line between potentially productive persistence and the stubborn refusal to change based upon wishful thinking. That difference may have more to do with the opportunities afforded within one's societal context than with either the talents present or the value of the goals one wishes to pursue.

Finding New Outlets for Current Skills and Values Along New Lines If finding new outlets for utilizing established talents toward long-held goals does not appear to be a viable option, it may be possible to employ existing skills in novel ways. This would require changes in the goals the person chooses to pursue. So long as the new goals are experienced as personally meaningful, the potential for continuing or reestablishing eudaimonic well-being is strong. However, here to, the opportunities afforded by the person's social context continue to be a crucial factor. If pursuing new goals is no more realistic than the continued pursuit of previously established goals, the prospects for success are dim, with inevitable negative consequence for well-being.

Identifying and Developing New Talents Considerably greater identity flexibility is required to put aside well-established talents and skills and take one's life in a different direction. This more extensive set of life changes may be the better course in instances of burnout and disillusionment. If, in effect, one has run out of new challenges one wishes to take on with respect to previously developed talents, the identification and development of new latent talents carries with it inherent increased challenge, the prospect of skill improvement, and accompanying subjective experiences of flow.

It should be recognized that with respect to personal potentials, it is not the case that there is one, and only one, latent talent capable of providing a foundation for eudaimonic well-being. Everyone has a range of potentials, some stronger than others, that can be experienced as personally expressive. The ones that were recognized in adolescence and emerging adulthood came to the fore in substantial part because of exposure to relevant activities and the opportunities to pursue them. That other latent talents, interests, and inclinations were not recognized at that time may have been a function of limited exposure, but was also likely due to focusing attention on those that were identified. Even in adolescence and emerging adulthood, time is a limited resource such that active pursuits in some areas are likely to preclude pursuing other possibilities. Now, with the recognition that there is a need to identify new areas of potential skills and interests, the person becomes open to seeing what else might be possible. And just as in adolescence and emerging adulthood exposure to a broad array of potential interests promotes the likelihood of finding personally expressive possibilities, so too in adulthood conscious efforts to encounter novel opportunities increases the likelihood of identifying previously unrecognized potential talents and interests.

Many individuals may be aware of alternative interests present in adolescence or emerging adulthood, or perhaps earlier, which were not pursued because decisions were made to go in a different, presumably more rewarding, direction. Present circumstances may provide opportunities to engage in activities along "the road not (previously) taken." It should be recognized that in starting over with the development of new skills, that one starts again as a relative novice and without an assurance of eventual success in achieving a high level of performance. This can be distressing for someone who has been performing very successfully along previous lines of endeavor. However, the recognition that those previous lines of endeavor are either no longer available or have grown stale make it easier to take the steps necessary to change one's life direction. Flow experiences and other feelings of personal expressiveness once again help to reinforce and thereby sustain the process of skill development.

Not everyone in adulthood will have identified potentially meaningful alternative paths that were put aside for one reason or another, but rather will find themselves with a stronger, more demanding question regarding "What do I do now?" The intensity of that question is indicative of the strength of the moratorium period that has been entered. The strategies that were used during adolescence and emerging adulthood to address the typically less intense and stage-characteristic question "What should I do?" are again applicable in adulthood. The goal is, once again, to identify activities consistent with one's underlying, personally expressive potentials. The intensity of the identity crisis can obscure recognition of cues associated with feelings of personal expressiveness, such that likelihood of success is enhanced if the current challenges experienced can be faced with a degree of calm, something easier to suggest than to achieve.

An individual's life experiences during the adult years, combined with identity flexibility, contribute to promoting a successful resolution of a renewed period of identity exploration. It is unrealistic to expect that all areas of one's life will be experienced as personally expressive; what is important for eudaimonic well-being is that at least some aspects of it are experienced in that way. Also, with life experience the person becomes increasingly likely to recognize differences between those things that are primarily under one's own control rather than contingent on the actions of others. To the extent that one can identify and develop skills that can be enacted irrespective of what others do, increased eudaimonic well-being becomes more likely.

Resetting Priorities and Improving Time Management to Promote Goal Attainment Time as a limited resource was identified as one of the challenges in adulthood to maintaining eudaimonic well-being. If someone has become bogged down in fulfilling obligations with respect to work, family, and/or community involving activities that are neither challenging nor closely related to personally expressive goals, eudaimonic well-being becomes difficult if not impossible to sustain. This is where resetting priorities and improving time management skills may prove beneficial in reestablishing opportunities for eudaimonic identity functioning. It is not that one should walk away from obligations one has taken on; the legitimate needs of others should matter. What is needed is the ability to balance being responsive to what others need with recognition that each person has a legitimate concern with having their own needs met. Viewing time management as a zero-sum arrangement, that is, time employed to pursue personally valued activities that comes at the expense of what one is obligated to do for others, increases the likelihood that frustration, burnout, and compromised well-being will be the outcome. It is instrumental in this context to recognize that the better one feels about one's life and oneself, the more likely it becomes to provide better quality support to others. I used the term "instrumental" in the previous sentence because I do not wish to convey the idea that one should do things for oneself *because* it will redound to the benefit of others. One should strive toward eudaimonic well-being because each individual's life matters. However, the recognition that caring for oneself does have benefits with respect to caring for others can be a useful initial step toward rejecting the perception of time as zero-sum arrangement.

Strictly speaking, changes with respect to priority setting and time management do not involve identity flexibility since new talents, interests, or inclinations are not involved nor are changes in the goals, values, and beliefs a person holds. Instead, the flexibility required here is a type of cognitive flexibility that involves a recognition of what is not working in a person's life and the ability to find a different strategy capable of increasing the likelihood of a more rewarding future.

Identity Statuses and Styles and Predictors of Identity Flexibility: The Past as Prologue

From the perspective of eudaimonic identity theory, several hypotheses can be advanced regarding predictions for the likelihood of effective use of identity flexibility in adulthood. Based upon Erikson's epigenetic principle, it is expected that the success that individuals have had with respect to addressing the questions posed during adolescence and emerging adulthood, the greater likelihood of success in addressing the questions being posed in adulthood that call for adaptive use of identity flexibility.

Identity Diffusion/the Diffuse-Avoidant Style Adults who have carried a legacy of identity diffusion and the diffuse-avoidant style forward from adolescence are unlikely to find a more successful identity in adulthood or to achieve eudaimonic well-being. They have not developed the skills required for the effective exploration of identity alternatives nor have they shown the dedicated motivation required to translate their personal potentials into genuine skills applied in the pursuit of personally meaningful goals. Just as they have allowed themselves to drift through earlier stages primarily responsive to the demands present in their immediate life circumstances, so too in adulthood, they can be expected to continue this pattern as adults. While the diffuse-avoidant style does allow for maximum flexibility as life circumstances change, such adaptability is unlikely to be productive in improving quality of life as the knowledge and skills required to make the most of new opportunities are largely missing.

Foreclosure Status/Normative Identity Style A distinction should be made here between those in the foreclosure status whose identity commitments in earlier years were consistent with intrinsic personal potentials and who have experienced eudaimonic well-being and those who carried identity commitments forward that were based primarily instrumental benefits and therefore unlikely to have direct personal experience of eudaimonic functioning. When faced with challenges in adulthood, individuals in the former group are aware of what is being put at risk, and if changes in their lives are required, they have an awareness of the type of functioning that they are seeking to maintain or if necessary restore. When those in the latter group are faced with similar challenges, their lack of experience with the benefits of eudaimonic functioning will make it unlikely they would seek for greater personal expressiveness in adulthood. Just as they have relied on the normative preferences for past identity decisions, they can be expected to follow that pattern as adults.

Life transitions from adolescence, through emerging adulthood, and into adulthood may proceed quite smoothly for individuals in both categories of foreclosure. They know what they want from life and are likely to have the motivation to develop their skills and pursue their goals, values, and beliefs with dedication. It is only when they encounter the challenges of adulthood that they will be called upon to adapt to changing circumstances. But in the absence of prior developmental experience having to deal with identity instability and the need to make choices among competing alternatives, they are at a disadvantage when trying to cope with the need for change. Further, the tendency in foreclosures toward cognitive rigidity and to see alternatives in dichotomous "right"/"wrong" categories compounds the difficulty of achieving effective identity flexibility. Thus, the functioning of foreclosures in the face of unemployment, divorce, or spiritual challenges is likely to be less effective than those who have dealt with identity uncertainty in early developmental stages.

The distinction between foreclosures who have and have not experienced personally expressive, eudaimonic functioning in their lives is relevant for the likelihood of successful responses to the challenges of adulthood. While relatively inexperienced in handling change, their knowledge of what is possible has the potential to provide greater motivation to stay with the task of maintaining or restoring a eudaimonic way of life. In the face of the failure of a normative style to provide stable identity commitments under changing life circumstances, the skills associated with an information processing style can still be acquired in adulthood.

Identity Achievement/Informational Processing Style Individuals who were functioning in the identity achievement status in adolescence and emerging adulthood, using an informational processing style, are best positioned to effectively employ identity flexibility when encountering the challenges of adulthood. These later challenges also involve making choices between alternatives available, something that they had dealt with successfully during prior stages. The distinction between identity achievers who have experienced personally expressive commitments and those whose commitments were instrumental, rather than expressive, is also relevant here. For individuals who have been functioning in terms of eudaimonic well-being, the incentive to maintain their existing commitments is particularly strong. Should that not be possible, their efforts to establish new commitments, whether in the same domain or some other domain, will in all likelihood be directed to achieving a similarly expressive outcome. This can be a quite complex task in that it may entail the identification of potentials not previously recognized or developed and may also involve rethinking goals and values through which those potentials may be expressed. In contrast, identity achievers whose previous commitments were primarily instrumental will be more likely to strive of other instrumental outcomes. In doing so, less attention may be paid to matters of personal potentials and personal satisfaction, making this a somewhat easier task as communities generally provide a fairly wide array of options that hold the promise for success. However, whether expressive or instrumental commitments are being sought, there remains the need to develop the requisite skills to take advantage of opportunities that may be available and to actually find and implement such opportunities. It should also be recognized that the opportunities that exist are not equally available to everyone, as discriminatory criteria may restrict who can and who cannot make use of them.

Other Predictors of the Successful Use of Identity Flexibility The likelihood of the successful use of identity flexibility will also be affected by the nature and timing of the identity challenges encountered. Some types of challenges will be more easily resolved than others, and this can be expected to vary with the age of the individual and the community supports available with the community. In general, it can be expected that the earlier in adulthood challenges are encountered, the greater the likelihood that those challenges will be handled effectively. With age, individuals are likely to assume greater responsibilities and obligations in their various roles that are not easily changed and that can conflict with identity changes being contemplated. In addition, with increasing age, adults are likely to become more entrenched in their traditional patterns of activity, making change more difficult. Another predictor of the likelihood of successfully maintaining or restoring the eudaimonic functioning is the number of different challenges encountered at any given point in time during the adult years. The greater the burden of challenges experienced simultaneously, the stress experienced will decrease the probability of the effective use of identity flexibility.

Conclusions

From the perspective of eudaimonic identity theory, achieving well-being involves the identification a person's best potentials, the development of skills and talents associated with those potentials, decisions concerning the goals toward which those talents are to be directed, and finding appropriate venues for the pursuit of those goals. These are the developmental tasks of the stages of adolescence and youth. These are the tasks of identity formation. Feelings of personal expressiveness including feeling a connection more strongly toward some activities, goals, values, and beliefs promote successful outcomes. However, the completion of these tasks is only the prelude to the developmental tasks of adulthood itself. At this stage, what is needed for achieving eudaimonic well-being is the successful implementation of the identity-related decisions previously made. In adulthood, there is an array of potential challenges that may be encountered; these challenges are varying by the identity domains of most salience for each person. Not everyone will face the same sets of challenges, and those challenges may vary in both their number, their severity, and their timing. If eudaimonic well-being is to be achieved and sustained, these challenges must be dealt with successfully. Consistent with the epigenetic principle, the stronger the developmental foundation brought forward from previous stages, the greater the likelihood of success in this regard. Key to successful outcomes is the adaptive use of identity flexibility, that is, the capacity to find new outlets for existing talents or to recognize, develop, and implement other talents in domains of identity salience. While the difficulties entailed in this process in adulthood should not be underestimated, each of the prior stages has involved its own set of developmental tasks and challenges that have had to be met and resolved. Adults who are living productive and expressive lives, whether with respect to rewarding vocational endeavors; mutually caring relationships in their families; the dedicated expression of religious, spiritual, philosophical, or political values; enthusiastic pursuit of avocational interests; and/or making meaningful contributions to their community, are a testament that eudaimonic well-being can be achieved. As no one is likely to go through life without encountering at least several of the challenges discussed in this chapter, such individuals can serve as models for the creative and adaptive use of identity flexibility in adulthood.

References

Ackrill, J. L. (1973). *Aristotle's ethics*. London: Faber and Faber.

Aristotle. (4th Century B.C.E./1985). *Nicomachean ethics*. (T. Irwin, Trans.). Indianapolis, IN: Hackett.

Berzonsky, M. D. (1989). Identity style: Conceptualization and measurement. *Journal of Adolescent Research, 4*, 267–281.

Berzonsky, M. D. (2011). A social-cognitive perspective on identity construction. In S. J. Schwartz, K. Luyckx, & V. L. Vignoles (Eds.), *Handbook of identity theory and research, Structures and processes* (Vol. 1, pp. 55–76). New York: Springer.

Cooper, J. (1975). *Reason and human good in Aristotle*. Cambridge, MA: Harvard University Press.

Csikszentmihalyi, M. (1990). *Flow: The psychology of optimal experience*. New York: Harper & Row.

Ericsson, K. A. (1990). Peak performance and age: An examination of peak performance in sports. In P. B. Baltes & M. M. Baltes (Eds.), *Successful aging: Perspectives from the behavioral sciences* (pp. 164–196). New York: Cambridge University Press.

Erikson, E. H. (1963). *Childhood and society* (2nd ed.). New York: Norton.

Erikson, E. H. (1968). *Identity: Youth and crisis*. New York: Norton.

Erikson, E. H. (1982). *The life cycle completed: A review*. New York: Norton.

Haybron, D. (2008). *The pursuit of unhappiness: The elusive psychology of well-being*. New York: Oxford University Press.

Keyes, C. L. M., & Annas, J. (2009). Feeling good and functioning well: Distinctive concepts in ancient philosophy and contemporary science. *Journal of Positive Psychology, 4*, 197–201.

Kraut, R. (1979). Two conceptions of happiness. *Philosophical Review, 87*, 167–196.

Kroger, J., & Marcia, J. E. (2011). The identity statuses: Origins, meanings, and interpretations. In S. J. Schwartz, K. Luyckx, & V. L. Vignoles (Eds.), *Handbook of identity theory and research, Structures and processes* (Vol. 1, pp. 31–53). New York: Springer.

Marcia, J. E. (1966). Development and validation of ego identity status. *Journal of Personality and Social Psychology, 3*, 551–558.

Marcia, J. E. (1980). Identity in adolescence. In J. Adelson (Ed.), *Handbook of adolescent psychology* (pp. 159–186). New York: Wiley.

Marcia, J. E. (1993). The status of the statuses: Research review. In J. E. Marcia, A. S. Waterman, D. R. Matteson, S. L. Archer, & J. L. Orlofsky (Eds.), *Ego identity: A handbook for psychosocial research* (pp. 22–41). New York: Springer.
Marcia, J. E., Waterman, A. S., Matteson, D. R., Archer, S. L., & Orlofsky, J. L. (1993). *Ego identity: A handbook for psychosocial research*. New York: Springer.
Maslow, A. H. (1970). *Motivation and personality* (2nd ed.). New York: Harper and Row.
McDowell, J. (1980). The role of eudaimonia in Aristotle's ethics. In A. O. Rorty (Ed.), *Essays on Aristotle's ethics* (pp. 359–376). Berkeley, CA: University of California Press.
Norton, D. L. (1976). *Personal destinies*. Princeton, NJ: Princeton University Press.
Rasmussen, D. B. (1999). Human flourishing and the appeal to human nature. *Social Philosophy and Policy, 16*, 1–43.
Schulz, R., & Curnow, C. (1988). Peak performance and age among superathletes: Track and field, swimming, baseball, tennis, and golf. *Journal of Gerontology, 43*(5), 113–120.
Stephen, J., Fraser, E., & Marcia, J. E. (1992). Moratorium-achievement (MAMA) cycles in lifespan identity development: Value orientation and reasoning system. *Journal of Adolescence, 15*, 283–300.
Tatarkiewicz, W. (1976). *Analysis of happiness*. The Hague, Netherlands: Martinus Nijhoff.
Waterman, A. S. (1982). Identity development from adolescence to adulthood: An extension of theory and a review of research. *Developmental Psychology, 1982*, 342–358.
Waterman, A. S. (1990). Personal expressiveness: Philosophical and psychological foundations. *Journal of Mind and Behavior, 11*, 47–74.
Waterman, A. S. (1992). Identity as an aspect of optimal psychological functioning. In G. R. Adams, T. Gullota, & R. Montemayor (Eds.), *Identity formation during adolescence. Advances in adolescent development* (Vol. 4, pp. 50–72). Newbury Park, CA: Sage.
Waterman, A. S. (1993a). Finding something to do or someone to be: A eudaimonist perspective on identity formation. In J. Kroger (Ed.), *Discussions on ego identity* (pp. 147–167). Hillsdale, NJ: Lawrence Erlbaum.
Waterman, A. S. (1993b). Two conceptions of happiness: Contrasts of personal expressiveness (eudaimonia) and hedonic enjoyment. *Journal of Personality and Social Psychology, 64*, 678–691.
Waterman, A. S. (2011). Eudaimonic identity theory: Identity as self-discovery. In S. J. Schwartz, K. Luyckx, & V. L. Vignoles (Eds.), *Handbook of identity theory and research, Structures and processes* (Vol. 1, pp. 357–379). New York: Springer.
Waterman, A. S., & Schwartz, S. J. (2013). Eudaimonic identity theory. In A. S. Waterman (Ed.), *The best within us: Positive psychology perspectives on eudaimona* (pp. 99–118). Washington, DC: American Psychological Association.

Index

A

Adolescents
- coregulating, 159–161
- principal task, 152

Adulthood, 120–122, 320
- cognitive development, 118–120
- eudaimonic well-being, domain-specific challenges, 320
- identity flexibility during, 319, 320
- personality development, 120
  - integrity *vs.* despair, 121, 122
  - six-foci model, 120
- spirituality, 116–118

Affective wisdom, 59
Alzheimer's disease, 20
American Academy of Pediatrics (AAP), 215
Anatta, 12, 311
Anicca, 311
Antifragility, 278–280
Architectural Design, 304
Autism, 20

B

Badagas, social identity, 130, 133–143
- method
  - becoming city Badaga (self-discovery), 141–143
  - being Badaga, 138–141
  - data collection and analysis, 134
  - findings, 134
  - living in Bangalore, 136–138
  - location, 133
  - participants and sampling, 133
  - social mobility, 135, 136

Baltimore Longitudinal Study of Aging (BLSA), 37
Bangalore, 136–138
Beyond Boredom and Anxiety, 213
Black Consciousness Movement (BCM), 240
Black immigrant identities, 83–95
- black racial identity, 86–92
- dreams of home, 83–95
- identity development, 85, 86
- immigrant incorporation/acculturation and identities, 92–95

Breadth processes, 62
Buddha, spirit and instruction of, 248
Buddhism, 12
- contemplate, 250
- contemplations, 250
- meditation, 250

Buddhist psychology, 249

C

Cancer, 309–312
Cancer effect on self-esteem, 310
Caregiver as woman's role, 293
Caregiver identity and flexibility, 289
- assessment, 296, 297
- development, 292–294
- future research, 297
- research, 294–296

Caregiver identity theory, 293, 296
Change, 290–292, 295, 296
Child development
- caring for infant, 154, 155
- coregulating adolescent, 159–161
- mentoring young adult, 161, 162

J.D. Sinnott (ed.), *Identity Flexibility During Adulthood*,
DOI 10.1007/978-3-319-55658-1

Child development (*cont.*)
 protecting and controlling preschooler, 155–157
 teaching, 157–159
Cognitive development, in adulthood, 118–120
Cognitive wisdom, 59
Confrontation
 identity inflexibility, 251
 potential for change, 252
 two-step process, 251
Consciousness-shaping, 179
Cotard's syndrome, 20
Cross' Nigrescence model, 88
Csikszentmihalyi's flow theory, 244

D
Deep mindfulness practice, 12
Dhammapada, 247
Diffuse-avoidant identity style, 57
Dissociation, 270–275, 278, 279, 281
Dissociative identity disorder, 265
Dual identities and artist
 accumulation of experience, 306
 in basic electronics, 304
 basic technical knowledge and quick learner, 304
 commercial art school, 304
 different playhouses, 306
 galleries, 306
 illustrator and a painter, 303
 in-house temporary employee, 305
 insurance company, 305
 Maryland Institute of Art and Basic Electronics, 304
 optimism and freshness, 307
 social group, 306
 South Bronx and Northwest Baltimore, 303
 special person, 305
 Towson University Department of Chemistry, 305
dukkha, 311

E
Ecclesiastes, 125
Ecstatic epilepsy, 20
Emerging adulthood, 158, 161
 choice, 72
 decision-making, 80
 definition of, 71
 developmental phase, 71
 dichotomies, 71
 DUI arrests, 79
 existential lens, 72–74
 exploration and experimentation, 79
 GCOS, 80
 growth experience, 77, 78, 80
 industrialized countries, 71, 81
 measurement, 76, 77
 narrative identity, 74, 75
 nongrowth experience, 77, 79
 participants, 75, 77
 procedure, 75–76
 quantitative techniques, 79
 self-determination, 80
Eminent elders
 adult identity flexibility, 241
 Alive with the Vanguard trio set, 237
 athlete, 236
 BCM, 240
 Black People's Convention, 242
 case studies, 245
 challenge and skill balances, 244
 Csikszentmihalyi's flow theory, 244
 evolving selves, 233
 flow
  experience, 234, 235
  research/ researchers, 234, 244
  theory, 239
 Fred Hersch, 236, 238
 individual musical performances, 237
 interviewees, 233
 intrinsic nature of flow activities, 235
 IUPsyS, 240
 life circumstances, 241
 longtime engineer, 238
 microflow and typical length flow experiences, 234
 Mihaly Csikszentmihalyi, 233
 My Coma Dreams, 239
 non-White, 242
 PERMA well-being theory, 235
 personal hygiene and maintenance activities, 236
 professional identity, 239
 PsySSA, 243
 self-consciousness disappears, 234
 teacher/parental praise, 235
 young adult, 243
Encounter stage, 86
Epic of Gilgamesh, 115
Erikson's theory of psychosocial development, 313
Eriksonian achievement scale, 185
Ethnic identity, 297
Ethnic racial identity, 321
Eudaimonic well-being, 315, 320, 322–330

challenges to sustaining, 322
age-related changes in opportunities and deterioration of skills, 323
burnout, 323
domain-specific challenges, 320
life disruptions, 323
problems of affordance, 322
resolutions, 324
time as limited resource, 324
identity and generativity, 319, 320
identity development, adolescence and emerging adulthood, 316–319
identity statuses/styles and predictors, identity flexibility, 328
foreclosure status/normative identity style, 328, 329
identity achievement/informational processing style, 329, 330
identity diffusion/diffuse-avoidant style, 328
predictors of use, 330
resolutions, 325
identifying and developing new talents, 326, 327
new outlets for current skills and values, 325, 326
resetting priorities and time management, 327

F
Families and schools, 216
Feelings of personal expressiveness, 316
Flexibility
altruism, 106, 107
audacity of hope, 112
beer making, 101, 102
case of Christine Bryden, 100
companies, 104
creative arts, 108, 109
de-emphasis, 100
dementia, 99
intergenerational programming, 107
learning, new language, 103–104
National Alzheimer's Project Act, 99
nursing home in Australia, 106
nursing home in Switzerland, 106
persons with dementia, 100, 101
price of, 111
resident-led activity programming, 104, 105
resident-led communities, 109–111
training dogs, 103
travel, 109
Flow
autoethnographic account, 226
divergent-convergent adjustments, 228
dynamic negotiation, 226
illumination, 227
leisure, 226
similarities, 226
Foundation of One's Self/Identity in Day-to-Day Life, 253

G
Gender, 163, 180, 181
Gender flexibility, 163, 164, 174
Gender identity, 163, 165–167, 170–173
among nonbinary transgender individuals, 165, 173
data analysis, 167
measures and procedure, 167
participant demographics and recruitment strategy, 165, 166
descriptions, 168
agender conceptualizations, 173
as blended, 170
as fluid, 171
as non-binary, 172
transgender as, 172
using binary terms of gender/sex, 170
historical and contemporary frameworks, 164, 165
labels, 168, 169
General causality orientation scale (GCOS), 75, 76, 80
General systems theory (GST), 29–31
General wisdom, 58
Generativity, 319, 320
Gerontology Research Center (GRC), 36–37
Growth-related personality, 60

H
Hippocampus, 15
Huntington's disease, 105

I
Identities, 152, 180, 181, 265–270, 276–278, 314
associated with marriage and family life, 321
attachment, dissociation, and, 273, 274
core disturbances, 276
disintegration, 278
identity alteration, 277

Identities (*cont.*)
identity confusion, 277
identity crisis, 276
identity diffusion, 276
identity distress, 276
negative identity, 277
transformation, 277
transition, 277
development, 289, 290
diffusion, 290
flexibility, 266, 290–292
autonomy and boundaries, 266–268
identity-based model of mind, 268–270
and generativity, 319, 320
hijacked in the society, 274, 275
identity-based model of mind, 271
and identity flexibility, 314
implications for healing, 280–283
religious/spiritual/philosophical, 321
resiliency or antifragility, 278–280
sociological and psychological properties, 269
statuses, 296
trauma, memory, and dissociation, 270–273
Identity flexibility, 23–28, 256, 314
adaptive transformation, 21
applications and research strategies, 43, 44
chaos speak to evolving identity, 22, 23
chaos theory, 31–34
cognitive pathology, 42
cognitive processes, 21
cognitively consistent, 43
complex postformal thought, 42
complexity theory, 31–34
contradiction, 259–262
failure to feel connection, 41
flexible adult self, 39–41
flexible identity, 21
human and nonhuman elements, 20
living systems, 22, 23
metatheory shift, 38
motivation factor, 41
multiple causality, 39
multiple methods, 39
multiple solutions, 38
neuropsychological insights, 20
neuroscience findings, 20
neuroscientists, 20
number of models, 21
paradox, 39
parameter setting, 38
physics models
adult identity flexibility, 23
electromagnetism, 25
gravitational fields, 27
interpersonal space, 28
intuitive and anthropomorphic generalizations, 24
lifespan development, 28
Lorentz transform, 26
measurement, 25
Newton's theory, 26
Newtonian physics, 24
Newtonian physics and calculus, 26
nonlocal causality, 28
parallel transport, 26
postformal thought, 27
pre-Einsteinian theories, 26
scientific hypothesis, 27
spirituality and organization management, 24
time element, 27
vector analysis and tensor analysis, 25
postformal cognition, 36–39
pragmatism, 39
problem definition, 38
process/product shift, 38
psychological research, 19
quantum physics, 19
quantum weirdness, 22, 23
reentry shock, 20
self-constructing systems, 19
self-organizing systems, 35
self-regulating systems, 31–36
three dynamic processes, 40
Identity flexibility and wisdom
adolescence and early adulthood, 54
benefits, 53
breadth processes, 62
contemplative identity processes, 64
contemplative pedagogy and psychology, 65
depth processes, 61
ego-identity, 54
growth-oriented identity style, 54, 58–60
identity status paradigm, 55
individual styles of coping, 55
integrative contemplative processes, 61
lifespan psychosocial development, 53
longitudinal research, 55
Marcia's Identity Status Interview, 54
processing, 55–58
static or outcome variables, 55
Identity interaction
brain disrupts memory, 13–16
cognitive damage, 6
cognitive deficits, 7
cognitive effects, 4

diffusion or moratorium prevails, 5
ego identity, 6
Erikson's highly influential theory, 5
external identity, 8–11
identity development, 4
identity formation, 6
individuation, 4
internal identity, 11–13
neurodegenerative diseases, 7
Self-Concept Scale, 4
self-esteem, 4
separation, 4
social cognition research, 6
stable identity, 4
Identity stories, 180, 181
art of possibility, 181
consciousness-shaping, 179
storytelling, 180
universe of possibility, 179
world of possibility, 181
Identity styles, 56
Illness, 310, 311
Immersion-emersion stage, 86
Impermanence, 310
Informational identity style, 57
Integrated wisdom, 58
Internal working models (IWM), 273
Internalization-commitment stage, 86
International Union of Psychological Sciences (IUPsyS), 240
Internationalization commitment status, 89
Interpretative phenomenological analysis (IPA), 221
Intrinsic person-environment connection, 217
Inventory of the dimensions of emerging adulthood (IDEA), 75, 76, 79
Isomorphic processes, 29

J
Jettison, 179
identity stories, 180, 181

L
Learning and creativity, 216
Leisure
flow experience, 221
idiographic/qualitative approach, 221
oppurtunities, 221–223
social integration, 223–226
spouse, 221–223
Lesbian, gay, bisexual, and transgender (LGBT) community, 164
Living with the Devil, 251
Lorentz transform, 25–26

M
Marcia's Identity Status Interview, 54
Maryland Institute of Art and Basic Electronics, 304
Medial temporal lobe, 15
Memory, 4, 6–9, 13
Memory criterion, 13
Metatheory shift, 119
Middle adulthood
energy and attention, 217
engagement, 217
intrinsic motivation, 218
learning and creativity, 218
person-environment transaction, 218
resources and energy, 216
self-actualization, 217
The Middle Length Discourses of the Buddha, 256
Migration, 130, 131, 133, 135, 139, 141, 143, 145, 146
Mindfulness, 258
Mindfulness of Dhammas, 249
Morality, 7, 8
Moratorium, 217
Multiple causality, 120
Multiple methods, 120
Multiple myeloma (MM), 309
Multiple solutions, 119

N
National Alzheimer's Project Act, 99
National Center for Education Statistics (NCES), 200
National Institute on Aging (NIA), 36
National Institutes of Health (NIH), 36
Negative identities, 275, 277
Nilgiri, 130–147
No Man Is an Island, 125
Normative identity style, 57

O
Olfaction, 6
Other specified dissociative disorders (OSDD), 265, 275

P
Paradox, 120
Parallel distributed processing (PDP), 272
Parameter setting, 119
Parental identity, 152, 153
  becoming parent, 153
  caring for infant, 154, 155
  coregulating adolescent, 159–161
  mentoring young adult, 161, 162
  protecting and controlling preschooler, 155–157
  teaching child, 157–159
Parenting, 153, 159, 161
Personal expressiveness, 218
Personality development in adulthood, 120
  integrity *vs.* despair, 121, 122
  six-foci model, 120
Personal wisdom, 58
Play (cost of play deprivation)
  biological and evolution-based process, 215
  cultural achievements, 213
  flexibility, 215
  healthy human development, 214
  human infants, 214
  momentary engagement, 214
  poverty, 215
  prototypical experience, 213
  research literature, 215
  SES families, 215
  sustenance and survival, 214
  underappreciation, 215
Political identity, 321
Positive disintegration, theory, 280
Possibility, 179, 181
Post-traumatic psychopathologies, 279
Post-traumatic stress disorder (PTSD), 265
Pragmatism, 119
Pre-encounter anti-Black identity, 87
Pre-encounter assimilation identity, 87
Pre-encounter stage, 86, 87
Problem definition, 119
Process/product shift, 119
Psychiatry, 265, 267, 272, 281
Psychological Society of South Africa (PsySSA), 240, 243

Q
Quality of life, 130–134, 136, 138, 145, 147

R
Race salience, 86
Racial Identity Attitudes Scale (RIAS), 89
Racial identity clusters, 296
Radical empiricist, 247
Religious/spiritual/philosophical identity, 321
Resiliency, 278–280
Reversible personality, 275

S
Sacred space, 217
Scale of existential thinking (SET), 75, 77
Schizophrenia, 20
Secretarial School, 304
Seeds of Contemplation, 116
Self-differentiation, 218–221, 223–226
Self-efficacy, 188, 189
Sick self
  dementia, 312
  multiple myeloma, 309
Social identity, 129
Social identity of Badagas, 130, 133–143
  method
    becoming city Badaga (self-discovery), 141–143
    being Badaga, 138–141
    data collection and analysis, 134
    findings, 134
    living in Bangalore, 136–138
    location, 133
    participants and sampling, 133
    social mobility, 135, 136
Social integration, 218–221, 223–226
Sociological self, 275, 279
Spirituality, 116
  development of felt connection, 122, 123
  existential questions, postformal thought, personality, and connections, 123, 124
  later adulthood, Merton, Rohr, and approach, 116–118
Storytelling, 180
Student to professional, 198–206
  clinical psychology, 197
  emerging adulthood, 198
  identity achievement, 198
  identity *vs.* role confusion stage, 198
  keys to success
    increasing knowledge, 204
    networking, 206
    self-care, 205, 206
    support systems, 203, 204
  prolonged adolescence, 198
  roadblocks
    cultivating, professional identity, 202, 203

diversity and generational differences, 200–202
impostor syndrome, 198, 199
shift of responsibilities, 199, 200
Surplus resource theory (SRT), 213–214

T
Tailoring identity
application, 219
circumstances, 211
commitment, 218
exploration/commitment dynamics, 218
and flow, 226–228
interpretive framework, 218–221
leisure, 221–228
play and possibility, 212–221
self-differentiation, 219
Transgender experience, historical and contemporary frameworks, 164, 165
Transitions, 152
child, 157
A Translation of the Majjhima Nikaya (MN), 256
Trauma, 266, 267, 269–273, 276, 277, 279–282
treatment, 282
Traumatic experiences, 266, 282
Traumatic stress, 283

U
Unconventional artists, 307

V
VC reports, 255
Vocational identity, 320

W
Who Is My Self, 258
Work and identity flexibility
accommodation, 189–191
carbon-based elements, 184
computer functions, 183
declines, 183
empirical testing, 185
employee flexibility, 184
identification, 186
industrial revolution, 183
industries and organizations, 183, 184
knowledge upgrading, 188–189
moral attitude, 185
openness to experience, 190, 191
postal workers, 183
reconstituting identity, 187, 188
somatic tension, social panic, and ego anxiety, 185
transitioning to other careers, 191, 192